INTEGRATED URBAN AGRICULTURE

INTEGRATED URBAN AGRICULTURE
Precedents, Practices, Prospects

Edited by Robert L. France

First published in 2016 by Green Frigate Books

Green Frigate is an imprint of Libri Publishing

Copyright © Libri Publishing Ltd.

Authors retain the rights to individual chapters.

ISBN: 978-0-9933706-2-5

The right of Robert L. France to be identified as the editor of this work has been asserted in accordance with the Copyright, Designs and Patents Act, 1988. All rights reserved. No part of this publication may be reproduced, stored in any retrieval system or transmitted in any form or by any means, electronic, mechanical, photocopying, recording or otherwise, without the prior written permission of the copyright holder for which application should be addressed in the first instance to the publishers. No liability shall be attached to the author, the copyright holder or the publishers for loss or damage of any nature suffered as a result of reliance on the reproduction of any of the contents of this publication or any errors or omissions in its contents.

A CIP catalogue record for this book is available from The British Library

Book and cover design by Carnegie Publishing

Libri Publishing
Brunel House
Volunteer Way
Faringdon
Oxfordshire
SN7 7YR

Tel: +44 (0)845 873 3837

www.libripublishing.co.uk

Dedication

To the agrarian memory of my grandfathers: William France (1909–2005), Sheffield urbanite and postwar editor of the British allotments magazine, who learned about the benefits of gardening while a POW in Stalag Luft III, from which the famous 'great escape' happened, and Peter Mazur (1896–1970), child immigrant from Poland and early homesteading farmer on the edge of the boreal forest and prairies in southeastern Manitoba, who endured the hardscrabble existence there until retiring to the city of Winnipeg where he would practice backyard gardening.

Contents

Contributor Information		ix
Preface	**Beyond Allotment and Community Gardens**	xvii
Introduction	**The Once and Future City Farm**	
	Robert France	1
Chapter 1	**Reading Urban Gardens and Farms: Literature, Layering and Largesse**	
	Robert France and Luc J. A. Mougeot	15
	Commentary – Urban agriculture and its role in transformational agriculture and gender equity: *Kathleen Kevany and Derek Lynch*	35
Chapter 2	**Public Produce: Food By the People, For the People**	
	Darrin Nordahl and Catherine Fisher	39
	Commentary – Imagining public livestock in the city: *Lorraine Johnson*	69
Chapter 3	**Making Agriculture Part of the City: Lessons from Research for Policy in the Global South**	
	Luc J. A. Mougeot	75
	Commentary – Some contemporary issues facing urban agriculture: *Mark Redwood*	149

CONTENTS

Chapter 4 **Designing Urban Agricultural Forms: History, Education, Proposals and Projects**
Robert France — 153

Commentary – Missing the gardener: *Laura Lawson* — 182

Chapter 5 **Urban Agriculture Linkages: Patterns, Education and Urban Planning**
Karen Landman — 187

Commentary – Globalization of a good food idea: Tracking the spread of a CSA from West to East: *Sarah Elton* — 250

Chapter 6 **Resilient City = Carrot City: Urban Agriculture Theories and Designs**
Mark Gorgolewski, June Komisar and Joe Nasr — 255

Commentary – Urban agriculture and desire: *Andre Viljoen and Katrin Bohn* — 278

Chapter 7 **Agricultural Urbanism: Building Sustainable Urban and Regional Food Systems for 21st-Century Cities**
Mark Holland and Janine de la Salle — 285

Commentary – Food regions, values and equity: *Betsy Donald* — 327

Chapter 8 **Urban Agriculture as a Response to the Great Recession**
Nevin Cohen — 331

Commentary – Will it last? Questions regarding the staying power of urban agriculture: *Jennifer Cockrall-King* — 353

Contributor Information

Katrin Bohn was born in East Germany and now lives in London and Berlin. She holds a Diploma in Architecture from the Bauhaus-Universität Weimar in Germany and a Master of Science in Low Energy Architecture from the University of East London, UK. After ten years of architectural lecturing in the UK, mainly at the University of Brighton, Katrin was in 2010 appointed a guest professor at the Technical University in Berlin where she heads the department 'City and Nutrition'. Since 1998, she also runs Bohn&Viljoen Architects with André Viljoen, a small London-based architectural practice and environmental consultancy. Bohn&Viljoen Architects have taught, lectured, published and exhibited widely on the design concept of CPUL [*Continuous Productive Urban Landscape*] which they contributed to the international urban design discourse in 2004.

Jennifer Cockrall-King is an independent food journalist who splits her time between Edmonton, Alberta, and Naramata, British Columbia. Though she grew up in the city, an early culinary education in the family's large veggie garden sparked a lifelong obsession with gardening, cooking, food systems, and food culture. Jennifer is the author of *Food and the City: Urban Agriculture and the New Food Revolution*, for which she received the Dave Greber Award for social justice writing in 2011/2012. She is the food columnist for *Eighteen Bridges* Magazine, and contributes to many magazines in Canada and the US. She is currently at work on a book about seeds, seed-saving and seed banks around the world.

CONTRIBUTOR INFORMATION

Nevin Cohen is an Assistant Professor of Environmental Studies at The New School, where he teaches courses in urban food systems, environmental studies, environmental planning, and environmental policy analysis, including cross-disciplinary courses that connect the fields of policy, planning, and design. Dr. Cohen's research focuses on the development of urban food policy, the use of urban space for food production, and planning for ecologically sound urban food systems. He has been involved in food policy development in New York City, and co-authored a study (*Five Borough Farm: Seeding the future of urban agriculture in New York City*) to support and strengthen New York City's urban agriculture system. Dr. Cohen is currently working on two book projects: a study of urban food policymaking in the US and Canada, and an analysis of urban agriculture projects that focus on social justice goals (*Beyond the Kale: Urban Agriculture and Social Justice Activism in New York City*, forthcoming, from the University of Georgia Press).

Betsy Donald is an Associate Professor in Geography at Queen's University and cross-appointed to the School of Urban and Regional Planning. She has written extensively about the creative food economy, food deserts, and food system planning in such journals as the *Journal of Economic Geography*, *Environment and Planning A*, *Economic Geography*, and *Regional Studies*. She has also edited a special issue of the *Cambridge Journal of Regions, Economy and Society* on 'Re-regionalizing the Food System'. Last year she was the Eccles Centre Visiting Professor in North American Studies at the British Library where she spent the year researching *The Rise and Fall of the American Industrial Foodscape*. She is inspired by Brazil's new food guidelines that emphasize simple things like preparing meals using fresh and staple foods and eating with others at home. As much as possible, Betsy tries to do this with her wonderful family in Kingston, Ontario.

Sarah Elton is a journalist and author of two bestselling books, *Consumed: Food for a Finite Planet* and *Locavore: From Farmers' Fields to Rooftop Gardens, How Canadians Are Changing the Way We Eat*. She is also an adjunct professor with the School of Environmental Design and Rural Development at the University of Guelph.

Contributor Information

Catherine Fisher is a graduate of Southern Oregon University with a BA in English Literature and History. She completed her postbaccalaureate from Western Illinois University in Zoology. Catherine currently resides in Florence, Oregon, with her three cats, where she enjoys research, writing and discovering new foods from the region.

Robert France is a professor of watershed management in the Faculty of Agriculture at Dalhousie University. He is the author of many technical papers and the author or editor of over a dozen books, including *Healing Natures, Repairing Relationships: New Perspectives on Restoring Ecological Spaces and Consciousness*, *Handbook of Regenerative Landscape Design*, and *Environmental Restoration and Design for Recreation and Ecotourism*. Dr. France has participated in award-winning urban planning and design projects around the world, and is currently at work on a book entitled *Regenerative Urban Agriculture: Projects Transforming Neglected or Damaged Landscapes, Lives and Livelihoods*. Robert is descended from Polish homesteaders on the Canadian prairies and others who played a role in the British post-war allotment movement. He grew up in the suburbs of Winnipeg, sustained by a large and healthy backyard garden.

Mark Gorgolewski is a Professor in the Department of Architectural Science at Ryerson University in Toronto. He has worked for many years as an architect, researcher and sustainable building consultant in Canada and the UK. He has been a director of the Canada Green Building Council and chair of the Association for Environment Conscious Building and is a LEED Accredited Professional. Dr Gorgolewski has written many papers and books on the subject of sustainable built environments. Currently areas of research include building performance, reuse of components and materials in buildings, and design for urban agriculture. He was co-curator of the exhibition *Carrot City: Designing for Urban Agriculture*, which has travelled around the world, and is co-author of the *Carrot City* book and website. Mark has participated in various sustainable building projects, including a winning design for the CMHC Equilibrium (net zero energy) Housing Competition and is also co-recipient of the 2007–2008 ACSA/AIA Housing Design Education Award.

CONTRIBUTOR INFORMATION

Mark Holland is Vice President of Development for New Monaco LP Inc – a company developing a large master-planned community in the heart of British Columbia's Okanagan wine country. He holds professional degrees in both Landscape Architecture, and Community and Regional Planning. He was raised in a log cabin on a homestead where his family grew most of the food they ate, and as a youth, he worked on many industrial farms in the BC interior. Mark then became an urbanite and dedicated his career to pursuing urban planning innovations in sustainability, health promotion, urban food systems and creating places that people love to be in. He coauthored the book, *Agricultural Urbanism* which is now used as a text in many universities on how to plan an optimum integration of food systems into cities. *Business in Vancouver* magazine named Mark one of Vancouver's Top 40 under 40, and a few years later, in 2010, he was named BC's Planner of the Year. Then in 2013, he was awarded the Queen's Diamond Jubilee Medal for his contributions to field of sustainability and planning for Canadian municipalities.

Lorraine Johnson is a Toronto-based writer and editor. She is the author of more than ten books (including *Green Future* and *Tending the Earth*), the most recent of which is *City Farmer: Adventures in Urban Food Growth*. She is currently writing a book on urban livestock. Active in the community gardening movement, Lorraine also advocates for the legalization of backyard chickens in Toronto. She is the editor of the magazine *Ground: Landscape Architect Quarterly* and teaches a course on native plant ecosystems at York University.

Kathleen Kevany is an Assistant Professor in Business and Social Sciences with Dalhousie along with being the Director of Adult Learning. Kathleen sees the Faculty of Agriculture, by nature and design, being accessible and innovative around an array of initiatives like urban agriculture and rural vibrancy. Kathleen's research focuses on enhancing individual and community well-being. She grew up in Southwestern Ontario with a father who had been transplanted from his own Irish farm. The family in Chatham was nourished with an abundance of substantial potatoes, succulent beefsteak tomatoes and peaches 'n cream corn. Not bad production for a yard with a large home on the main street of the city.

CONTRIBUTOR INFORMATION

June Komisar is an Architect and an Associate Professor in the Department of Architectural Science at Ryerson University. At Ryerson she is currently an Associate of the Centre for Studies in Food Security and the Principal Investigator of a multidisciplinary research group called the REAL lab as well as a member of the Architectural APP research group. Along with Joe Nasr and Mark Gorgolewski she has co-curated the exhibit *Carrot City: Designing for Urban Agriculture* that has been touring Europe and North America for about five years. She is an advisor for the Ryerson productive landscape initiative called Rye's HomeGrown and a member of the Toronto Food Policy Council. She has served on the scientific committees for several architectural conferences and is a past board member of ICOMOS Canada. Recent publications include the book *Carrot City* with the same collaborators as the exhibition of the same name, and a chapter in *Architectura: Elements of Architectural Style*. She is currently writing a book on Brazilian architecture. Her doctoral research on Brazilian architecture earned her a Montequin fellowship from the Society of Architectural Historians and a distinguished dissertation award.

Karen Landman is a professor of Landscape Architecture in the School of Environmental Design & Rural Development at the University of Guelph. Her background is in horticulture, landscape architecture, planning and cultural geography. Current research interests include urban agriculture design, food systems, green infrastructure, landscape stewardship and pollination habitat. Many of Karen's landscape architecture students are interested in UA design, and some have even become urban farmers. Karen grew up on a dairy farm; her parents had immigrated to Canada from Friesland (from whence came the Holstein-Friesian cow).

Laura Lawson is Professor and Chair in the Department of Landscape Architecture at Rutgers, The State University of New Jersey. Her research includes historical and contemporary community open space, with particular focus on community gardens and the changing roles of parks in low-income communities. Dr. Lawson teaches community-based design studios and seminars focused on research methods, social issues in design and planning, and the public landscape. Her scholarship includes *City Bountiful: A Century of Community Gardening in America* (2005), *Greening Cities, Growing Communities: Urban Community Gardens in Seattle* (co-authored with Hou and Johnson, 2009), and numerous articles and chapters in edited books.

Derek Lynch is Associate Professor and Canada Research Chair in Organic Agriculture at Dalhousie University in Halifax, Canada. His teaching and research interests include organic and low input agricultural systems, environmental and ecological impact of farming systems, soil management and urban agriculture. He is currently president of the Canadian Society of Agronomy and is widely published on issues concerning the environmental impacts and long-term sustainability of organic agriculture. Derek grew up in Dublin, where as a young teenager he dug up the backyard and planted vegetables for sale, a decidedly odd act in a family with no farming or gardening history. He is more than ever convinced that urban centres, and their rapidly growing populations, have a central role to play in a new transformative agriculture, which combines a redesign of agro-ecosystems and of our communal relationships to, and via, food.

Luc J. A. Mougeot is currently a senior program specialist with Canada's International Development Research Centre (IDRC), where he led the Centre's Urban Environment Management research program (1993–1995) and its Cities Feeding People (CFP) research program (1996–2004). CFP supported over 90 projects on urban agriculture in more than 40 countries in the global South. Luc created and led a donor agencies' Support Group on Urban Agriculture, a graduate field-research fellowship program and a research report series on urban agriculture. Luc helped design and manage three regional training courses on urban agriculture in West Africa, East Africa and Latin America, as well as collaborations with programs of United Nations Habitat and the Food and Agriculture Organization. He has served on international advisory boards for UN-HABITAT's State of the World Cities Report and for the Worldwatch Institute's State of the World Report. He sits on the Board of Trustees of the RUAF Foundation, which supports a global network of resource centers on urban agriculture. Luc has authored or edited over 60 publications, including *For Hunger-Proof Cities: Sustainable Urban Food Systems*, *AGROPOLIS: the Social, Environmental, and Political Dimensions of Urban Agriculture*, and *Growing Better Cities*. He is a contributor to *Cities Feeding People*, to *African Urban Harvest*, and to *Food and the City* (in press).

Contributor Information

Joe Nasr is an independent scholar, lecturer and consultant based in Toronto, with a doctorate in urban and regional planning from the University of Pennsylvania. Having grown up in Beirut, he discovered urban agriculture over two decades ago through the late Jac Smit while helping him research what became the seminal book *Urban Agriculture: Food, Jobs and Sustainable Cities*. He co-curated the exhibit *Carrot City: Designing for Urban Agriculture*, which has travelled to over 20 cities so far and been turned into a book and website. He coordinated the programming committee for the *Urban Agriculture Summit* in August 2012 in Toronto. Joe has taught at a number of universities in several countries and has been awarded several postdoctoral fellowships, most recently in New York and Paris. He teaches regularly online courses on Urban food security and Urban agriculture through Ryerson University, where he is an Associate at the Centre for Studies in Food Security. He coordinated a training course on urban agriculture in the Middle East and North Africa. He is co-author or co-editor of four books and dozens of articles, and recently became co-editor of a new Urban Agriculture Book Series at Springer.

Darrin Nordahl loves to eat food, talk and write about food, and grow food. He is the author of *Public Produce* and *Eating Appalachia*, and a native of the San Francisco Bay Area, where locally grown produce has been a staple in his life. Darrin graduated from the University of California at Davis with a Bachelor's degree in Landscape Architecture, and then from Cal-Berkeley with a Master's in Urban Design. When Darrin is not espousing the joys and benefits of eating locally sourced, sustainably raised produce, he is likely writing and speaking about public transit. Someday, Darrin will merge his two passions and make eating good food aboard public transit a requisite in the United States.

Mark Redwood is the Program Leader of the Climate Change and Water initiative at Canada's International Development Research Centre (IDRC). He has ten years of experience in environmental planning and is a specialist on urban planning, water management, and climate change. As Program Leader, Redwood manages an international team of specialists on water and a portfolio of eighty active research projects on climate change in more than two dozen countries. Redwood is an urban planning expert and has contributed to numerous conferences and peer-review journals, most recently editing the book *Agriculture and Urban Planning* and co-editing the book *Wastewater Irrigation and Health*. His current area of interest is on the safe use of wastewater in order to mitigate the impacts of climate change in developing countries.

Jennifer de la Salle has a decade of experience in building sustainable urban and regional food systems with municipalities, regional districts, developers, non-profits and universities. As principal of Urban Food Strategies, Janine collaborates with interdisciplinary teams to develop food and agriculture strategies, policies, and plans, neighbourhood designs that consider food and agriculture, local food economy assessments, and farm park designs. In addition to delivering many presentations and producing professional plans, she is co-author of the book *Agricultural Urbanism*. Recently, Janine was part of the project team that developed *Fresh*, the City of Edmonton's urban agriculture and food system strategy that won a planning merit award from the Alberta Professional Planning Institute.

Andre Viljoen was born in Cape Town, studied architecture in Dublin and lives in London. He holds a Diploma in Architecture from the Dublin Institute of Technology in Ireland and a Master of Science in Low Energy Architecture from the University of East London. While completing his Master's he met Katrin Bohn with whom he has been working since. Andre has taught in several Schools of Architecture and is currently a Principal Lecturer at the University of Brighton. With Katrin Bohn he has just completed a follow up to their seminal work *Continuous Productive Urban Landscapes: Designing Urban Agriculture for Sustainable Cities*. The new book is titled, *Second Nature Urban Agriculture: Designing Productive Cities*. In 2013 he was appointed Chair of the Association of European School of Planning (AESOP) Sustainable Food Planning Thematic Group, which runs the annual European Sustainable Food Planning Conferences.

PREFACE

BEYOND ALLOTMENT AND COMMUNITY GARDENS

ORIGIN OF THE BOOK

During the harvest season of 2010, a symposium was held at the Nova Scotia Agricultural College (now Dalhousie University's Faculty of Agriculture) and the Faculty of Architecture at Dalhousie University. Titled 'Planning Urban Agricultural Systems for the 21st Century,' this gathering was sponsored by the Nova Scotia Department of Agriculture and brought together nine experts from across North America who had published or established academic courses/programs that contribute to the developing practice and emerging scholarship of urban agriculture (UA). The purpose of the symposium was to catch the rising tide of UA as it moves beyond issues concerned with the establishment and operation of allotment and community gardens; in other words, as it evolves from being a sustenance provider for private citizens into becoming a recognizable and valued professional practice and academic discipline in contemporary urban planning and design (e.g. *Agricultural Urbanism: Handbook for Building Sustainable Food & Agriculture Systems in 21st Century Cities*, de la Salle and Holland, 2010, Green Frigate Books; and *Urban Agriculture: Growing Healthy, Sustainable Places*, K. Hodgson, M. Campbell and M. Bailkey, 2011, American Planning Association). Emphasis was therefore placed on highlighting the comprehensiveness of the discipline, the shift from urban agriculture to urban agriculture *systems*, or as posited in the Introduction and title to this resulting volume, *integrated* urban agriculture.

The symposium was therefore perhaps most successful in demonstrating the extremely broad range of interests and professional approaches encompassed within the discipline and practice of UA. In this regard, the following disciplines were represented by the presenters and panelists at the symposium and by the writers of the resulting book: international development, city governance, urban planning, social science, botany, soil science, water management, landscape architecture, health care, landscape history, geography, journalism, architecture, urban design, sustainable management, urban policy, and ecology.

The symposium was attended by over a hundred practitioners, academics, students, government officials, farmers, and interested private citizens. Following a day of presentations at the agriculture campus in Truro that focused on the theory, history, and illustrative examples of UA, a workshop was convened the next day in downtown Halifax at which those involved in the planning and implementation of UA projects in the city discussed their work with the visiting experts and concerned citizens and students. At the same time, representative selections from the 'Carrot City' exhibition of Ryerson University (see Chapter 6) were mounted to stimulate discussions of innovative urban design.

Purpose of the Book

The present book is designed to introduce, describe, and demonstrate new interpretations to UA in a form to engage the broadest audience possible. A few readers will find familiar elements here, but even those most educated about UA will be surprised at the variety of novel ideas and approaches explored and developed within these pages. This collection of papers – all of which have been substantially updated from the earlier versions presented at the symposium – pushes the frontiers of UA toward new directions, challenging readers into abandoning the comfortable safety of business-as-usual within narrow disciplinary confines, and instead directing views outward to the exciting and incompletely mapped regions of true interdisciplinary or *integrated* urban agriculture. Represented in these pages are the pioneering efforts and opinions of those practitioners and scholars working at the intersections of paradigms, those very regions where, as Thomas Kuhn informs, visionary insight and conceptual evolution are most likely to occur.

STRUCTURE OF THE BOOK

The book contains eight chapters developed from presentations and the accompanying exhibition at the UA Symposium. All chapter authors were asked to expand upon the concepts originally presented, and in particular and most importantly, to focus on providing new information arising since the 2010 meeting. Ten writers and scholars of agriculture and food issues were then invited to comment upon the various chapters. These individuals, all published authors, of whom five are academics, three are professional writers/journalists, and one is each a practitioner and an international developer, were asked to springboard out from their assigned chapter into whatever new direction in which they found themselves inspired.

In the Introduction, France explores the shift in the conception of UA from oxymoron to opportunity. This is demonstrated through the dramatic rise that has occurred in the popularity of UA as reflected by specialized conferences and books on the subject leading up to the Dalhousie conference. Urban agriculture, the author argues, also plays a philosophical role in challenging three prevailed myths on human–nature relationships. A brief review is presented of the unified history of food and cities. Finally, parallels are drawn between the shifting focus of urban agriculture and stormwater management, leading to positing the new, more holistic discipline of *integrated* urban agriculture.

France and Mougeot, in Chapter 1, highlight how UA has developed into a horizon issue of emerging societal import by demonstrating a quadrupling of published books over the last decade. To introduce readers who may be arriving new to this rapidly expanding literature, the authors provide an annotated bibliography of fifteen representative books from which more than seventy-five salient points are extracted to illustrate the wide diversity of topics under the umbrella concept of UA.

In their commentary to Chapter 1, Kevany and Lynch emphasize the transformative nature of UA in the context of its multifaceted nature that results in it being a complex socio-ecological system capable of addressing sustainability concerns. For agriculture to truly thrive in cities, it is suggested that more study is needed of anthropedology, the character and management of soils in urban landscapes. The authors also make the compelling point about the under-recognized, undervalued, and understudied issue of gender in UA, to which end they introduce another book specifically about this important topic.

Nordhal and Fisher, in Chapter 2, discuss a new trend in UA – public produce – in which citizens and public officials dedicate and operate accessible space for anyone to harvest, free of charge (this is in contrast to allotments and community gardens in which space is allocated to individuals who sometimes defend it with a territorial zeal worthy of Medieval overlords). Public produce is becoming increasingly popular, the authors believe, due to a set of push and pull issues; push: food insecurity in North America, in particular concerns about food safety; and lack of daily access to affordable and nutritious food compared to 'junk' food, leading to the obesity epidemic; and pull: the growing fascination and demand for local produce; and the embrace of food literacy programs in education.

In her commentary to Chapter 2, Johnson expands the discussion into the occasionally thorny issue of public livestock in cities (every city these days seems to have as a press foil, its own resident 'chicken lady'). Not sidestepping the messy reality about slaughtering animals in cities, the author imagines a future scenario of publicly regulated urban livestock in which demonstration farms play a role in fostering food literacy.

Mougeot, in Chapter 3, focuses on initiatives and implementations of UA in the global South, providing a critically important perspective from a region where growing food in cities is an unromantic necessity of life (not just a utopian dream of sustainability of the affluent North). The author provides a detailed overview of agriculture and cities through Western history and then creates a list of principles of how these ancient practices can contribute to contemporary UA. For those in the South, the continual growth in UA is driven by growing urban markets, recurring crises, and persistent poverty. A series of case studies is presented from around the world that demonstrate the importance of governance and financial support and most especially public policy in successful UA programs.

In his commentary to Chapter 3, Redwood makes the point that the biggest threat to the widespread implementation of UA may be skyrocketing real estate values in cities, resulting in their being fewer and fewer pieces of undeveloped land suitable for farming. Two other complicating factors raised by the author are climate-induced alterations in the hydrological cycle, and the growing sensitivity of commodity pricing associated with global trends in fossil fuel costs.

France, in Chapter 4, explores the role of landscape architecture in UA, first, through several historical examples from a time when there was no division between productive and ornamental gardens, and second, today as UA is a feature of sustainable urbanism taught in many design school curricula. The author reviews examples of proposed projects and is critical of some outlandish designs (e.g. vertical farming) and more supportive of the reality shown by others (e.g. 'agrarian urbanism'). Drawing the parallel in the recent transition in urban stormwater management from constructing treatment wetlands to creating wetland treatment *parks*, the point is made of the need to move UA from being regarded as a last resort for marginalized land to being a lasting resource in the design of high visibility urban greenspace.

In her commentary to Chapter 4, Lawson reminds that during the last century there are examples when landscape architecture was either ambivalent or outright critical of productive gardens; only recently has the profession embraced UA. However, for UA to be successful, considerable knowledge is required about cultivation, climate, and labour. In short, landscape architecture must acknowledge the physicality of the act of gardening if it is to participate in the evolution of UA; i.e. focusing on design alone will not be enough.

Landman, in Chapter 5, describes a road tour across North America that reveals the exponential blossoming of UA at the grassroots level and the consequent rich diversity represented by projects created for academic research, community greenspace planning, commercial produce production, neighbourhood gardens, and school farms. The author highlights the growing significance of UA in many academic disciplines and its increasing role as a resource for grade-school education.

In her commentary to Chapter 5, Elton describes how North American principles of UA are being exported. One example of this is China's first community-supported agriculture (CSA) farm at the edge of Beijing which was created by a student returning home after studying in America. The author predicts that such CSAs will grow in popularity in China due to food safety scandals and concerns about deteriorating environmental quality.

Gorgolewski, Komisar and Nasr, in Chapter 6, insert UA into the discussion about global sustainability, in particular the movement in urban planning to create resilient cities which can adopt and effectively operate robustly under conditions of distress. Ensuring an adequate food supply by growing food in or near cities is a central tenet of the self-sufficiency embedded in resiliency. The authors review key developments and case studies of alternative thinking that have focused on food and explore the growing role of urban design in increasing the visibility of UA, drawing on examples of repurposing 'junk' spaces, the resource of roofs as productive spaces, and the establishment of farming subdivisions.

In their commentary to Chapter 6, Viljoen and Bohn focus on the multi-faceted desires behind UA, particularly the 'wicked' problem of developing a more equitable and sustainable food system. Such UA projects generate more than just food; they provide emergent social benefits in the creation of public open space. The authors reflect on moving UA from design to action, touching upon issues of citizen mobilization, project visualization, community capacity building, and research templates.

Holland and de la Salle, in Chapter 7, advance a holistic perspective by emphasizing that food is part of agri-*culture* through which 'agricultural urbanism' becomes the key strategy in developing Sustainable Urban and Regional Food Systems. Scalar issues of geography and jurisdiction are discussed and the concept of 'food hubs' – concentrations of many food system elements in one location – is advanced as a convenient and highly visible planning tool. The authors review examples and lessons from detailed case studies in the implementation of agricultural urbanism.

In her commentary to Chapter 7, Donald emphasizes the importance of planning for regional food systems. In this respect, we need to shift our focus from considering UA in terms of production to a more holistic approach that considers marketing, economics, and other value-added benefits. The author believes UA, through dealing with the issue of access to food, has a great role to play in addressing the comprehensive issue of poverty in cities.

Cohen, in Chapter 8, discusses how UA responded to the economic austerity resulting from the financial crisis of 2007, in terms of rising food security concerns, increased reliance on subsistence income and food self-sufficiency, and the availability of emergency funding packages provided by the government for job creation. Examples are reviewed of the complicated and tenuous relationships between land tenure and food production on suddenly undeveloped properties or temporarily stalled development sites during the recession. The author considers the policy implications of relations between food and economic development for small businesses, and the use of UA in building healthier communities through green infrastructure.

In her commentary to Chapter 8, Cockrall-King echoes the ephemeral nature of UA as a response to cyclical financial prosperity but adds that shifts in social attitudes and values that accompany UA are just as important as structural changes. In this regard, the author provides an optimistic outlook for the future in her belief that increased citizen empowerment in decision-making and the formation of their urban spaces, coupled with the rising popularity of food in grade-school education means that, like recycling and smoking ban bylaws, UA is here to stay.

ACKNOWLEDGEMENTS

Richard Donald and Peter Havard are thanked for providing the funding and Theresa O'Brien, Susan Guppy and Jennifer Watts for helping to facilitate the urban agriculture symposium from which this book originated. I would like to express my sincere thanks to the contributors through whose work, included in these pages, I have been inspired: Andre Viljoen, Mark Redwood, Darrin Nordhal, Joe Nasr, Luc Mougeot, Derek Lynch, Laura Lawson, Karen Landman, June Komisar, Kathleen Kevany, Lorraine Johnson, Mark Holland, Mark Gorgolewski, Sarah Elton, Betsy Donald, Janine de la Salle, Jennifer Cockrall-King, Nevin Cohen, and Katrin Bohn.

And to my contributors I would like to offer the following in gratitude, echoed from a previous compilation edited by me (*Handbook of Regenerative Design*, 2008, CRC Press) from which I was similarly inspired: to participate in integrated urban agriculture it is necessary to wish for and move toward an imagined future state as captured in the spirit of William Morris writing at a time when Blake's 'dark Satanic mills' were coming to be recognized for their toll being exacted upon the well-being of both urban land and life: 'Dreamer of dreams, born out of my own due time, why do I strive to set the crooked straight?' The concepts and case-studies presented in this book can be regarded as inspirational dreams well on their way to becoming pragmatic realities, and thus can be satisfying answers to Morris' formerly open-ended question.

INTRODUCTION

THE ONCE AND FUTURE CITY FARM

ROBERT FRANCE

FROM OXYMORON TO OPPORTUNITY: THE PHILOSOPHY AND POPULARITY OF URBAN AGRICULTURE

Urban agriculture (UA), besides providing food security for a significant portion of the world's population and generating a wide array of ancillary social benefits, also plays an important role in defining how humans interact with nature.

Humans love to categorize their world. One ramification of this is the false dichotomy held by many regarding what is referred to as *either* 'nature' *or* 'culture.' Increasingly, however, environmental historians and philosophers have contested the Nature ≠ Culture Myth (Wilson 1991; Evernden 1992; Cronon 1996). In reality, conceptual Nature (with a capital 'N') is as much a cultural construct as is physical nature a real entity. All locations can be positioned somewhere along a nature–culture gradient depending on the duration and intensity of human contact (Steedman 2005; France 2012). Some people have difficulty with such a unification and might intone, as I imagined in my introductory presentation to the UA conference from which this book derived (France 2010): *'Fine, I can accept (albeit begrudgingly!) that nature maybe – OK, is – cultured, but by no means does that imply that the reciprocal follows; i.e. that culture can be naturalized.'* But in point of fact, it can be, and indeed often is.

Nowhere is the false dichotomization between nature and culture emphasized more strongly than with regard to the way we set up the Nature ≠ Non-Nature (i.e. Cities) Myth (France 2008). After all, cities are for people whereas the countryside is where all that messy nature stuff belongs. However, since the time when academic ecologists living in West Berlin were forced to conduct their field studies in their urban neighbourhoods, we have come to realize that cities are in fact functioning ecosystems (Spirn 1984; Hough 1995) that are filled with nature (e.g. Houck and Cody 2000) to a degree that concepts such as 'city wilds' or 'urban ecology' have become accepted fields of professional planning and academic study (Dixon 2002; Marzluff et al. 2008; Gaston 2010). Accepting such a perspective, our imaginary sceptic might then emote: *'Fine, you have convinced me about cities and nature not being mutually exclusive. However, whereas I can accept that plants in cities might provide sustenance for wildlife, it is quite another thing altogether to infer from that that plants are capable of providing sustenance, of a physical not merely an emotional kind, for humans in cities. Come*

Fig. 1. Popular television shows predicated on the comedic contrasting of urban and rural lifestyles and prejudices.

The Once and Future City Farm

Fig. 2. Landscape art project, *Wheatfield – A confrontation*, 1982, by Agnes Denes, in lower Manhattan, based on the forced juxtaposition of rural and urban enterprises. Permission courtesy of Agnes Denes and Leslie Tonokonow Artworks and Projects.

on, get real!' (France 2010). And so, it is at this point that UA enters the discussion.

Agriculture, or 'agri-culture,' we must not forget, is just as much about the active culture around food, as for example, tourism (Hall et al. 2003) or art (Pearson and Nasby 2008), as it is about the activity of cultivating food. It is only recently that we have created the last dichotomous mindset, the artificial separation of cultivated nature from cultural habitation, in other words, the Farm ≠ City Myth. As a result, we find nothing odd in the humorous morphing of Grant Wood's famous *American Gothic* painting to showcase, in the most stereotypic way, either sophisticated urbanites making fun of simple country bumpkins or world-wise farmers flummoxed at the haplessness of superficial city dwellers (Fig. 1). The idea of food grown in cities has become so incongruous that it can form the basis of landscape art installations that purposely exploit the edgy juxtapositions, such as Agnes

Denes' famous *Wheatfield – A Confrontation* (Fig. 2). It was of course, not always this way.

Urban living and growing food have until recently always been tightly decoupled. The world's first cities in Mesopotamia were characterized by dense settlements in which food-producing fields, fruit orchards, ornamental gardens, and phyto-remedial green infrastructure for waste treatment were mixed together (Hamblin 1973; Dersin et al. 1993: Leick 2001). Medieval European towns (Matthew 1983; Gies and Gies 2000; Frugoni 2006) were closely associated with defensible farmed fields and much agricultural activity took place either within or abutting their boundaries, as shown in early paintings and by modern vestiges (Figs. 3, 4). Today, whereas UA is often regarded as an oxymoron or novelty in Western cities, it is de rigueur for much of the rest of the world where it is estimated to produce between 15 and 20% of the world's food while employing more than 200 million people (Mougeot 2005, 2006).

Fig. 3. Vestiges of a medieval farm located in the centre of the abbey town of Much Wenlock, England. An information sign contains the following statement: 'A rare surviving farm within a town. The farm buildings are gathered around the fold yard and are of traditional local materials, the timber framed barn being a typical 3-bay Shropshire example. The stack yard and garden form the outer perimeter. The fields are scattered outside the town.'

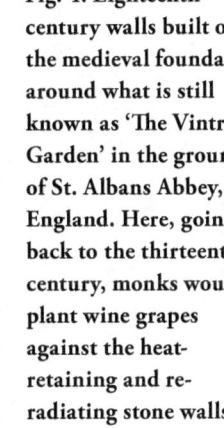

Fig. 4. Eighteenth-century walls built over the medieval foundations around what is still known as 'The Vintry Garden' in the grounds of St. Albans Abbey, England. Here, going back to the thirteenth-century, monks would plant wine grapes against the heat-retaining and re-radiating stone walls.

Interest in all things related to food has undergone a recent and remarkable resurgence in the West, with a deluge of television shows, popular books, and documentaries being produced every year. 'Eating healthy' and 'eating local' have become quasi-religious mantras mouthed by 'foodies' flocking to markets that satisfy their desires (Fig. 5). Mirroring these trends has been the increasing popularity in UA, not just in terms of actual gardens and farms being created but also in the scholarly studies being published. For the latter, Redwood (2008) presents a figure indicating that the number of peer-reviewed articles with 'UA' in their title has grown from 9 between 1985–1990, to 43 between 1991–1996, to 77 between 1997–2002, to 110 between 2003–2008. And Chapter 1 in the present book diagrams the quadrupling of UA books that have been published over the last decade. Planners, despite being slow to join the UA resurgence (see below), have become active participants in disseminating information about the practice

Fig. 5. Labelling of local and sustainably produced food at a market in Nova Scotia.

in the decade prior to the Dalhousie/NSAC conference from which the present book originated, as for example:
- July 2000: International Symposium Urban Agriculture and Horticulture: The Linkage With Urban Planning (TRAILOG; Berlin)
- July 2003: 'Food and planning' (S. Guppy at CIP; Halifax)
- June 2005: CPULS Continuous Productive Urban Landscapes (A. Viljoen* and K. Bohn*)
- July 2007: Policy Guide on Community and Regional Food Planning (APA)
- May 2008: The Role of Food and Agriculture in the Design and Planning of Buildings and Cities (Ryerson Univ.*)
- July 2008: Planning for Agriculture and Food (CIP; Winnipeg)
- Feb. 2009: Carrot City: Designing for Urban Agriculture (Ryerson Univ.*)
- Nov. 2009: Opportunities for Action: An Urban Agriculture Symposium (Univ. Guelph, K. Landman*)
- Nov. 2009: Re-Imagining Cities: Designing Urban Farms to Feed Our Cities (MAS Jane Jacobs Forum, NYC, N. Cohen*)

- Feb. 2010: Food Security: From Feast to Famine (St. Mary's Univ.)
- Aug. 2010: *Re-Regionalizing the Food System* (Special Issue of Cambridge J. Regions, Economy, & Society; B. Donald*)
- Aug. 2010: Museum of Vancouver photo exhibition on UA – Home Grown: Local Sustainability
- Oct. 2010: AESOP 2nd European Sustainable Food Planning Conference (Univ. Brighton, A. Viljoen*)

...with asterisks noting contributors to the present book. Indeed, the pace of publication and pedagogy about UA is rapidly accelerating, as for example witnessed in the single year leading up to the Dalhousie/NSAC conference (again, with asterisks noting contributors to the present book):

- Sept. 2009
  - 7th: Food Forms: Agriculture and Urban Systems (Harvard GSD course; Imbert & Fultineer)
- Oct. 2009
  - 1st: *Greening Cities, Growing Communities: Learning from Seattlle's Urban Community Gardens* (Hou, L. Lawson* et al.)
  - 21st: *Public Produce: The New Urban Agriculture* (D. Nordahl*)
- Feb. 2010
  - 1st: *Urban Agriculture: Diverse Activities and Benefits for City Society* (Pearson)
- Mar. 2010
  - 8th: *Locavore: From Farmer's Fields to Rooftop Gardens – How Canadians are Changing the Way We Eat* (S. Elton*)
- April 2010
  - 1st: *Agricultural Urbanism: Handbook for Building Sustainable Food & Agriculture Systems in 21st Century Cities* (J. de la Salle* & M. Holland*)
  - 27th: *My Empire of Dirt: How One Man Turned His Big-City Backyard into a Farm* (Howard)
- May 2010
  - 7th: *Smart Cities + Eco-Warriors* (Lim & Lu)
  - 15th: *City Farmer: Adventures in Urban Food Growing* (L. Johnson*)
- Sept. 2010
  - 5th: Theory and Principles of Sustainable Urban Agriculture and Horticulture; Sustainable Urban Crop Production (Univ. Guelph Urban Agriculture Certificate; K. Landman*)

In order to catch this rising crest of the UA wave, a conference was hosted by the Nova Scotia Agricultural College in association with Dalhousie University and the Halifax Regional Municipality in late September to early October 2010. The goal of the conference was to bring together leading North American scholars of UA and have them present ideas to an audience of academics and practitioners about what might be referred to as '*integrated* urban agriculture.'

Once More, the Wheel: Reinventing Integrated Urban Agriculture for the 21st Century

As modern civilization strived for and embraced efficiency as its ultimate Sangreal, forgotten was the wisdom that the much better metric for sustainable living and indeed for all relationships, be they human to nature or human to human, is effectiveness, not efficiency. Scratch the surface of any 'new' green technology championed as part of sustainable design, as for example in green architecture and landscape architecture, environmental and civil engineering, or environmental land-use planning for housing, forestry and agriculture, and one will often find a long-established and richly-diverse history of the effective use of the same technology at some time in the past. Much of sustainable living and design therefore amounts to reinventing the tried and proven effectiveness of that old wheel through the application of modern, efficient methods (spokes?). The same is true for growing and distributing food in cities.

The brief reemergence of UA in the 20th century as a national imperative for sustenance during challenging times of war and recovery has been well documented (Crouch and Ward 2003; Lawson 2005; Carriker 2010). When those times of self-reliant need had passed, city dwellers, hoping to put such memories behind them, embraced the convenience of supermarket grocery shopping. After all, growing one's own food, as had been done on the old family farm by one's parents or grandparents, was like turning the clock back and certainly not something to be countenanced by the nouveau suburban sophisticates (try to imagine if you will, Don Draper, the lead character in the television period show of the 1950s–1960s, *Mad Men*, planting and harvesting produce from his own backyard kitchen garden). Whereas the disenfranchised as well as new immigrants certainly continued private kitchen gardens throughout the latter half of the 20th century, community or allotment gardens and farmers' markets became something that could pejoratively be identified with those having anachronistic yearnings or those on the fringe of respectability; i.e. utopian back-to-the-earthers or antiquated hippies growing tomatoes in between their dope plants. It became, and sometimes still is, all too easy to poke fun in popular venues at the over-earnestness of these individuals, wherein, as for example, squabbling (Richler 2010) can sometimes lead to murder (Shelton 2010, 2011a,b; Acorn Media 2006). In recent times, however, the perception of UA has undergone a dramatic change.

Urban agriculture has moved beyond its private gardening phase and is becoming a recognized professional practice believed by many to be capable of contributing to the righting of many urban woes. Urban planners of North American and European cities, following the lead of those in international development, are now taking an active role in the emerging profession. But this has been a long time coming. As recently as a decade-and-a-half ago, Pothukuchi and Kaufman (2000), in a provocatively titled paper, 'The food system: A stranger to the planning field', threw down the gauntlet with quotes like the following:

- 'Most planning literature ignores food issues.'
- 'The food system, however, is notable by its absence from the writing of planning scholars, from the plans prepared by planning practitioners, and from the classrooms in which planning students are taught.'
- 'This low level of involvement is perplexing because the food system is a significant metropolitan system, and because planning claims to promote quality and livable settlements that meet basic needs and is concerned with connections between community systems.'

This failure by those charged with the planning and running of Western cities to adequately and effectively address food systems was so glaring that it led one observer, even a decade later, to pen the following criticism (Johnson 2010):

> 'It is one of the great ironies of urban life that although food – its production, processing, storage, consumption, marketing, transportation, and waste management – impacts so much of our existence in cities, there is actually very little deliberate and conscious shaping of our cities for food. The planning profession – the people who shape the policies that guide virtually every aspect of urban development – and the engineering profession – the people who shape the infrastructure that delivers the services that make our cities tick – have, for decades, almost completely ignored issues related to food and the food system. Roads,

housing, parks, zoning, water, transportation, waste, all are on the radar, but it is only relatively recently that food has explicitly entered the equation.'

And indeed UA has recently entered the equation of the planning profession in a significant way. Hodgson et al.'s (2011) seminal overview *Urban Agriculture: Growing Healthy, Sustainable Places*, shows how urban food planning has come of age in its holistic embrace of issues of food justice, brownfield regeneration, and societal well-being. In other words, today, the one-time, frequently (but not always) dilettantism of UA is maturing into the formalized discipline of 'agricultural urbanism' (*sensu* de al Salle and Holland 2010), or its derivative 'agrarian urbanism' (*sensu* Duany 2011). The major difference between UA and agricultural urbanism is the shift in the scale and complexity of the focus from site-specific urban gardens or farms to entire urban food *systems*. And it is here where one can envision the paradigm of *'Integrated* Urban Agriculture,' as reflected by the topics covered in the chapters of the present volume.

The progressive transition from simple UA to integrated UA during the 2000s parallels a similar shift that took place in the field of water management over the previous decade. For much of the 1980s and the early 1990s, watershed management was largely a techno-fix discipline in which environmental engineering played the dominant role. With the inclusion of a whole suite of social issues (reviewed in France 2002, and France 2005a, b), the field morphed into the more holistic *integrated* watershed management (e.g. Healthcote 1998; Lal 2000). Today, it is acknowledged that the latter, now universally recognized by its anagram 'IWM,' is, due to its more comprehensive nature, the only satisfactory approach for addressing complex issues of sustainability (e.g. Merry et al. 2005; Forch 2009; Wani 2011). Integrated urban agriculture (IUA), like it sibling discipline IWM, is based on environmental, social, and economic components; i.e. the famous three-legged sustainability stool. And it is worth noting that for some, IUA can be regarded as being a form of old wine in a new bottle given that progressive thinkers (e.g. Butler and Maronek in CAST 2002; Fig. 6) have been emphasizing the need for just such a more holistic conceptualization of peri-urban and urban agriculture for more than a decade (see also Mougeot 2006; Redwood 2008). Integrated urban agriculture in its various forms, as for example, agricultural urbanism, can be regarded as a form of agricultural 'LUSA' or land-use systems analysis (e.g. van Duivenbooden

Fig. 6. 'Today's urban agriculture system is a complex system composed of a central core of activities along with a wide variety of services and outcomes that support the total population.' (from CAST 2002. *Urban and agricultural communities: Opportunities for common ground.* Task Force Report 138; used with permission).

1995; Guhathakurta 2010), in that it too is based on much more than the nuts-and-bolts operations involved with the growing of food. Integrated urban agriculture is thus firmly rooted in Lyson's (2004) concepts of 'civic' or citizen-based agriculture.

References

Acorn Media. 2006. Rosemary & Thyme: Mysteries grow around them. The complete collection. Acorn Media DVDs.

Carriker, R.M. 2010. Urban farming in the west: A New Deal experiment in subsistence homesteads. Univ. Arizona Press.

Council for Agricultural Science and Technology (Butler, A. and B. Maronek). 2002. Urban and agricultural communities: Opportunities for common ground. Task Force Report 138. CAST.

Cronon, W. (Ed.) 1996. Uncommon ground: Rethinking the human place in nature. W.W. Norton.

Crouch, C. and C. Ward. 1997. The allotment: Its landscape and culture. Five Leaves Publ.

de la Salle, J. and M. Holland. 2010. Agricultural urbanism: Handbook for building sustainable food & agriculture systems in 21st century cities. Green Frigate Books.

Dersin, D., C. Hagner and D. Johnston. 1993. Summer: The cities of Eden. Time-Life Books.

Dixon, T.F. 2002. City wilds: Essays and stories about urban nature. Univ. Georgia Press.

Duany, A. 2011. Garden cities: Theory & practice of agrarian urbanism. The Prince's Found. Built Environ.

Evernden, N. 1992. The social creation of nature. John Hopkins Univ. Press.

Forch, G. 2009. Integrated watershed management: A successful tool for adaptation to climate change. Rural 43:22-25.

France, R.L. 2002. Background – Perspectives of water management: Representative examples from the recent literature. *In* France, R.L. (Ed.) Handbook of water sensitive planning and design. Lewis Publ.

France, R. 2005a. Introduction: Topics and challenges in watershed management – A literature review. *In* France, R. (Ed.) Facilitating watershed management: Fostering awareness and stewardship. Rowman & Littlefield.

France, R. 2005b. Introduction: Developing a plurality of voices for watershed stewardship – A literature review. *In* France, R.L. (Ed.) Facilitating watershed management: Fostering awareness and stewardship. Rowman & Littlefield.

France, R. 2008. Environmental restoration with people in mind: Regenerative landscape design at the interface of nature and culture. *In* France, R.L. (Ed.) Handbook of regenerative landscape design. CRC Press.

France, R. 2010. Setting the stage: City farms and gardens of eatin'. Introductory presentation at the Planning Urban Agricultural Systems for the 21st Century conference. NSAC/Dalhousie, Truro, NS, Sept., Oct.

France, R.L. 2012. Environmental restoration and design for recreation and ecotourism. CRC Press.

Frugoni, C. 2006. A day in a medieval city. Univ. Chicago Press.

Gaston, K.J. (Ed.) 2010. Urban ecology. Cambridge Univ. Press.

Gies, F. and J. Gies. 2000. Daily life in medieval times. Barnes and Noble.

Guhathakurta, S. 2010. Integrated land use and environmental models: a survey of current applications and research. Springer.

Hamblin, D.J. 1973. The first cities. Time-Life Books.

Hall, C.M., L. Sharples, R. Mitchell, N. Macionis and B. Cambourne. (Eds.) 2003. Food tourism around the world: Development, management and markets. BH Publishers.

Heathcote, I.W. 1998. Integrated watershed management: Principles and practices. Wiley.

Hodgson, K., M. C. Campbell and M. Bailkey. 2011. Urban Agriculture: Growing healthy, sustainable places. Amer. Planning Assoc.

Houck, M. and M. Cody. 2000. Wild in the city: A guide to Portland's natural areas. Oregon Historical Society Press.

Hough, M. 1995. Cities and natural process. Routledge.

Johnson, L. 2010. City farmer: Adventures in urban food growing. Greystone Books.

Lal, R.J. (Ed.) 2000. Integrated watershed management in the global ecosystem. CRC Press.

Lawson, L. 2005. City bountiful: A century of community gardening in America. Univ. Calif. Press.

Leick, G. 2001. Mesopotamia: The invention of the city. Penguin Books.

Lyson, T. 2004. Civic agriculture: Reconnecting farm, food, and community. Tufts Univ. Press.

Marzluff, J.M. and others. 2008. (Eds.) Urban ecology: An international perspective on the interaction between humans and nature. Springer.

Matthew, D. 1983. Atlas of medieval Europe. Facts on File, Inc.

Merry, D.J. and others. 2005. Integrating 'livelihoods' into integrated water resources management: Taking into consideration the integration paradigm to its logical next step for developing countries. Reg. Environ. Change 5:197-204.

Mougeot, L.J.A. 2005. Agropolis: the social, political, and environmental dimensions of urban agriculture. Earthscan.

Mougeot, L.J.A. 2006. Growing better cities: Urban agriculture for sustainable development. Can. Internat. Develop. Res. Cen.

Pearson, C. and J. Nasby. 2008. The cultivated landscape: An exploration of art and agriculture. McGill-Queens Univ. Press.

Pothukuchi, and Kaufman. 2000. The food system: A stranger to the planning field. J. Amer. Plan. Assoc. 66:113-124.

Redwood, M. 2008. (ED.) Agriculture in urban planning: Generating livelihoods and food security. Earthscan.

Richler, N. 2010. Farmers' markets are SO stressful: In principle I love the idea of fresh local produce, but…get your hands of my peas! Maclean's Magazine: May 31 issue.

Shelton, P. 2010. Farm fresh murder: A farmers' market mystery. Berkley.

Shelton, P. 2011a. Crops and robbers: A farmers' market mystery. Berkley.

Shelton, P. 2011b. Fruit of all evil: A farmers' market mystery. Berkley.

Sprin, A.W. 1984. The granite garden: Urban nature and human design. Basic Books.

Steedman, R.J. 2005. Buzzwords and benchmarks: Ecosystem health as a management tool. *In* France, R.L. (Ed.) Facilitating watershed management: Fostering awareness and stewardship. Rowan & Littlefield.

van Duivenbooden, N. 1995. Land use systems analysis as a tool in land use planning: with special reference to North and West African agro-ecosystems. Ph.D. Wageningen Agricultural Univ.

Wani, S.P. and others. 2011. Farmer-participatory integrated watershed management: Adarsha watershed, Kothapally India – an innovative and upscalable approach. J. SAT Ag. Res. 2:1-27.

Wilson, A. 1991. The culture of nature: North American landscape from Disney to the Exon Valdez. Harper Collins,

Chapter 1

Reading Urban Gardens and Farms: Literature, Layering and Largesse

Robert L. France and Luc J.A. Mougeot

As urban agriculture (UA) rises in popularity (France – Introduction), as reflected by the increasing number of academic and magazine articles, so has the publication of like-themed books mirrored this trend (Fig. 1.1). These works, some of which are identified in Table 1, generally fall into the categories of travel-based surveys, site-specific narratives, academic analyses, or how-to guides. If there is a single common element shared by all these books, it is the inherent belief and frequent intoning by the authors that urban gardens and farms are much more than merely pieces of cultivated cityscape without ancillary benefits. Instead, such locations, by accumulating human experience, become transformed from being physical *spaces* into becoming social *places* (see, for example, Tuan 2001 for further elaboration of the difference between these two geography terms).

The purpose of this chapter is to bring readers new to the field of UA quickly up to date, by introducing some of the salient features of this rapidly expanding literature. We do this, using the methodology employed for the same purpose in other introductory literature reviews contained in books (France 2002, 2005, 2006, 2008), by summarizing representative publications through a series of bulleted points of interest that emerge from each

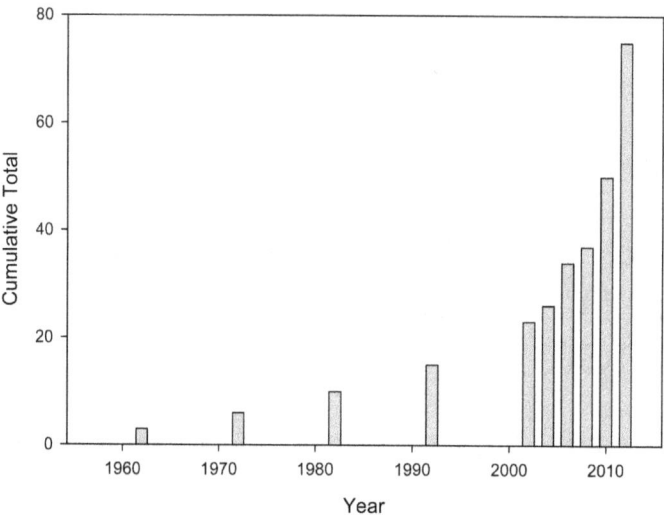

Fig. 1.1. Cumulative total of English-language books about urban agriculture, community gardens, and city farms over the last half century that can be easily purchased from electronic bookshops. Note the number of published UA books has quadrupled over the last decade.

work. The present volume is authored by some of leading thinkers and writers in the field of UA, who together have published more than a dozen reports and books. Because aspects of their work are presented within these pages in their respective chapters or commentaries, the examples below focus on the publications of other scholars and practitioners.

Table 1.1. Selected examples from the expanding urban agriculture literature over the last two decades. * = authors contributing to the present volume, and # = books discussed in the text of this chapter.

Year	Title	Author(s)
1993	*Creating Community in the City: Cooperatives and Community Gardens in Washington, D.C.*	Ward
1997	*The Allotment: Its Landscape and Culture*#	Landman
1998	*On Good Land: The Autobiography of an Urban Farm*	Ableman

Year	Title	Author(s)
2002	Urban and Agricultural Communities: Opportunities for Common Ground#	Butler & Maronek
	The Struggle for Eden: Community Gardens in New York City#	Von Hassel
2003	Agriculture in the City: A Key to Sustainability in Havana, Cuba	Cruz
2004	Civic Agriculture: Reconnecting Farm, Food, and Community#	Lyson
2005	CPULS – Continuous Productive Urban Landscapes: Designing Urban Agriculture for Sustainable Cities	Viljoen* & Bohn*
	Agropolis: The Social, Environmental, and Political Dimensions of Urban Agriculture	Mougeot*
	City Bountiful: A Century of Community Gardening in America	Lawson*
	Community Gardens: A Celebration of the People, Recipes and Plants	Woodward & Vardy
2006	Growing Better Cities: Urban Agriculture for Sustainable Development	Mougeot*
	Food Not Lawns: How to Turn Your Yard Into a Garden and Your Neighborhood Into a Community	Flores
2008	Agriculture in Urban Planning: Generating Livelihoods and Food Security	Redwood*
	Cracks in the Asphalt: Community Gardens of San Francisco	Hatch et al.
2009	Public Produce: The New Urban Agriculture	Nordhal*
	Greening Cities, Growing Communities: Learning From Seattle's Urban Community Gardens	Hou, Johnson & Lawson*
	Farm City: The Education of an Urban Farmer#	Carpenter
	My Empire of Dirt: How One Man Turned his Big-City Backyard into a Farm#	Howard
	The Allotment Experience: Everything You Need to Know about Allotment Gardening - Direct from the Plot	Binney
2010	Locavore: From Farmer's Fields to Rooftop Gardens – How Canadians are Changing the Way We Eat	Elton*
	City Farmer: Adventures in Urban Food Growing	Johnson*
	Agricultural Urbanism: Handbook for Building Sustainable Food and Agriculture Systems in 21st Century Cities	de la Salle* & Holland*

Year	Title	Author(s)
	Urban Farming in the West: A New Deal Experiment in Subsistence Homesteads#	Carriker
	Smartcities + Eco-Warriors#	Lim & Liu
	Urban Agriculture: Diverse Activities and Benefits for City Society#	Pearson et al.
	African Urban Harvest: Agriculture in the Cities of Cameroon, Kenya and Uganda	Prain et al.
	The Vertical Farm: Feeding the World in the 21st Century#	Despommier
2011	Food and the City: Urban Agriculture and the New Food Revolution	Cockrall-King*
	The Urban Food Revolution	Ladner
	Carrot City: Creating Places for Urban Agriculture	Gorgolewski*, Komisar* & Nasr*
	Reclaiming Our Food: How the Grassroots Food Movement is Changing the Way We Eat#	Cobb
	Responsiveness of Town Planning to Urban Agriculture: Kwa-Mashu, SA#	Magidmisha
	Garden Cities: Theory and Practice of Agrarian Urbanism	Duany & DPZ
	Sustainable Urban Agriculture in Cuba#	Koont
	Urban Agriculture: Growing Healthy, Sustainable Places	Hodgson et al.
	The Urban Farm Handbook: City-Slicker Resources for Growing, Raising, Sourcing, Trading, and Preparing What You Eat	Cottrell et al.
	Urban Farming: Sustainable City Living in Your Backyard, in Your Community, and in the World	Fox
2012	Urban Farms#	Rich & Benson
	Breaking Through the Concrete: Building an Urban Farm Revival#	Hanson et al.
	Sowing Change: The Making of Havana's Urban Agriculture	Premat
	Urban Agriculture in South Africa: A Study of the Eastern Cape Province	Thornton
	Edible Landscaping: Urban Food Gardens That Look Great	Lindsay
	Urban Kitchen Garden: Grow and Cook Your Own Food in the City	Moggash

Year	Title	Author(s)
2013	*Designing Urban Agriculture: A Complete Guide to the Design, Construction, Maintenance and Management of Edible Landscapes*	Philips
	Urban Agriculture: Case Studies of Accra, Bangalore, Lima, and Nairobi and a Global Review	Hoornweg et al.
	Digging the City: An Urban Agriculture Manifesto	McAdam
	From the Ground Up: Community Gardens in New York City and the Politics of Spatial Transformation	Eizenberg

England's three-hundred year old experience with rural and urban allotment plots (small parcels of land rented to individuals for growing food crops) has been foundational to many emulations in the global North, but also to the urban agriculture movement in global South cities. *The Allotment: Its Landscape and Culture* (Crouch and Ward 2003) has been reprinted three times since first published in 1997 and remains a rich exploration into the local history and cultural diversity of the English urban allotment experiment. Beyond the locational peculiarities of the English allotment, we have chosen to highlight findings with international resonance.

- The number of allotments in England has fluctuated over time, peaking during WWI and the economic depression of the 1930s, and reaching a historic high during WWII, followed by a lower peak during the early 1970s economic crisis, and declining further in the late 1990s.
- Tension between sector-specific official promotion versus multiple functions motivating practitioners: for the majority of allotment holders since the mid-20th century, economic benefits by and large have not been their driving motivation. Official reviews of the allotment programs have generally downplayed this reality and a better case must be made for policy design to embrace multiple roles that allotments fulfil for both tenants and communities.
- Local government commitment and support to promoting and managing allotments in their jurisdiction is critical for these to cater to local demand and fulfil their intended roles.
- In periods of national crisis, central government initiatives are essential for up-scaling. Initial legislative innovations for local authorities to provide allotments for labouring populations later were reinforced, granting to local authorities powers to take over any unoccupied land for

allotments, and this without its owner's consent. The 'labouring population' qualifier for eligibility was dropped and even when peace returned additional measures were passed to safeguard allotments. In recent decades, however, the allotment and larger UA movement has changed in tune with practitioners' motivations, and the movement has been struggling to press government authorities to transit toward more comprehensive, multi-sector, policy-making initiatives on allotments.
- There is a need for organizational visioning to re-invent the allotment movement. Two major organizations merged into a new entity which did lobby effectively but which has been unable to secure continuous national funding or to push for regulatory measures to strengthen the movement including maintaining obligations from local authorities toward allotment programs. By the late 1990s only a fraction of allotment holders were members of the movement's only society. A chasm had opened between the movement's society and the motivations and needs of new local entrants.
- Policy development in England, like that in Germany, Holland, Denmark and Sweden reveals a common struggle in getting allotment gardening accepted as an activity under town planning legislation.

The U.S. Council for Agriculture Science and Technology's *Urban and Agricultural Communities: Opportunities for Common Ground* (CAST 2002) was an important early discussion of UA from a systems analysis perspective.
- We need to broaden society's perceptions of agriculture beyond its traditional rural roots and commodity production focus.
- Interestingly, the demarcation between urban and rural agriculture now may exist more profoundly in the mind than on the land due to the physical blending of long-distance commuting, migration, immigration, etc.
- Understanding the functionality of the interface between rural and urban agriculture is needed to determine the areas of common ground in order to ensure the health of the entire agro-ecosystem. Potentially shared goods and services issues between rural and urban agriculture include restoration and remediation, ornamental horticulture and landscape services, and education and human capital development. Potentially shared problems include those related to sprawl, pollution and water resources. And potentially shared benefits include community and individual health, and business and economics.

- Contemporary UA is therefore a complex system encompassing a full spectrum of interests, including: production, marketing, distribution, and consumption; recreation and leisure (u-pick farming, agritourism); business entrepreneurship and economic vitality (horticulture, green industries, farmers' markets); neighbourhood beautification (sense of place); environmental planning (stormwater management, brownfields remediation, waste recycling, heat island modulation, sprawl restriction); and Individual and community health and well-being (plant and gardening therapy, quality of life, good food).

Community gardens often possess fascinating histories. And rarely are these histories ones of continued success after success with no difficulties circumvented along the way. Indeed, occasionally such histories take on the overtones of a Greek tragedy wherein gardening proponents become engaged in a process that can resemble the labours of Sisyphus. *The Struggle for Eden: Community Gardens in New York City* (Von Hassel 2002) demonstrates, as few other published case studies have, the importance of stepping back from the oftimes contentious fray and using an anthropological approach to describe and examine the *process* of developing such gardens, instead of merely focusing on only their end-products.

- Community gardens in New York City should be examined through a contextualized history that considers the following aspects: organization, internal politics, children, aesthetics, pageants, associated initiatives, food production, urban development, immigrants, economics, activism, sustainability, alternative society, spirituality and cartography.
- It is important to acknowledge that most community gardens are cherished and contested spaces, are city-owned with insecure tenure, and are part of a larger social movement.
- Intriguingly, community gardens epitomize the paradoxical possibility of urban spaces in which individuality in all its myriad forms can exist in the context of a community without being subsumed by it.
- With respect to New York City, the history of community gardens is 'a medley of lies, confusion, and betrayal involving political power and corruption.' Strong opinions developed leading to antagonisms. Mayor Giuliani, for example, before bulldozing gardens with no warning, told community gardeners that they were not living in a realistic world as they were 'stuck in the era of communism'. This criticism was embraced by garden proponents who adopted the marching song *Our Gardens Make Us*

Strong used by the Industrial Workers of the World (a.k.a. the Wobblies) during the early decades of the 20th century: 'The Earth is being murdered by the greed of man alone / They dig the mines and rape the fields and spread the cancer stones / Now it's time to stand together to defend our only home / And our gardens make us strong / Chorus: Solidarity forever (three times) / For our gardens make us strong!' sung to the tune of *John Brown's Body*.

- Community gardens claim, reshape and recycle the city landscape and also provide context for development of ideas and concepts. Additionally, they are battlefields for the emergence of new sets of ideas on how to live in cities. In other words, 'community gardens are not attempts to escape the city, but rather attempts to live within it, to confront it, and to selectively reject and appropriate aspects of its structures and dynamics.'
- Community gardens express the notion of battle on all fronts, which some believe to be a fight for an entire way of life rather than an assortment of single issues. In such cases, gardens become an ideological sword at the heart of people's self-imagined struggle to define themselves.

―

Cornell University's Thomas Lyson was one of the first academics to explore the modern linkages between food and people through a comprehensive systems analysis perspective. His 2004 book, *Civic Agriculture: Reconnecting Farm, Food, and Community*, is most important in highlighting the importance of studying the sociological in addition to the physical attributes of such systems.

- 'Civic agriculture' it is important to note is not exclusively nor even necessarily city agriculture but is rather *civitas* or citizen agriculture. In this sense, civic agriculture represents the rebirth of locally based agriculture and food production where these activities are tightly linked to a community's social and economic development as operationalized through farmers' markets, community gardens, and community-supported agriculture.
- In short, civic agriculture calls for the regeneration of a more socially and environmentally integrated food system. It becomes a powerful template around which to build non- or extra-market relationships between persons, social groups, and institutions that have been distanced from each other.
- In comparison to conventional agriculture, civic agriculture is based on a model of sustainability, holistic ecology, social and economic equity,

community welfare, localism, dispersed political power, grass-roots engagement, and the development of an educated food citizenry.

Urban agriculture in North America is still very much in its infancy at least in terms of its publication corpus. If one popular form of book has recently been the cross-system travelogue with succinct introductions to a suite of inspiring projects scattered around the world, another has been the site-specific, first-person narrative of the (mis)adventures involved with growing urban food. Two such works, written for a populist audience, are *Farm City: The Education of an Urban Farmer* (Carpenter 2009) and *My Empire of Dirt: How One Man Turned his Big-City Backyard into a Farm* (Howard 2009), dealing respectively with Oakland and New York City.

- Locavorism and the concept of 'food miles' have replaced organic agriculture as the rallying points for food discussions.
- The quest for backyard self-sufficiency, particularly pertaining to animal husbandry, is a difficult and sometimes expensive undertaking. Attempts at a closed system are plagued by problems in dealing with excrement from farm animals.
- Urban farming is not an easy endeavour. Often an important degree of humour is required to carry one over hurdles such as escaping livestock and dying plants, degraded or contaminated soil, and battles with disease, pests, predators, and politicians, in addition to a suite of legal obstacles.
- Just as important to nurture from the start is a healthy degree of scepticism to counter the often grandiose claims made about the ensuing benefits and managerial ease of urban farming. Above all, reality therapy needs to intercede to ground-truth flights of agrarian romanticism.
- For novices, searching for useful information is difficult. To circumvent contemporary knowledge gaps about backyard farming, one has to turn to century-old manuals on rearing and growing.
- An attitude of capitalizing on one's dilettantism by treating urban farming as a series of experiments is a healthy approach to prevent disappointment.
- Project success of such private enterprises can be made or broken by the support, ambivalence, or opposition offered by abutting neighbours. In this regard, dealing with flies attracted to manure can be a real thorny problem.

In *Urban Farming in the West: A New Deal Experiment in Subsistence Homesteads,* Carriker (2010) fills a longstanding gap in the scholarly study of New Deal communities. After the Great Depression, the U.S. government's Division of Subsistence Homesteads (DSH) and its successor, the Resettlement Administration (RA), built thirty-four New Deal homestead communities to provide a healthier and more secure life for disadvantaged Americans. The settlements would combine rural and urban living benefits through part-time farming, positive social functions, and affordable homes. Drawing extensively on local to state and federal archives, homesteader associations' proceedings, and photographic records, Carriker concludes that in many ways the Far West projects were the DSH's most successful initiatives.

- The original DHS was born out of a national industrial recovery act approved in the aftermath of the 1929 stock market crash. It built on an already vocal back-to-the-land social movement as a response to urban plight plaguing major urban centres at the time wherein two-thirds of industrial workers lived in substandard housing and less than half of all families owned a house.

- Informed vision and political savvy are critical to designing and securing support for publicly financed experiments. The case for federal political support for the subsistence homestead program was based on championing its multiple benefits, from child-rearing to secure retirement. Still, the proposal met with fierce criticism and failed to be funded as a stand-alone initiative. Rather, it was subsumed into a section of the National Industry Recovery Act and a lack of specific direction at the outset would eventually contribute to its undoing.

- The relative success of the four Western schemes in delivering on the original DHS vision is attributed to their having applied judiciously the DSH's standards of local organization, uncomplicated combination of part-time gardening, reasonable access to urban or industrial work, thoughtful home designs, family stability, and programmatic fiscal responsibility.

- With limited funding, the DHS focused on the demonstrative value of these settlements. In Phoenix, not only did the homestead project prove financially viable and affordable to homeowners, it also created a vibrant community association, and its design was found superior in many ways to rural resettlements implemented later under an agricultural cooperative model by the RA (which had replaced the DSH) as manager of the homesteads. Los Angeles County's allegiances to small farm homes were fuelled by the agrarian experiments there and advocacy continued for this movement with more people choosing the 'rurban' homestead as a way of life. Homesteaders selling their produce at public markets encouraged others to emulate them. These projects overall were celebrated, eyed with regional pride, house designs were prized, and one site was declared a national historic district. Today, 70 years after their creation, much of the land still remains under cultivation.

- The demise of the subsistence homestead experiment is attributed to confusion over critical aspects of the program. The name 'subsistence' caused many to envision a stop-gap relief program. And its mission was too ambitious, benefiting a wide range of groups needing assistance, well beyond its means.
- The Far West subsistence homesteads definitely did not fit into the utopian mission of the back-to-the-landers whose mission catered to national development priorities in terms of promoting more cohesive land-use planning, creating a sense of community among residents, and emphasizing home ownership as a boon to the national economy. The latter was probably the one priority most satisfied by the Far West industrial homesteads which fared better than many of the DSH's other projects because they were sited outside cities with industrial economies wherein employment created a financially stable population with low turnover. Homesteads of entirely rural nature were much more problematic and less successful.

Urban agriculture has the potential to be a high-design element in city planning, as shown in *Smartcities + Ecowarriors* (Lim and Liu 2010) and *The Vertical Farm: Feeding the World in the 21st Century* (Despommier 2010). To anchor their conceptual designs, these authors make some interesting points about the role of UA in sustainability.

- Urban agriculture is situated along a continuum of ideological planning extending backward from new urbanism to the garden city movement. Smart cities are those that address nature and society through ecological symbiosis and the built form.
- Food connects people and communities. It transcends class, age, culture and gender, and if it is belittled into nothing more than an abstraction due to mass production, processing, and packaging, we lose the best chance we have of adopting sustainable lifestyles. Most importantly, the

implementation of UA – which involves processing and distribution of food as well as its cultivation – makes these processes transparent and offers a means for the reestablishing of food and its production as a social relationship rather than just a commodity.
- Successful UA is based on closing the loop between production and waste recycling and reuse.
- Proponents of UA and local food sourcing should look to the French concept of *terroir* which considers climate, topography, soil, and sense of place when discussing wine production. Such locations might be called 'sitopias' or food-places, from the Greek *sitos* (food) and *topos* (place). Ideas of 'ecogastronomy' and agritourism, as developed in rural Europe, could be adapted to UA.
- Agriculture is responsible for more ecosystem disruption than any other form of pollution, If the built environment imitated and integrated more ecosystem functions, life for all would be more environmentally and ecologically sustainable.
- Indoor, hydroponic-based UA in specially designed, 'high-tech' greenhouse buildings will present multitudinous environmental benefits compared to traditional, soil-based farming in peri-urban areas.

Urban Agriculture: Diverse Activities and Benefits for City Society (Pearson et al. 2010), reprinted from a special issue of the *International Journal of Agricultural Sustainability*, is a compilation of papers from an international group of scholars that showcases the range of activities subsumed under the umbrella term 'urban agriculture.'
- Urban agriculture is not a single entity. It encompasses peri-urban farmland, small community gardens, personally managed allotments, home gardens, portions of parks, roadside reserves, greenhouses, and green roofs and living walls.
- Urban agriculture is frequently championed by social scientists as playing a central role in community development. It is now time for environmental scientists to join the discussion. Environmentally, in addition to providing food, UA has landscape impacts – mostly beneficial – on site aesthetics and ambient water and air quality. It is therefore important to recognize UA as a positive environmental act which can, for example, help with sanitation with respect to the disposal of biosolid waste or to provide a riparian buffer for flood control.
- The paramount issue regarding the long-term sustainability of UA is the

social one of how to protect urban land for greenspace and food production. This necessitates the following: acceptance of agriculture as a legitimate and protected land use within cities, promotion and maintenance of thriving food markets, and establishment of food policy councils to coordinate municipal responses to urban food security.
- There is a strategic need to identify principles of sustainability that help policy makers to design resilient cities such as, for example, the idea of 'food-prone areas' that can be prioritized for the production and employment.
- Another research priority is to explore the operational use of innovative institutional mechanisms to promote and preserve UA such as differential land taxes or payment incentives for ecosystem goods and services.

As urban farming continues to grow in popularity, it is important to collate and champion the many successes in order to provide encouragement and also education about the lessons learned concerning the best means of implementing these projects. One such book that accomplishes these objectives through an overview of many case studies is the richly illustrated *Reclaiming Our Food: How the Grassroots Food Movement is Changing the Way We Eat* (Cobb 2011).
- Fully one-third of American households grow and consume food from backyard gardens. As such, we need to shift focus from discussions about 100-mile diets to those about 100-foot diets.
- The historic progression toward banning farm animals in cities had less to do with sanitation than with development priorities concerned with impressions of backwardness and sophistication.
- Productivity of urban farms is often higher than rural ones due to heat island effects.
- Community gardens are increasingly being considered as part of comprehensive urban and peri-urban planning, including green/affordable housing and land conservation. Some development projects now include agriculture not as an afterthought but as the central focus.
- A recipe for success in developing and sustaining a community garden includes: community organizing, tenacity, patience, central focus on agriculture, partnerships, clustered housing, land trusts, accessibility, government support, and belief in the goals.
- Community gardens are catalysts for social change involving social justice, economic development, and public health.

- One important lesson learned from running a successful community garden is that if it is to help a community the individuals must assume ownership of the project from the very beginning; i.e. they must own, design, build, and maintain the space.
- Urban farms provide resilience to the local food system and educate about community spirit and connections to the natural world.
- One of the best interim uses for a brownfield site prior to its eventual decontamination and redevelopment is as an urban farm.
- Landscape architecture has begun to embrace the concept of edible landscape design.
- Urban farms are means towards ends of effective urban revitalization and regeneration.

Sustainable Urban Agriculture in Cuba (Knoot 2011) provides the most comprehensive account published to date on the Cuban UA model, probably the most complex and integrated of any national public program in existence today which has been inspiring a growing number of initiatives throughout the Americas and beyond. The book discusses the historical background to the program and its organization; the foundational role played by pre-existing infrastructure for education, research and development; adjustments that have been brought to worker training, preparatory education and material inputs for UA; systems and processes of material and moral incentives introduced to motivate workers; examples of technological innovation in UA; and case studies based on field visits which show how the support system has combined with capacities and consciousness on the ground to enable agricultural transformation. The book concludes with an evaluation of the model's success to date and looks at the future of urban and sustainable agriculture in Cuba and beyond.

- Similarly to England and other western countries, an economic and food-rationing crisis prompted the national government to develop grassroots UA in Cuba.
- Success has been uneven across the production systems: high with fruits and vegetables in cities, but more modest with livestock raising and with making rural agriculture more sustainable.
- Prerequisites critical to the success of the Cuban UA program include infrastructure for human resource formation, a strong and coherent gender-, work- and territorially based social organization, and a centrally

- directed organization supporting a decentralized network of production units.
- Cuba's National UA Group's definition of what constitutes UA is broad, including all agricultural lands within certain distances of cities and towns of a thousand or more people, as well as kitchen gardens in settlements of at least fifteen houses.
- The organic character of UA was imposed by circumstances, not developed in response to market demand. And it stemmed from the need to rely on locally available or developable resources.
- Cuba has demonstrated, out of necessity, that a transition to agro-ecological production is possible. Should conventional agriculture under free market trade return to Cuba, the Cuban UA movement leadership believes its model can be sustained under certain conditions. The opportunity cost of labour in other economies, as in the Cuban economy, will remain a key factor in shaping the viability of particular practices within UA systems. However, public agencies have been investing in innovations to increase efficiencies of agro-ecological practices, with success, as for example, monitoring returns across several dimensions beyond yields to account more fully for their economic merit. Cuba now exports some of its agro-ecological services and products. A new program of suburban agriculture started in 2009 should help urban innovations to spread to the rest of Cuban agriculture.
- Cuba's national UA program does show that, with vision and coordination, a comprehensive approach is technically feasible at very low marginal cost and can achieve impressive results on multiple fronts. Although it should not be expected to supply all of the food consumed by cities, the Cuban experience shows that UA can become an important tool to improve food security (and sovereignty), human and environmental health, usefully occupy young talents, at the same time as building stronger communities.

In *Responsiveness of Town Planning to Urban Agriculture: Kwa-Mashu, SA*, Magidimisha (2011) asks why South African town planning has largely been unresponsive to the growth of UA. She selected the municipality of eThekwini and drew on municipal maps, a small-sample survey of households in low-income neighbourhoods, interviews with senior municipal officials, and observation participants to review the South African experience through the lens of modernist town planning and sustainable livelihoods.

- South African government policies and legal instruments (Local Government and Public Health Acts) do allow particular types of farming to be practised in and around cities under certain conditions.
- Town planning in South Africa has been greatly influenced by the modernist school for orderly and functional settlements; it has resorted to zoning, massive slum clearance, public housing (e.g. Soweto) and town planning schemes ruled by apartheid-era principles. This blending of modernism with apartheid led to a racially segregated and spatially fragmented urban form. It also prevented the establishment of UA in areas classified as urban; i.e. agriculture was viewed as a rural activity which should not be practised in urban areas.
- This planning approach has discouraged attention to a sustainable livelihood approach to urban development, where people's own capabilities might be supported by government policies to help them participate better in the urban economy.
- With the exception of Johannesburg and Cape Town, few cities in South Africa have regarded UA as a legitimate urban land use. UA is not recognized as such because it is viewed as secondary and momentary. Producers cannot obtain long-term leases, make firm commitments, and solicit grants. Regulatory and bureaucratic hurdles place legal UA opportunities beyond the reach of ordinary poor people. No support or training is provided to urban producers.
- In eThekwini there is poor local management of UA and related issues. Plans do not define UA uses spatially. Authorities have been tolerating UA activities on an ad hoc basis (for a fee), mostly on right-of-ways and easements, as well as on un-built areas slated for other uses. Inadequate zoning for UA has led to competition for space with other urban needs. Planners seem to view the odours produced by poultry and goat rearing in residential areas as the responsibility of other departments.

The vividly illustrated *Urban Farms* (Rich 2012) surveys in a very compelling way the nascent urban farming movement in the U.S., in particular the origin, strategies, accomplishments and challenges of initiatives in the major cities of Boston, New York, Philadelphia, Washington, Detroit, Chicago, Milwaukee, New Orleans, Los Angeles, and Oakland. These case studies are interspersed with contributions by various writer-practitioners on the roles and benefits of urban farms for education, entrepreneurship, public health, artistic expression, and homesteading systems. A sister publication, *Breaking Through Concrete: Building an Urban Farm Revival*, by Hanson and Marty (2012), covers different sites in Brooklyn, Chicago, New Orleans, as well as other cities: Seattle, Birmingham, Santa Cruz, Santa Barbara, Denver, and Kansas City.

- Urban garden or urban farm? A garden is a leisurely, optional use of one's time, whereas a farm is driven by the need for sustenance that it fulfils. Sustenance should not be equated with self-sufficiency, as urban farms are hardly the farmers' sole source of subsistence or income; nor are benefits exclusive to that particular form of UA. A more refined definition of the urban farm is needed. In this respect, urban farms are more business-oriented than gardens and normally require larger areas or space than gardens, allowing them to accommodate a broader range of interacting production systems (including several types of livestock) and other compatible urban activities to encourage synergies between these and farming itself. Urban homesteading encompasses, beyond urban farming, a broader range of do-it-yourself (artisanal) activities for a more self-reliant life-style, however one that is still dependent on amenities offered by the city. Finally, urban farming is more an aim or purpose, rather than a physically distinct UA system.
- While urban farms involve managers, staff or volunteers in planning and working the plots for market sales, the community garden allots small beds to individuals who apply for them, pay a small fee, adhere to shared guidelines, and grow for their own needs.
- The multiple functions of urban farms are often reflected in the very diverse partnerships formed with other urban sectors: use of abandoned or under-utilized lots and buildings, growing media imported from local cemeteries, zoos, breweries, and municipal tree-maintenance services, contributions from city nurseries (trees), restaurants (grease for biodiesel), animal and motorized power from police departments, and manpower from shelters, local volunteers, universities, and youth. They attract funding for rain catchments, outdoor education, school meals, and community health and well-being initiatives. In return they supply food to shelters, food banks, restaurants, local health clinics, schools, and consumers at designated points of sale.
- Gaining a voice at City Hall is important for the longevity and success of grass-root UA initiatives, as exemplified by Seattle's 40 year-old P-Patch system of 73 community gardens over 23 acres and supported by a senior urban planner who led an effort to recognize and define UA in the city.
- The broadly defined educational function of urban farms often stands out as the single most important entry point or catalyst for urban farmers in U.S. cities to gain local political support, strike partnerships with public

programs, secure financial support from both private and public entities, press for regulatory innovation, and develop other functions in the process. Engaging school children in urban farms redresses the balance between technology-oriented and outdoor-based learning.

- In many cases, urban farms have contributed to re-using under or unused, abandoned and contaminated ground areas. Hydroponics are a good way of using areas where in-ground planting is not appropriate due to soil contamination.
- Urban farms are mostly civic businesses. By combining public with private good functions, many urban farms rely on a fairly robust financing model which pools public subsidies with market income and makes their operations viable. Even so, most urban farms strive to become more self-reliant.
- Innovative policy making can be critical to success. For example, Seattle in the 1970s and Washington in the early 1980s launched programs to make better and more systematic use of the city's empty lots and vacant land. In Chicago, City Farm has a unique arrangement with the city: it does not buy or lease the land for its crops but uses it at the discretion of developers and city officials, with commitment to vacate if land is needed for development. This had led its operators to design the farm to be fully mobile. Cities are being pressed to set up one-stop shops for urban farms, like for small business development, where urban farmers can address zoning, home business regulations, nuisance laws and the like all in one place.
- Crises can spark renewed policy interest in UA. Recently, exposure to food supply and demand disruptions triggered by extreme natural events and economic recession in the US have led cities such as Seattle to revisit their reliance on long-distance food sources. As a result, Seattle changed its zoning codes to remove all barriers to growing and selling food to citizens, while ensuring public health and safety. The planning process initiated in 2010 has now turned to looking beyond production and at the whole of the local food system (distribution, education, awareness).
- A highly educated new generation is leading the growth of urban farms in the U.S. Architects, agro-ecology engineers, agronomists, business managers, and lawyers volunteer time to design, run, promote and protect urban farms, In cities with high unemployment and abundant abandoned land (such as Detroit), a new generation of local graduates and transplants from other cities have been lured by low housing prices and low cost of living to move in, renovate properties, and revitalize neighbourhoods anchored around development of UA. However, these new urban farmers rarely possess agricultural training or background, and even when they

do, these usually are more suited to rural rather than for urban settings. As such, there is still a huge gap to be filled in our training systems before we can match opportunities in urban farming with a supply of knowledgeable practitioners.

References

Council for Agricultural Science and Technology (Butler, A. and B. Maronek). 2002. Urban and agricultural communities: Opportunities for common ground. Task Force Report 138. CAST.

Carriker, R.M. 2010. Urban farming in the west: A New Deal experiment in subsistence homesteads. Univ. Arizona Press.

Carpenter, N. 2009. Farm city: The education of an urban farmer. Penguin Press.

Cobb, T.D. 2011. Reclaiming our food: How the grassroots food movement is changing the way we eat. Storey Publ.

Crouch, C. and C. Ward. 2003. The allotment: Its landscape and culture. Five Leaves Publ.

Despommier, D. 2010. The vertical farm: Feeding the world in the 21st century. Thomas Dunn Books.

France, R.L. 2002. Background – Perspectives of water management: Representative examples form the recent literature. p. 1-8 *In* France, R.L. (Ed.) Handbook of water sensitive planning and design. Lewis Publ.

France, R.L. 2005. Topics and challenges in watershed management – A literature review; and Developing a plurality of voices for watershed stewardship – A literature review. p. 1-14 *In* France, R.L. (Ed.) Facilitating watershed management: Fostering awareness and stewardship. Rowman & Littlefield.

France, R.L. 2006. Ideas and concerns in environmental education: A literature review. p. 19-23 *In* France, R. Introduction to watershed development: Understanding and managing the impacts of sprawl. Rowman & Littlefield.

France, R.L. 2008. The muddy, messy means and mores of 'restoring' a broken world: A literature review. p. 232-235 *In* France, R.L. (Ed.) Healing natures, repairing relationships: New perspectives on restoring ecological spaces and consciousness. Green Frigate Books.

Hanson, D. and E. Marty. 2012. Breaking through the concrete: Building an urban farm revival. Univ. California Press.

Howard, M. 2009. My empire of dirt: How one man turned his big-city backyard into a farm. Scribner.

Koont, S. 2011. Sustainable urban agriculture in Cuba. Univ. Press Florida.

Lim, C.J. and E. Lu. 2010. Smartcities + ecowarriors. Routledge.

Lyson, T. 2004. Civic agriculture: Reconnecting farm, food, and community.

Tufts Univ. Press.

Magidmisha, H.H. 2001. Responsiveness of town planning to urban agriculture: Kwa-Mashu, SA. VDM Verlag.

Pearson, C.J., S. Pilgrim and J. Pretty. (Eds.) 2010. Urban agriculture: Diverse activities and benefits for city society. Routledge.

Philips, A. 2013. Designing urban agriculture: A complete guide to the design, construction, maintenance and management of edible landscapes. Wiley.

Rich, S. 2012. Urban farms. H. N. Abrams.

Tuan, Y-F. 2001. Space and place: The perspective of experience. Univ. Minnesota Press.

von Hassel, M. 2002. The struggle for Eden: Community gardens in New York City. Praeger.

Commentary – Urban agriculture and its role in transformational agriculture and gender equality

Kevany, K. and Lynch, D.

Recognizing, articulating, and celebrating the many benefits of UA necessitate, as France and Mougeot argue, a greater appreciation of the physical spaces and social places that constitute UA. Effective policy design and planning would incorporate the multiple roles that UA allotments fulfill and problems they may help mitigate. Issues that engage the imaginations of urban and rural farmers and dwellers might be addressing their shared problems of sprawl, pollution and water resources, as the authors contest. Multiple benefits too could be shared, those of enhancing community and individual health, expanding business opportunities and economic return as well as contributing to environmental protections and facilitating social benefits like through 'citizen agriculture' as promoted by Lyson (2004). Challenges in urban agriculture, like battles with *disease, pests, predators, and politicians*, need a variety of strategies, including a sense of humour, as the authors of this chapter exemplify.

As noted also above, France and Mougeot have highlighted very well how publications on UA to date have tracked the role of UA in 'reestablishing food and its production as a social relationship rather than just a commodity' and its role in community development. Indeed it can be viewed as a form of 'civic agriculture' first elaborated by Lyson (2004) and has thus engaged the attention of social scientists throughout its development. Importantly, however, they also highlight the clear need for environmental scientists and ecologists to now contribute to our understanding of the benefits of UA. Urban agriculture's role in protection of the landscape, and likely benefits to ambient water and air quality are noted. To this list could be added examination of the important potential benefits of vegetative and faunal biodiversity including managed or native pollinators, plus the, until recently, neglected study of 'Anthropedology'; i.e. the character and management of soils in urban landscapes and the services they provide. Environmental benefits from UA will not be limited to land-based operations however, and innovations (often patented) in energy and water conservation and waste use and recycling are being developed currently by rooftop and greenhouse UA ventures, a commercial example of which is Lufa farms in inner-city Montreal.

Reganold et al. (2011) argue that since agriculture is a complex socio-ecological system, multiple sustainability concerns can only be addressed through a transformative, whole system redesign that engages all stakeholders, rather than more incremental and solely technological approaches. A broader question thus is whether UA can be considered part of a spectrum of such a needed transformation of agriculture, combining UA, Fair Trade and Organic Agriculture, and not restricted solely to considerations of location. All these overlapping systems in common 'promote agricultural literacy by directly linking consumers to producers' or awareness of their production systems, and a 'more socially and environmentally integrated food system' (Lyson 2004). Lynch et al (2013) undertook an integrated examination of the social, environmental and economic benefits associated with organic agriculture in the Canadian context. Documented gains in environmental/ecological goods and services included enhanced biodiversity. Socially, knowledge production and social learning opportunities are enhanced by the shared and knowledge intensive nature of organic farming, and organic farmers appear to be more engaged locally and contribute more to rural community sustainability. However, with some exceptions, while 'organic agriculture can offer an opportunity for addressing rural gender relations this opportunity has often been squandered' (Sumner & Llewelyn, 2011), a failing in recognition of gender issues in common with UA as noted above. Proactive gender strategies are needed to enable all alternative forms of agriculture to achieve their full potential.

Understanding UA and organic agriculture as a form of the civil commons may help to influence the recognition and acceptance of the suite of benefits such transformative agriculture provides. Building on Lynch et al. (2013), integrated and multi-disciplinary approaches help elaborate how transformative agriculture forms, such as UA and organic agriculture, can be considered sustainable to the degree that they promote a 'civil commons' – a co-operative human construct that protects and/or enables universal access to a variety of life goods and services (Sumner 2005), whether these be the minimization of soil degradation and erosion, decreased pollution, increased energy efficiency and a sustainable livelihood, and the creation of a knowledge commons that inform and fuel advances in gender equality.

While the specific and very important issue of gender in UA was not addressed in the books reviewed by France and Mougeot, the potential for social transformation and gender equality are germinating in UA. In the book, *Women Feeding Cities*, the authors provide substantive evidence for the social, economic, and public good that are cultivated through women nurturing the soils and feeding their families and communities. Over ten thousand years, wherever humans have settled, women have been pivotal in growing agriculture. Today, it is largely women, whether urban or rural, that cultivate small family farms and transport foodstuffs on their backs or on public transport as they actively sustain family food sources and base income as 'market women'. Much of this work by women is insufficiently calculated and valued in food and agriculture policies. This contradiction in effort and attention 'has contributed to the invisibility of women's role in provisioning cities with food' (Hovorka, de Zeeuw, & Njenga, 2009, p. xiiii). Large scale food production, processes, and packaging have largely become disassociated from communities, from the infusion of feminine leadership and have revealed less sustainable ecological patterns and less 'civilized' social systems. To address marginalization and inequality faced by women, authors Hovorka, de Zeeuw, and Njenga identify tools and solutions from case studies in an array of developing countries. Even with some resistance in urban settings where restrictive bylaws strive to prohibit urban agriculture, growing campaigns are evident. Rising from patches of these cultivated lands are the ingredients for healthy social change, social justice, economic and social development and these give rise to the seeds for greater public health and community vitality and well-being. These authors contend that 'urban agriculture should be recognized as an integral and permanent element of the urban socio-economic and ecological system' (p. 5). For it is through urban agriculture that a large number of urban poor sustain themselves and their livelihood.

These stories of valuing women's roles in urban and rural agriculture are corroborated in a special collection of papers on 'Water, Women, Waste, Wisdom, and Wealth' Kevany et al. (2013). These papers reveal the need for proactive planning to mitigate disruptions when women and men face more complex and dynamic social and economic processes moving from rural into evolving urban structures and systems. The papers also address the gender bias evident in the health risks faced by women and girls and the roles filled by women in preserving the integrity of ecosystems. On a daily basis, it is often women who are contending with social and political practices in urban agriculture. When women are engaged in feeding cities they also are contributing to family stability and health, job creation, bolstering self-confidence and ecological improvements. These authors concur that more attention needs to be given to the critical role women fulfill in urban agriculture and ecosystem management. This special collection offers an array of strategies to recalibrate approaches to produce food while caring for the environment and the community. Through the emerging insights from fifteen years of study on women feeding families and cities, we have the insights to incorporate proactive gender strategies and to facilitate interventions that strengthen the resiliency, prosperity, vibrancy, and sustainability of urban agriculture.

References

Hovorka, A., de Zeeuw, H., and Njenga, M. (eds.), 2009. Women feeding cities: Mainstreaming gender in urban agriculture and food security. Practical Action Publishing.

Kevany, K., Siebel, M., Hyde, K., Nazer, D., and Huisingh, D. 2013. Special volume: Water, women, waste, wisdom and wealth, Journal of Cleaner Production 60: 1-230

Lynch D. H., Sumner, J. and Martin, R.C. 2013. Framing the social, ecological and economic goods and services derived from organic agriculture in the Canadian context *In* S. Bellon, S. Penvern (eds.), Organic Farming, Prototype for Sustainable Agricultures, 1 DOI 10.1007/978-94-007-7927-3_19, © Springer Science+Business Media Dordrecht 2014

Lyson. T, 2004. Civic agriculture: Reconnecting farm, food, and community. Thomas University Press of New England, Lebanon, NH.

Reganold JP, Jackson-Smith D, Batie SS, Harwood RR, Kornegay JL, Bucks D, Flora CB, Hanson JC, Jury WA, Meyer D, Schumacher JrA, Sehmsdorf H, Shennan C, Thrupp LA, and Willis P. 2011. Transforming US agriculture. Science, 332:670-671.

Sumner, J. 2005. Sustainability and the civil commons: Rural communities in the age of globalization. Toronto: University of Toronto Press.

Sumner J., Llewelyn, S. 2011. Organic solutions? Gender and organic farming in the age of industrial agriculture. Capitalism, Nature, Socialism, 22:100-118.

CHAPTER 2

Public Produce: Food By the People, For the People

Darrin Nordahl and Catherine Fisher

Introduction

Imagine walking around downtown in any major North American city. You will see many shops, cafés, an art gallery or two, a trendy restaurant, and other places to spend time and money. On your stroll, you spot something mid-block, sandwiched between that trendy restaurant and a cute dress boutique. At a quick glance, it appears to be a farmers' market, but where the tomatoes, lettuce, bok choy, and radishes are growing *in situ*. Though you see what appear to be farmers or gardeners tending the produce, you realize there are no places to conduct commerce; no tables, cash drawers, or even merchants to take your money. That is because this place is a free produce market, where the cost of organically grown fruits and vegetables is only your willingness to harvest them yourself.

If you are now wondering if such a place exists outside your imagination, let us assure you, it does. Kamloops, British Columbia might very well be a fresh produce lover's Xanadu. In January of 2011, a community group, with the help of the Kamloops Food Policy Council and the Thompson-Shuswap Master Gardeners, earnestly transformed an unused parcel of land on Victoria Street in downtown into a public edible garden. The plan had been in the making for a long time before this, the leaders gathering their information and inspiration from the Victory Gardens in San Francisco and

Fig. 2.1. Kamloops' downtown public produce project is one part vegetable garden and one part community gathering space (image courtesy of Kendra Besanger)

Darrin Nordahl's book *Public Produce: The New Urban Agriculture*. It all came together when the gardeners association received a food-safety grant from the Interior Health Authority, and a local property owner allowed his vacant land to be cultivated.

By the summer of 2011, a robust garden was thriving on that vacant lot, offering fresh, free produce to passersby. Hand-lettered signs introduce folks to the garden's various produce items, and tell them when to pick and how. Children pick chard alongside college students and suited business men and women pluck zucchini with the down-and-out (Fig. 2.1).

And the thrill of such an experience caught on. In the following years, Kamloops public food gardens have spread. Public vegetables have been planted in front of City Hall; in decorative sidewalk planters along Victoria Street; on a vacant parcel in a residential neighbourhood; and in two city parks.

The Kamloops gardens are an example of a new trend in urban agriculture, commonly referred to as *public produce*. Here, local citizens, working with public officials, have taken a publicly accessible space and are growing food for the public – for anyone to harvest, free of charge. It is a trend we are seeing across North America, from Vancouver to Halifax, and from Seattle to Baltimore.

But what is the motivation for growing food in public space for free public consumption? One is a growing attitude that in our now mechanized and global food supply, everyone should have the opportunity to taste a perfectly ripe tomato picked moments from the vine. But this attitude underscores a more pervasive concern. The biggest motivator of public produce is food security. Food security issues are having a profoundly negative impact on our health, environment, and pocketbook in North America, and public produce, such as those examples in Kamloops, can provide relief.

FOOD INSECURITY IN NORTH AMERICA

Before we outline what the specific food security issues are in the U.S. and Canada, let's begin with a definition. Food security, as commonly defined, is the daily access to *adequate, safe, affordable and nutritious* food. Let's start with that first component of our definition: daily access to *adequate* food. According to the United States' Centers for Disease Control and Prevention (CDC), only one in four American adults consume the recommended daily servings of vegetables, and only one in three meets their recommended daily allowance for fruits. Stated another way, the overwhelming majority of Americans are not meeting the minimum levels of nutrition supplied by fruits and vegetables.[1]

Then there is that second component of food security: *safety*. While it is now common knowledge that undercooked meat and eggs pose great health risks, we are now witnessing large outbreaks of food-borne illness from contaminated fruits, vegetables, and even nuts. The pathogens of *E. coli* and *Salmonella* – two types of bacteria that are commonly found in raw meat and eggs – are now finding their way onto our fresh produce items. *TIME* magazine ranked leafy greens, perhaps the most nutritious stuff we can eat as humans, as one of the top 10 most dangerous foods.[2] In 2006, for example, *E. coli* contaminated fresh spinach from California, sickening almost 200 people across 26 states. Three of those infected – two elderly and a two-year old child – died.[3]

But it isn't just leafy greens that are dangerous. During the summer of 2008, North America witnessed what we call the 'Great Salsa Scare.' *Salmonella* var. 'Saintpaul' was sickening people in Texas and across the southwest. The U.S. Food and Drug Administration (FDA) first believed that tomatoes were the source of the bacteria, and advised people to stop eating fresh roma, plum, and round tomatoes. Still more people were infected and in many more states. Tainted tomatoes were never discovered, but the FDA did discover a link between salsa and *Salmonella*, meaning cilantro and peppers were possible culprits. Finally, the FDA traced the source of contamination to jalapeño and serrano peppers from a packing plant in Texas.[4] At the end of the outbreak, 1,442 people were infected across 43 states and parts of Canada.[5] As soon as that *Salmonella* outbreak was contained, another outbreak emerged, this time from the variant *Salmonella* 'Typhimurium' Thirty-million pounds of tainted peanut products were recalled from a single processor in Georgia during late 2008 and early 2009, but not before 700 people across 46 states were sickened. Nine of those people died.[6] Then, in the spring of 2009, *Salmonella* var. 'Saintpaul' returned, this time contaminating alfalfa, and sickening over 200 people across 14 states.[7] And in April of 2011, romaine lettuce was found contaminated with another virulent strain of *E. coli*. Over the next eleven months, five-dozen Americans across 9 states became sickened from *E. coli*-contaminated Romaine lettuce.[8]

So why are pathogens like E. coli and Salmonella more prevalent in our factory-farmed, corporate-scale agriculture? Because of the massive scale at which fruits and vegetables are grown.

'The bigger and more global the trade in food,' food journalist Michael Pollan contends, 'the more vulnerable the system is to catastrophe.'[9] A decentralized system of many small, local farms and garden plots simply could never have the potential of infecting that many people over so large a geographic area. It was this very pattern of widespread infection that led health officials to conclude that, amid the thousands of people falling ill during the Salmonella 'Saintpaul' outbreak, produce from local gardens was safe.[10]

Salmonella and E. coli are bacteria found in the intestines of animals and humans. So how do they get into our spinach, pepper, peanut, alfalfa, and other produce crops? Usually they come from the feces of animals, meaning that these bacteria can be found in the soil of our 'pristine' farm fields (as is the case when fields are fertilized with manure). Or, even more treacherous, bacteria breeds in the water supply used to irrigate the crops. Indeed, irrigation water is a common source of microbial contamination of fresh produce. Large farm fields in the warmer and drier parts of the country (where most of our year-round fresh produce is derived) requires irrigation through large bodies of open water, such as canals and ponds. Open bodies of water present a potential health hazard, as they receive untreated stormwater runoff. When that stormwater finds its way into canals and ponds – after it has been in contact with chicken ranches, feed lots, cow pastures, and other places where concentrations of animal dung can be found – there exists a real risk of contamination. In fact, FDA officials traced the source of the Salmonella 'Saintpaul' strain that infected serrano peppers to a holding pond used for irrigation.[11] Unlike their rural food-producing counterparts, urban agricultural efforts are at less risk from waterborne pathogens because they are not irrigated by large bodies of open water. Urban gardens are typically irrigated by rainfall and closed sources of potable water, delivered directly to the plants from city waterlines. The chance of contamination from water, therefore, is quite limited.

THE COST OF HEALTHY CALORIES

Colin Beavan, known by many as No Impact Man, set out on a year-long journey to find homeostasis, an equilibrium between his consumerist way of life and environmentalist ideals. His goal was deceptively modest: to sustain a simple life in New York City without making any net impact on the environment. To Beavan, that meant 'no trash, no carbon emissions, no toxins in the water, no elevators, no subway, no products in packaging, no plastics, no air conditioning, no TV, no toilets. . . .'[12] And it also meant a very different way of eating. Beavan needed to eschew fast and processed foods, and only consume locally raised, organically grown foods to be honest to the No Impact Man project. At the end of his experiment, Beavan realized that 'Eating local is a no-brainer if you live in a rich neighbourhood with the cool, local-food farmers' market nearby.' Beavan has been criticized that his experiment was bourgeois, and he now understands why. 'Not consuming resources is no problem if a life of purchasing power has provided you with most of what you need,' he admits. It is quite perplexing that to live a simple lifestyle in North America is beyond the financial means of many. It is easy to say that we all should buy more organic, locally grown produce. It is quite another to be able to do so. And as Beavan has discovered, 'Nutritious, local food should not just be available to the wealthy while the poor are left with McDonalds and KFC.'[13]

Beavan's discovery of the conundrum between local, organically grown food and its high cost brings us to another important consideration in food security, and that is public health, which is directly tied to that last component of our definition: *affordable* AND *nutritious* food. We've all seen the emaciated bodies of starving people living in countries crippled by food insecurity. It is oxymoronic that obesity is the result of food insecurity here in North America. It is not the inaccessibility of food calories in this continent that is problematic. Rather, it is the abundance of cheap calories derived from processed and fast food vis-à-vis the inaccessibility of fresh, wholesome, nutrient-dense foods at an affordable price that is responsible for the poor health of our citizens.

The rapid rise in obesity in the North America largely coincides with the increase of energy-dense, processed foods in our diet over the past two decades. And the change in our health during that short time span is mind-boggling. In 1990, not a single state in the United States reported a prevalence of obesity greater than 14% of its adult population. Today, not a single state can make that claim. Colorado has the lowest prevalence of obesity, with 15-19% of its adult population. For states throughout the South and parts of the Midwest, 1 in 3 adults are obese.[14] Fig 2.2).

But the increased prevalence of obesity is not just a problem in the States. While the U.S. population is certainly fatter than Canada, Canadians are increasing in size as well. According to a 2012 Policy Brief from the

Fig. 2.2. These two diagrams profoundly illustrate the rapid rise in adult obesity in the United States (maps from the Centers for Disease Control and Prevention)

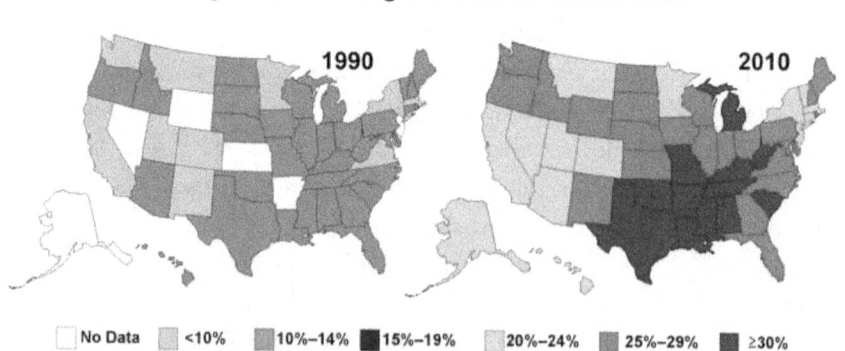

Organisation for Economic Co-Operation and Development (OECD), two out of three Canadian men are overweight, and one in four Canadian adults are obese.[15] (*Obese* is generally defined as having a Body Mass Index, or BMI, greater than 30. *Overweight* is a BMI score of 25–29.9. You can find BMI calculators online; simply enter your weight and height and your BMI will be instantly calculated.)

The obesity epidemic is alarming, because obesity increases our risk of a whole host of ills, such as Type 2 diabetes, heart disease, stroke, and variety of cancers.[16] In Huntington, West Virginia, for example, the city that the CDC labeled the unhealthiest in the U.S., people in their thirties – what should be the prime of their life – are undergoing open heart surgery.[17] This new generation, it is predicted, will live sicker and die younger than their parents; the first time in the modern history of North America.[18]

What is particularly frustrating is that these illnesses are not the result of nature, but of our own actions. They are entirely preventable, if only we could eat more sensibly, and to increase fruits and vegetables in our diet. But for many people, they have no choice but to eat a poor diet. They cannot afford to eat healthy, and that is the real shame in this so-called 'Land of Plenty.'

GROWING FASCINATION AND DEMAND FOR LOCAL PRODUCE

Aside from issues of food security, there is a growing fascination and demand for local agriculture. There are environmental, physiological, economical, and even psychological reasons for eating local produce. With regard to the environment, *food miles* – the distance between the farm and your plate – have become a big concern. As most have heard, the average produce item in a Canadian or American supermarket (unless you live in California) comes from over 1,500 miles away. We're now regularly importing produce items from Mexico, Peru, Chile, China, and New Zealand. And with the increase in food miles comes an increase in concern over our environment. There is a considerable amount of greenhouse gases being spewed into the atmosphere to transport our food.

Take Chicago, for example, a huge city surrounded by hundreds of thousands of acres of the most fertile soil in North America. Grapes and broccoli, on average, travel over 2,000 miles to get to Chicago. Asparagus and apples travel over 1,500 miles to reach the Chicago terminal market. Mexico provides Chicagoans with 37% of their asparagus and 43% of their squash. And perhaps most confounding is sweet corn. Illinois is the 2nd largest producer of corn in the United States, behind Iowa. Yet, on average, sweet corn travels over 800 miles to reach Chicagoans.[19] Keep in mind all of these produce items grow quite well in Illinois, but because of today's agricultural policies, government subsidies, and economic structure, almost everything now is imported.

Increased food miles also reduce the flavour, suppleness, and nutrition of many produce items. In order for produce to travel such long distances without bruising or spoiling, farmers are growing varieties with tougher skin, that pack tighter, and have a longer shelf life. To make that journey from across the country, or Mexico, South America, or New Zealand, fruits and vegetables have to be picked well before they are ripe, and then artificially ripened with ethylene gas when they reach the terminal market. What does this do? For one, it reduces the flavour potential of our food. And it also reduces the amount of nutrients available.

Here's a question for you: what's the difference between a red bell pepper and a green one? Ripeness. A green bell pepper is simply an under-ripe red bell pepper. Red bell peppers have four times the Vitamin C as green peppers, eleven times more beta carotene, and red bell peppers have the antioxidant lycopene, which is absent in the under-ripe green bell pepper.[20] The same nutrient-to-ripeness relationship holds true with other fruits and vegetables. Picking produce before it is fully ripe often means there will be less phytochemicals, micronutrients, vitamins, and antioxidants compared to ripe produce.

We are also rediscovering the beauty of agriculture. The prominent New Urbanist planner Andres Duany once quipped that 'agriculture is quite good-looking' and remarked that 'agriculture is the new golf.'[21] Developers across the continent are now looking at subdivisions not ringing the golf course, as what once was considered the norm, but now ringing organic farms. A great example of this can be found just outside of St. Louis, in a development called New Town at St. Charles (which was designed by Duany). Troy Gardens in Madison is another example of this trend, as well as one in False Creek, Vancouver (see Chapter 7).

Coinciding with this growing fascination and demand for local produce, 'U-Pick' operations have exploded in popularity throughout the U.S and

Fig. 2.3. A common message on so-called 'community' gardens (photo by author, Davenport, Iowa)

Canada. Urbanites today crave an agrarian experience, and are looking to pick or harvest fresh food for themselves. In the San Francisco Bay Area, for example, folks will drive *two hours* for the simple pleasure of picking apples from an orchard!

Unfortunately, high demand for fresh local produce also has a seedy side. We've all witnessed this before: so-called 'community' garden plots with blatant signs notifying other members of the community to 'Keep Out.' (Fig 2.3). Such displays point to the obvious: fresh, locally grown produce is in such high demand, people have to resort to stealing it. If we could provide a system of public produce, so that a diversity of garden items are readily available to the public, people wouldn't have to pilfer the veggies from somebody's community garden plot.

Which brings us to what public officials are doing across the U.S. and Canada to do just that, provide readily accessible produce for the public at large.

Examples of Public Produce

Nathan Murray is not your typical farmer. Sure, he has the stocky build of a man who works the land. But he is a white collar, green thumber, who tends his crops in Dockers, loafers, and a Van Heusen. Murray's smart casual attire – perhaps a bit spiffy for growing vegetables – is actually mandatory. He is a representative of City Hall, after all.

'Pansies have their place, but I prefer looking at tomatoes,' Murray admits. Murray – a City Planner for the City of Provo, Utah – is referring to the view out his cubicle window. The raised brick planters dotting the plaza on the south side of City Hall used to be planted with the usual flashy suspects: pansies, petunias, and marigolds. But those showy flowers have long been replaced by equally showy fruits, like tomatoes, peppers, and eggplant. And Murray is the reason for the change in the landscape's visage.

Murray's transformation of City Hall's landscape was sparked by an all-too-familiar story. During the economic freefall that tipped in 2008, municipalities across the nation tightened their belts (see Chapter 8). In an effort to reduce cost, 'minimum maintenance' became the mantra bellowed from the halls of every municipal building in America. Budgets for

Fig. 2.4. Seedlings germinating in a cubicle under fluorescent lights in the City of Provo's City Hall (image courtesy of Nathan Murray, City of Provo, Utah)

landscaping the City's public spaces and buildings were slashed. Flowers were luxuries municipalities couldn't afford. Even if they could, such displays were certainly not evocative of fiscally prudent budget managers.

But Murray didn't want to look out his cubicle window and see empty dirt. Besides, this was City Hall, a prestigious civic building that should convey a friendly and inviting message to the public, not an austere one.

Murray had just finished reading a book on guerilla gardening, and that sprouted an idea. He would commandeer those empty planters and fill them with vegetables. His goals were quite simple: to provide a bit of greenery to soften the stark plaza around City Hall, and to show folks just how much food can be produced from a little bit of dirt.

He began by germinating vegetable seeds in a makeshift greenhouse – in this case his cubicle. With the office thermostat set to 72 degrees and the flood of light from the overhead fluorescent tubes, Murray's cubicle proved an ideal environment to sprout tomatoes, peppers, melons, squash, eggplant, beans, and all sorts of heat-loving plants…even in the dead of winter. Once the danger of frost had passed, Murray and a couple of co-workers transplanted their City Hall seedlings outside. They may not have realized it at the time, but their simple act of planting food in public space would prove wildly popular (Fig 2.4).

Murray and his colleagues started the City Hall veggie patch in spring of 2009, and they've never looked back. The vegetables immediately garnered the admiration of co-workers, the mayor (who lauded the garden in his blog[22]), the public, and news crews throughout Provo. Murray and his gardening crew have been featured in numerous blogs, newspapers, and television news segments. It seems growing food in public space for the benefit of the public has great appeal to the folks of Provo.

During that first year, Murray harvested about 300 pounds of produce, which was donated to the local food bank. In 2010, Murray *doubled* the harvest. By 2012, Murray and his co-workers were able to coax 1,200 pounds of vegetables from those same planters, which – when the surface area is aggregated – totals a scant 250 square feet of dirt. Murray's thumb became forest green in just a few short years. Not only that, but he realized his goal: you *can* grow an awful lot of food in a small amount of space.

Since the garden had been so successful the first few years, in 2013 Murray decided to relocate to a vacant lot three blocks away. The parcel gave him far more real estate to work with, and planting a garden could do a lot to improve the public image of the neglected site. But Murray learned an invaluable lesson that year: site selection for public produce is paramount for its success.

'People didn't see the garden has having as much significance,' noted Murray. 'It wasn't as special, having vegetables growing on a vacant lot versus City Hall.'[23] Indeed, vacant lot gardening, though a fantastic endeavour for land that otherwise lies fallow, doesn't make us do a double-take, pause, and think the way that seeing growing food in true civic space does. There is tremendous power in the example. Like First Lady Michelle Obama's garden on the South Lawn at the White House, growing vegetables at City Hall sends a symbolic message about food and our food culture. 'Gosh, if City Hall is advocating fresh, locally grown tomatoes, zucchini, and cucumbers, maybe I should think twice about ordering that double cheeseburger for lunch. And maybe I should start gardening, too.'

Murray also noticed that the vacant lot garden was more difficult to maintain than the City Hall planters. Because the garden wasn't deemed as special, it was tougher for Murray to motivate co-workers to help tend crops. Not only that, but gardening is much more convenient when it is right outside your door. Pulling the occasional weed as you return to the office from lunch, or turning on the hose during your morning break are tasks that become almost effortless, simply because you are passing by the garden multiple times each day. The new garden was a short walk from City Hall. But it doesn't matter. As soon as you have to go out of your way to weed, water, or even harvest ripe produce, gardening becomes a chore.

For 2014, Murray admitted the garden needs to return to City Hall; not only for the prestige, but for ease of maintenance. And speaking of maintenance, it should be noted that Murray and his colleagues tend the crops on their own time, usually before or after work, and sometimes on their lunch break. This is quite generous of the City Planners in Provo, but I (DN) ask Murray, 'Doesn't that consume a lot of your free time?'

'I'm surprised how much can be done with just a little bit of effort,' Murray told me. 'It doesn't take much to turn over a section of dirt, throw in some seeds, and remember to water. If you can weed every now and again, all the better, and the yield is rather remarkable.'[24]

What Murray has learned is that a lot of food and community good can be nurtured with just a little time and a modest patch of dirt. As a public official, Murray is one of the many stewards of public space in his city, and his many years of growing food in those civic planters has changed Murray's attitude about urban space. 'The space we planted was grossly underutilized, as are a lot of city owned spaces,' Murray admitted. 'It was good to put it to a higher and better use.'

Now, whenever he passes by some underutilized piece of land, like an empty corner in a park or a forgotten parking strip along the street, Murray says 'I just want to throw some strawberries in there.'[25]

When folks hear 'urban agriculture,' what often comes to mind are community gardens on vacant parcels in distressed neighbourhoods, similar to what Murray planted in 2013. But urban agriculture is much more diverse. Former San Francisco mayor Gavin Newsom once said, 'Urban agriculture is about far more than growing vegetables on an empty lot. It's about revitalizing and transforming unused public spaces, connecting city residents with their neighbourhoods in a new way and promoting healthier eating and living for everyone.'[26]

Newsom's statement was in reference to a pioneering food policy he was championing in 2009. At the time, Newsom was urging municipalities to lead the fight against food insecurity. The mayor laid out a comprehensive agriculture plan for the city, to bolster access to fresh fruits and vegetables and reshape how San Franciscans think about food.

Newsom kicked off his agricultural plan with an Executive Directive, which declares that 'Access to safe, nutritious, and culturally acceptable food is a basic human right and is essential to both human health and ecological sustainability. The City and County of San Francisco recognizes that hunger, food insecurity, and poor nutrition are pressing health issues that require immediate action.' The Directive then states that 'Food production and horticulture education will be encouraged within the City and, to the extent feasible, on City owned land, through urban agriculture including community, backyard, rooftop, and school gardens; edible landscaping, and agricultural incubator projects.' The Directive concludes with a set of action steps, the first one stating 'all [City] departments having jurisdiction over property will conduct an audit of their land suitable for or actively used for food producing gardens or other agricultural purposes.'[27] This meant the Department of Public Works would look at the potential to grow food on land they oversee, namely streets. Recreation and Parks would look at city parks; the Planning Department would look at vacant parcels they have acquired; the Public Library would analyze the grounds around their buildings to grow food; and so on.

Newsom's Directive might be ahead of its time; but only slightly. The declining health of our nation is directly linked to our poor diet, and as Newsom noted, requires immediate action. Every municipality aims to improve the quality of life for its citizens, and one of the surest, most effective strategies to achieve such an aim is to adopt a similar urban agriculture policy that Newsom has outlined for San Francisco.

Newsom's Directive illustrates the variety of public spaces worthy of agricultural exploration. Though the community garden on the vacant lot will likely continue to epitomize urban agriculture, as the practice evolves it will become clear that the diversity of public space within cities presents a diversity of food-growing opportunities.

We should clarify that by 'public space,' we are referring to those places that are freely accessible to the public, whether they are truly public or merely perceived to be. True public spaces include those properties owned and maintained by the municipality, such as streets and sidewalks, parks, squares and plazas, parking lots, and municipal buildings (libraries, city halls, and police and fire stations, for example, and the landscaped grounds that surround them). Civic institutions not owned by the municipality, but by other government or public agencies, may also be public, such as the grounds around courthouses, universities, and grade schools. Then there are those spaces that are privately owned, but where permission to pass is explicitly stated or implied. Hospitals, business parks, churches, corporate plazas, retail and commercial parking lots are examples of privately owned spaces where the public freely enters, and is often encouraged to do so. Even floodplains and transportation and utility easements, where structures are not allowed to be built, can be great opportunities for food production. In essence, any space where the public can enter throughout the day without being charged an admission fee (even if that space is privately owned and maintained), and that is suitable for growing food, is worthy of inclusion into a network of public produce.

We are not advocating the removal of fountains, benches, paving, sculpture, playground equipment, picnic tables, and other public-space amenities that attract people for the sake of urban agriculture. Quite the contrary. We are interested in ways of attracting *more* people, by providing additional reasons for folks to frequent public space: namely, wholesome sustenance, food education, and a sense of self-sufficiency.

In the design of public spaces, there are many variables that, when properly identified and accommodated for, work together to create vivacity. Food is often one of those variables. This was something the late preeminent people-watcher William H. Whyte recognized over thirty years ago. In his seminal book *The Social Life of Small Urban Spaces*, Whyte proffered, 'If you want to seed a place with activity, put out food.' That's because, he writes, 'Food attracts people who attract more people.' Whyte was so convinced of the positive impacts food has on the attractiveness of public space that he reiterated, just a couple paragraphs later, 'Food, to repeat, draws people, and they draw more people.'[28]

What Whyte was speaking about in particular was food prepared and sold from vendors, which helps make the many street corners and plazas in Manhattan so attractive to the passerby. But we are starting to witness an utter fascination with the *growing* of food as well. Gardens and orchards can be community gathering places, and food – even fresh produce in its natural habitat – can improve the attractiveness of public space, and its ability to create a sense of conviviality.

Regardless if the space is truly public or only semipublic, municipal government is going to have to play a leading role in shaping food policy, as Mayor Newsom argued. Programs, policies, funding strategies, and maintenance regimens of any urban agriculture endeavour will be difficult to implement and sustain if the largest landowner in the city is indifferent. If public officials want a healthier, more prosperous citizenry, and believe that access to fresh, locally sourced, wholesome, and affordable food is good for both the individual citizen and the community at large, then public officials can no longer remain idle. In the face of rising food insecurity and declining public health stemming from a poor diet, public officials need to provide better food choices in their community.

Which is exactly what the City of Calgary is doing.

The same year Nathan Murray started his City Hall veggie patch, the City of Calgary broke ground on the Community Orchard Research Project, a five-year pilot program testing public fruit trees and their ability to thrive in urban settings and a harsh climate. 'We have a grassland landscape, not a woodland landscape,' noted Jill Spence, Lead Urban Forester with the City of Calgary, as she outlined the challenges of growing fruit trees in her region. 'Plus, it gets very cold here, then you have Chinooks which can wreak havoc on the budding cycle of fruit trees.'

Such natural constraints would be enough for most municipal governments to forego any attempt to plant fruit trees for the community. Heck, even in cities with mild climates, most public officials wouldn't entertain an opportunity to plant produce in public settings. But the City of Calgary sees food differently. 'Food in Calgary is a priority,' Spence said. 'It improves our urban forest, engages our community, and improves our image. For Calgarians, this is important.'[29]

The idea for the orchards didn't come from Spence, or the City of Calgary. Rather, it came from the community. Though you might expect most bureaucrats to rattle off a litany of reasons why fruit trees shouldn't be planted in public spaces, the City of Calgary listened to their citizens. Spence then engaged the experts at the University of Saskatchewan to determine which fruit trees and shrubs might do best in Calgary's challenging environment. Apples, pears, apricots, honeyberries, hazelnuts, gooseberries, and cherries were some of the fruits recommended by the university.

So Spence and her crew set to work planting orchards in four public parks. And they didn't start timidly. For the Sunnyside Community Orchard, thirty apple, three pear, thirty cherry, five apricot, seventy-eight honeyberry, fifty-five strawberry, seventeen gooseberry, and six hazelnut trees and shrubs were planted. We're not talking a few fruit trees to appease a citizen request, but a veritable fruit farm that rivals any small commercial orchard.

In fact, it was precisely the commercial orchard that the City of Calgary modeled their pilot project after. 'We are taking a different approach from a hobby garden,' says Russell Friesen, an urban forester who works under Spence. 'We are trying to take a more economic approach and something closer to commercial orchards, using commercial varieties.'

Friesen noted that the apple varieties used for the City's orchard project use dwarf root stock, meaning the trees will only get to be six or seven feet tall. 'They are easy picking, and these dwarf trees invest more energy in the fruit than they do in the wood,' says Friesen. 'They're not particularly esthetically pleasing: they look weird. But for the purposes of a community orchard, the best practice is to grow on these dwarf root stocks, with each dwarf apple tree expected to eventually produce twenty pounds of easy-to-harvest fruit.'[30]

The City of Calgary is so serious about fruit production, that they are encouraging citizens to take up a hobby that has generated a bad buzz for American municipalities: beekeeping. Fruit trees need pollinators, and most varieties are pollinated by bees. Unfortunately, there has been a serious decline in honeybee populations throughout North America due to a number of factors, such as liberal pesticide use, climate change, loss of habitat, and predatory mites. In conjunction with the fruit tree plantings, the Urban Forestry Division introduced native mason bees at each orchard site to ensure pollination. (Mason bees, unlike honeybees, are solitary and nonaggressive. They will sting, but only as a response to being squeezed or stepped on.) The City even published an informational brochure teaching homeowners a simple, step-by-step process to build houses for mason bees.[31]

Calgary's community orchard pilot program ended in 2014, and Spence said the program was a success. Spence learned quite a bit during the five-year pilot. Pears, for example, fared quite poorly in Calgary's climate. Some varieties had a zero survivability rate. But apples, cherries, and hazelnuts did quite well. She also learned that orchards that are planted in parks without an associative community group don't thrive like those planted in parks where there is already a large contingent of community gardeners. When you already have a group of people in the area gardening, they naturally look after the orchards. These gardeners prune, thin, harvest, and keep pests away. The trees in the stand-alone park, the one without any community association tied to it, saw heavy damage from deer and low-fruit yields. Spence also sees a great opportunity to use the orchards as teaching tools. Parks' staff train citizens on how to prune the trees and thin for higher fruit yields. Citizens then train other citizens. The result is healthy public fruit trees maintained by citizens without financial burden on City staff.

When Spence was asked about the future of community orchards in Calgary, especially amid perennial concerns over lean municipal budgets, she said, 'Funding is always a matter of prioritizing. Community orchards are community gathering places, and we listen to our community. These orchards are a priority.'[32]

Provo provides public vegetables and Calgary offers public fruits. In the central Ohio town of Worthington, one elected official says both are needed for community well-being.

Fig. 2.5. Councilman Doug Smith and his daughter find black walnuts in a public park in Worthington, Ohio

City Councilman Doug Smith is pioneering *transitional* gardens in Worthington – a strategy to make the community happier, stronger, and more resilient in the face of a potentially fragile environment. *Transition* initiatives are responses to the challenges of an uncertain climate, economy, and resource supply. And public fruits and vegetables, in Councilman Smith's eyes, are resources that can help folks get by a little easier.

But Smith doesn't necessarily envision fruit trees planted like commercial orchards or vegetables replacing petunias outside of City Hall. Rather, Smith sees an opportunity to work with nature to allow underutilized public space throughout the city to feed folks, with little effort expended from Staff. 'The idea is to allow nature to 'do its thing' with minimal attention from the community and minimal resources from the city,' said Smith. 'Worthington is the perfect community in central Ohio to begin a transitional garden. We have public space that can sustain edible plants, and a lot of residents are happy to participate to increase community sustainability.'[33]

This means planting mulberry, serviceberry, walnut, hickory, and pawpaw trees, because these species are native to central Ohio. And it means planting them in wooded thickets and along river banks, because these are the native habitats of these plants. The result is a large network of food bearing plants that thrive because they are perfectly suited for their location (Fig. 2.5).

The first phase of Smith's idea was completed in 2013, when the city mapped the existing fruit and nut trees in town. Residents can simply go online and navigate a Google map to find local raspberries, walnuts, pawpaws, and apples. The website also helps residents with fruits they may not be familiar with. What are serviceberries, for example? A lot like blueberries, only a bit sweeter and mealier. You can eat them fresh from the bush, or you can visit the Worthington Resource Site to find recipes for serviceberry jam, spicy serviceberries, and serviceberry relish.[34] Providing information about serviceberries along with recipes takes the mystery out this native-but-now-forgotten fruit, and it gets folks excited to forage for these new flavours.

The next phase of Smith's transitional gardens will be to plant more trees and shrubs throughout the city. Sure, seeding your public spaces with food helps feed people at little cost to the municipality. This is certainly a great benefit to the community. But Smith sees another great value of the public produce. For him, transitional gardens provide 'a start to a long-term culture shift in Worthington to be closer to nature.'

Across the continent, folks are demanding ready access to fresh, locally grown produce. It is becoming apparent that in the near future, municipalities will need to address urban agriculture as an important component of urban infrastructure, much like housing, transportation, and education. By simply allowing, encouraging, and implementing food gardens in public space, cities can meet that public demand, and in a fiscally responsible manner. Some municipal officials – like those in Provo, San Francisco, Calgary, Worthington, and Kamloops – have already recognized this, and have taken an active approach in the management of food-producing efforts in public space. And through these efforts, these municipalities are telling the world this: food system planning *is* the responsibility of City Government. Food system planning can be a core component of a broader policy to reduce social inequity and increase quality of life for citizens. Access to healthy, low- or no-cost fruits and vegetables helps assure the health, safety, and welfare of the public, every bit as much as providing clean drinking water, protection from crime and catastrophe, sewage treatment, garbage collection, shelters and housing programs, and pot-hole free streets.

And these communities have also proven that public parks, wooded river banks, downtowns, and even the grounds around city hall are fantastic places to cultivate fruits and vegetables.

Food Literacy

Peanuts do not grow on trees, nor do pineapples. Green bell peppers are underripe red bell peppers. Parsnips are not related to parsley, but they are related to carrots. Not all potatoes come from Idaho. Ask a nine-year-old where an apple comes from, and he or she will likely respond, 'The grocery store.'

People today are food illiterate. For a continent rooted in agrarianism, it is frightening how ignorant of food we have become. Our Big-Ag brand of food production has given us unprecedented convenience, from fast-food and prepackaged meals (so that we do not have to learn to cook) to year-round mangoes and asparagus (so that we do not have to worry about what grows in our corner of the world or at what time).

Public produce can help us regain that great agrarian knowledge our forefathers possessed. The trees, shrubs, rambling vines and showy annuals we choose to adorn our streets, parks, plazas, and city squares can offer visual delight as well as lessons on healthy eating. But we need to get back to basics. A growing number of Canadians and Americans have never seen fruits and vegetables in their native habitat, much less plucked them from the vine.

Once we start seeding our public landscapes with fresh produce, we will have to learn how to distinguish food from ornamentals (and remember they can be both). We will have to learn what parts of a plant are edible, and which are not (rhubarb, for example, has toxic leaves; only the petioles – the red stalks – should be eaten). We will have to learn when to expect those fruits and vegetables (apples in autumn, citrus in winter, asparagus in spring, and summer squash in, well, you get the idea). And we will have to learn to appreciate those forgotten foods that were once commonly enjoyed, but have disappeared from our diet (like juneberries, hickory nuts, and pawpaw) as well as the culturally diverse foods that more accurately reflect the eating habits of our melting pot nations.

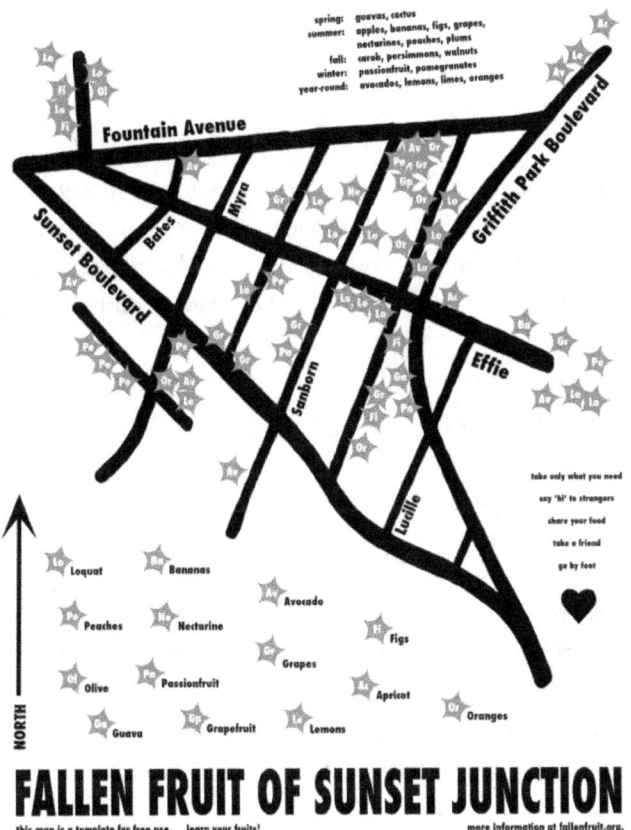

Fig. 2.6. Example of a public fruit map for the Sunset Junction neighbourhood of Los Angeles (map courtesy of Fallen Fruit: http://www.fallenfruit.org/index.php/media/maps/)

Bolstering the depth and breadth of our food knowledge is a daunting endeavour. But getting back to basics doesn't mean municipal employees have to create a food curriculum from scratch, or become experts themselves. Municipal budgets are lean, and city staff are stretched. Luckily, public officials can draw from the knowledge and passion of others in their community to help citizens become more food literate. Gardening clubs, zealous parents and teachers, farmers markets, and nonprofit groups committed to locally grown produce and healthy eating reside in every community, and each can partner with the municipality to help lessen our food ignorance.

An artist group known as *Fallen Fruit* has taken up that challenge of educating people about food, and has prepared neighbourhood fruit maps for various Los Angeles neighbourhoods. These fruit maps show folks not only where to find fruit, but when it is in season.[35] These maps also illustrate the diversity of food that can grow in Los Angeles, such as bananas, guavas, figs, persimmons, carob, passion fruit, avocados, pomegranate, citrus, peaches, and plums (Fig. 2.6). The maps have become so popular, that residents in countries around the world – Denmark, Austria, Colombia, and Sweden – have contributed fruit maps for their own communities, all posted on *Fallen Fruit's* website.[36]

The idea for *Fallen Fruit's* maps came from an arcane law in Los Angeles – a usufruct law – that states if fruit overhangs a public space, even if the tree, vine or shrub is on private property, the public has right to that fruit (so long as the private property is not damaged). In a city where fresh produce is prized – yet also quite expensive – *Fallen Fruit* had an ingenious solution: show people where they can eat for free. *Fallen Fruit* also organizes harvesting parties where people roam the neighbourhoods of LA, harvesting fruit that overhangs the streets and alleys. It should be noted that this practice is beneficial to the property owner as well. Most fruit trees produce much more fruit than can be consumed by a single family. Harvesting the surplus saves the property owner from having to clean up undesired fruit that would have otherwise fallen to the ground.

A San Francisco group has a new take on neighbourhood fruit maps. They have developed an App for the iPhone. The idea is that, regardless of where you are in the United States, you can just pull up an area on your phone and find all the publicly accessible fruit in the neighbourhood. Currently, over 10,000 trees with publicly accessible fruit across the country has been registered and mapped in this App.[37]

The nonprofit Center for Urban Education about Sustainable Agriculture (CUESA) has a website full of great ideas that municipalities could easily adapt for their own purposes. CUESA, which manages San Francisco's Ferry Plaza Farmers Market, packs its website chock-a-block with all sorts of food and agricultural content in a mouthwatering manner. From the Glossary page, which succinctly teaches the difference between *heirloom*, *heritage*, and *hybrid*, to the A to Z Sustainability Guide, CUESA offers provocative content paired with delicious photography, infused with soul-enriching philosophy.

For us, CUESA's most valuable online resource is their seasonality charts, which we think of as fruit, nut, and vegetable calendars. These charts help consumers better understand their agricultural geography, by teaching them what grows where when. Bay Area consumers can find out just when those prized California artichokes, pistachios, or fava beans are available at the Ferry Plaza farmers' market by logging on to www.cuesa.org. These calendars also list a variety of unusual crops that reflect both the ethnic diversity and the adventurous foodie spirit that prevails in San Francisco. Produce such as cactus pads and pears, cardoons, burdock, salsify, feijoas, jujubes, and cherimoyas are listed among the more familiar avocados, fennel, figs, bok choy, shallots, and tomatillos.

Of course, California's mild climate enables a tantalizing array of food to be grown throughout the year. But it is just as important for Manitobans to understand what grows in their neck of the woods and when it is ripe, so that they, too, can cultivate an interest in food and appreciation for the unique environment in which they live.

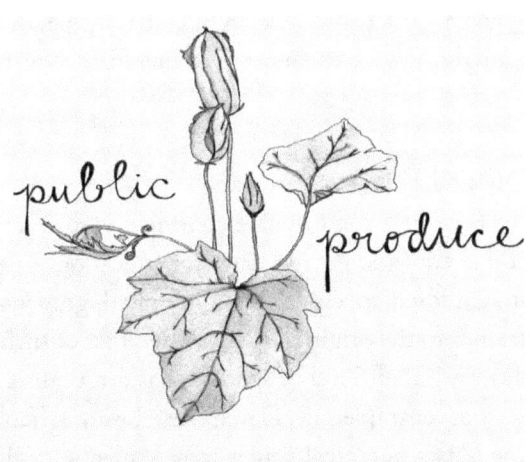

Fig. 2.7. This Kamloops *How-To* guide provides invaluable lessons to any municipality interested in establishing a public produce program. The guide is available through the Kamloops Food Policy Council website: http://kamloopsfoodpolicycouncil.com/ (cover image courtesy of Elaine Sedgman.)

Social and digital media – Facebook, Twitter, blogs and websites – are perhaps the most effective ways to spread the word among your citizenry about the availability of public produce. And they can be great educational tools as well. The extraordinary success of this public produce gardens in Kamloops, for example, is not because Kamloopsians enjoy fresh produce more than their compatriots. Public produce is successful in Kamloops because it is in the public consciousness, thanks to the tireless advocacy of the Kamloops Food Policy Council (KFPC). The group printed posters and passed them out around town, announcing the arrival of the public produce gardens. Presentations were given to various community groups and municipal staff. Television and newspaper reporters were invited to cover the public produce efforts. KFPC created a blog and a Facebook page to announce various public produce events, post sumptuous pictures of ripe produce, and offer lessons on growing food and healthy eating. They even published what might be the definitive *How To* guide for public produce. This inspiring manual – written by Elaine Sedgman, a Master Gardener and co-creator of Kamloops' public produce gardens – offers lessons and expert insights any municipality on any continent would find useful (available from KFPC's website: http://kamloopsfoodpolicycouncil.com/).

Utilizing every available media outlet available, KFPC has helped to ensure citizens of Kamloops might now be the most food literate in North America (Fig. 2.7).

Children and Food Literacy

The most effective manner to become a food literate continent is to teach children, and require that edible education – like physical education – be part of the school curriculum. Children are especially smitten with growing food plants, as their only reference to the origin of food is often that of their home kitchens or school cafeterias. Their level of ignorance is astounding, and even a bit frightening. For example, in Davenport, Iowa, school children on a field trip to the City's botanical center were shown a small orange tree. One student asked if the oranges were pumpkins or watermelons. Another student, when seeing sunflowers being grown, asked if they would produce those 'ranch-dressing flavoured seeds,' which were his favorite. Children today have little clue about food, what it looks like, or where it comes from.

The late Euell Gibbons – often called the Father of Environmentalism

– had a great strategy for getting children excited to learn about food. In his book *Stalking the Wild Asparagus*, Gibbons capitalized on the joys of discovering wild foods – those that thrive naturally, right near your home. What child doesn't like to go 'exploring' in his or her surrounds? Gibbons said he has 'seen several feeding problems cured merely by interesting the child in the gathering and preparation of wild food plants.'[38]

Of course, Gibbons' method of instruction supposes that every child lives quite close to relatively undisturbed patches of nature, where an abundance of berries, wild plums, and other edible plants thrive. Obviously many children do not have access to such bounties of nature. But what if food could be brought into the classroom? This is exactly the idea that is transforming the school curriculum in cities from coast to coast.

Shortly after President Kennedy was elected, he became appalled at the lack of physical fitness of American youth. Kennedy was instrumental in establishing physical education as core component of the classroom curricula. Today, many are also realizing how woefully ignorant our kids are of food, and are pushing for the addition of an edible education in schools as well. Edible schoolyards are sprouting across North America, but the exemplar is one for the Martin Luther King middle school in Berkeley, California, started by famed chef Alice Waters of Chez Panisse.[39]

The Edible Schoolyard, as it is known, is a one-acre organic garden and kitchen classroom. Before the garden was created, the grounds around the school were comprised of asphalt, dried lawn, and leggy perennials – certainly not the sort of landscape that inspires learning. Today, a veritable oasis of organic produce encourages children, teachers, and parents to learn more about food, nature, and healthy eating. The garden is planted with seasonal produce, herbs, berries, and fruit trees. There is also a tool shed, seed propagation table, chicken coop, and a pizza oven.

The Edible Schoolyard is part of the curriculum for all students at King Middle School. When finished with the curriculum, the students will have gained a complete seed-to-table experience, which begins by preparing and seeding the planting beds and concludes with a sit-down meal at the table, complete with flowers from the garden. And, the children even participate in the cleanup. Throughout the school year, the program exposes children to food production, ecology, nutrition, and fosters an appreciation of meaningful work, and of fresh and natural food.[40]

Obviously, a full-fledged edible schoolyard on the scale of King Middle

School is a massive undertaking. But even one small garden plot can offer profound lessons to children (and parents) on food. Setting aside an hour to plant seeds, and a few minutes each week to water, weed, and study how food evolves in a patch of dirt, can have an immensely positive impact on even the youngest grade-school children.

Outside my (Nordahl's) daughter's kindergarten class in northern California, there was talk one day between some of the parents about establishing a small garden plot. Food is important in this region, and many parents have urged the school to adopt a healthier attitude toward food. But with any project, there were hurdles to clear.

Our problem wasn't the usual one when trying to start a garden: infrastructure. We had water. We also had a tool shed. In fact, we even had a raised garden box filled with soil. What we didn't have was gumption. The teacher wasn't enthused about incorporating gardening into the school curriculum, but offered, 'If this is something parents wish to do, I will support you guys in your efforts.'

So I (DN) and another parent purchased some seeds and seedlings, and then took an hour out of our day and held a gardening workshop for the kids. We planted fun stuff we thought kids would enjoy to look at, like rainbow chard, yellow, red and purple carrots, orange cauliflower, red radishes, and green peas. We planted stuff that was fun to touch and smell, like sage. We planted stevia, because we thought kids would be amazed that something green and leafy could taste like candy. And we even planted the strange: Brussels sprouts. The kids learned about food and where it comes from. They also learned about roots and flowers and leaves and dirt. And they had a blast.

The two of us watered the box regularly, and managed the weeds and bugs. But what had sprouted was more than we could have hoped for. When the seedlings emerged, so did the teacher's enthusiasm for the garden. She started helping out with the watering. She helped kids pick radishes and she even took handfuls of chard home to her family on occasion. Many of the other parents became intrigued with the garden as well, as they often gathered around the plot and ogled the growing vegetables while they waited for their kids to get out of school. The amount of food the garden yielded was modest. But the joy it brought kids and parents, and the interest in fresh vegetables that the garden sparked, was immeasurable (Fig. 2.8).

Fig. 2.8. Author Darrin Nordahl and a group of kindergarten children plant vegetables in a garden outside the classroom. He has dubbed the group the KinderGardeners.

We would like to conclude this chapter with this reflection. During World War II, the public gardening campaign known as Victory Gardens supplied the United States with 40% of its fresh vegetables.[41] It is staggering how much food can be grown from small scale gardening efforts on public land, with a little bit of organization and encouragement from our government officials. The time is ripe to revisit public space gardening, and its potential to bring people together in a wholesome manner, while bolstering health and prosperity, both for the individual and the community.

NOTES

1. Centers for Disease Control and Prevention, 'Majority of Americans not Meeting Recommendations for Fruit and Vegetable Consumption.' *CDC Newsroom* (September 29, 2009): http://www.cdc.gov/media/pressrel/2009/r090929.htm (last accessed January 14, 2015).
2. Frances Romero, 'Top 10 Most Dangerous Foods,' *TIME*, February 22, 2010. http://www.time.com/time/specials/packages/article/0,28804,1967235_1967238_1967213,00.html (last accessed January 14, 2015).
3. Centers for Disease Control and Prevention, 'Update on Multi-State

Outbreak of *E. coli* O157:H7 Infections From Fresh Spinach, October 6, 2006' http://www.cdc.gov/ecoli/2006/september/updates/100606.htm (last accessed January 14, 2015).
4   U.S. Food and Drug Administration, 'FDA Extends Consumer Warning on Serrano Peppers from Mexico,' July 30, 2008: http://www.fda.gov/NewsEvents/Newsroom/PressAnnouncements/2008/ucm116929.htm (last accessed January 14, 2015).
5   Centers for Disease Control and Prevention, 'Investigation of Outbreak of Infections Caused by *Salmonella* Saintpaul' August 28, 2008: http://www.cdc.gov/salmonella/saintpaul/jalapeno/ (last accessed January 14, 2015).
6   Centers for Disease Control and Prevention, 'Investigation Update: Outbreak of *Salmonella* Typhimurium Infections, 2008–2009,' April 29, 2009: http://www.cdc.gov/salmonella/typhimurium/update.html (last accessed January 14, 2015).
7   Centers for Disease Control and Prevention, 'Investigation of an Outbreak of *Salmonella* Saintpaul Infections Linked to Raw Alfalfa Sprouts,' May 8, 2009: http://www.cdc.gov/salmonella/saintpaul/alfalfa/ (last accessed January 14, 2015).
8   Centers for Disease Control and Prevention, 'Investigation Update: Multistate Outbreak of *E. coli* O157:H7 Infections Linked to Romaine Lettuce,' March 23, 2012: http://www.cdc.gov/ecoli/2011/ecoliO157/romainelettuce/032312/index.html (last accessed January 14, 2015).
9   Pollan, 'Farmer in Chief.'
10 Amanda Gardner, 'FDA Expands Tomato Warning Nationwide,' HealthDayNews, June 10, 2008, http://www.healthday.com/Article.asp?AID=616391 (last accessed November 28, 2008).
11 Centers for Disease Control and Prevention, 'Outbreak of Salmonella Serotype Saintpaul Infections Associated with Multiple Raw Produce Items – United States, 2008,' *Morbidity and Mortality Weekly Report 57*, no. 34 (August 29, 2008), 929–34.
12 Colin Beavan, 'The No Impact Experiment,' *The No Impact Man Blog*, entry posted February 21, 2007, http://noimpactman.typepad.com/blog/2007/02/the_no_impact_e.html (last accessed February 3, 2014).
13 Colin Beaven, 'Like falling off a log,' *The No Impact Man Blog*, entry posted March 21, 2008, http://noimpactman.typepad.com/blog/2008/03/like-falling-of.html (last accessed February 3, 2014).
14 Obesity trend data collected through the CDC's Behavioral Risk Factor Surveillance System (BRFSS), on the basis of self-reported weight and height. Each year, state health departments use standard procedures to collect data through a series of monthly telephone interviews with U.S. adults. Prevalence estimates generated for the maps may vary slightly from

those generated for the states by the BRFSS as slightly different analytic methods are used.: http://www.cdc.gov/obesity/data/adult.html/ (last accessed July 13, 2012).

15   OECD, 'Obesity and Economics of Prevention: Fit not Fat,' February 21, 2012: http://www.oecd.org/dataoecd/0/60/49712071.pdf (last accessed July 13, 2012).

16   For a list of obesity trends and associated malady's, see the CDC's 'Overweight and Obesity' webpage: http://www.cdc.gov/obesity/data/adult.html/ (last accessed July 13, 2012).

17   Associated Press, 'CDC: Huntington, W. Va. Nation's Unhealthiest City,' *Fox News*, November 16, 2008: http://www.foxnews.com/story/0,2933,452864,00.html (last accessed July 13, 2012).

18   Pam Belluck, 'Children's Life Expectancy Being Cut Short by Obesity,' *New York Times*, March 17, 2005: http://www.nytimes.com/2005/03/17/health/17obese.html (last accessed July 13, 2012).

19   Rich Pirog, Timothy Van Pelt, Kamyar Enshayan, Ellen Cook, 'Food, Fuel, and Freeways: An Iowa perspective on how far food travels, fuel usage, and greenhouse gas emissions,' *Leopold Center for Sustainable Agriculture*, June 2001: http://www.leopold.iastate.edu/sites/default/files/pubs-and-papers/2011-06-food-fuel-and-freeways-iowa-perspective-how-far-food-travels-fuel-usage-and-greenhouse-gas-emissions.pdf (last accessed July 13, 2012).

20   Centers for Disease Control and Prevention, 'Vegetable of the Month: Bell Pepper,' http://www.fruitsandveggiesmatter.gov/month/bell_pepper.html (last accessed July 14, 2012).

21   Robert Steuteville, 'Old McDonald had an organic TND?' *New Urban News*, December 2008, 13.

22   http://provomayor.com/2010/07/21/what-s-that-growing-on-the-patio/

23   Nathan Murray, in a telephone conversation with the author, January 9, 2014.

24   Nathan Murray, in an e-mail to the first author, October 14, 2013.

25   Sam Penrod, 'Provo City puts garden to good use,' KSL-TV, July 10, 2011: http://www.ksl.com/?sid=16321964 (last accessed January 27, 2014).

26   Heather Knight, 'Mayor's agricultural plan soon to bear fruit,' *San Francisco Chronicle––SFGate*, March 23, 2010: http://www.sfgate.com/homeandgarden/article/Mayor-s-agriculture-plan-soon-to-bear-fruit-3195585.php (last accessed January 27, 2014).

27   The full executive directive, which was issued by San Francisco Mayor Gavin Newsom on July 9, 2009, can be viewed here: http://www.sfgov3.org/Modules/ShowDocument.aspx?documentid=74 (last accessed January 27, 2014).

28 William H. Whyte, *The Social Life of Small Urban Spaces* (New York: Project for Public Spaces, 1980), 50–53.
29 Jill Spence, in a telephone conversation with Darrin Nordahl, January 15, 2014.
30 Jacqueline Louie, 'Community Orchards: Nature's store,' *Calgary Herald*, September 30, 2011: http://www.calgaryherald.com/travel/community+orchards/5484344/story.html (last accessed January 27, 2014).
31 Interested in building your own mason bee house? You can download the City of Calgary's easy, step-by-step instructions here: http://www.calgary.ca/CSPS/Parks/Documents/Programs/Community-Orchards/mason-bee-house.pdf (last accessed January 27, 2014).
32 All of Jill-Anne Spence's quotes transcribed from a telephone conversation with Darrin Nordahl on January 15, 2014.
33 Worthington Resource Site, 'Transitional Gardens in Worthington,' http://dsmi51.wix.com/worthingtonohio#!transitional-gardens/cx84 (last accessed January 28, 2014).
34 http://dsmi51.wix.com/worthingtonohio#!serviceberry-recipe/c1jt (last accessed January 28, 2014).
35 An assortment of *Fallen Fruit's* neighborhood maps can be see on the group's website: http://www.fallenfruit.org/index.php/media/maps/ (last accessed July 14, 2012).
36 The myriad fruit maps from around the world can be seen on this page of Fallen Fruit's website: http://www.fallenfruit.org/index.php/media/maps/ (last accessed August 30, 2012).
37 The name of the App is 'Find Fruit,' and it's available through Apple's iTunes. More information about the app can be found on the Developer website Neighborhood Fruit: http://neighborhoodfruit.com/iphoneapp (last accessed July 14, 2012).
38 Euell Gibbons, *Stalking the Wild Asparagus* (Chambersburg, Pennsylvania: Alan C. Hood & Company, Inc., 1962), 3.
39 To learn more about Alice Waters' Edible Schoolyards – and to see inspirational videos – visit the Edible Schoolyard website: http://edibleschoolyard.org/ (last accessed July 14, 2012).
40 Text about the Martin Luther King Jr. Middle School Edible Schoolyard adapted from my book: Darrin Nordahl, *Public Produce: The new urban agriculture* (Washington DC: Island Press, 2009), 130-131.
41 Laura J. Lawson, *City Bountiful* (Berkeley: University of California Press, 2005), 171.

Commentary – Imagining Public Livestock

Lorraine Johnson

'Death is never easy,' said my friend Matt, moments after we had chopped the head off one of my backyard chickens. We had two more to 'do' (i.e. kill) and we were still shaking. The chicken herself had stopped shaking – for what felt like minutes but was probably just 30 seconds she had flapped her wings (or tried to – I was holding them tightly to her warm body), even though her head was severed from the rest of her.

'Death is never easy.'

Never easy, but necessary if we choose to eat meat.

I rarely choose to eat meat, though, strangely, I've become more carnivorous since I started keeping backyard hens for eggs. Over the years, I've had many hens of different heritage and conventional breeds, but these most recent three had not produced many eggs at all over their months of tenure in my coop, and so I decided to eat them.

I would never say that I took any pleasure in ending my hens' lives, but I did feel a kind of solemn completeness in participating in the deed. Not ease – my shaking hands betrayed conflict with the concept and the act – but grim recognition that death, never easy, can be if not exactly embraced then at least to some degree honoured, and done as humanely as killing a living creature can ever be. Matt and my Sunday morning three-hen slaughter felt something like meat consecration, almost ritualistic. As I pulled out feathers by the fistful (discovering a meditative rhythm I found calming), I participated in a process of transforming 'my' hens (living, autonomous creatures) into my dinner – and it felt right.

What Matt and I did is something that happens day in and day out on farms and at slaughter houses everywhere. But it is usually out of sight for city dwellers who, in effect, subcontract the messy stuff of death to others. How does an urban backyard context transform the act into something very different? Crucially, I think, it brings the reality of death – necessary for meat dinners – closer to home. We might think of our urban backyards as private places, but ending a hen's life twenty feet away from a downtown sidewalk is an assertion, indeed an insertion, of a messy meat truth into the urban realm: Death is never easy. (The mess, by the way, was emotional, not physical. The neck chop was swift and clean – Matt is an expert – and the blood went into a bucket.)

Darrin Nordahl and Catherine Fisher have advocated eloquently and persuasively for public produce – fruits and vegetables grown in public places and available for all, free for the taking. How might we extend at least some of this food ethic and approach to urban livestock? Should it even be a goal? And what would a city that explored opportunities for public livestock look like?

Right from the start it has to be said (obviously but crucially) that animals are living, feeling, sentient creatures who deserve to live a healthy, safe and happy life. Calling animals livestock in no way absolves us of the responsibility to provide them with the good care that is their right and our duty. What I hope for, for every creature I eat, is that in a life of health, safety and happiness, it has just one bad minute – the moment of its death. And taking responsibility for the death of a food animal – particularly in a public place, not hidden – is one way, among many, to ensure that this is indeed the case.

Not only do most North American city dwellers subcontract the messy stuff of death to others, but we are also removed from the reality of the lives that our food animals live. In terms of the hens that lay the eggs we eat, for example, industrial production allows us to ignore the appalling conditions that the vast majority of chickens are subjected to – tiny enclosures, little room to move, clipped beaks, no access to the outdoors, no freedom to express their natural behaviours, and on and on. For all the squeamishness so many of us exhibit at the thought of actually killing an animal for food, I'd say that we've grossly misplaced most of our discomfort. It is to their lives that we should also direct our scrutiny. And one of the many ways this could happen is if we embraced the notion of raising at least some of our food animals in the places where many of us live – in our cities, in our backyards. Close to home.

So, taking a cue from Nordahl and Fisher's public produce vision and extending it to chickens, as an example, here's what public livestock could look like.

Imagine a park. Children play on the swings; parents and care-givers sit on benches nearby. Some children, though, aren't in the playground – they're gathered around an adult in a fenced-off area of the park where a flock of hens is scratching away at the ground. The children are excited but quiet, mesmerized by the creatures at their feet. The hens are quiet, too, focused on foraging for insects. The adult, a volunteer responsible for caring for this park's flock, hands each child a lettuce leaf and shows them how to hold it out for the hens. Soon, the chickens are pecking off little pieces of the leaves and gobbling them down. The children squeal with a mixture of nervousness and delight, some getting braver and patting their hands along the hens' feathered backs. This is the closest most of these kids have ever been to a farm animal and they are transfixed. They are even more transfixed when each child is given an egg to take home.

Many North American cities already have demonstration farms. The city where I live, Toronto, has Riverdale Farm, and scenes like the one described above happen every day. The only differences are that the person showing the chickens to the kids is a parks employee, not a volunteer from a community group; the farm is managed by the City; and visitors are not given free eggs to take home.

Toronto is full of community gardens and has a very active and vibrant urban agriculture scene, including many people who consider themselves city farmers. Some, like me, keep chickens in their backyards. However, because chicken-keeping is illegal in Toronto, you won't find *public* hens in any community-run gardens or community-run farms here. But it's not for lack of desire, motivation or skill.

What are the possibilities for public chickens (and other urban livestock), beyond the model of a City-run demonstration farm like Riverdale? Imagine a school, for example, where the students already have a garden in which they raise vegetables, manage the compost bins, and learn about food, nutrition and soil. Imagine that they also have a coop with a small flock of hens. They've researched coop design and built the structure in shop class. They've had a visiting farmer in to do a presentation. In science class, they've researched nutrition. In biology class, they've learned about the life cycle of chickens (they now know, for example, that a rooster is not necessary in order for a hen to lay eggs – something that many urban dwellers are unaware of). They've set up a schedule for weekend care of the flock and have a clear protocol for emergencies. In short, they've taken all the steps required of responsible animal keepers before bringing these creatures into the schoolground environment. And now they are stewards, kids who are growing up exposed to the reality of what it takes to have eggs on their breakfast tables. I'd even go so far as to assert that their potential for growing into compassionate adults – people alert to and concerned about suffering – is nurtured and enhanced by their experience with the hens.

These school kids' exercise in compassion could also take on a more immediate and public expression as they consider what to do with the eggs produced by their flock. Give them to a food bank or a local community group for free distribution to those in need? Host a weekly give-away day, open to anyone in the community? The possibilities are endless.

The kids will also be exposed to the uncomfortable question of what to do with the hens when they stop producing eggs. This issue often rears its head in debates over the wisdom of allowing backyard hens (and other food animals) in the city. Public health officials and animal welfare groups are understandably concerned with backyard slaughter. How can we ensure that these animals' deaths are humane and that the broader imperative of community health is not endangered in the process?

Again, Nordahl and Fisher's emphasis on the possibilities of *public* food production is instructive. *Public* doesn't necessarily mean a sanctioned free-for-all, in which anyone and everyone could take up an axe. It could, for example, mean publicly *regulated*, with courses, workshops or certification programs, so that only those people who are trained in safe and humane methods of animal slaughter are given permits to carry out the deed in urban backyards or public places.

No doubt, small enterprises offering backyard slaughter services would develop. Or, as an alternative to slaughter, systems could be set up whereby rural farmers willing to offer boarding services/retirement homes could be enlisted. Indeed, one pro-chicken city councilor in Toronto has been engaged in such discussion and found a rural host.

Such willingness suggests that the public danger of unwanted chickens being abandoned to the streets is inflated. Although chicken abandonment is an issue often raised by the anti-urban chicken faction, it is a concern mired in hyperbole. The summer of 2013 saw a media-induced panic over irresponsible people simply offloading their past-prime chickens onto the public, letting hens loose on city streets so that someone else has to deal with them (municipal animal control crews or, in a more grisly food-chain outcome, to be consumed by raccoons, foxes or hawks). Media stories gave the impression that there was a loose-chicken epidemic, but how many on-the-lam hens have you seen on your city's streets? There is no doubt a danger that some irresponsible chicken keepers will resort to this desperate and insupportable 'solution.' And no doubt that some already have. But is this grounds for outlawing a whole category of urban animal-keeping activity? We haven't done so for cats and dogs, and surely the loose cat and dog problem *is* an epidemic, certainly more so than the phantom loose hens.

There is no concern over urban livestock that can't be addressed, reasonably debated, and resolved using the public mechanisms already in place to deal with the whole host of uniquely urban dangers and annoyances that arise from living in close proximity with animals. North American cities already have bylaws and ordinances covering noise, odour and pests, all of which could be applied to any potential livestock problems. As well, most North American cities that currently allow certain types of livestock have clearly defined regulations, covering numbers of animals allowed, setbacks from neighbours, minimum sizes of animal housing, etc.

Hidden activities, closed off from public scrutiny, are those that diminish our shared capacity for positive community experiences and, instead, often lead to problems. Public activities, on the other hand, open to scrutiny, are those that allow for full debate and reasoned negotiation. Inserting livestock into the discussion of cultivating food in public places for free public consumption takes us one step closer to the imperative goal of food security for everyone. And, crucially, closer to the imperative goal of better lives and deaths for the animals we choose to eat.

Chapter 3

Making Agriculture Part of the City: Lessons from Research for Policy in the Global South

Luc J.A. Mougeot

Introduction

This chapter reviews a range of initiatives which global-South local governments have developed over a period of fifteen years to make agriculture part of the city. Emphasis is placed on the role of evidence-based policy-making. Rather than discussing strengths and weaknesses of specific projects or programs, an attempt is made to draw collective wisdom from policy research carried out by various organizations in different regions of the world, often with support from Canada's International Development Research Center (IDRC). IDRC has supported over a hundred projects on urban agriculture in some fifty countries since the late 1980s, most of them between 1993 and 2010.

The chapter is organised in two parts. It starts with reviewing past civilizations' approaches to integrating agriculture into their cities, a record from which robust principles are drawn, deemed fundamental to our making agriculture part of our cities in the 21st century. A definition of contemporary urban agriculture (UA) in the global South is proposed, with particular attention to what distinguishes it from its rural counterpart.

Against this background, the chapter then turns to the rise of government attention to public policy on UA in recent times. A review of UA's growth in the global South, its benefits and challenges, sets the scene for examining the role of research in supporting recent public policy initiatives on UA. A broad base of project experience spanning a period of fifteen years or so speaks to questions such as:

How has UA surfaced on cities' policy agendas?
- What has been the merit of demand versus supply-driven policy research?
- Are there any advantages to multiple-city over single-city initiatives?
- What have been the risks associated with policy research in this area?
- What have been useful survey designs and
- What protocols have been particularly effective for research-policy interactions?

Finally, the chapter recapitulates the contribution of this policy research to knowledge on UA and anticipates upcoming developments on urban design and policy fronts.

I. Urban Agriculture: The Return of the Ostracized

Since When Has Agriculture Been Part of the City?

We have been here before. Archaeological and ethnographic records from ancient and medieval cities in the Hindus valley, Mesopotamia, Eastern Europe, the Mediterranean, North, Central and South America and Africa, suggest that the city's divorce from agriculture historically is very recent. Globally, it has remained fairly confined. In diverse world regions, cultures and epochs, our more advanced urban settlements greatly valued prudent measures of self-reliance against external shocks. This, even though they often controlled extensive territories. Such provisions consistently included agriculture and food production in particular (Steel, 2008), as a subsidiary though vital urban function. This function was often associated with massive and ingenious earth- and waterworks, within and on the edge of the built-up area.

Cities on the Indus River, such as Harappa and Mohenjo Daro, discovered under the shifting muds of the river, were once specialized agro-urban centers. Uruk, the most important city in 4000 BC Mesopotamia (possibly with 50,000 people), extended over 445 hectares, a third of which was covered with palm groves. The large majority of Uruk's working adults were engaged in primary agricultural production on their holdings, on allotments of land from temples, or as independent retainers on large estates; they also had occupations other than agriculture (Adams 1994).

The Neolithic Cretan settlement of Knossos developed mixed farming (wheat, barley, lentils, sheep, goats, pigs and some cattle); the Minoan town spread over 75 hectares with a population of 12,000. Knossos had isolated farms on its edge (Rodenbeck 1991). Minoan palaces had a central court around which were grouped storage and production areas; rulers probably controlled much of the agriculture in the surrounding region of Knossos, about 1000 hectares (Warren 1994).

Under Persian emperor Darius, enclosed gardens or pairidaeza ('paradises') were associated with hydraulic facilities, thereby exploiting water resources more fully. In Thebes, capital of a new kingdom in 1500 BC, walled gardens of prosperous Egyptians provided fruits for the household (including indigenous vine, pomegranate, imported apple and almond varieties), sycamores, dates and down palms, and fresh fish from lotus-covered pools; larger gardens with water tanks had ducks (Jellicoe, 1989). Much in the same way, aristocratic gardens under France's New Regime would welcome exotic food plants and fruit trees and trialed technical innovations (Quellier 2012). In the capital city of Akhenatan, Egypt, gardens were everywhere, with additional spaces reserved for storage, underground cellars, breweries and animal dens (Courtlandt and Kocybala 1990). In Egyptian cities – which, some argue, spurred the domestication of the cat to deal with rodents – temples distributed land to urban households for their provisioning. In medieval Egypt, the city of Fustat (200,000 people), centre of the Islamic culture for three centuries, already in the 11th century boasted 14-storey high buildings with top-story roof gardens and ox-drawn water wheels for irrigating them.[1]

Water shortages may have curtailed urban horticulture in ancient Greece, but ingenious use was made of water, wherever some was available. On Crete, the large inland city of Eleutherna was important until the Late Roman period and had a vaulted aqueduct taking water from cisterns under the acropolis and to extensive fields for crops, terraced down along the limestone spur on which the city was erected. Some terraces are still cultivated (Rodenbeck 1991). Greek city states were self-supplied with goat milk and olive-oil fuel for house lighting.

Vast agricultural drainage schemes have been revealed on imperial Roman sites of Timgad in Algeria and of Volubilis in Morocco. Near the mouth of the Tiber River, in the densely settled ancient Roman port of Ostia, a planned complex of garden houses, surprisingly similar to contemporary counterparts, was erected in ca. 128 BC. The complex was more likely built for middle and lower classes, with 40-100 apartments which probably housed 400-700 people. All that remains of its original gardens are the six fountains from which residents drew their water (Watts and Watts 1994). The coastal city of Cosa, 140 km north of Rome, at its height in 100 BC, had its harbour linked by artificial and natural channels to a commercial fishery in a lagoon. The catch was dried, pickled or salted and shipped in amphorae. The fish farm had tanks more than 100 meter long, covering about one hectare at one end of the adjacent lagoon. Some of the catch of eel, grey mullet, sea bass, gilthead and sole would have been eaten by the local population. A modern lagoon fishery was still in operation at the nearby town of Orbetello in the mid-1990s (McCann 1994). Elsewhere, Andalusia cities had houses surrounded by gardens and orchards.

In medieval Europe, local food supply systems actively engaged a rural-urban continuum of sub-systems. Susan Reynolds (1984, 200) writes: 'The provision of food in sufficient quantity, sufficiently fresh, and at a reasonable price, was a constant anxiety...'Crop-rotation systems were being tested in farms and fields of monasteries, walled cities and castles. Medieval tapestries suggest ladies' castle gardens included herbs on raised beds and rabbit hutches (Jellicoe 1989). A fifteenth-century College of the Vicars Choral in the city of York, England, had a building surrounding a garden; behind it laid orchards (Addyman 1994). Nearly perfectly preserved medieval Novgorod in Russia is depicted in an XVIIth-century icon, showing well-spaced housing, gardens and orchards, both within its outer and its inner walls (Yanin 1994).

In North America, four thousand years ago in the pre-Olmec Valley of Mexico, small towns on stone-faced terraces, such as Tlatilco and Ticoman, farmed vegetables and raised dogs and turkeys (Burland 1976). In the Mississippi culture (peak 1050–1250 BC),intensive riverine horticulture supported what Butland (cited in Coe et al. 1986) qualifies as true preindustrial cities, in the rich alluvial valleys of the Mississippi, Ohio, Tennessee, Arkansas and Red rivers and their tributaries. One of them, the ten-thousand people city of Cahokia in Illinois, was the largest pre-Columbian urban centre north of Mexico. Also, in the middle course of the Mississippi, the Moundville site (pop. 3000) in Alabama contains borrow-pits apparently used to store live fish, which were part of the food needed to support its people (Coe et al. 1986). In the Yucatan peninsula, subject to seasonal rains and with difficult access to underground water, whole cities such as Tikal were designed by the Mayas to capture rainwater and store it in reservoirs, some located on hilltops, for drinking and for irrigating crops through complex canal systems (Peterson and Haug 2011). Authority was also exerted to terrace steep hills and drain swamps into fields, as on the edge of Nohmul. This was a large late pre-classic city near the Belize-Mexico border. Discovered in 2004, the Maya metropolis of Caracol in western Belize had been one of the largest pre-Columbian cities. In ca 650 its more than 120,000 people cultivated land, traded and prospered within the perimeter of the city-state (Johns 2008). At the city of Edzna, on the coastal plain of Campeche, waterworks of staggering proportions (2.25 million cubic meters of water storage) supported a highly organized agricultural economy (Hammond 1994).

The Aztec civilization depended partly on food grown and raised within and on the periphery of its city-states such as Teotihuacán and Tenochtitlán, the capital city sited south-west of the former on an island was expanded on Lake Mexico (Anton 1993). In these city-states each skilled and unskilled artisan and merchant received a house and a field which he or she had to farm or else have someone else do it for him/her. Otherwise it would be taken back by the State (Gendron 2011). In 1519, the *conquistador* Bernal Díaz del Castillo marvelled at the agricultural nature of the city which he discovered: an island capital extending over 20 square miles, with five times the population of Henry VII's London (Redclift 1987). Teotihuacan itself, at the height of its power (500 BC), with more than 4000 buildings and 50–100,000 people, had been larger than imperial Rome (Millon 1994). Millon's maps of Teotihuacan (125–250,000 people) at the time of the Spanish conquest clearly indicate *chinampas* in one section of the city: these were 'rectangular raised-beds anchored with planted fences of willows, filled in and periodically fertilised with piles of marshy vegetation removed through canal-cutting, topped with canal-bottom mud.' (Coe et al. 1986).

Chinampas carried fruits, vegetables, trees and houses, supplied most of the produce consumed in the city at the time of the discovery and still supplied some vegetables as late as 1900. Animals were kept and their manure and that of humans applied to organic gardens (Redclift 1987). Highly fertile and productive *chinampas* were found in Xochimilco (surviving to the present), towns on southern shores of Lake Xochimilco, and in most of the island of Tenochtitlan-Tlatelolco. A plan to recover the Xochimilco region has prompted new interest for the *chinampa* economy which has survived to the present (Millon 1994; see also Canabal 1992). A 15-km long dyke, built across Lake Texcoco, protects *chinampas* from rising saltwater to irrigate a hilltop orchard in the northeast of Tenochtitlan (Haas 1993). The well-spaced layout of outer house mounds probably enabled each home to have its own garden (Burland 1976). In Haas' Gardens of Mexico (1993), a nineteenth century painting depicts a woman in her central Mexico City rooftop garden, attended by her mestizo and native maids, and a water seller approaching the group. Haas finds that secure rooftop potted plants are an enduring phenomenon in provincial and rented houses of Mexico.

At Tairona's Buritaca 200 site in Colombia's Sierra Nevada, an elaborate landscape of retention walls, canals, and drainage systems afforded in-city cropping (Coe et al. 1986); Burland 1976). In the Peruvian Andes, central plazas of U-shaped structures might have been irrigated or flooded and crops possibly grown; large ceremonial complexes were usually adjacent to cultivated fields (guinea pig bones found earlier than 1800 BC at Culebras, half-way between Trujillo and Lima) (Coe et al. 1986). At Cuzco and Machu Picchu, extensive retention walls, terrace gravel beds and stone-lined drainage afforded intensive farming of steep slopes (Fig. 3.1). Inca city building obeyed strict rules which included slope-terracing for crops indispensable to city supply, as at Choqek'iraw, a ceremonial center , royal residence and bastion near Machu Picchu, which boasts nearly 150 terraces farmed with probably maize, quinoa and other vital staples, even possibly coca (Lecoq 2011). In the Upper Xingu (Brazilian Amazon), GPS assisted mapping and fieldwork in the last ten years have enabled archaeologist Heckenberger (2011) to unravel a pre-Columbian network of garden cities (and villages) centered on the city of Kuhikugu on Lake Lamakuka. The population of these cities probably exceeded 1000 people, comparable in size to their medieval Europe counterparts. The urban sites were walled, with housing sectors inside sited on black earth, a fertile soil enriched with domestic wastes.

While in XVIth-century Europe cities of 20,000 people or more were still the exception, pre-colonial Africa boasted cities averaging 15–25,000 residents. Locals themselves had terms to distinguish cities from big villages.

Fig.3.1: 15th-century citadel of Machu Picchu

Similar to their European counterparts most were highly dependent on agrarian production (Coquery-Vidrovitch 1993). Some cities were temporary, seasonal, rose and declined but many of the more important sacral, political and economic centers maintained agricultural functions within their walls, even though they commanded considerable military might, industry (textiles and metals) or trading areas.

In Central Africa the spatial organization of urban areas was distinct from European models, as it provided spaces for specialized trades, cult, fallows, sacred woodland, fuel reserves and food supply. According to Coquery-Vidrovitch (1993), any agglomeration of importance implied innovation of an agricultural nature. Mbanza Kongo, capital of a powerful state south of the Congo River (in today's Angola) had walled compounds with enough space for livestock and garden farming, plus room for more extensive agriculture. In western Transvaal, Kurrichane, an industrious iron-age city of 16,000, agriculture remained essential with terraced crop fields extending beyond the urban settlement proper (Coquery-Vidrovitch 1993). The first capital cities of Central Africa were built around a palace and its livestock corrals within its walls; in Hull's words reported by Coquery-Vidrovitch, they 'minimized urbanity in order to maximize the urban space: spaces for markets, meetings, crops, life in general'. Considered as undeniably urban as of the XIXth century, Buganda, with its nearly 70,000 souls at the turn of the XXth century, devoted considerable space to fruit trees (Coquery-Vidrovitch 1993).

In northern Nigeria, much agricultural land was enclosed within the impressive outer walls of Kano, a major Hausa city ; even after it became a central marketplace for food trade in the early XIXth century, the 'custom of farming within the walls remained pivotal' (Freund 2007, 33). In southern Nigeria, Yoruba urban centers, such as the capital city of Ilesha, provided for households to have access to fields for their sustenance and the market (ibid.; Adams 1994). In the XVIIth century Cape Town, a pivotal link on the Netherlands-East Indies trading route, next to its massive castle the other 'most critical focal point' were its gardens nearby: in the post-slavery era, land loans gave way to land purchases and peri-urban agriculture developed for its urban population to become more autonomous to feed itself (Freund 2007).

What Guidance from Ancient Urban Agriculture for Contemporary Urban Agriculture?

These cities' collective experience suggests foundational principles that enabled them to make agriculture part of urbanity. In very diverse geographical and cultural settings, cities made UA work for them because they followed principles so universal that, I would contend, these remain appropriate even for their latest descendants, our 21st century urban centres. These principles are an enduring heritage which contemporary policy should not only acknowledge but also promote, wherever it is now disregarded, and preserve wherever it is still followed, in order to make agriculture part of our cities in a way that will render them more beautiful, liveable, safe and prosperous.

1. Urban agriculture was associated with functionally sophisticated urban centres. Strikingly, much of the best archaeological evidence we have of agricultural activity in ancient cities comes from centers of power, cult and wealth in their respective societies. These cities were anything but shantytowns when and where they existed. And in those advanced settlements, agriculture was not a rare, temporary activity sited haphazardly in the urban fabric. Much agriculture in and around such cities was not socially demeaning or technically primitive at the time it was practiced.[2]

2. In order to become part of the city, agriculture needed to be valued by authorities. Cities have always been systems highly vulnerable to disruption. City authorities ensured the city would set aside and control a minimum area from which it could reliably draw a reasonable share of all the food required to feed its inhabitants. Food production was not only carried out by better-off individuals; those in authority also commissioned, built and managed massive food-producing systems, even making room for food production when designing lower-class living quarters.[3]

3. Urban agriculture was used to draw meaningful benefits from land investments in other urban functions. Advanced ancient cities sought to maximize self-reliance returns, when investing in large and ingenious earth and waterworks, within their walls and on their edge. And these, to varying extents, were designed to grow: crops for food, feed, fodder ; wood for fuel, tools, furniture, building, shade, fencing, and windbreaks; shrubs, ornamental, medicinal, and other useful plants; and raise livestock for food, materials, traction, transport, and trade, savings, sacrifices and status.[4]

4. The morphology and dynamics of the city stimulated the diversification of space and time-specific agricultural systems. Urban food production took a variety of forms, making ingenious use of space, site conditions, exposure to natural elements, proximity to equipment, facilities and markets, water, soil and waste resources, and seasons. The scarcer these resources were, the greater was the pressure to innovate and the more valuable were the products grown or raised by city dwellers.[5]

5. The urban economy pushed the limits of the technically possible in agriculture. Although innovations also arose in rural areas, cities provided the best incentives, resources, markets and sites for more intensive and productive farming systems to be designed and tested, perfected and disseminated. Technological breakthroughs included: sun reflectors; water collection, storage, and distribution; frost protection; wetland drainage and slope terracing; *chinampa*-style raised beds for multiple cropping.[6]

Our ancient societies' stock of science and technology was then much more limited than is ours today, but UA back then was being done with no less ingeniousness and for reasons which in many parts of the world have endured up to our days.

Why UA has been disregarded by governments and planners of western urban economies has yet to be clarified. Segregating colonized locals away from the City? Creating captive consumer markets for the agro-industry? Sanitizing urban agglomerations against diseases? Lee-Smith and Memon (1994) argued that the exclusion of agriculture as a permanent urban function in western contemporary urbanism can be explained by cultural connotations assigned to country and city, dating back to the Greco-Roman period, later reinforced by Industrial Revolution urbanism.

Still, Greco-Roman archaeological remains, current liberal practices in the Mediterranean rim, plus garden-city paradigms transferred from Europe to colonies or ex-colonies (greenbelt towns of the USA and garden-city colonial cores of Asian and African cities) point to a very complex arena of visions. Zoning started to sanitize the medieval core of Dutch cities as early as in the XVIIth century (Wagenaar 1992). But agriculture never disappeared from Dutch cities and the country today is re-valorizing its UA tradition, with a fledgling UA entrepreneurial sector already apparent in cities such as Rotterdam.

The sanitation argument of West European colonial powers that discouraged food production in colonial cities was aimed wrongly. In the industrializing metropolises of the North, pathologies and epidemics had their origins more in pollution-prone manufacturing technologies and in workers' substandard living conditions than in urban food production itself. Following nearly two centuries of plague outbreaks, imperial French and Ottoman rule enforced drastic measures in burgeoning Cairo against the discharge of human and animal wastes in public areas. As a result, risks of epidemics were greatly reduced, while small livestock-raising, fowl in particular, remains quite common, despite it being illegal and under-reported (Gertel and Samir 2000). Pathway research on health risks linked with some UA systems and practices lends arguments for cities to clean up their act on other fronts, such as how they manage their liquid and solid wastes as well as airborne emissions.

The prevailing XVIIIth-century philosophical view in Western Europe was one which opposed natural to artificial, nature to civilization, natural man to urban man (Marshall 1992). This view, along with the privatisation of land ownership and the elite's privilege to grow food on private land, may better explain the divorce between city and agriculture. This separation was being formalized when cities and urban workers could have gained much from UA (See Introduction). War-time rationing included exceptions to this rule in Europe and North America, not dissimilarly to situations which post-colonial African cities have been facing more enduringly.

In the global North and South, particularly over the last forty years, urbanisation has been challenging cities' growing reliance on often distant and unreliable food producing areas. Urbanisation has also been challenging the morality of depriving the urban poor from accessing un-built urban land for feeding themselves and others.

The divorce is being revisited and changes are being promoted, albeit based on different arguments in the global North and in the global South, given the larger measure of urban poverty in the latter. In the urban areas of newly independent countries in the South, particularly those where local governance has become representative and progressive, bylaws inherited from the colonial era are being changed and urban food production is tolerated, if not supported. In the North, urban governments are rediscovering UA as a means to recover and utilize more fully resources such as space and energy. In both North and South UA is helping cities reduce long-distance sourcing of fresh and nutritious perishable food, while extending the useful life of the water and organic resources which they consume.

How Different is UA from Rural Agriculture?

Studies by the CIRAD (Centre de coopération internationale en recherche agronomique pour le développement) in central Africa and in South-East Asia (Moustier 1998, 2006, 2007) and by the Urban Vegetable Production Project (UVPP) of Tanzania's Ministry of Agriculture and Co-operatives and the German cooperation agency GTZ (Deutsche Gesellschaft für Internationale Zusammenarbeit) (Stevenson et al. 1996) have shown that rural and urban agriculture participate in a same system logic. Both constantly vie to complement each other in a way that evolves according to various factors, including international trade. The Government of Guinea-Bissau supported the development of urban vegetable irrigated farming in Bissau to reduce imports from neighbouring countries and price peaks during the local off-season (Lourenço-Lindell 1995) and more countries have done the same to dampen seasonal price fluctuations or longer-term price spikes, as observed in recent years.

When compared to its rural sister, UA always has been technically more vanguard. As the cradle for innovations, including those in agriculture, the city supplies protection, expertise and funding needed, as well as demand and competition, for pressing agriculture to relentlessly push back the limits of its diversity, quality and yields. While rural yields are measured by the hectare, yields in the city are so by the square meter or cubic meter.

When conditions in rural areas become suitable technical advances that were incubated in and around urban areas can be taken up in rural areas. Even today agricultural innovation centers are located in or near cities. Metropolitan agriculture remains the most performing one in the USA (Laweil and Nierenberg 2007). Despite its 12 million people, France's Isle de France has 45% of its land under cultivation; the Isle is the nation's first producer of watercress, second for decorative flowers, third for salads and thirteenth for wheat (Bhatt and Farah, 2009). The agro-food biotechnology industry has been using peri-urban fields as launching pads for their genetically modified products, as in Harare (Gabel 2005).

The geography of UA is far more opportunistic, and makes use of much smaller areas. Its distribution is more scattered, but also more dynamic over time and mobile throughout the seasons and the years. If one holds the area constant, UA will be consistently more intensive and diversified – more than 40 systems and sub-systems were inventoried by UNDP (1996) in a same city. Creative ways have been found to circumvent constraints affecting access to and tenure of land available at attractive locations. Examples of such creativity abound in the literature of the global South.[7] In terms of employment, UA is a second-order strategy for most urban producers in the global South, even though it is the main source of income for a growing minority. In terms of its social acceptance, the viewpoints on its place in the city vary according to culture but are often divided, when not contrasted. People tend to accept more easily non-food productions than food production, and within the later, plant crops rather than animal husbandry, and then, more so small rather than large livestock. However, in arid and semi-arid climates, urban livestock is culturally more tolerated and is more widespread than food plant cultivation. In terms of access to urban resources, agro-food production faces stiffer competition, from other agricultural activities but particularly from non-agricultural activities. Market vegetable gardening is very intensive with high-input content; it eliminates fallows and produces on demand. It is the pay-per-view version of agriculture, running year-round where conditions permit. In cities, a very large percentage of urban producers use land which they do not own or to which they have no rights, hence exposed to greater tenure insecurity (theft or destruction of harvests or equipment, evictions or seizure of animals). Wage labour is more expensive than in rural areas but costs are kept low in several ways; cash flow is quicker and marketing costs lower, as value chains are shorter (Moustier 2007). As a result, income by the square or cubic meter and profit margins are generally higher for the urban producer.

Market UA production tends to be ruled more by local urban demand, particularly of large high-income consumer markets nearby. However, given its proximity to transportation terminals, any high-value surplus can be easily exported (cut-flowers from Bogota or Cochabamba to the US market). This demand varies seasonally and favours a specialisation in fresh, perishable foodstuff (small livestock, dairy products, leafy vegetables, fresh fish, flowers, fine herbs, etc.) or in specialty foods with high seasonal demand (often linked to cultural celebrations, as the Tabaski religious holiday in Dakar or Círio de Nazaré pilgrimage in Belém, Brazil). As to support structures, except for the capital-intensive private sector, research, technical and financial services are usually less accessible to UA. On the policy front, national governments tend to grant lesser priority to UA, if any. And even though municipalities are paying more attention to UA, in most cases regulatory systems in place still remain very compartmented, confusing and inadequate (Campilan et al. 2001).

WHAT IS URBAN AGRICULTURE TODAY?

From a review of definitions in the literature the following was proposed in 2000:

> 'Urban agriculture is an industry located within (intra-urban) or on the fringe (peri-urban) of a town, a city or a metropolis, which grows and raises, processes and distributes a diversity of food and non-food products, (re-)using largely human and material resources, products and services found in and around that urban area, and in turn supplying human and material resources, products and services largely to that urban area.' (Mougeot, 2000)[8]

However, as more disciplinary fields seek to mainstream UA into their own research and practice, new definitions should contribute to enrich existing ones. For instance, agricultural urbanism, as proposed by food system planners and landscape architects, is concerned with 'developing a wide range of sustainable food and agriculture systems elements into multiple community scales.' (de la Salle and Holland 2010; see Chapter 7). Using techniques ruled by principles of integrated resource recovery, agricultural urbanism promotes compatibility and interconnection in order to close the loop on material flows at different scales in the city (e.g.: district energy systems). The American Planning Association for its part issued a planning advisory report in 2011 which defines UA as comprising production-to-marketing activities for food and other products that are located 'within the cores of metropolitan areas' (Hodgson et al. 2011).

Beyond a more over-arching concept, operational definitions of UA do vary from one case to another. Such definitions seek to account for the interests of particular actors, be these researchers, activists, authorities, entrepreneurs or producers (Quon 1999). Premat's discourse analysis in Cuba (2005) has shown that, even within the same city, how one defines UA, its usefulness and the roles of various actors, is a question whose answers can vary widely, when they do not contradict one another, even within government and depending on who is the respondent.

UA is practised everywhere in and around urban areas, on rooftops, balconies, terraces, window sills, shelves, stairs, underneath stairways and counters, on pillars, ceilings and floors, walls and fences, in basements and attics, in front and back yards, in pens, cages, tanks, on right-of-ways, water bodies, vacant or built lots, combined or not with other space uses.

But the mere fact that agriculture is located within or bordering an urban area does not itself suffice to distinguish UA from its rural counterpart. If location were its only difference UA would not survive in the city. Crops and husbandry must critically mesh with urban dynamics, if they are to prosper in the city.

The urbanity of agriculture is defined by how closely and broadly it interacts with the rest of the urban ecology and economy. How can it do this? By tapping on resources (human and material, under- used or unused), inputs (from seeds to containers, including tools and other equipment) and services (veterinaries, agronomists, community services, funds for small enterprises) which are concentrated in that urban area. In return, UA provides this same urban area with resources (green spaces, micro-climates), products (food and others) and services (education, recreation, sanitation, therapy, agro-tourism, etc.). From a geographic, economic or ecological perspective, if not from a political standpoint, contemporary UA expresses itself quite differently from what Ebenezer George Howard (1902) envisaged in its Garden Cities of Tomorrow.

A case of greater integration would be: a small enterprise run by city-born and trained individuals uses a vacant ground area of a city school property, relies on city-based technical extension, product inspection and market price information, applies inputs and seeds purchased from urban outlets and disposed of by urban industries, plus treated school wastewater, and grows organically short-cycle, high value vegetables which it sells to city supermarkets and other urban consumers on a daily basis. It then applies incomes to re-investment into ornamentals, and the purchase of goods and services produced or sold by city outlets. The enterprise uses student interns, supports school events and donates to a local soup kitchen.

By contrast, a case of lesser integration would be: a recent arrival to the city, settled on its periphery, cultivates on an adjacent un-built lot a low-value, rain fed crop, relying on seeds, know-how, tools and other inputs brought from the rural area. The activity taps very little on urban-based services; the crop goes to self-provisioning the household, at most bartering for other food brought in by visiting rural relatives. There are some savings on food purchases but little extra income available to purchase city-based services or goods, and none to re-invest (Mougeot 1999).

The principle of agriculture's integration into the urban ecosystem is critical to its conceptual identity, its civic usefulness and political viability in the city. For this reason, much recent research on UA has focused on developing approaches to integration, from physical planning, economic development and multi-functional viewpoints. Agriculture seeks to integrate itself to the city at different scales and in different ways. Largely driven by practitioners themselves, this integration can be supported and improved through collaboration with others urban actors and appropriate policy support. Research for policy has been focusing on informing and influencing public actions to promote the integration of agriculture in the city.

Growth of Urban Agriculture in the Global South

'UPA (urban and peri-urban agriculture) is already an important reality in developing countries. As urbanization will likely accelerate in the decades ahead, its contribution will be even more significant. Consequently, governments and city administrations must recognize the opportunities offered by UA to improve urban food security and livelihoods. By adopting policy responses that better integrate agriculture into urban development, developing countries can reap considerable benefits, especially enhancements in social, economic and environmental sustainability.' (FAO 2012, 216).

The practice of urban agriculture (UA) and its contribution to urban food supply particularly in the global South will grow at least over the next two generations, whether some like it or not. The UNDP (1996) estimated that, in that year, some 800 million urbanites worldwide were then already engaged in food crop growing and livestock raising in and around urban areas, 200 million of whom for the market. This represented 30.8 percent of the 1996 global urban population (2.6 billion), a ratio that, if applied to the mid-2011 global urban population estimate (3.69 billion), would give 1.1 billion people in 2011 engaged in some form of urban agriculture (UA), including over one-quarter of a billion who are doing this for trade. In terms of area used by UA, a conservative estimate by Thebo et al. (2014) puts the maximum area solely under rain-fed or irrigated crops within urban settlements of 50,000 people or more, at some 67.4 million hectares globally in 2000. This excludes an additional 272 million hectares found within a 10 km radius of those urban areas. Three mega-drivers are at work.

Growing urban markets

For one, the world is becoming more urban, thanks to a population transfer from rural to urban areas and to natural growth of urban populations (over 50% in 2007, could be 70% by 2050). The spatial distribution of food production to supply these urban areas is adjusting accordingly. This is consistent with land rent and market access principles ruling the geography of agricultural commodities (Huriot 1994). More of the higher-valued foodstuff will be produced close to or within urban areas and regions, as these grow in population and in market potential for such commodities. Even if exposure to systemic shocks were limited, (discussed below), it is difficult to imagine how a re-regionalization or re-localization of food systems will not imply a greater role for UA in the future (McClintock 2010).

SYSTEMIC EXPOSURE TO CRISES

In an increasingly interdependent world economy, climatic, energy and financial crises are having widespread impacts on cities' lifelines (Satterthwaite et al. 2010). Historically, surges in the practice of urban agriculture – and in supportive public policies – have been linked to such crises. But as cities grow more exposed to frequent and far-reaching crises over which they have little control, it is making more economic and security sense by the day for these cities, most of which are in the global South, to produce nearby, when not within their own limits, as much food as they can to feed their own people, rather than rely heavily on supplies from far away. This is particularly true for the more perishable and nutritious foodstuff. Over the last thirty years, people have not waited for their governments' green light to make their city's food system more self-reliant. And even if today more city governments are buttressing these efforts than was the case decades ago, global agricultural institutions have yet to 'adequately approach urbanization of agriculture and food systems holistically.' (Forster, 2011).

PERSISTENT URBAN POVERTY

Fuelled by the previous drivers, a third one which, in the global South, explains the sustained growth of UA beyond crisis-driven surges is the rising level of urban poverty. Now estimated at 30% globally, it is predicted to continue to grow over the next 20 years, possibly reaching 50% by 2035 (UN Habitat 2004). Nearly all of this growth will take place in less developed countries; while India is at 30%, some of the poorer Sub-Saharan Africa countries, as well as the Caribbean countries, are already passed the 50% level. Without remedial action, the population living in slums is estimated to increase from 32% of the world's urban population in 2001 to about 41% in 2030. For the urban poor, food has become a 'basic luxury', with households from Calcutta to Kinshasa, from Lagos to Lima, spending as much as 80% of their income on food. A review of data from 19 countries showed urban poverty rates to be very close to rural poverty rates in many cases (Kessides 2006, quoted by Prain 2010, 3); a breakdown of urban poverty rates between slum and non-slum populations would probably show rates for the slum population equal or higher than mean rural poverty rates.

According to some reports, the 2007-8 food price shock by itself would have increased global poverty then by between 3-5%, deepening rural poverty and adding 'new poor' in urban areas (Compton et al. 2010). Low-income households are particularly vulnerable to disruptions in food supply; with a rise in food staple prices of 29% some 44 million people are estimated to have fallen below the poverty line in 2010 (Cohen and Garrett 2009). UNICEF estimated, from a sample of 58 countries, that food staple prices were 55% higher in November 2010 than they were in May 2007 (Ortiz et al. 2011). Food staple output is now barely sufficient to attend world demand and prices increased again by 10% within a month-span in mid-2012, with the World Bank blaming it on drought in major producing regions. But this was the third price spike in less than five years, and prices could as much as double over the next twenty years, affecting particularly the poor, according to an OXFAM report.[9] In Indonesia, as elsewhere in times of similar crises, President Yudhoyono pressed families to grow some of their food to ease demand (Ortiz et al. 2011). And like Save the Children already had observed in Kampala during civil strife under the Idi Amin presidency, the Red Cross also recognized more recently that during the civil war in Sierra Leone, Freetown had managed to feed itself relatively well, thanks to urban food growing.

Poverty levels could be fuelled by the fact that 'more than half of the world's urban population currently lives in cities of less than five hundred thousand people (and) (s)maller cities are expected to absorb half of urban population growth between 2005 and 2015, yet their capacity to manage this process with services and policies is weak' (UNFPA 2007, 9). In 2008, an estimated one third of all urban residents were poor (Ravallion, Chen, and Sangraula 2007, quoted by Garland et al., 2007). 'Many of these are in small cities and towns where the incidence of poverty tends to be higher than in big cities. While these proportions have not changed dramatically in the last ten years, with continued urbanization, the numbers of the urban poor are predicted to rise and poverty will increasingly be an urban phenomenon.' (Baker 2008, 11).

UA has been positioning itself on the agenda of at least one international conference every year, and this since the congress of the International Union of Local Authorities in 1993. At the time of the Symposium for this book in September 2010, at least two other international events were going on. UA is now featured in yearbooks of a growing number of UN agencies (FAO, UNDP, UNEP, UN Habitat). FAO and Habitat clarified their corporate policy on UA in the late 1990s and early 2000s, both looking to complement each other in mutual respect of their respective mandates (FAO 1999; Okpala 2003). After the 2004 edition of the UN Habitat World Urban Forum devoted a first panel to it, UA was abundantly present on the program of its 2006 edition (Vancouver) and was assigned a session in 2008 (Nanjing) (Campbell et al. 2010). The Worldwatch Institute devoted an entire chapter to it in its State of the World in 2007 (Halweil and Nierenberg 2007) and has been reporting on its developments ever since. The International Food Policy and Research Institute and the World Meteorological Organization have been promoting UA as a tool to make cities resilient to climate change (Campbell et al. 2010).

A major break with historical trends over the last 40 years: although global data are unavailable, field studies indicate that agro-urban productions have increased considerably their share of total urban food supply, largely due to the proliferation of small producers who grow food in areas, in and around cities, which they do not own.

WHAT IS URBAN AGRICULTURE'S IMPACT ON LIVES NOW?

This is considerable in the global South. I will answer the question largely by drawing on my analysis of late 1990s data from surveys in twenty-four cities and in urban areas of three countries published elsewhere (Mougeot 2005). The cities are: Accra, Addis Ababa, Antananarivo, Bandim, Bangui, Bissau, Brazzaville, Cagayan de Oro, Dakar, Dar es Salaam, Hanoi, Harare, Jakarta, Kampala, Kumasi, La Habana, London, New York (1849), Nouakchott, Shanghai, Sofia, St Petersburg, urban areas of Bulgaria, Romania, and Russia. The findings from those surveys indicate that:

(a) Every year in any of those cities, various types of UA yield thousands of metric tons of produce and millions of liters of milk, worth tens of millions of dollars.[10]

(b) Households that grow food make up an important minority or a large majority of all households in any given city.

(c) These households produce a significant share of all the food that they consume, and this share is even larger for the poorer households.[11]

(d) Where data are available, the relative share of UA in a city's total food supply tends to increase over time.[12]

(e) Where poor households who do not practice UA are compared with poor households who do, those who do are found to be more food secure (e.g.: Kampala, Nairobi, Harare).[13]

The practice of UA also helps to reduce urban poverty. Again, late 1990s surveys in twenty-four cities and in urban areas of one country indicate that UA can provide sizeable employment and income. The cities are: Accra, Addis Ababa, Bamako, Cagayan de Oro, Cairo, Calcutta, Dakar, Dar es Salaam, Harare, Jakarta, Kumasi, La Habana, Lomé, London, Lusaka, Mexico City, Moscow, Nairobi, Nakuru, Port Sudan, Santiago (Dom Rep), Shanghai, Sofia, Thiés, and urban areas of Russia (Mougeot 2005). The findings indicate that:

(a) At any given time and in any of those cities, thousands of farmers and tens of thousands of workers may be engaged in a particular type of UA production at any time.[14]

(b) UA is more widespread as a second or third source of income, a relatively easy entry into the job market for youths.[15]

(c) Generally, the higher the market value of the produce, the greater its contribution to the producer's household income.

(d) Market UA tends to afford higher incomes and wages than unskilled construction work; incomes often are even higher than wages of mid-level civil servants.[16]

(e) Annual savings in food purchases amount to several months of the minimum wage.

In less consolidated settlements, savings or profits from home-based UA allow women to invest in other home-based business that improve household well-being. This comes handy in cultures where adult and married women cannot work away from home or in public places. Also, economic crises – including recent food price hikes and shortages – tend to drive growth in UA employment and output. Cuba's recovery in the late 1990s reduced areas under crops and jobs in UA, while productivity was increased, output was sustained and higher-valued (small livestock) systems expanded (Cruz and Sanchez 2001). In Uruguay and Argentina, post-crisis UA provides less but more productive employment, now established as a permanent sector interacting with new partners (Santandreu et al. 2010).

Why Do Governments Pay Attention to Urban Agriculture?

Local governments have rightly been concerned with risks associated with the growth of UA in their city: sub-optimal use of urban resources, health risks posed to food products grown in a contaminated environment, health risks posed to producers and consumers by UA mis-practices, and conflicts over access and tenure of resources used in particular UA. All such risks are well documented in the literature and have been a persistent focus of applied research over the last couple of decades (Mougeot 2000; Dubbeling and de Zeeuw 2007; de Zeeuw et al. 2011).

What has changed over the last fifteen years or so are the attitude and disposition of a growing number of governments at all levels to tackle these risks in a constructive way. At least three trends have been gathering in recent decades which are leading local governments in the global South in particular to be more aware of UA's role in urban development, more supportive of UA initiatives, more engaged in leading some themselves.

(A) EMANCIPATION OF MUNICIPAL GOVERNMENTS:

Municipal decentralization: in the 1990s national governments delegated to local governments a series of responsibilities without necessarily sharing needed funds, capacities and skills, or allowing municipalities to raise these resources in order to comply.

Municipal self-reliance: as a result, local governments have increasingly turned to tapping on assets and resources within their own jurisdiction to promote territorial development, including 'municipal agriculture' or 'metropolitan agriculture'.

Municipal networking: The 1990s witnessed a marked development of national, regional, global associations, federations and confederations of local governments, to share expertise and experiences in dealing with common challenges. The former International Union of Local Authorities (IULA) – now United Cities and Local Governments (UCLG) – held a panel on urban agriculture as early as in 1993, at its conference in Toronto, Canada.

Municipalities as interlocutors on world stage: The 1990s were also a decade during which local governments gained official national delegation status at UN global summits. UNDP sponsored international colloquia of local government officials in NYC. The UN Habitat created a Sustainable Cities Program and an Urban Management Program, and the agency later was granted higher status in the UN system. Both UN Habitat programs would collaborate with IDRC over more than a decade to support evidence-based policy making on UA in Latin America and the Caribbean and Sub-Saharan Africa.

(B) INTERNATIONAL ASSISTANCE:
The UNDP commissioned a world survey of UA, published in the aftermath of the UN Habitat Conference in Istanbul, in 1996. Canada's IDRC created a research program dedicated partly (1993-6), then wholly (1996-2005) to UA in developing regions. With other donors that Centre created a global support group on UA to coordinate actions. The Dutch international cooperation agency DGIS and IDRC jointly core-funded the creation of the Resource Centers for Urban Agriculture and Food Security (RUAF), originally coordinated by ETC International in the Netherlands. Over a decade RUAF developed into a global network, with hubs in all major regions of the world. By the late 90s the FAO had over a dozen units tackling different aspects of UA and the agency consolidated an interdisciplinary program on urban and peri-urban agriculture (UPA), setting up more recently a Food for the Cities Secretariat, to better coordinate its assistance to national governments in this sector. The CGIAR created in 2000 a Strategic Initiative on Urban and Peri-Urban Agriculture (SIUPA), later renamed Urban Harvest, to address several research issues. Its Sub-Saharan Africa coordinating office, supported by the IDRC, lent strong support to policy development in cities such as Kampala and Nairobi. In the early 2000s the WHO decided to revise its norms for wastewater reuse in agriculture, and for this received IDRC support. In different regions of the world, UN agencies with their regional partners organized international conferences, convening national ministries and municipal governments to address UA issues. Officials committed to policy development on UA, with dozens of cities now having endorsed the Quito Declaration in Latin America and the Caribbean. Over the last five years, some central governments have been drafting or have approved blue-prints for national UA policies.

Sources of financial support for such initiatives have also diversified away from official development assistance agencies. Local foundations have started to mobilize resources for UA as a means to pursue various agendas (civil rights, food sovereignty, community and enterprise development), such as the Fundación Rosario in Argentina, the Metcalf Foundation in

Toronto, and the Real Estate Foundation in Vancouver (Santandreu et al. 2010; Nasr et al. 2010). Likewise, governments of high-income countries, as part of international cooperation programs on climate change, are assessing the contribution which UA can make to resilient urban development (e.g.: Germany's Federal Ministry of Education and Research (BMBF), as per Han and Pieschel 2010, Dubbeling 2013).

(C) COMMUNITY OF PRACTICE:
Partnerships among initially a small group of institutions and agencies, as in Sub-Saharan Africa over 2000-2008 (Prain 2010), have enabled growth in the range of disciplines, of organizations in research and training, and of policy issues and measures addressed. The IDRC supported the creation of regional networks made up of researchers, civil society practitioners and policy-makers, in Latin America, North and West Africa, the Middle East and Asia. With others, it supported several regional courses for city teams of Latin America, French and English speaking Africa and the Middle East (2000-2005). These activities reinforced one another over time.

Both the IDRC and UN HABITAT – particularly its Urban Management Programme – in collaboration with regional anchoring institutions, such as Promoción del Desarrollo Sostenible (IPES) in Lima, the Institut africain de Gestion urbaine in Dakar, and Municipal Development Partnerships for East and Southern Africa in Harare, supported policy and planning projects that involved groups of cities in order to accelerate mutual learning and innovation.

The RUAF network has been publishing the Urban Agriculture Magazine, a high-quality science magazine which distils scholarly research into language accessible to various stakeholder groups in the UA sector. Its theme-specific issues have become a global platform for reporting and networking among the world community of researchers, practitioners and policymakers. Published in various languages, regional editions also feature regional content. A growing number of scholarly journals are producing special issues on UA topics, including Sitopolis, launched in late 2014 and focusing on urban agriculture and regional food systems.

Latin American and Caribbean municipalities issued their own set of policy guidelines in 2003, based on a collective review of individual experiences to draw good practices. The set has been translated into four languages, and has been used as a reference for municipalities in other world regions to develop their own guidelines. UN HABITAT's World Urban Forums put UA on their agenda, for the first time in Barcelona 2004, and with a panel of mayors from cities on four continents at its Vancouver 2006 edition.

The American Planning Association adopted a policy in 2007 to encourage its members to engage in food-system building with other professions (Dubbeling et al. 2009), later issuing guidelines for the zoning of urban agriculture (Mukerji and Morales, 2010).

Undergraduate courses and graduate concentration programs on UA are now being offered in a growing number of disciplinary fields at European and North American universities (Ryerson University in Toronto, Washington University in St Louis, George Washington University in Washington D.C.). Beijing's University of Agriculture now has a Graduate School of Urban Agriculture. Training centers for urban producers are being set up in cities of both the global South, as in Nakuru, Kenya, and in the global North. In New York, the South Side Community Land Trust has a city farm which also operates as a training center.

RESEARCH FOR POLICY ON URBAN AGRICULTURE: SOME LESSONS

HOW DOES URBAN AGRICULTURE SURFACE ON THE PUBLIC POLICY AGENDA?

A city where agriculture is highly integrated to its economy and ecology would be either one which has UA as a distinct policy sector that interacts in its own right with other relevant sectors, or one which has UA as a cross-cutting dimension or subsector in all relevant sector policies. Unfortunately, a more common situation is exemplified by the city of Pune, India, where the Department of Gardens does not include low-income households and organic waste recycling in its UA projects, because waste management falls under the purview of the Health Department, uninterested yet in such synergies (Behmanesh 2010). Cohen (Chapter 8) discusses how Seattle's government works its UA program through the functions of various departments; water rate adjustments, gleaning as waste management, allowing rooftop greenhouses to exceed height limits, keeping of pigmy goats in backyards, UA integrated into public housing (rooftop, terrace, on ground).

Major metropolitan centers in the global North have used the creation of food policy or sustainability councils for more systematic attention to UA across policy sectors. Cities in the global South have created committees, programs, offices for coordinating the activities of several departments in UA. Local coalitions representing a wide span of stakeholders (research and civic organizations, public agencies, consumer and producer groups, industry) have been a driving force for the creation of such instances. Although pathways to policy response do vary from place to place, what cities seem to share is the fact that agendas are rarely driven to meet primarily the interests of the agriculture sector itself, even though this is an essential player in such policy developments. A failure of municipal government to support and engage with local coalitions and vice-versa can greatly hinder policy progress, despite pro-active programming by civil society and higher-level government agencies, as observed in Cali, Colombia in 2012.

Cities face many development problems but, at any given point in time, only a very few can be expected to graduate and become public policy issues. Others may never do so. Very often, some stay on the waiting list for so long as to render solutions intractable by the time they become issues. Problems become public policy issues when, often sensitized by the media and lobbies, politicians (elected government officials) more so than managers or technocrats, realize the scale or significance of adversities which particular problems are causing or may cause to groups in society. They also realize that these could seriously affect the government's power base if left unattended to. Governments of course can and often do have a lead role in inducing public opinion to perceive particular problems as public policy issues. This may seem like circular logic but it is a strategy to which governments are also entitled, like any other stakeholder. This applies as much to UA as it does to other sectors. When a problem becomes an issue, policy intervention is required on part of the government in order to move attitudes, behaviour or their consequences, and make the outcome fairer, more viable and sustainable under the public's microscope.

Issues leading to policy initiatives on UA are of at least two orders. They can spring either from problems originally found in sectors other than UA, or directly from problems largely attributable to UA itself (mis-practices). This is at least as far as perceptions go, and perceptions are a big part of any politician's world.

In the former case, UA may come into the picture as part of a problem which has turned into a policy issue. For instance, the Public Health Department is concerned with the quality of food sold in open markets, some of which, it is known, is leafy produce which people tend to eat raw and which is grown by local urban farmers who irrigate crops with untreated sewage water. These groups are part of the problem, but their business also creates employment for which the city is in dire need, earns them an income and help them sustain families. The growers may or may not have influence or support from other actors. The issue may have been raised by the media or consumers and pits the general public against the various actors involved in producing and marketing the food. In this case a particular form of UA in the city may be one of the culprits of a food safety risk. In Accra, a project team from the Noguchi Memorial Institute for Medical Research of the University of Ghana looked into this issue and dismissed an early claim that the urban producers were the main culprits for the contaminated produce sold at local markets. They found that, although producers' ways were part of the problem, produce from both rural and urban growing areas and sold on markets throughout the city were equally contaminated; more critical factors, they found, were the handling and watering practices of the produce vendors themselves. Several measures were proposed to abate health risks to consumers.

Conversely, UA may come in the picture as part of the solution. For instance, the Department of Social and Economic Development is concerned with the growing ranks of idle youth which pose an increasing security risk to citizens, as they engage in delinquent and criminal activities. The issue pits unemployed youths against property owners in particular. In this case a programme to employ youths in community gardens may contribute to increase their self-esteem, usefully employ their idle time, raise an income and learn a trade in the process; other solutions might be to provide training and help groups of youth set up service or artisanal cooperatives. One of the Harare projects documented the early experience of Harare City Council (Department of Community Services) with this, and the National Police of Nicaragua in mid-2010 was considering a similar program to be sited quite visibly in downtown Managua.

Several projects have dealt with instances where UA is brought into the picture as a useful ingredient to resolve issues of concern primarily to sectors of urban management other than UA itself. The tri-city project in Latin America and the Caribbean, headed by UN Habitat-UMP and IPES, used

UA to improve urban food security and participatory urban governance.

Issues leading to public policy initiatives on UA can also stem from problems directly linked with some UA activities themselves: access to and tenure of land and water, natural resource management, including the use of agrochemicals, the disposal of wastes and other nuisances, health risks posed by particular sites and practices. These are all problems which, with the correct blend of scale, duration, press coverage and major incidents (unsafe food or water-related epidemics), can become issues by themselves.

In both types of situations where UA is part of the issue, it is very important from a policy viewpoint to specify which UA systems or practices may be part of the problem or part of the solution. UA is an overarching concept which means different things to different people. In fact, policy projects supported by IDRC over the years have used different specifications of what they meant by UA. Some focused on on-plot (e.g.: inside residential lots), others on off-plot (e.g.: outside residential lots) activities, while others looked at both. The same could be said of focus on intra-urban as opposed to peri-urban, or on crops versus livestock or other systems. Other projects dealt with activities aimed at provisioning the household essentially, while others were more interested in market-oriented activities. Some dwelled exclusively on production, while others needed to address processing and distribution as well. It all depends on the nature of the issue, which needs to be well circumscribed before anything else.

Maps of Harare (Fig. 3.2) may not show the location of all agriculture within city limits, for very good reasons. The policy issue here was the rapid expansion of open space cultivation in recent years, conflicts and risks associated with this growth. The two maps therefore focus on that particular type of UA and show that total open space area under cultivation within city limits doubled in just four years (from 8 to 16% percent of the whole area within city limits), thanks to various climatic and policy factors (Gumbo and Ndiripo, 1999). They display only a very conservative picture of the full growth of UA which such problems may have triggered in the city. The maps disregard all on-plot (e.g. backyard) agriculture in residential and other built-up plots, as well as all livestock and fisheries on and off-plot. They could also underrate the true extent of open space cultivation itself since, excluded from the maps are any fallows at the time of the survey, as well portions of those cultivated open spaces shown on the maps which actually extend beyond the city border line. The maps show that between

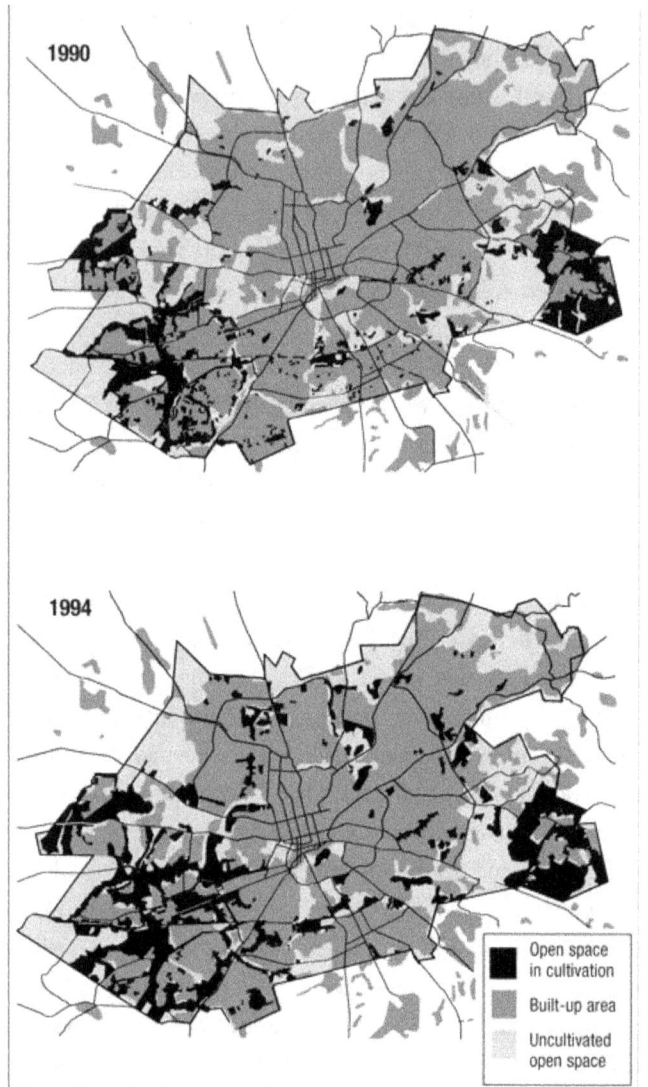

Fig. 3.2: Open space in cultivation spaces within city limits of Harare, Zimbabwe, 1990 and 1994. (Source: Gumbo and Ndiripo 1999)

1990 and 1994 smaller cultivated areas had coalesced into larger ones by 1994; other open spaces were being cultivated in better-off wards in 1994, such as Mount Pleasant, where there had been hardly any such activity in 1990.

In Rosario, Argentina, the Municipality saw community gardens as the best form of UA to improve food security and income. Therefore, the mapping focused on the spatial distribution of current community gardens.

This exercise revealed areas well and less well served by community gardens, and the availability or not of supporting infrastructure locally. Sectors of the city were identified for greater support to the establishment of community gardens, leaving out on-plot agriculture.

In contrast, in a city with much vacant land on residential plots, mapping of on-plot agricultural land uses afforded information on how people of different socio-economic status were using on-plot areas for UA. It helped the local government realize how important agricultural production is to low-income households, even where space is limited, how much they try to make the best use of small spaces, through rapid-growth plants and small livestock, as opposed to trees and ornamentals. It made the government realize how much more these people could do if they could secure access to larger areas. This motivated the Municipality to look for ways to improve the poor's access to suitable vacant areas found to be abundant in the city (on and off-plot).

To circumscribe clearly the policy issue we are concerned with is extremely important. This is not only to diagnose properly the nature and extent of the issue, as well as potential actors affected or benefited by it. It is also needed to devise solutions which will stand a chance of correcting the problems in an effective and lasting way, by engaging the right actors in identifying solutions and by sharing both their costs and benefits in a fair way. This will also ensure that diagnoses do not miss the real culprits and do not present as culprits parts of the UA sector (practices or actors) that, even if they are not part of the problem, might still end up being penalized by indiscriminate restrictions.

This unfortunately has happened too often. Field visits organized by ENDA-Zimbabwe (1996) during the second Harare project enabled both producers and city councillors to verify that initial allegations that farmers at one major site had cut down whole trees to clear ground for their crops, were unfounded: farmers were actually using areas timbered by the electricity utility because trees stood in the right-of- way of future power lines. The same project also found that chemical contamination of freshwater impoundments supplying the city was caused by industrial effluents much more than by riparian farming itself; similar results were found in Dar es Salaam (Kishimba 1996). On the other hand, in that city as in Dakar (Niang 1999; Niang and Gaye 2002), the studies did confirm that, for instance, market vegetables grown using groundwater next to derelict wastewater plants had pathogens concentrations well in excess of tolerable levels for unrestricted irrigation.

Municipal councils and managers often have condemned or repressed much larger universes of UA systems, practices and actors than actually warranted by the problems and issues themselves. This is, usually to little avail. Projects supported by IDRC show that many municipal governments are changing their ways. Sound research can help to better scope policy issues, identify stakeholders, inform their proceedings to define interests, roles, consider alternative solutions, prioritize and share actions, and monitor results of actions taken. This can make policies more effective and fairer to people engaged in UA to feed themselves, earn a living or complement their incomes, supply food to others and in the process make cities safer, greener and more liveable.

Practically this means, for instance, that in some parts of the city large cattle rearing should be replaced with smaller livestock, instead of banning all types of livestock altogether. In others, zero-grazing (stall-feeding) and proper waste disposal can be made mandatory, rather than closing all operations. In others, ornamental plant irrigation could be allowed to circumvent the food contamination issue, or low-lying instead of tall-stem crops may be permitted in open spaces at road intersections or near residential areas, to reduce risk of causing traffic accidents or being used as hide-outs by delinquents.

It is important for both policy-makers and researchers to understand that UA is a useful concept but one that is operationally meaningless if not properly specified, in legislative and regulatory terms. It encompasses a wide variety of production systems, actors, practices, and types of activities: from seed and breed production to growing or raising, harvesting, storage, processing, marketing and distribution, consumption and recycling of waste by-products. It is therefore very easy for any generic policy resolution to go awfully wrong for being too vague, too lax or restrictive, and more often than not, unenforceable.

One should be reminded that some forms of UA have been regulated and acceptable for a long time while others not. Municipalities will often allow some gardening, even small livestock on private residential plots, and institutions and even factories and public utilities have been directly engaged in growing crops and raising animals on their estates. This agriculture is largely regulated.

The kind of UA which has been presenting new policy issues over the last few decades is the one carried out by poor and not so poor people, in all sorts of open spaces other than on strictly private residential or institutional lots. In the global South, off-plot UA is often spatially more important than that carried out on private residential plots. Also, systems used both on- and off-plot have diversified well beyond those traditionally allowed. The conditions under which such systems operate also have changed. At the same time, authorities are forced to recognize that this growth and diversification, however problematic in some cases, does clearly respond to social and economic, even environmental, demands. A growing number of governments are also aware that these demands have not been met otherwise and hardly can be so at a lower cost, possibly for decades to come, either exclusively or primarily through means other than UA. Repression would only build up pressure and this may have to be released in much less harmless ways, as through food riots for instance.

For researchers who support policy processes, the previous discussion underlines the capital importance of paying attention to the policy context in which they are likely to work. Is it enabling or not? If so, why and how? If not, why not and hence, what is possible? The factors which may make a particular context more amenable than otherwise are many: the socio-economic conjuncture, such as acute and widespread impoverishment (Tanzania, Ecuador, Argentina), food scarcity (due to failure of imports in Cuba, domestic production decline in Zimbabwe); a central government sector priority as entry point (solid waste management in Dominican Republic, water demand management in Jordan, wastewater treatment and use in Senegal, productive greening of open spaces in Brazil or in South Africa), political support (Senegal, Ecuador), relevant experience available from other cities (financing, physical planning), conditions for inclusive governance (municipal decentralization, civic organization, participatory budgeting).

For both policy-makers and researchers the environment may be enabling for certain policy advances, less so for others at any given time or location. The extent to which a city may progress on the way to full institutionalisation of UA in its policies may vary, depending on where it currently stands. If it does not have a database of areas available and suitable for UA, it may want to do this first, as in Bulawayo, Zimbabwe, or Governador Valadares, Brazil. It may then want to identify particular systems and issues, revise or create regulations, enforce measures which curb some problems or promote some benefits. Next to handling these from a sector perspective, it then may want to consolidate various initiatives under an inter-sector programme, as in Cuenca, Ecuador, or Kampala, Uganda.

The speed at which uptake (institutionalization) moves along this spectrum will very much depend on resources and political will. For instance, it is only in 2011 that a new administration of the City of Metropolitan Lima, Peru, made UA a priority on its policy agenda. This will build on initiatives carried out by various municipalities of metro Lima over more than a decade, with support from local and international organizations. The City has invited an expert from a lead local NGO, IPES, to coordinate its UA program; municipal funds have been assigned and the program was being designed at the time of writing. Like multi-actor coalitions in cities as diverse as Vancouver and Kampala, the Alliance for Urban Agriculture in Metropolitan Lima was a major driver behind the creation of Lima's own program and it will support its implementation (personal communication of Gunther Merzthal, 28 April 2011).

An extreme example is provided by Cuba, a centralized economy which put in place a highly coordinated and localized national programme in record time, actually in response to popular pressure. Argentina's national Pro-Huerta programme is more recent and is increasingly buttressed by municipal policies (Casale 2006). Brazil's federal government over the last decade has been developing a national program, drawing on the learning from municipal programs implemented in several states over more than twenty years (Fig. 3.3).

In the global South and after Argentina, Cuba and Brazil in South America, Sub-Saharan Africa is likely to stage interesting premieres. In both Kenya and Uganda, policy processes in primate and secondary cities are now turning into springboards for national policy proposals, this even despite limited initiative in some cities. Differently from experience in higher-income economies so far, in both Kenya and Uganda the Ministry of Agriculture is the key protagonist. That sector ministry has been participating actively and learning from city-level policy exercises in Nairobi and Kampala. In Uganda, the Ministry's involvement probably drove the country's national agriculture research organization to acknowledge the livelihood value of UA practised in Kampala. This also may explain why, despite Kampala's platform of actors having been less active since new UA bylaw issuance, a central government initiative to develop a national UA policy has been proceeding apace. In Kenya, the Ministry of Agriculture and Livestock has been a longstanding actor in the UA sector: urban producers have been for many years the main clientele of its Nairobi provincial directorate's extension agents. The Ministry was involved in UA policy discussions from the very first local forum on UA held in 2004 (following a regional event in 2002), made input into UA courses and by 2005 was calling for a constructive regulatory framework for UA. Even when local politics in Nairobi did not favour rapid policy progress on UA in that city, the Ministry forged ahead with inviting civil society actors from the Nairobi platform to join the Steering Committee of the National Agriculture and Livestock Extension program; the Ministry has been leading the drafting of an inter-ministerial national policy for UA (Lee-Smith 2013).

Fig. 3.3: Brazil's national urban agriculture program

Brazil is one of a few countries with a federal public agency now charged with coordinating its national program in UA.

Lodged in the Ministry for Social Development and Fight Against Hunger, the General Coordinating Office for Urban and Peri- urban Agriculture was created with an annual budget of 6 m USD, of which renewal is guaranteed by federal budget legislation.

In 2008, organizations involved created an operational network of centers of assistance to urban and peri-urban agriculture, now established in 14 metropolitan centers. Over 2003-8 the program reportedly assisted directly more than 100,000 households (Moreira, 2010).

This national program and its coordinating office are only the latest developments in a strategy originally informed by a 2006 national survey; this had identified more than 600 UA initiatives in 11 metro arweas in the five regions of the country (Merzthal 2006). The survey was conducted by organizations supported by FAO and IDRC.

Brazil's national strategy actually builds on several municipal initiatives which have come on stream over the last twenty years. In 1986 Terezina (Piaui)'s municipal Secretariat of Agriculture and Supply launched a UA program in partnership with state enterprises. In the early 2000s, Porto Alegre (Rio Grande do Sul) published UN Habitat-IPES policy guidelines in Portuguese. In 2004 Recife (Pernambuco)'s Secretariat for Economic Development also launched a program. Sao Paulo included UA in its municipal strategic master plan. In 2003-4 Governador Valadares (Minas Gerais) adopted ordinances to buttress its municipal UA program and master plan.

In these as in many other countries, the assets in place for supporting a national UA policy are more considerable and comprehensive than often thought. New investment tends to be less critical than changes in mental models ruling institutional cultures. This is what policy processes can bring about, through promoting common vision, coordinated mandates, shared plans and collaborative ground-level interventions.

A good example is Kenya's Draft National Urban and Peri-Urban Agriculture and Livestock (UPAL) Policy (Republic of Kenya, 2009). Yet to be adopted, this draft is being co-proposed by the Ministers for Agriculture, for Livestock Development, for Public Health and Sanitation and for Local Development. For the first time ever in Kenya, this draft recognizes the contribution urban and peri-urban agriculture (UPA) can make, as an 'organized urban land use', to the country's Agricultural Sector Development Strategy (ASDS) 2009-2020. The draft clearly outlines challenges faced by the UPA sub-sector, identifies key policy interventions to address them, as well as essential stakeholder communities (government ministries, public enterprises, international research institutions, processors, input suppliers, producer associations, financial institutions, CBOs, NGOs and development partners). When drafting this policy the ministries involved tapped on the results of more than twenty years of research on UA in the country and the region. If the bill were passed, a national UPAL Steering Committee would be set up, with departments of agriculture and livestock created in each municipal and town council. As in other countries, the Kenyan exercise builds on UA activity and policy initiatives put forward by important urban centers in Kenya in recent years, initiatives which have either been influenced by similar processes (Cape Town) or have themselves influenced others (Kampala) in Eastern and Southern Africa.

However, still more often than not, particular cities are the ones launching their own programmes in the absence of any national policy. In the same way that national policies build on a stock of municipal initiatives, municipal initiatives tend to build on the record of more localized initiatives led by various actors over the years, as was the case in Cuenca, Ecuador. Noteworthy is that any particular policy step should be framed by a vision for more, not less, policy attention to UA and to its relationships with other aspects of urban development over time. So that, if and when the opportunity arises, current advances can support new ones. This is the way municipal governments in both developed and developing countries have been moving.

WHAT ROLE FOR DEMAND VERSUS SUPPLY RESEARCH?

The effectiveness or uptake of policy-oriented research seems to greatly depend on whether the policy authority has influence over the agenda and the process of the research. A gradation of influence associated with the role played by the policy authority in the research process is clearly recognizable from projects supported by the IDRC. At the lower end, the policy authority acted as simple informant or discussant, as in early demand-driven projects in Africa, Latin America and the Middle East; while at the upper end, government was engaged as project designer and co-implementer. The municipal administration led the research and was its main end user in more recent demand-driven projects.

Unsolicited, supply-driven research is one in which scientists engage to advance the knowledge commons on a particular topic. This research is done quite regardless of whether there is or could be, in the short term, any specific demand on part of a policy agency for the information. Supply-driven research was a trademark of most early research supported by the IDRC and others on UA (until mid-1990s), for instance in Nairobi, Kampala, Harare and Dar es Salaam. Most of current UA research worldwide still fits this category. This kind of research is not useless, as it can eventually be retrieved when the political climate becomes ripe for policy interventions. But there are obvious costs to relevance, reliability and usefulness when an uptake of the original results is delayed considerably. Demand-driven research tends to be taken up more quickly.

Given the relative novelty of UA as a policy issue, official local statistics remain few and far between, very partial at best and they still usually under-estimate greatly the reality of some UA systems. Supply-driven local surveys often are a logical first step to fill this gap. For which the initiative of carrying it lies mainly with the researchers. Not a minor detail. The IDRC's experience is that in those cities where conditions later became mature for demand-driven research, pioneer baseline information was valued and retrieved. Otherwise survey data remained shelved, with little or no incidence.

That a 'shelving' risk is greater with supply than with demand-driven research is an obvious statement. But this should be of particular concern to low and middle-income countries, where it is critical that scarce public funding be spent on research that directly helps to tackle development problems. And development problems turned into policy issues are those that are more likely to call for research use to be addressed. Policy research does not need to be costly or cutting-edge science to be effective.

The kind of supply-driven research funded by the IDRC initially involved baseline field surveys which usually required the collection and analysis of large databases, geographically and statistically representative of larger populations and fit for various types of comparative analysis. These are typically the most expensive component of any research. In the first Harare project, airborne photography, restitution, interpretation, mapping and selective ground checks for the entire urban area of Harare alone cost 30,000 CAD in the early 1990s. The data were published, publicized internationally and used by several international and local public agencies. But the investment had little immediate local policy impact, other than lead to the creation of an ad hoc committee by the Harare City Council to monitor the agricultural use of public open spaces. Parliamentarians, city councillors and managers did attend project workshops but the project itself was not formally embedded in any municipal or other official policy exercise. The context would be very different in a later project in the early 2000s, when the Harare City Council was engaged in drafting a new urban development strategy.

The retrieval of baseline data often happens many years after the survey has been completed. One may need to sustain a research effort to inform and keep the public debate alive before a problem can turn into a policy issue. In such instances, it is certainly easier to assess how much credit for change can rightly be attributed to recent rather than earlier research investments. For instance, collaboration between, on one hand, the CGIAR's Urban Harvest initiative and a UN Habitat regional workshop on UA in Sub-Saharan Africa, and on the other, City Councils of Nairobi and Kampala, certainly has had more influence on the drafting of new bylaws on UA than surveys carried out in these cities ten or twenty years earlier.

Nevertheless, steadfastness has been a key vector for supply-driven research to be gradually replaced with demand-driven policy research over time. In these long-term dynamics, one should not underestimate the influence which the commitment and professionalism of steadfast individuals and institutions can have in bringing local authorities to account for the stock of information on the local scene and other cities, when they take up UA policy issues in their own city. The fact that scholars in Nairobi,

Dar es Salaam, Dakar, Amman, or Lima, were involved in the initial baselines and, over the years, have continued their research and supported others, engaging with a wide range of actors and remaining opened to assist governments of all political stripes, certainly brought credibility to their advice and participation in policy exercises.

SINGLE-CITY OR MULTIPLE-CITY INITIATIVES?

Demand-driven research became a trademark of UA projects supported by the IDRC up to 2010. In instances where the city site for the project was selected deliberately in terms of policy uptake potential, a research process could be blended into current policy exercises and the returns were reaped more rapidly than through a separate supply-driven approach. Follow-ups to baselines and new research in specific cities were either designed from the onset to support ongoing urban policy processes (Dar, Kampala, Santiago de los Caballeros, Dakar, Quito, Rosario, Valadares, Cienfuegos, Fortaleza), or else were modified after their inception in order to do so (Harare, Havana).

The architecture of inter-city relationships in a policy project does influence policy uptake by individual cities involved. Where a demand-driven project in a particular city provides for that city to interact with 'less advanced or ripe' city contexts, this can accelerate policy change in the latter. Also, the IDRC's shift from single-city to multi-city projects clearly sped up policy changes in cities involved, when compared with the pace of change observed in cities involved in single-city projects. It is not that inter-city exchanges did not take place in single-city projects, but these tended to be fewer, opportunistic and often out of sync with policy windows which could have enabled one city to timely draw on the experience of others. This was the case with exchanges between the single-city projects in Havana and Santiago de los Caballeros, or between those in Dar es Salaam and Harare.

By contrast, projects that involved several cities and formally provided for face-to-face interaction among peers at critical moments, tended to be more effective within the lifespan of the project. For instance, this enabled a Guatemalan utility to strike a cooperation agreement with a Costa Rican counterpart to assist on a study to treat and use municipal wastewaters in agriculture (CEPIS 2002). Quito sought the assistance of a Brasilia programme to design and provide training on the financing of small urban agro-industries for its Panecillo pilot project. Rosario's first agro-industry for urban produce also learned from the Brasilia programme. Governador Valadares learned from Rosario's municipal programme to use GIS and incorporate UA in its land-use planning; it also learned from Teresina's community gardens programme. Sao Paulo's proposed municipal programme benefited from the results of a tri-city project on the productive use of vacant open spaces. Nouakchot (Mauritania) learned from Dakar on how to devise wastewater treatment and use such systems for peri-urban agriculture.

Projects which formally provided for exchanges of experiences and visits between cities were clearly of mutual benefit to quicken changes in attitude and behaviour by political and policy circles of cities involved. This was the case with the IAGU project, which carried out city consultations in several West African cities, and with the UN-Habitat project led by UMP and IPES in LAC. The latter led to a regional course for city teams, plus a tri-city project in Cienfuegos (Cuba), Rosario (Argentina) and G. Valadares (Brazil) on how to integrate UA into physical urban planning.

One should not discount opportunities that may arise, during or after the project has been designed and approved, initiated or completed. Project process and results were able to interact and influence the outcomes of originally unrelated exercises. The policy process which initially framed the Santiago project was a new city strategic urban development plan, but the national plan for the integrated management of solid wastes ended up overtaking the former as the one framework affording the best potential for immediate local policy uptake of research results. This induced a re-orientation of the project strategy: both the research institution and the City Council came to see the municipal waste issue as the more promising window through which introduce new policy on UA. This would be done through emphasizing UA's waste recycling, community-building and food-provisioning functions, particularly in low-income areas of the city.

Demand-driven policy research does not go without city commitment and a competitive city selection has been a good way to ensure this. It makes all the difference in the world when a policy research is actually requested by government, instead of simply securing its endorsement. Various selection criteria were used in the IDRC projects and these varied from project to project, depending on the needs of particular projects. But in all cases official written commitments, particularly when international funders or their intermediaries are involved, are usually honoured by local governments, as in projects led by IAGU, MDP and UN-HABITAT – UMP. The selection process must be as transparent as possible, so that cities not selected can see why they were not so and can improve their standing in future competitions. At all costs all competing cities should be kept on the distribution list of the project, if not invited to attend stock-taking events. This recommendation is not only useful to development agencies or research institutions but also to major cities or national associations and international federations of cities, particularly well positioned to host such multi-city events. The principle here is that selection is dictated by the need for tangible learning and new know-how, along with diffusion of innovations within a reasonable period of time. And as always, resources are limited. The goal should be a process that fosters a community of inclusion, not exclusion, in which cities should be able to engage in various capacities.

Risks of Demand-driven Policy Research

There are risks to demand-driven policy research which should not be ignored. These instead should be acknowledged and addressed with provisions, to avoid or minimise any undesirable consequences. Scientists tend to stress these often to stay clear from such type of research. But there are also risks to confining oneself to supply-driven research. Scientists sometimes overlook the fact that risks of a political nature are a daily currency for other professionals too, particularly those charged with prioritizing, formulating and implementing public policies, some of which end up affecting scientists themselves in one way or another. In the same way that scientists may see themselves as running risks by having their research subordinated to the needs of a policy process, policy processes whose progress relies variously on subsidiary research do present risks to policy-makers themselves.

The IDRC projects on UA contain numerous examples of risks associated with demand-driven policy research. Proper and timely data collection may be curtailed or delayed by some emerging political crisis or urgency, as in Dar es Salaam and Lima, where a couple of surveys originally should have been scheduled to be carried out outside election periods. Also, research results may end up being used in a repressive rather than a constructive way by different areas or levels of government, as in Harare, or in a partisan way to chastise the administration of the day, as in Santiago de los Caballeros.

In Cochabamba, the project coordinator had to seek political support from the provincial government when a change in the local city administration moved the project from the front to the back-burner of its agenda. The Sokoine field survey in six Tanzanian cities was hindered somewhat by the fact that Government was at the time exploring various ways of raising Government revenues (individuals not paying taxes from part-time incomes, including livestock keeping in urban areas). However, it can safely be said that overall such political incidents were limited and did not undermine the process and outcomes of projects in any significant measure.

In no project that I am aware of did the researchers report to the IDRC any pressure put on them by policy or political actors involved to 'doctor' either their data collection, analyses or reporting. This does not mean that it never happens; increasingly, researchers are developing principles of engagement to which commissioning governments should agree. Shortcomings, and there were some as in all field research, were more due to teams having fewer resources, skills or less equipment than ideal, rather than due to partisan lobbying. In the business of research for development, scientists have much to learn from engaging with other professionals in policy processes. The research is usually more confined and targeted than would be academically ideal, since it is dictated by purposeful information needs, uses scarce resources and has its timeline ruled by the decision-making schedule itself. On the other hand, in order to adequately inform a policy process, public authorities are often more willing than not to facilitate access to a mix of expertise, equipment or data which otherwise would not readily be made available to researchers for a supply-driven research.

Who Should Respond for Policy Research that Is Demand-driven?

Different types of organizations can in principle be charged with carrying out and reporting research aimed at informing a policy exercise. But some clearly are better skilled, more experienced, and lend more credibility to research results than others. The IDRC's experience with UA in the global South is that research, when carried out by development NGO s, tends to have less legitimacy in governmental circles than when it is so by universities or recognized research institutes. NGOs have had a very important role in assisting with project design, data collection, capacity building activities and other ground-level interventions, public awareness campaigns, multi-stakeholder workshops and advocacy. But from a governmental perspective, even when the research which they produce is of good quality, and few in UA had enough capacity of their own for this, findings do not garner the kind of recognition and trust which is bestowed on institutions and organizations mandated for scientific research.

In the few cases where development NGOs led the research, these were usually unable to commit to quality research without bringing on board researchers from universities or research institutes. This was the case with projects in Haiti, Zimbabwe, Peru, Bolivia, Brazil, Cuba, and Senegal. More importantly, public policy outcomes tended also to be more limited. The stronger projects, as far as on-the-ground policy results are concerned, were those where universities or research institutions teamed up with NGOs and even CBOs, as in Haiti, Brazil, Senegal and Jordan. A good example is the tri-city project of UN-Habitat-IPES, which used a city team approach bringing together academia, civil society and government. Reflecting on this experience, the UN-Habitat project coordinator Marielle Dubbeling (2003, 61) wrote:

> 'The involvement of university staff in each project team strengthened the scientific quality of the research. The presence and political will of the government bodies has shown to be essential for the elaboration, appropriation and future application of the proposed legal/normative framework. The experience of the NGO s with community participation and popular education was invaluable in the process... The incorporation of producer groups in the project allowed responding to their demands and making optimum use of their knowledge.'

While it is important for research-mandated institutions or organizations to be key research players in the policy exercise, this does not mean that they should lead the policy exercise itself. In fact they probably should not, as this is a role for the governmental entity itself, which should have control over agendas and timelines. This is to ensure that research supports the proceedings of the policy exercise in a way that is as relevant, timely, and effective as conditions permit.

Policy-makers can make research bear on particular policy exercises in various ways. The sectors which can benefit from research on UA are many, from the productive use and protection of open space in a temporary or permanent way (Harare, Dar es Salaam), to solid waste management (Santiago, Kumasi) and poverty alleviation (Camilo Aldao, Rosario, Santiago, Teresina in Brazil), to income generation and enterprise development (Brasilia, Quito, Gaborone) and food security (Kampala, Havana, Port-au-Prince), to safe reuse of wastewaters in food production (Lima, Fortaleza, Amman) or the rehabilitation of mentally or physically challenged population groups (Santo Domingo, Lima, Nairobi, Toronto).

Clearly, cities which have successfully integrated UA into municipal policies are those that clearly see UA as helping them to address a range of sector-specific issues. Such a perspective actually makes UA more defensible in both the political and administrative spheres of municipal government. The multi-sector contribution of UA is a dimension which is valued by many cities with UA programmes in the North (St Petersburg, Stockholm, Berlin, Montreal, Vancouver, New York) but also in the South (Cagayan del Oro in the Philippines, Accra in Ghana, Cuenca in Ecuador, Rosario in Argentina, Habana in Cuba, Kampala in Uganda, Quito in Ecuador, Valadares in Brazil, Texcoco in Mexico).

What Types of Research Can Be Useful?

The types of research which public policy exercises can use are many. Baseline descriptions of UA are more appropriate earlier than later in policy research; they can be done by well-supervised students as part of their degree programme. Several mayors in the international seminar-workshop held in Quito in 2000 told me they had not realized until then how this was definitely one way in which they could tap on local university capacity.

The purpose of a baseline survey should be clear, as this will affect its design and eventually the relevance of its findings and conclusions. It is well known that surveys are expensive and policy processes often draw on supply-driven surveys, with some risks. Such surveys are normally carried out without any policy purpose in mind, or may have been so with one that differs greatly from the purpose which is of current policy interest. The surveys supported by the IDRC are of the two kinds; an obvious lesson is that policymakers using supply-driven surveys should be aware of their limitations. This is true of both types of surveys but is more of a concern with those surveys designed with no policy purpose in mind.

This can be better illustrated by a set of UA surveys supported by the IDRC over the years (Fig. 3.4). Early ones were broadly defined, with no particular policy use in mind (Nairobi, Dar, Kampala), while others were designed with information needs in mind for particular policy processes (Santiago, Governador Valadares, Amman). Figure 3.4 shows how the survey design (sampling framework) can affect the statistical domain and pertinence of findings from a particular survey.

Fig. 3.4: Household Surveys from IDRC-funded research in selected cities on practice of urban agriculture and its economic importance

Cities /Year	Types of UA Surveyed	Numbers (valid) of Households Surveyed	Sample Statistics Apply to:	% of Hshlds Practising UA	Economic Importance of Production
Six cities in Kenya, 1985	food crops livestock, fish, bees urban areas on and off-plot	1576[17]	all households, in all urban areas of Kenya	29 % in food cropping 17% in livestock keeping	21 m USD/year (4 m in crops, 17 m in livestock)
Six cities in Tanzania, 1987-8	crops, mostly livestock, on-and off-plot, intra and peri-urban areas,	1820[18]	urban producers only, bias toward high-density, farmers, males, in all urban areas of Tanzania	68% of urban producers in livestock keeping	revenue from UA (livestock) higher than salary for 66% producers
Dar es Salaam, 1990-1 (Kinondoni District)	crops, livestock, off-plot (open space), intra-urban areas	260 on-farm[19] (from a producer list of 580)	urban producers only, men and women, bias toward producers farming in low-density (high income) areas	73.6% of urban producers in livestock keeping	10-30% of food consumed in 88% households (UA revenue greater than salary for 66.7% of producers)
Kampala, 1989 (urban area of Kampala District)	crops and livestock, on and off-plot, intra-urban areas	150 producer households[20] at home and in open spaces	urban producers only	36% in some form of UA (based on producers' estimates)	45% of food consumed by producer households 40-100% of food consumed in 55.6% households

Cities /Year	Types of UA Surveyed	Numbers (valid) of Households Surveyed	Sample Statistics Apply to:	% of Hshlds Practising UA	Economic Importance of Production
Harare, 1994	food crops, off-plot, intra-urban areas	1784[21] urban producer households	off-plot producers in major cultivated open space areas	-	4 423 tons of maize (1994 harvest) 85% of maize harvested consumed by producers
1996-7	food crops and livestock, on and off-plot, intra-urban areas	475[22] households	all socio-economic categories of wards	65% in on-plot UA 19.8% in off-plot UA	annual food savings eq to 2.0 monthly incomes (on-plot crops), from sales eq to 5 (off-plot crops) or a net 0.8 (chickens) monthly incomes
Santiago de los Caballeros, 1998	off-plot food crops, intra-urban	110 producer households[23] in intra-urban area	off-plot urban producers in all socio-economic categories of city blocks	3000 households involved in off-plot UA	17 m DR$ annual worth (10 major crops) average monthly worth is eq to 83% of minimal monthly salary (40% if only food crops)
Governador Valadares, Brazil, 2002	on-plot, crops (food, medicinal, ornamental), livestock, fisheries, intra-urban and peri-urban	9281[24] 167	on-plot producers in all intra and peri-urban wards of different socio-economic status	52% engaged in some UA	ca. 2 m USD/ year
Amman, 1998	food crops (vegetables, medicinal, fruits), livestock, flowers intra and peri-urban	13,000[25] 2711 1458	all households of greater municipality of Amman	50,097 or 20% of all hshlds	10.9 m CAD / year (market value of products) produce mainly for self-provisioning in 50% of hshlds

For instance, a 1987–8 sample of Dar es Salaam deliberately targeted men and on-plot activities, which is why the percentage of women included was lower, compared to other surveys. This may be useful for policy interventions to assist male livestock keepers, but less so women involved in this activity, who moreover have much less access to land ownership in that country. Both the 1987–8 and 1990–1 surveys in Dar were somewhat biased toward better-off urban producers, reflecting preferences of local officials who produced the statistical population listings for the researchers. This may explain why the percentage of urban producers who declared having purchased their cultivated plot, was higher in these surveys than in others that were more representative of the general city population. Obviously, such surveys substantiated the fact that UA is not only a poor man's business, contrarily to what some still believe. Findings on the environmental aspects of livestock keeping may inform policies aimed at the better-off practitioners. But the Dar surveys probably would not help much a policy exercise interested in increasing the urban poor's access to open spaces for livestock raising or food crop cultivation, for instance.

The latter objective could be well served by the Kampala survey. This originally faced a bias similar to the Dar surveys, here corrected through revisiting the officials' listings; the survey for instance included areas where producers used open spaces, not covered in the original listings. The final socio-economic profile of the sample was found to be representative of the city's population. In the Santiago de los Caballeros survey, the low percentage of women reported to be engaged in UA was almost certainly due to all on-plot UA activities having been excluded from the working definition of UA; also, a majority of the off-plot cultivated areas were found to be located at a distance from producers' residences, in the same ward or in other (better-off) residential neighbourhoods. At the very least this does point to a major difference in the types of systems in which women and men engage in Santiago. This survey was suited to inform off-plot policies (e.g. community gardens), while being less useful for interventions to promote on-plot systems led by women.

This latter policy goal would be well served by the 1998 Amman survey, which focused on on-plot activities. This revealed a higher participation of women, with fruit trees as the main use, both in spatial and value terms, as well as extensive livestock rearing. Researchers also found that in Amman 62,096 heads of nine different types of livestock (from horses to pigeons) were being kept in the 50,000 home yards or so surveyed. Jordan's Department of Statistics wanted to document the scale and nature of on-plot cultivation and livestock keeping in the city, still disregarded by official censuses. The project was interested in the self- provisioning and health aspects of UA practices by different socio-economic groups, their use of scarce water resources, and their current and potential recycling of household solid and liquid wastes. This survey would be followed by a project which introduced a domestic gray water treatment system for the irrigation of on-plot crops.

In any event, no matter how researchers have cut their samples, these all informed policies to strengthen food and economic security among different population groups; a great majority of practitioners clearly valued UA for self-provisioning and income.

Different socio-economic groups are engaged in UA in any given city. Most surveys and sampling designs were stratified by socio-economic categories. Samples were distributed among these categories either proportionally or disproportionally to the weight of particular categories in the overall population. In the former case, results could be directly generalized to that population, not so in the latter. Several surveys gave more weight to non-poor groups, not only by under-selecting them but also by focusing on on-plot production. However, in both cases surveys did point that poor producers have access to smaller land areas on their residential plot, when they do have access to some (as many tend to be lodgers or tenants), and tend to use a much higher share of this area for food production. In Amman it was found that some 554 households with no on-plot land available had set up a garden in the built-up space of the plot (e.g. rooftops, etc.).

In such initial research, government officials can provide data early on (as in Governador Valadares) and/or discuss end findings (as in Kampala). More importantly they can look at such surveys as a way to test, at low cost to them, data collection instruments which could inform the adaptation or creation of census-taking systems to capture aspects of UA relevant to policy-making at various levels. This is what UN Habitat-UMP did at the end of its good-practice project, when it recommended to its head office the use of a UA indicator to monitor Agenda 21 progress in the Latin American and Caribbean region.

Beyond baseline surveys, the more research is expected to influence policy the more it must be contemporary or simultaneous to the policy exercise itself. An example of protocol is provided later in this chapter. The more research must formally interact with policy, the closer should be the match between the domain and evolution of the research and the domain and progress of the policy exercise itself, so that research can inform the policy process at some moments and be guided by it at others.

This is why it is less appropriate and feasible for research entities to captain the policy process. The University of Dar es Salaam in Tanzania, the Makerere Institute of Social Research in Uganda, the Pontifícia Universidad Católica Madre Maestra in the Dominican Republic, the University Cheik Anta Diop in Senegal, the Universidad Central in Ecuador, the Universidad de la República in Uruguay, and others had no problem in recognizing this. The reason is a difference in mandates and capacities. The convening power and the legitimacy required to engage diverse actors and move a public policy process ahead does not usually fall within universities or research institutes' attributions. This does not mean that governments should not seek the collaboration of such organizations to provide venues, equipment or personnel; exercises where governments and research institutions team up for policy exercises actually can only gain in credibility and earn respect from other actors.

Which Disciplines Should Go Into Demand-Driven Research for Policy on Urban Agriculture?

This will depend very much on the nature of the issue. What can be said is that, of all IDRC projects on UA, no single demand-driven policy research was carried out by one researcher alone. All projects involved teams of researchers with different areas of expertise. Expertise is not something which is improvised and teams unable to secure particular experts did feel it. The Care Haïti project had to de-emphasize the marketing side of UA. In the project led by the Panamerican Centre for Sanitary Engineering and Environmental Science (CEPIS), city teams which lacked social science expertise did not treat the relationships between wastewater treatment and/or reuse schemes and their host communities as satisfactorily as did teams with such expertise. Economists are still a rare commodity in Cuba and one could not be replaced on the team, after he eventually left the project to work with a company; economic analyses had to be curtailed in that project.

A good example is provided by the tri-city project with Rosario, Governador Valadares and Cienfuegos in Latin America. The three cities assembled multi-disciplinary and multi-actor teams, composed of government representatives, local university researchers, ,NGO staff, in order to obtain a good mix of political, scientific and technical expertise and deliver high quality and credible products and tools. Individuals had expertise in GIS, urban planning, agronomy, participatory research and planning methods. To be operational and functional, local core teams numbered 4-8 persons but worked together with a wide range of institutions for specific tasks, follow-up and advocacy. This strategy is reflected in other projects in Santiago de los Caballeros, Quito, in the regional CEPIS project, as well as in Dar es Salaam and Dakar.

As we have seen, UA can address several urban challenges and connect with the agenda of different sectors of government at any given time. The right mix of disciplinary expertise is often hard to secure, either because some of it is not available locally, or simply because there is a lack of tradition in collaboration across certain areas of knowledge. UA requires agriculture-related and urban management related expertise to work together. This is more easily said than done, but possible and certainly desirable. IDRC projects found that there was little if any tradition of working together in these two communities of expertise, this even in cities with significant UA activity. This required the project teams to initially spend some time developing a common vocabulary. It was essential for a Cuban project on UA in Habana, which assembled a team of 15 members (seven women and eight men) with a wide range of expertise (agronomy, livestock, sociology, urban economy, geography, biology, water engineering, computer analysis) to address policy issues ranging from technological systems to types of producer associations, as well as economic, social and environmental benefits and adversities, support and collaboration among different actors, and use of waste and water resources.

Communications between government sectors dealing with agriculture and cities also remain limited in most countries where the IDRC has worked. Projects in UA thus have served as platforms for testing such collaborations. This has led some municipalities to create inter-sector programmes on UA and food security. This collaboration is essential for mapping areas with agricultural potential and for defining the nature and scale of production systems which should suit particular city sites and sectors. Collaboration is also important to tailor technical assistance to particular groups and encourage synergies between agricultural and other proximate urban activities.

Governments know that multi-actor participation makes up for better resourced, more comprehensive and robust interventions. IDRC projects show that although many key urban actors in UA wished to impress public policy changes, none was able to achieve these individually. In most cities urban producers, particularly the poor, are usually not a recognized political constituency. They may be a clientele for the Department of Agriculture, particularly its local offices, but not so for City Council, the immediate ruling instance in urban areas. Although the numbers of urban producers may be quite large, they are not a statistical entity in most censuses; for many it is their second or third occupation, most are not organized in registered groups, although recent studies show that more are organized in at least some way than originally thought. But even in countries which do possess UA policies, as in Cuba, some groups of urban producers may still fall out of official purview.

Women are often numerous, if not a majority, of producers in many UA systems, and often dominate in processing and marketing stages of UA value chains, as shown by several projects. Projects on space-confined and home-based systems in Haiti, Peru and Ivory Coast, as well as on community gardens in Governador Valadares, Rosario and Quito, have shown a high involvement of women. Both research and policy must pay particular attention to gendered practices, benefits and challenges, which requires the inclusion of gender expertise in both research and policy processes. Research supported by IDRC shows that there can be considerable gender differences in access to and tenure of resources, in actual use of resources, production systems preferred and destination of the produce. Premat (2005) in Habana found that gender unawareness can lead officials to discount women's substantive role in UA, while Hovorka (2005) in Gaborone observed that financing programmes un-sensitive to gender differences can miss out on small women-run UA enterprises' potential contribution to urban food supply and local economic growth.

ANY EFFECTIVE PROTOCOL FOR RESEARCH-POLICY INTERACTIONS?

Over the years, IDRC and its partners have experienced with various approaches for research and policy to best interact in UA. This has included projects in Sub-Saharan Africa, followed by projects in LAC.

What is clear from this experience is that: (a) recent projects have succeeded in encompassing an ever broader spectrum of the public policy cycle; (b) however, few were long enough to monitor, review or adjust UA policy initiatives either recommended by or initiated during the lifespan of the project itself; (c) some projects did review the performance of policies inspired by non-IDRC funded research (Dar es Salaam, La Habana); (d) projects including policy steps beyond baseline surveys have used participatory methods; (e) the degree to which disadvantaged groups (poor urban producers) have been represented – and the effectiveness with which their concerns have been addressed – varied from project to project and tended to be greater in more recent projects (Santiago, Quito, Rosario, Dakar, Amman); (f) at issue-scoping and diagnosis stages of the policy cycle, such groups seem to have been engaged more effectively in Harare than in Santiago de los Caballeros, possibly depending on the mandate of the lead agency (an NGO in Harare) and producers' own degree of organization (higher in Harare); (g) producers' involvement later on in the process, at priority-setting and action-planning stages, was greater in Quito than in Dar es Salaam; here, this could be due to a topically and spatially more focused policy exercise in Quito. The Rosario-Cienfuegos-Valadares project, where producers' participation was more important than in any earlier projects, combined a strong set of conditions for their involvement through all stages of the policy process (mandate of lead agency, level of organization, topical and geographic focus).

Governmental institutions' involvement with research linked to the policy exercise varied very much in selected IDRC projects on UA. From this range of experiences:

(a) It is important for the research project to connect with the governmental agenda and to commit the government to the project. Projects responding to a governmental institution's request and/ or which secured a written commitment from it do display a higher degree of governmental involvement throughout the research.

(b) Research must use a methodology which engages the government throughout: recent policy-oriented projects delivered more diverse policy outputs within a shorter period of time. This seems to be related to executing agencies' ability to engage government in more stages of the research throughout the policy cycle.

(c) Government should be the one to convene stakeholders and should focus policy exercises on UA. Projects which were led by a governmental authority and focused specifically on UA (and its interactions with other issues and sectors) were more likely to engage the government throughout the various stages of the research and lead this to use findings for specific UA policy, programs and projects.

(d) Research projects should provide for inter-city sharing of experiences and expertise to inspire or press governments to acknowledge, respond to, and deliver. Local processes developed as components of regional projects delivered UA policy outputs more quickly than others carried out in isolation.

(e) Crisis awareness or a link with a separate major development project, such as a World Bank project in Kampala or the UN Habitat Sustainable Dar es Salaam Project, were not sufficient drivers for short-term policy developments on UA.

The role of peer networking to speed up the adoption of innovations, observed in the IDRC's work with global South municipal governments on UA, is a condition which seems to apply to other sectors as well, as suggested by the Nova Scotia conference on which this book is based. Different categories of actors/organizations in society are more inclined to learn from their peers in other cities than from other types of actors in their own community (e.g.: mayor of Chicago learning from counterparts' green rooftop initiatives in Germany; Dalhousie University's learning from McGill University's edible landscape project; New School in New York learning from Ryerson University's exhibit in Toronto, Capital Health in Halifax learning from a Toronto hospital 's farmers market initiative).

If this is true, then innovation diffusion pathways within specific sectors do affect how networking for innovation by a range of local actors should be promoted and supported in any given city. For instance, policy research initiatives to generate innovations and their adoption by different groups of local actors should actively involve in their design and conduct organizations drawn from the very sectors which they aim to influence (rather than expect members of other sectors to lead or mediate communications with such audiences).

IDRC's experience with UA policy-oriented research initiatives is that participatory protocols have been more effective than directive ones. Such protocols should contain basic features: (a) a city consultation for issue scoping, assessment of stakeholders' capacities and resources; (b) partnerships for implementation and funding; (c) prioritization over time for effectiveness, including short-listing, timetable, assignments, periodic reporting and adjustments; and (d) a strategy of incremental results (staggering of goals) to sustain commitment. Demo projects act as catalyzers, regular peer exchanges between governments are useful for know-how transfer, out and up-scaling, and institutionalisation.

In line with the urban planning focus of this book, one good example of a participatory protocol for interaction between research and policy on UA is provided by the Rosario-Cienfuegos-Valadares project. This project sought to optimize the use of vacant space for UA, with the policy goal of strengthening urban food security and municipal governance (Dubbeling 2003). Similar projects supported by IDRC have positioned themselves at various moments of this stem protocol which I break down here into seven steps:

STEP 1: BEFORE ANYTHING COULD START IN THE THREE CITIES

In each of the three participant cities, collaboration among local partners was formalized through support letters and inter-actor agreements, which assisted in mobilizing local resources. This enabled the project to make optimum use of local capacities and increase chances for uptake and the institutionalisation of results. The project coordinating entity, UN-Habitat's Urban Management Programme (regional office in Quito) possessed solid expertise with such provisions. A detailed technical note and a methodological note were developed by the coordination to serve as terms of reference for the city teams. The technical note dealt with concepts that required local discussion and definition (e.g.: urban agriculture, open and vacant spaces, etc.), steps in running a participatory consultative process and action planning on current and potential use of land, access to land and land management. The latter note discussed optional methods and techniques for the different activities outlined, stressing the fair and effective participation of urban producers and community actors in both consultation and planning.

Based on the technical and methodological notes, each city team drafted their respective work plan, identified actors to be involved, working methodology, expected outputs and time frame. Each city team made a PowerPoint presentation on its proposal at a regional planning workshop. Policy Briefs out of a previous regional review of municipal initiatives assisted teams in defining expected project results. In the weeks following the workshop, local work plans were revised, inter-actor agreements and contracts were finalized and signed. A regional electronic platform was set up for exchanges among cities and with coordination and an interactive website enabled the three cities and others involved with a regional City Working Group on UA to collect and share various databases (visual, bibliographic, messages and contacts). A list of ten different expected outputs and results was drawn by the city teams.

STEP 2: AWARENESS RAISING, MOBILISATION, MOTIVATION AND TRAINING (THROUGHOUT)

Compared to other IDRC-supported projects, this one on UA was especially rich in the number and diversity of municipal actors involved. In Cienfuegos, training on the use of GIS and its use in urban management and planning drew on experiences from elsewhere in LAC. In Rosario and Governador Valadares project folders were developed with the community and urban producers. As a variant on this phase, a more recent project (Tramel 2010) in Cagayan de Oro, Philippines, combined training with issue scoping; local participation was spurred by organizers' commitment to issue certificates to participants.

STEP 3: ELABORATION OF LAND USE MAPS, ANALYSIS, VERIFICATION AND DIGITISING OF DATA

Baseline information was collected in the three cities from secondary sources. The Valadares team found that its municipal legal and normative framework was somewhat related to UA; however, this was not reflected in its framework for physical urban planning. Proposals were drawn, as well as in Rosario, with the help from a research unit of a local university. One proposal aimed at creating ecological and productive corridors in the city, while the other looked at how to include productive spaces into sustainable housing developments. Field visits and workshops were needed to update the information from secondary sources. All three cities selected specific study zones for further ground work (four popular councils in Cienfuegos, four out of the six city districts in Rosario, five neighbourhoods in Valadares). The areas were selected to represent a spectrum of intra and peri-urban sites and socioeconomic levels. Actions for scaling up from these study areas to the entire city were later proposed by all city teams, as part of their action plans.

The coordinating team also provided city teams with a typology of vacant and open spaces developed during a regional course in Quito (previous IDRC project). This was adapted to local circumstances, with studies focusing on the more relevant types in each city (un-built municipal or state owned land, private household plots, public or private institutional land, protected land areas, land that cannot be built upon, communal areas, areas for waste treatment, peri-urban agricultural land). Cienfuegos focused on areas over 1000m^2, the minimum area for a single-family organic garden, while in Rosario the focus was on areas over 2500 m^2 (intra urban) and 5000 m^2 (peri-urban) for community gardens for groups of 5-10 people (500m^2 was the minimum estimated by the project for a person to grow enough produce that allows, through sales, to earn an income above the unemployment subsidy). In Valadares no specific unit size was defined but work eventually focused on private household plots, the most common type of area used for UA in that city.

Each city then worked on the details of vacant and agricultural land areas within their study zones. The cities found that UA land use was not officially included in any of the land use categories defined by their planning department. However, these frameworks did provide opportunity to incorporate UA land uses either as a specific category or as a sub-category under the 'green spaces' or 'non-urbanisable' categories. Enabling cities to recognize and incorporate UA in city master plans and land use plans was seen as a necessary first step. None of the three cities could come up with land use maps for the entire municipal area, within the confines of the project. Rather, based on information from the study zones, work focused on how to address UA use on different types of land rather than on how to design and plan specific micro-sites.

The cities moved forward the elaboration of legal and normative proposals to facilitate access to and use of these specific categories of land, a reference for all similar land types throughout the city. All cities concentrated on land and soil use related to production activities, less so on the use of aquatic spaces, built-up areas, or processing and marketing activities. Cities used different computer soft-wares to develop their GIS database on UA (Software MapInfo professional in Cienfuegos, AutoCAD/ArchView and Corel Draw 10.0, MaxiCad and AutoCad, then ArchView, in Valadares). Municipal maps (1:100,000), neighbourhood maps (1:10,000) and maps in the range of 1:2000-1:10,000 were used to identify and typify vacant land areas, as well as communication tools during workshops where participants validated the cartographic information.

STEP 4: PARTICIPATORY CONSULTATION AND DIAGNOSIS

This process was carried out in the three cities and helped to discuss, validate and analyse information, debate actors' opinions and perceptions of land use, access and tenure problems, scope and investigate specific issues, as well as propose potential solutions.

In Rosario for instance, three workshops were held over a period of four months in each district or study zone, with 55–90 urban producers participating in each one. The first wave of workshops focused on diagnosis of access to and tenure of off-plot lands under cultivation, while the second dealt with on-plot activities; the third zeroed in on problems with accessing different land areas for UA. The project found that, in that city, 47% of the community gardens were sited on informal waste dumps and some 40% of their area counted with large quantities of construction debris. It was agreed that soil analyses would be carried out to develop soil rehabilitation strategies. Maps were validated and updated by the community and a glossary of terms was developed, defining local residents' understanding of access, security of tenure, user rights, etc. A series of solutions were proposed to deal with specific problems, including the elaboration of two new regulations, one for the creation of a municipal databank of vacant spaces, the other for the granting of temporary land use permits.

In Valadares a rapid participatory appraisal was carried out in each of the five study zones to generate and analyse data on vacant lands, the importance of current UA and its impacts. A large amount of data needed to be collected in Valadares, where there had been no previous studies on UA. It was found that UA was basically limited to private plots: the limited area available on these plots was identified as the major constraint, while large areas of public land remained vacant.

Out of the research carried out in all three cities, this phase of the project enabled all three cities to collectively refine the concept of optimisation, in terms of spatial use and temporal use of vacant lands. Optimisation of land use further needed to pay attention to aptness or suitability, feasibility (inputs, security, proximity) and accessibility (legal aspects).

STEP 5: ELABORATION AND IMPLEMENTATION OF LOCAL ACTION PLANS

Both consultation and baseline studies led to the formulation of action plans to eliminate bottlenecks and facilitate access to land by the urban poor. The actions plans included generally six different lines of action: (a) further action research on new or current issues; (b) implementation of projects and programmes to start up or strengthen project activities on the ground; (c) elaboration of legal-normative proposals; (d) definition of new financial frameworks or budgetary provisions; (e) institutionalisation of participatory frameworks (working groups, commissions, fora); and (f) preparation of information and training materials to support awareness and capacity building.

The Action Plan of Valadares focused on providing economic and fiscal incentives for UA production on different land areas (mainly private household plots and institutional estates), while Rosario moved forward on providing and legalizing temporary user rights on municipal vacant land areas.

All plans stressed the institutionalisation of UA, in either land use or city development plans, and provided tools and instruments for achieving this. Both Rosario and Valadares advanced in implementing priority projects and programmes. These produced tangible results in the short term which helped to sustain commitment and participation on part of actors involved. Such activities were largely co-financed by local actors themselves. In Rosario, 800 community gardens were set up over the last eighteen months of the project, with over 10,000 people involved in urban farming by the end of it. Four weekly open markets were set up, the first social urban agro-industry was established in the central city, in a revamped railway storehouse, next to the river and a farmers' market. The agro-industry employed 18 people, trained to safely process city-grown vegetables. By the end of the project, contacts had been made with local shops and super-markets to sell the products, to be marketed under a specific label.

In Valadares, thirteen community gardens were set up and an association was created. By the end of the project the first small producers market was inaugurated with support from the Food Supply Programme of the Ministry for Environment, Agriculture and Food Supply.

STEP 6: DOCUMENTATION AND SYSTEMATISATION OF INFORMATION

Draft reports from the city teams were reviewed by the project coordination and the methods and gender advisers, then were finalized. Preliminary versions were distributed among the cities. A regional workshop was held in Rosario, which brought 50 participants from eight cities and national and regional organizations. Other cities funded their own participation (Sao Paulo, Montevideo, Camilo Aldao, Mar del Plata and Villa Maria del Triunfo-Lima). One of the coordinating institutions, IPES, decided to create a specific and separate working area in UA (currently a program with a staff of eight). This reportedly was the first time a regional UA event in Latin America and the Caribbean counted with such a diverse membership. The three cities' action proposals were greatly improved and other proposals were also debated. These included: a law project for the creation of a (peri)urban agriculture programme in Sao Paulo, including several project elements and the signing of an agreement with private entities for their temporarily ceding land areas to organized groups for UA; proposals for the productive use of land in Montevideo through articulation between producers and land owners; the integration of UA in the general city plan of Villa Maria del Triunfo, in metropolitan Lima; training on design of housing settlements with UA production by the National Movement of Struggle for Housing in Brazil (Movimento Nacional de Luta pela Moradia).

It was decided that, instead of engaging the second part of the project in one city only, all three original cities would participate, given the complementarity of instruments proposed by each one. The workshop in Rosario also interacted with local urban producers and the municipal UA programme in three separate moments. The project and workshop were explained to 250 community, civil society and government representatives. Various community gardens and producer groups were visited and the workshop was officially closed before an audience of more than 600 urban producers. Workshop results were shared with them and a video on the municipal programme was shown. During the entire event, producers had organized a market and an exposition of posters. The project more generally enabled low-income urban producer groups to influence local decision-making, thus reinforcing the economic development trust of local strategic planning, priority setting and capital investments.

Members of the Rosario city team presented their experience in this project as part of an event organized by UN-Habitat and IPES in Quito in mid-2003, to review some twenty-one city consultations. This seminar gave visibility to the Rosario process and generated demand for its support to local UA programmes in cities such as Neiva (Colombia), León (Nicaragua), Maracaibo (Venezuela) and Porto Alegre (Brazil). A proposal was negotiated with the University of Harvard, with funds from the David Rockefeller Foundation, to build on the Cienfuegos study and address the land use management systems of three other Cuban cities.

When reviewing more recent research-development partnerships in three major urban centres of Sub-Saharan Africa (Nairobi, Kampala and Yaoundé), Lee-Smith and Prain (2010) underscored ingredients of this general protocol that are critical for effective research-policy interactions: (a) the importance of external facilitation to convene a regional stakeholder meeting , build platforms or groups of collaborating local stakeholders, identify broad areas of concern and convert these into research areas and proposals; (b) the importance for such development-oriented proposals to build on a track record of research and civil society and local government activity; (c) the importance of connecting UA to the right policy issue, in order to mobilize policy circles (e.g.: a partnership geared toward technology and enterprise development may be less compelling that one aimed at resolving public health risks, for instance); and (d) building stakeholder platforms that are inter-disciplinary and inter-agency, as a prelude to policy and institutional building.

STEP 7: MONITORING, EVALUATION AND COURSE ADJUSTMENTS

Monitoring helps municipal governments learn from early policy implementation and make adjustments as required and possible. When prefacing RUAF's review of the field in 2006 de Zeeuw (2006) underscored the need for monitoring the impacts of innovative policies and programs on UA informed by research.

Such monitoring updates remain few and far between but have started to appear in the literature. Lee-Smith (2010) reported on policy development at national level in Uganda, as well as risks presented by the current approach of the Kampala City Council to enforcing new ordinances. Anguelovksi (2010) followed progress made by the AGRUPAR program of Quito's metropolitan agency for economic development, despite the lack of recognition of UA as a legitimate urban land use. Santandreu et al. (2010) documented the post-crisis evolution of publicly-supported UA in Rosario, Argentina. A new generation of researchers is now positioned to monitor and reflect, as well as propose further improvements to a slate of innovative local UA policies which now have been operational for some time. For this, they have access to a stock of knowledge today unprecedented in scale and depth.

Conclusion

This chapter has examined a range of initiatives which global-South local governments have developed over the last fifteen years to make agriculture part of the city. Initially, a review of historical evidence from past civilizations' own approaches to integrating agriculture into their cities pointed to principles that remain appropriate and relevant to contemporary efforts. Ancient cities did manage to associate agriculture with sophisticated urban functions, and in order to achieve this agriculture needed to be valued by authorities, being used to draw meaningful benefits from land investments in other urban functions. Cities' morphology and dynamics drove the diversification of their agricultural systems and practices, while the urban economy kept pushing the limits of the technically possible in this agriculture.

The chapter further discussed macro-trends spurring the growth of UA in the global South in recent decades (growing urban markets, systemic exposure to crises and persistent urban poverty), pointing to the many ways in which, despite often adverse policy settings, this UA has been contributing to food and economic security in global South cities. In this context governments, particularly local governments, at last have started introducing novel policies to mitigate adversities of this largely unregulated agriculture and enhance its ability to help cities address multiple challenges. Enabling factors responsible for growth in official attention to the sector range from an emancipation of municipal governments to dedicated international assistance and emerging communities of practice.

Investment in applied research and the generation of relevant knowledge has been critical to informing and influencing policy innovation on UA in global South cities. This is why the chapter lastly drew collective wisdom from a range of policy research, carried out by diverse organizations in different regions of the global South. It examined the merit of demand versus supply-driven policy research and the advantages to multiple-city over single-city initiatives. It identified risks associated with policy research in this area and characterized purpose-specific survey designs, as well as protocols that have been particularly effective for research-policy interactions.

In hindsight, and perhaps unsurprisingly, one must admit that, although cities of the global North undeniably hold much policy capital in this sector (some now even promoting regional food systems – Mansfield and Wendes 2013), very little of it has been found to be directly or easily transferable to global-South cities. This is less due to a lack of awareness – a majority of initiatives here involved international expertise – and more so to different capacities and resources, needs and constraints faced by global South cities. For instance, community garden models, for long an iconic fixture of UA programs in the global North, overall have had little traction in most global South cities reviewed; on the other hand, market-oriented farming has been much more extensive in these cities. Inclusive and participatory approaches followed in these initiatives ensured that they would prioritize local relevance for uptake. The diversity of actors, tenure modalities, sites used and systems at work in global South cities far outstrips the usual landscape in global North counterparts.

This said, for a variety of reasons, interest for mutual exchanges, networking, learning and collaboration between the North and the South is growing, as demonstrated by the conference behind this book, and others since then. Long left to their own devices, global South cities are now finding ears with global-North cities. It is my hope that this chapter, commissioned to focus on recent global South experience, shall contribute to this much needed dialogue.

References

Adams, R.M. 1994. The origin of Cities. Scientific American (special issue): 12-19

Addyman, P.V. 1994. Eburacum, Jorvik, York. Scientific American (special issue): 108-118.

Ali, M., H. de Bon and P. Moustier. 2006. Pour la promotion d'une agriculture urbaine et péri-urbaine multifonctionnelle à Hanoi. Magazine Agriculture urbaine 15: 9-11.

Anguelovski, I. 2010. Édification de la résilience des communautés vulnérables à Quito: Adaptation du système alimentaire local au changement climatique. Magazine Agriculture urbaine 22: 23-25.

Anton, D. 1993. Thirsty Cities: Urban Environments and Water Supply in Latin America. Ottawa: International Development Research Centre.

Bhatt, V. and L.M. Farah. 2009. Editorial – Designing Edible Landscapes. Open House International 34 (2): 4-7.

Bemanesh, S. 2010. Gestion Municipal de Residuos Sólidos como un Incentivo para la agricultura urbana en Pune. Revista Agricultura urbana 23: 27-28.

Burland, C.A. 1976. People of the Sun: the Civilizations of pre-Columbian America. New York: Praeger Publishers Inc.

Cabannes, Y. and M. Dubbeling. 2001. Urban agriculture, food security and urban management. In Urban Agriculture in Cities of the 21st Century: Innovative Approaches by Local Governments of Latin America and the Caribbean, working paper 84. Quito: Urban Management Programme – Latin America and the Caribbean, UN-HABITAT.

Campbell, M. C., M. Dubbeling, F. Hoekstra and R. van Veenhuizen. 2010. L'édification de villes résilientes. Magazine Agriculture urbaine 22: 3-14.

Campilan, D, P. Dreschel and D. Jocker. 2001. Urban Agriculture Magazine 5 http://www.ruaf.org/topic-paper-5-monitoring-and-evaluationMonitoring and Evaluation.

Canabal Cristiani, B. 1992. La ciudad y sus chinampas. Mexico City: Universidad Autonoma Metropolitana – Unidad Xochimilco.

Casale, K. 2006. Jardins démonstratifs à Almirante Brown en Argentine. Magazine Agriculture urbaine 15 (July): 23-24.

Centro Panamericano de Ingeniería Sanitaria y Ciencias Ambientales (CEPIS). 2002. Guidelines for the formulation of projects. Lima: CEPIS. (IDRC 100123)

Coe, M., D. Snow and E. Benson. 1986. An Atlas of Ancient America. Oxford: Equinox.

Cofie. O., R. van Veenhuizen, V. de Vreede, S. Maessen. 2010. Gestión de Residuos para la Recuperación de Nutrientes: Opciones y desafíos para la agricultura urbana. Urban Agriculture Magazine 23: 3-7.

Compton, J., S. Wiuggins, and S. Keats. 2010. Impact of the Global Food Crisis on the Poor: What is the Evidence? London: Overseas Development Institute. www/odi.org.uk/resources/download/5187.pdf

Coquery-Virdovitch, C. 1993. Histoire des villes d'Afrique noire. Des origines à la colonisation. Paris: Albin Michel.

Courtlandt, C. with A. Kocybala. 1990. A Guide to the Archaeological Sites of Israel, Egypt and North Africa. New York: Facts on File.

Cohen, M. & J. Garrett. 2009. The food price crisis and urban food insecurity. London: International Institute for Environment and Development.

Cruz, M.C. and R. Sanchez Medina. 2001. Agriculture in the City: A Key to Sustainability in Havana, Cuba. Kingston, Jamaica, and Ottawa: Ian Randle Publishers and International Development Research Centre.

David, S., D. Lee-Smith, J. Kyaligonza, W. Mangeni, S. Kimeze, L. Aliguma, A. Lubowa, and G. W. Nasinyama. 2010. Changing trends in urban Agriculture in Kampala. In African Urban Harvest: Agriculture in the Cities of Cameroon, Kenya and Uganda, ed. G. Prain, N. Karanja and D. Lee-Smith, 97-122. New York, Ottawa, Lima: Springer, International Development Research Centre, International Potato Center.

De la Salle, J. and M. Holland. 2010. Agricultural urbanism in a Nutshell. In Agricultural Urbanism: Handbook for Building Sustainable Food & Agriculture Systems in 21st Century Cities, ed. J. de la Salle and M. Holland with contributors, 30-35. Green Frigate Books and HB Lanark.

Del Rosario, P.J. Y Cornelio, L. Jímenez Polanco, A. Russell, H. López, P. Escarramán. 1999. Manejo de Residuos Sólidos y Agricultura Urbana en la Ciudad de Santiago de Los Caballeros. Santiago de los Caballeros, República Dominicana: Centro de Estudios Urbanos y Regionales, Pontifícia Universidad Católica Madre y Maestra. (IDRC 002759).

Despommier, D. 2010. The Vertical Farm – Feeding the world in the 21st century. New York: St Martin's Press.

de Zeeuw 2006, H. 2006. Preface. In Cities Farming for the Future: Urban Agriculture for Green and Productive Cities, ed. R. can Veenhuizen, xi-xiii. Ottawa: RUAF Foundation, International Institute for Rural Reconstruction and International Development Research Centre.

de Zeeuw, H., R. van Veenhuizen and M. Dubbeling. 2011. Foresight Project on Global Food and Farming Futures: The role of urban agriculture in building resilient cities in developing countries. Journal of Agricultural Science: 1-11.

Di Bernardo, E., L. Bracalenti, L. Lagorio, V. Lamas, and M. Rodríguez. 2003. Optimización del uso de suelos para la agricultura urbana en el município de Rosario. Fase 1 Consulta sobre acceso y tenencia de la tierra y uso del suelo. Rosario, Argentina: Centro de Estudios de Producciones Agroecológicas (CEPAR). Facultad de Arquitectura, Planeamiento y Diseño, Universidad Nacional de Rosario (UNR), Municipalidad de Rosario. (IDRC 100983)

Dreschel , P. 2010. Agriculture urbaine et Sécurité alimentaire des ménages. Magazine Agriculture urbaine 22: 8.

Drescher, A.W. 2001. Urban and peri-urban agriculture – A briefing guide for the successful implementation of urban and peri-urban agriculture in developing countries and countries in transition. Special Programme for Food Security SPFS/DOC/27.8 Revision 2, Handbook Series Volume III. Rome: Food and Agriculture Organization.

Dubbeling, M. 2013. Urban and Peri-urban Agriculture as a Means to Advance Disaster Risk Reduction and Adaptation to Climate Change. Regional Development Dialogue 34(1): 134-149.

Dubbeling, M., L. Bracalenti and L. Lagorio. 2009. Participatory Design of Public Spaces for Urban Agriculture, Rosario, Argentina. Open House International 34(2): 36-49

Dubbeling, M. 2003. Optimizing use of vacant space for urban agriculture through participatory planning processes – a strategy to strengthen urban food security and municipal participatory governance. Technical progress report May 2002-Jne 2003. Quito: Urban Management Programme, Latin America and the Caribbean (UMP-LAC), UN-Habitat. (IDRC 100983)

Dubbeling, M. and H. de Zeeuw. 2007. Multi-stakeholder policy formulation and action planning for sustainable urban agriculture development. RUAF Working Paper No. 1. Leusden: RUAF Foundation. http://www.ruaf.org/taxonomy/term/45/0?page=1

Dunnett, N. and N. Kingsbury. 2004. Planting Green Roofs and Living Walls. Portland: Timber Press.

Environment and Development Activities – Zimbabwe (ENDA-ZW). 1996. Urban Agriculture in Zimbabwe: realities and prospects. Proceedings of a workshop organized by ETC International and ENDA-Zimbabwe. Harare: ENDA-ZW. (IDRC 95-0007)

Environment and Development Activities – Zimbabwe (ENDA-ZW). 1994. Urban Agriculture in Harare. Final report. Harare: ENDA-ZW. (IDRC 93-0024).

FAO (Food and Agriculture Organization). 2012. Statistical Yearbook. Rome: Food and Agriculture Organization.

FAO (Food and Agriculture Organization). 1999. Urban and peri-urban agriculture. COAG/99/10. Presented and approved at 15th Session of the Committee on Agriculture (COAG), FAO, Rome, 25-29 January 1999. Rome: Food and Agriculture Organization.

Forster, T. 2011. Food, agriculture and cities. FAO Food for the Cities – Multidisciplinary Initiative. Rome: FAO (draft August 2, 2011).

Freund, B. 2007. The African City: A History. New York: Cambridge University Press.

Gabel, S. 2005. Exploring the gender Dimensions of urban Open-Space Cultivation in Harare, Zimbabwe. In AGROPOLIS: the social, political and environmental dimensions of urban agriculture, ed. Luc J.A. Mougeot, 107-136. London and Ottawa: Earthscan and International Development Research Centre.

Gendron, F. 2011. Le monde précolombien, entre démocraties et empires. Dossier pour la science 72: 58-59.

Gertel, J. and S. Samir. 2000. Cairo: urban agriculture and visions for a 'modern city'.' In Growing Cities, Growing Food: Urban Agriculture on the Policy Agenda, ed. by N. Bakker, M. Dubbeling, S. Guednel, U. Sabel-Koschella and H. de Zeeuw, 209-234. Feldafing, Germany: German Foundation for International Development.

Heckenberger, M. 2011. Les cités perdues d'Amazonie. Dossier pour la science, 72: 110-117.

Gough, K.V. and P. Kellett. 2001. Housing Consolidation and Home-based Income Generation. Cities 18(4): 235-247.

Gumbo, D. J. and T. W. Ndiripo. 1996. Open Space Cultivation in Zimbabwe: A Case Study of Harare, Zimbabwe. In African Urban Quarterly 11(2-3): 210-217. (IDRC 93-0024)

Hammond, N. 1994. The Emergence of Maya Civilization. Scientific American (special issue): 128-137.

Haas, A. 1993. Gardens of Mexico. New York: Rizzoli.

Han, S.M. and M. Pieschel. 2010. Développement durable des mégapoles du futur: Infrastructures écologiques pour Casablanca, Maroc. Magazine Agriculture urbaine 22: 26-29.

Hodgson, K., Campbell, M.C., and Bailey, M. 2011. Urban Agriculture: Growing Healthy Sustainable Places. Planning Advisory Service Report no. 563. Chicago: American Planning Association.

Hovorka, A. J., H. de Zeeuw and M. Njenga. 2009. Women feeding cities: mainstreaming gender in urban agriculture and food security. Warwickshire: Practical Action Publishing,

Hovorka, A. 2005. Gender, Commercial Urban Agriculture and Urban Food Supply in Greater Gaborone, Botswana. In AGROPOLIS: the social, political and environmental dimensions of urban agriculture, ed. by Luc J.A. Mougeot, 137-152. London and Ottawa: Earthscan and International Development Research Centre.

Howard, E.G. 1902. Garden Cities of Tomorrow. London: S. Sonnenschein & Co., Ltd. (originally published in 1898 under a different tile).

Huriot, J. M. 1994. Von Thünen: économie et espace. Paris: Economica.

Jellicoe, G. 1989. The Landscape of Civilization. Northiam: Garden Art Press.

Johns, C., chief ed. 2008. Les mystères des Mayas. L'essor, la gloire et la chute d'une civilisation. National Geographic, Collection no. 6.

Kessides, C. 2006. The urban transition in Sub-Saharan Africa. Implications for economic growth and poverty reduction. Washington, D.C.: Cities Alliance, Swedish International Development Agency, World Bank.

Kishimba, M.A. 1996. Urban Agriculture in Dar es Salaam: How Polluted Are the Irrigation Waters? Dar es Salaam: Chemistry Department, University of Dar es Salaam. (IDRC 93 – 0037)

Kinver, M. 2014. Global importance of urban agriculture 'underestimated'. BBC News. http://www.bbc.com/news/science-environment-30182326

Larsen, K. and F. Barker-Reid. 2010. L'adaptation au changement climatique et le renforcement de la résilience urbaine en Australie. Magazine Agriculture urbaine 22: 19-22.

Laweil, B. and D. Nierenberg. 2007. Farming the Cities. In 2007 State of the World: Our Urban Future, 48-56. New York and London: The Worldwatch Institute, digital edition.

Lee-Smith, D. 2010. Cities feeding people: an update on urban agriculture in equatorial Africa. Environment & Urbanization 22(2): 483-499.

Lee-Smith, D. 2013 Which Way for UPA in Africa? City: analysis of urban trends, culture, theory, policy action 17(1): 69-84.

Lee-Smith, D., N. Karanja, M. Njenga, T. Dongmo and G. Prain. 2010. Ciclos de Nutrientes en Tres Ciudades Africanas. Revista Agricultura urbana 23: 17-19.

Lee-Smith, D. and G. Prain. 2010. The Contributions of Research-Development Partnerships to Building Urban Agriculture Policy. In African Urban Harvest: Agriculture in the Cities of Cameroon, Kenya and Uganda, ed. G. Prain, N. Karanja and D. Lee-Smith, 287-308. New York, Ottawa, Lima: Springer, International Development Research Centre, International Potato Center.

Lecoq, P. 2011. Le site inca des lamas sacrés. Dossier pour la science 72: 44-51.

Lee-Smith, D. and P.A. Memon. 1994. Urban Agriculture in Kenya. In Cities Feeding People: An Examination of Urban Agriculture in East Africa, 67-84. Ottawa: International Development Research Centre.

Losada, H., J. Rivera, J. Vieyra, J. Cortés. 2010. El Papel de la Agricultura Urbana en la Gestión de Residuos en Ciudad de México. Revista Agricultura urbana 23: 40-41.

Losada, H., H. Martinez, J. Vieyra, R. Pealing and J. Cortés. 1998. Urban agriculture in the metropolitan zone of Mexico: changes over time in urban, suburban and peri-urban areas. Environment & Urbanization 10(2): 37-54.

Lourenço-Lindell, I. 1995. The Informal Urban Food Economy in a Peripheral Urban District: The Case of Bandim District, Bissau. Habitat International 19(2): 195-208.

Lovo, I.C., K.M. Silveira Pessoa, E.J. Soares, Z.R. Pereira Costa. 2003. Otimiçaçao do uso de espaços vazios para Agricultura urbana através de planos participativos, planificaçao e gestao para promover a segurança alimentar e gobernabilidade participativa municipal. Governador Valadares, Brazil: Associaçao das Hortas Comunitárias de Governador Valadares,

Diocese de Governador Valadares, Universidade Vale do Rio Doce, Doce Rio Consultoria, Assessoria e Projetos Ltda., Associaçao Habitacional Governador Valadares. (IDRC 100983)

Mansfield, B. and W. Mendes. 2013. Municipal Food Strategies and Integrated Approaches to Urban Agriculture: Exploring Three Cases from the Global North. International Planning Studies 18(1): 37-60. http://www.tandfonline.com/doi/abs/10.1080/13563475.2013.750942

Marshall, P. 1992. Nature's Web: An Exploration of Ecological Thinking. London: Simon & Schuster.

McCann, A.M. 1994. The Roman Port of Cosa. Scientific American (special issue): 13-18.

McClintock, N. 2010. Why farm the city? Theorizing urban agriculture through a lens of metabolic rift. Cambridge Journal of Regions, Economy and Society 3(2): 191-207.

Merzthal, G. 2006. Technical Report 2006 for Latin America and the Caribbean. Lima: RUAF Foundation-IPES.

Millon, R. 1994. Teotihuacan. Scientific American (special issue): 138-148.

Mkwambisi, D. D., E. D. G. Fraser, A. J. McDougall. 2011. Urban agriculture and poverty reduction: Evaluating how food production in cities contributes to food security, employment and income in Malawi. Journal of International Development 23(2): 181-203.

Montangero, A. 2010. Cerrando el Ciclo del Fósforo en Hanoi, Vietnam. Revista Agricultura urbana 23: 13-14.

Moreira, C. 2010. Interview de Crispim Moreira. Magazine Agriculture urbaine 22: 18.

Mougeot, L. J. A. 2006. Cultiver de meilleures villes. Ottawa: Centre de Recherches pour le Développement international.

Mougeot, L. J. A. 2005. Urban Agriculture and the Millenium Development Goals. In AGROPOLIS: The Social, Political and Environmental Dimensions of Urban Agriculture, ed. idem, 4-11. London and Ottawa: Eartshcan and International Development Research Centre.

Mougeot, L. J. A. 2000. Urban Agriculture: Definition, Presence, Potentials and Risks. In Growing Cities, Growing Food: Urban Agriculture on the Policy Agenda, ed. N. Bakker, M. Dubbeling, S. Guednel, U. Sabel-Koschella and H. de Zeeuw, 1-42. Feldafing, Germany: German Foundation for International Development.

Mougeot, L. J.A. 1999. Urban Agriculture: Definition, Presence, Potentials and Risks, and Policy Challenges. Cities Feeding People Series Report 31. Ottawa: International Development Research Centre.

Moustier, P. 2007. Urban horticulture in Africa and Asia: an efficient corner food supplier. Acta Horticulturae 762: 145-158.

Moustier, P. 2006. Le développement commercial des produits frais périurbains: Synthèse des activités du projet SUSPER (Sustainable Development of Peri-urban Agriculture in South-East Asia Project). Montpellier: Centre de coopération internationale en recherche agronomique pour le développement.

Moustier, P. and A. Salam Fall. 2004. Les dynamiques de l'agriculture urbaine: caractérisation et évaluation. » In Développement durable de l'agriculture urbaine en Afrique francophone. Enjeux, concepts et méthodes, ed. O.B. Smith, P. Moustier, L. J. A. Mougeot and A. Salam Fall, 23-43. Montpellier and Ottawa: Centre de coopération international en recherche agronomique pour le développement and Centre de Recherches pour le Développement international.

Moustier, P. 1998. La complémentarité entre agriculture urbaine et agriculture rurale. In Agriculture urbaine en Afrique de l'Ouest: une contribution à la sécurité alimentaire et à l'assainissement des villes, ed. O. B. Smith, 41-55. Ottawa: International Development Research Centre. (IDRC 004080)

Mukerji, N. and A. Morales. 2010. Zoning for urban agriculture. Zoning Practice 3. Chicago: American Planning Association.

Mutonodzo, C. 2009. The Social and Economic Implications of Urban Agriculture on Food Security in Harare, Zimbabwe. In Agriculture and Urban Planning: Generating Livelihoods and Food Security, ed. Mark Redwood, 73-90. London and Ottawa: Earthscan and International Development Research Centre.

Nasr, J., R. MacRae and J. Kuhns. 2010. Scaling Up Urban Agriculture in Toronto: Building the Infrastructure. Metcalf Food Solutions. Toronto: George Cedric Metcalf Charitable Foundation.

Niang, S. and M. Gaye, coords. 2002. L'épuration extensive des eaux usées pour la réutilisation dans l'agriculture urbaine: des technologies appropriées en zone sahélienne pour la lutte contre la pauvreté. Scientific report of Institut fondamental d'Afrique noire (IFAN), and ENDA Tiers-Monde/Relais pour le Développement Participatif. Dakar: IFAN and ENDA Tiers-Monde. (IDRC 004367).

Niang, S. 1996. Épuration et réutilisation des eaux usées domestiques en maraîchage périurbain à Dakar, Sénégal. African Urban Quarterly 11(2-3): 250-257.

Okpala, D. 2003. Urban agriculture: what limits? Habitat Debate 9(4): 1-3.

Ortiz, I., J. Cai, and M. Cummins. 2011. Escalating food prices: The threat to poor households and policies to safeguard a recovery for all. Social and Economic policy Working Paper, UNICEF Policy and practice (February). New York: United Nations Children's Fund.

Peterson, L. and G. Haug. 2011. Pourquoi les Mayas ont disparu. Dossier pour la science 72: 90-95.

Prain, G. 2010. The Institutional and Regional Context. In African Urban Harvest: Agriculture in the Cities of Cameroon, Kenya and Uganda, ed. G. Prain, N. Karanja and D. Lee-Smith, 1-11. New York, Ottawa, Lima: Springer, International Development Research Centre, International Potato Center.

Premat, A. 2005. Moving between the Plan and the Ground: Shifting perspectives on Urban Agriculture in Havana, Cuba. In AGROPOLIS, ed. L. J. A. Mougeot, 153-186. London and Ottawa: Earthscan and International Development Research Centre.

Quellier, F. 2012. Paris is a land of plenty: Kitchen Gardens as a Major Urban Phenomenon in a Modern European City (16th-18th centuries). Paper presented at Food and the City Symposium, Dumbarton Oaks, Washington, D.C., 3-5 May.

Quon, S. 1999. Planning for urban agriculture: a review of tools and strategies for urban planners. Cities Feeding People Series Report 28. Ottawa: International Development Research Centre.

Redclift, M. 1987. Sustainable Development: Exploring the Contradictions. London: Routledge.

Redwood, M. 2009. Introduction. In Agriculture and Urban Planning: Generating Livelihoods and Food Security, ed. M. Redwood, 1-20. Ottawa and London: International Development Research Centre and Earthscan.

Republic of Kenya. 2009. Draft National Urban and Peri-Urban Agriculture and Livestock Policy (First Draft, August). Nairobi: Ministry of Agriculture, 41 pp.

Reynolds, S. 1984. Kingdoms and Communities in Western Europe 900-1300. Oxford: Clarendon Press.

Rodenbeck, M. 1991. Egypt from the Air. Thames and Hudson: Editions Didier Miller.

Santandreu, A., A. Gómez, R. T. Perazolli and M. Ponce. 2010. L'agriculture urbaine à Montevideo et à Rosario: réaction face à la crise ou une composante du paysage urbain? Magazine Agriculture urbaine 22: 15-17.

Satterthwaite, D., G. McGranahan and C. Tacoli. 2010. Urbanization and its implications for food and farming. Philosophical Transactions of the Royal Society B 365: 2809-2820.

Schiere, H., E. Thys, F. Matthys, B. Rischkowsky, J. Schiere. 2006. Livestock Keeping in Urbanised Areas, Does History Repeat Itself? In Cities Farming for the Future: Urban Agriculture for Green and Productive Cities, ed. R. van Veenhuizen, 350-366. Ottawa: RUAF Foundation, International Institute for Rural Reconstruction and International Development Research Centre.

Sithole, D. 1998. Heavy Metal Toxicity and Urban Agriculture Products. Presented at Environmental and Socio-economic Impacts of Urban Agriculture Workshop, 14-15 May. Harare: ENDA-Zimbabwe. (IDRC 95-0007)

Slater, R. and J. Mitchell. 2009. Economic Dimensions of Urban Agriculture in the Context of Urban Poverty Reduction Strategies: Final Scoping Study (November). London: Overseas Development Institute. (IDRC 105186-002)

Steel, C. 2008. Hungry city: how food shapes our lives. London: Chatto and Windus.

Stevenson, C., P. Xavery, and A. Wendeline . 1996. Market production and vegetables in the peri-urban area of Dar es Salaam, Tanzania. Dar es Salaam: Urban Vegetable Production Project, Ministry of Agriculture and Co-operatives/GTZ.

Tallaki, K. 2005. The Pest-control System in the Market Gardens of Lomé, Togo. In AGROPOLIS: the social, political and environmental dimensions of urban agriculture, ed. L. J. A. Mougeot, 51-87. London and Ottawa: Earthscan and International Development Research Centre.

Thebo, A.L., P. Dreschel and E.F. Lambin. 2014. Global assessment of urban and peri-urban agriculture: irrigated and rainfed croplands. Environmental Research Letters 9(11). http://iopscience.iop.org/1748-9326/9/11/114002/article

Tramhel, J. M. E. 2010. Uso del Diseño Urbano Participativo para 'Cerrar el Ciclo de Nutrientes': Un Estudio de Caso en Las Filipinas. Revista Agricultura urbana 23: 31-33.

UNDP (United Nations Development Programme). 1996. Urban Agriculture: Food, Jobs and Sustainable Cities. United Nations Development Programme, Publication Series for Habitat II, Volume One. New York: UNDP.

UNFPA UN Population Fund. 2007. State of the World Population: Unleashing the Potential of Urban Growth. New York: UNFPA. UN HABITAT. 2004. Dialogue on Urban Realities. Working paper of the Committee of Permanent Representatives to UN-HABITAT for World Urban Forum 2004 (HSP/WUF/2/5, draft 17/03/04).

van Veenhuizen, R. 2006. Cities Farming for the Future. In Cities Farming for the Future: Urban Agriculture for Green and Productive Cities, ed. R. van Veenhuizen, 2-17. Ottawa: RUAF Foundation, International Institute for Rural Reconstruction, International Development Research Centre.

Viljoen, A. ed. 2005. Continuous Productive Urban Landscapes: Designing Urban Agriculture for Sustainable Cities. Amsterdam: Elsevier.

Wagenaar, M. 1992. From hidden hand to public intervention. Land use and zoning strategies in the liberal and post-liberal city (1875-1914). In

Economic Policy in Europe since the late Middle Ages: The Visible Hand and the Fortune of Cities, ed. H. Diederiks, P. Hohenberg and M. Wagenaar, 165-176. Leicester: Leicester University Press.

Warren, P.M. 1994. Minoan Palaces. Scientific American (special issue): 46-57.

Watts, D.J. and C.M. Watts. 1994. A Roman Apartment Complex. Scientific American (special issue): 86-91.

Werner, C. 2004. Ecosan – principles, urban applications & challenges. Presentation at the United Nations Commission on Sustainable Development, 12th Session, New York, 14-30 April.

Yanin, V.L. 1994. The Archaeology of Novgorod. Scientific American (special issue): 120-127.

Zezza, A. and L. Tasciotti .2008. Does urban agriculture enhance dietary diversity? Empirical evidence from a sample of developing countries. Paper for presentation at the 12th EAAE Congress on 'People, Food and Environments: Global Trends and European Strategies', Ghent, Belgium, August 2008. http://purl.umn.edu/44390.

Zhang, F., J. Cai and G. Liu. 2009. How Urban Agriculture is Reshaping Peri-Urban Beijing? Open House International 34(2): 15-24.

NOTES

1 See : http://en.wikipedia.org/wiki/Roof_garden#History.

2 Even today, cutting-edge innovations in UA policy and technology continue to emanate from the more important urban centers, in the USA as much as in Uganda or Ecuador. World- class metropolitan centers, such as New York, Berlin and London, tend to innovate with frameworks for UA which smaller urban centers look up to and tend to emulate later on.

3 In today's Tanzania and Uganda, the fact that urban elites are visibly engaged in UA is considered by lower-income groups as an asset for policy progress to their benefit; there would be less hope for it if elite groups did not practice some form of UA or benefit from it in any way. In Uganda and dating back to the Buganda-Kingdom era, UA has been associated with royal power and status in Kampala (David et al. 2010). Landscape architect D. Imbert reviewed iconic UA models in France, led by both the royalty (Potager du Roy in late XVIIth-century Versailles) and private developers (e.g.: the *maçonnerie* walls of Montreuil, provided hundreds of hectares of vine-growing surface during the XVIIth-XIXth centuries).

4 Even in today's global South cities, various forms of agriculture are sited next to, when not linked to or embedded in, major public works (transportation terminals), infrastructure networks (treatment plants, transportation corridors) other non-agricultural land uses (institutional and industrial estates). In many more ways, informal UA makes every effort to tap on land

investments such as wastewater pipelines, sanitary landfills or unregulated discharges, food fairs and water reservoirs.

5   Today, in global South cities, it is not uncommon for different UA production systems to make use of the same space at different times of the year, depending on rainfall and weather, but also on fluctuations in access to inputs or to consumer groups.

6   Today, dwarf animal and crop varieties, bio-engineered food plants, hydro and aqua-ponic systems, biogas-heated greenhouses, portable chicken coops continue to be designed, tested and applied in urban and peri-urban settings. Not only have our cities preserved production systems well suited to urban conditions but they have invested in improving such systems. For instance, guinea pigs, a delicatessen praised by North Andeans since pre-Inca times have seen local breeds improved by the Instituto Nacional de Innovación Agraria (INIA) in Lima and disseminated with World Food Program assistance, through NGOs working with schools and women's groups in major cities of Ecuador and Peru. As iconic ancient cities once did, today's metropolises will continue to breed innovations in UA: landscape and structural architecture, as well as the wide field of engineering and biogenetics are now engaged in bettering the resource circuitry of the built environment and the role which UA can play in it, through productive landscapes, vegetated structures, ecological buildings and vertical farm prototypes (Dunnett and Kingsbury, 2004; Viljoen, 2005; Despommier, 2010). In the context of climate change, as one reviewer pointed out, UA offers the possibility for new designs for urban producers on small areas with intensive management to withstand weather extremes.

7   Landscape architect S. Fultineer referred to several US examples of portable growing systems that accommodate different measures of land tenure security (tons of produce harvested from a mulched medium on pavement at Added Value Farm of Red Hook in Brooklyn, N.Y.; in Providence, community gardens on pavement make temporary use of land to be developed, with sown-up roofing membranes used as containers that can easily be taken away).

8   This definition has been used in technical assistance publications of UN-HABITAT's Urban Management Programme (Cabannes and Dubbeling 2001), training guides of FAO (Food and Agriculture Organisation)'s Special Programme for Food Security (Drescher 2001) and of research centres such as the CIRAD (Moustier and Salam Fall 2004), plus research collections edited by the CGIAR (Consultative Group on International Agricultural Research) 's Urban Harvest Programme (Prain 2010) and IDRC's Urban Poverty and Environment Programme (Redwood 2009), as well as RUAF (Resource Centers on Urban Agriculture & Food

Security)'s state-of-the-art review (van Veenhuizen 2006).

9   Desrosiers, E. (2012) "Pour une stratégie concertée contre la faim." Le Devoir, CIII/201 (September 5th) : B-1 and B-2.
10 In some cases, UA may contribute a sizeable share of a municipality's agricultural gross domestic product – it was equal to more than half of rural agriculture's own share of municipal gross domestic product in Governador Valadares, Brazil (Lovo et al. 2003).
11 There is no such thing as subsistence agriculture in the city, where expenditure substitution (fungibility) through UA can be very high. Because poor households spend so much on food, with absolutely little left for many other expenses, any savings on food costs, even if limited as noted by a recent ODI review (Slater and Mitchell 2009, 7), is highly valued because the opportunity cost of not doing so can be quite high. In Kumasi and Accra, even households who backyard-garden for their own needs will trade or sell any surplus; self-provisioning may be more significant as a share of the total weight than as a share of the total retail value of the food consumed by the household where food staples represent important items of the grocery bill, such as rain-fed grain and tuber foods (Mutonodzo 2009; Dreschel et al., insert in Campbell et al. 2010).
12 Still, data are few and far between. A more systematic effort is needed to improve the breadth, periodicity and consistency of statistical monitoring of UA production. In early 2000s this share stood at ca. 44% for Hanoi (2.8 m people in 2001): the city then produced within its urban and peri-urban limits nearly half of its cereals, vegetables, pork, beef and poultry meat, as well as a surplus of root crops (Ali and Moustier 2006).
13 In Harare, sample sizes were too small for statistically significant differences. A recent international comparative analysis of fifteen developing or transition countries found that, when other factors are held equal, involvement in UA is associated with a more diverse diet in ten of those countries (Zezza and Tasciotti 2008).
14 Middle and high-income producer households in Lilongwe and Blantyre, Malawi, were found to hire significant numbers of unskilled workers (Mkwambisi et al. 2011). In Gaborone, small UA enterprises have emerged, with low-income women operating highly efficient and effective broiler production systems out of their own resources (Hovorka 2005; Hovorka et al. 2009).
15 Some UA value chains have a significant multiplier effect: In South-East Asian cities, aquatic production systems generate income and jobs at as many as six levels between farmer and consumer.
16 The capacity of market-oriented UA systems to absorb urban workers from other activities can be considerable. For instance, official statistics on

employment in Lomé's market vegetable-growing business grew nearly fivefold in seven years, from 620 in 1987 to 3000 in 1994, in response to reduced food imports and rising local unemployment. In Lomé, only 6% of the growers out of a field sample of 102 surveyed in mid-2000 had previous primary-sector work experience. The great majority, mostly men, were then occupied full time in vegetable growing (Tallaki 2005).

17 Kenya: cities of Nairobi, Mombasa, Kitui, Kisumu, Kakamega and Isiolo of were chosen to represent different city sizes, agro-climatic zones and socio-cultural identities; proportional stratified sampling framework in three stages, according to city size interval, income category and population of sub-locations within city.

18 Tanzania: cities were chosen to represent different city sizes, pace of urban growth, agro-climatic zones; combined stratified sampling framework in five stages, with sample proportionally distributed according to city size interval, then in each city disproportionally to over-represent certain characteristics (high density wards (5:1), farmers (2:1), non-leaders (3:1) and men (4:1)).

19 Dar es Salaam: Kinondoni District selected for intra-urban location, large population (46% of Dar pop. In 1988), good residential planning, large share of urban producers; within Kinondoni, three- stage sampling framework, with disproportional inclusion of high, medium and low density wards (to allow for comparisons), and within each ward a list of producers representing pre-set types of producers was established by local household-group leaders; from those lists urban producers were selected through systematic list sampling, with numbers proportional to population size of ward. Sample biased toward better-off farmers.

20 Kampala: five Resistance Council zones selected to represent range of socio-economic categories; stratified random sampling of households, representative of a mix of socio-economic categories of zones in the urban area (from producer lists provided by local Resistance Council officials), complemented with random sampling of major open spaces under cultivation, which tended to be more centrally located.

21 Harare (1994): sampling framework targeting cultivated open space areas found in wards of low, medium and high densities, sampling numbers proportionate to population size of ward.

22 Harare (1996-7): four wards of Highfield, Dzivarasekwa, Braeside and Mabelreign selected to represent range of population densities; in each ward, street-by-street random sampling, proportional to ward population, to select producers and non producers with a least one child under age 5 (nutrition impact).

23 Santiago de los Caballeros: sampling framework stratified according to socio-economic status of city block with off-plot UA, then random selection

of one producer per city block (probable under-representation of poor, which tend to live in smaller, more crowded housing).

24 Governador Valadares: five wards selected to represent different urban zones and socio-economic status: stratified proportional random sampling framework, according to population size of each ward (listing of statistical population from municipal sources).

25 Amman: data is drawn from two surveys. The first survey on basic household data used a proportional stratified random sampling: the population was divided into six strata (six socioeconomic, plus a nearby town and one Amman suburb). A more or less even number of clusters (100 houses each) were selected from the four first strata, plus 8 and 32 for the fifth and sixth strata for a total of 120 clusters (results possibly biased toward upper socio-economic groups). All 13000 households in those clusters were interviewed in these clusters. A second survey on agricultural production itself in two rounds included all gardens over 200m2 and all gardens with livestock and a sample of 25% of all gardens under 200m2 selected in a systematic way.

Commentary – Some Contemporary Issues Facing Urban Agriculture

Mark Redwood

Across the globe, city and development planners have been unable to keep pace with demographic change. The transition of people from rural areas to cities, and the growth within cities challenges even wealthier emerging market countries such as Brazil, China and India, let alone resource poor countries in Africa and parts of Asia. Moreover, international land markets have become extremely adverse to the protection of land for agricultural and other 'non-built' land uses in and around cities. The profit potential of building far exceeds the financial value of agricultural production in and around cities. It is in this context that both the promise of urban agriculture on one hand and the threats to locally produced food coincide.

Luc Mougeot's chapter on how research has helped to specify the value and appeal of urban agriculture in city and national development strategies is exhaustive in its account of how urban agriculture has grown in recognition and prominence, hand in hand with the rapid urbanization seen across the globe, but particularly in Africa and Asia. And he would know: Mougeot has been at the centre of discussions and debate on urban agriculture since the early 1990's when the curious nature of urban and peri-urban farming started to be seen as both a development challenge and opportunity. His chapter also highlights some of the problems cum opportunities that are fundamental in debates about urban agriculture. For instance, poorly/un-treated wastewater is commonly used in many contexts as a source of water for farming. In this sense, it is one way urban agriculture contributes to environmental management and nutrient recycling. Of course, untreated wastewater irrigation can carry huge costs in terms of illness and so must be managed carefully or controlled.

Mougeot's chapter touches on the historical origins of agriculture in cities, but only briefly touches on more recent (at least, comparatively recent: the last 100 years) – trends in planning. With land values skyrocketing, it may be that only state intervention in the protection and zoning of vacant land for agricultural use is the only option available to optimize the value of urban agriculture. Modern planning, however, has had an ambivalent relationship with city farming. The celebrated Garden City concept of Ebenezer Howard was less about producing food, and more about escaping urban pollution and about finding balance between industry, agriculture and residency. Le Corbusier, the influential visionary pushed boundaries by conceiving of urban growth as upward into high towers, with green spaces in between, but focused his concern on mobility and fresh air more than productive uses of land. Until recently, architects and planners have rarely actually proposed the integration of food production with cities; they have, instead, focused on recreation and parkland. The notable exception in the West had been periods of crises (World War II Victory Gardens, for instance) where conflict, demographic pressure and other crises led to an often desperate need for food. Utopian in character, the notion of self-sufficient, vibrant and balanced cities is still the basis of the planning profession. Unfortunately, as is well known and documented, rapid growth, low investment in public space and transit, the rise of the car and weak to non-existent and often misguided planning has resulted in many cities being chaotic. Nowhere are cities more chaotic than in developing countries where rapid growth, poverty and low public investment have conspired to make many cities packed, costly and polluted.

Mougeot is correct that the 1990s and 2000s have heralded a shift in perception of urban agriculture, particularly in the developing world. Torrid growth in many countries, population expansion, volatile commodity markets (leading to high food prices), income inequality and urbanization provide fertile ground for not only many to move into agriculture in and around cities, but also for those groups that have been farming for decades and sometimes centuries, to be noticed.

Modern agriculture is no longer local as markets for international products expands, and transport remains comparatively cheap, however, growing interest in minimizing ones 'food footprint' by eating local has taken hold. But there are contradicting trends that are not always easy to reconcile. For instance, movements such as the '100 Mile Diet', and *locavore* trends are common in developed countries, and yet the thirst for exotic products from the far off tropics is seemingly insatiable. The range of available foods has skyrocketed where it is not even a question that one can buy mangoes, apples, walnuts and other foods, regardless of where one is in the world. In major crises, such as the food price spikes of the 1980s, and more recently in 2008, this flow of trade has been arrested for a variety of reasons. Increasingly, self-reliance has become an important motivator for city action. As Mougeot puts it, local governments have become more interested in 'tapping assets and resources within their own jurisdiction', and of course, control. By being local, by controlling the means of production, and by being less dependent on international commodity/food markets, urban agriculture is an extremely resilient approach to food security.

While we have certainly conceived of urban systems incorporating agricultural land use, how widespread is this? Is our cognizance of urban agriculture leading to a shift to its preservation and growth? I believe that cities will be divided on this. Some cities struggle with the most basic tenants of urban governance and growth, let alone planning for local food production. Other cities have seen a perfect confluence of political will, innovation, and popular support and as a result have become leaders of the new urbanism that includes food. We may have touched the tip of the iceberg and these few leading cities will reap the benefit of innovation.

On the basis of this chapter, it is clear that research has conclusively assessed the presence and character of urban agriculture, as well as ideas about how to optimize its value, and minimize negative side effects. So now, what next for scientists? I would argue that three major trends have not yet been studied enough in the context of urban agriculture. The first is a threat: the growth of real estate values is a trend that probably poses the biggest threat to the possibilities of urban agriculture. The second two trends are well researched, but not in the context of urban agriculture. And in fact, climate change and the crises posed by reliance on fossil fuels for energy are most likely to encourage the pace of urban agriculture's adoption.

REAL ESTATE MARKETS

The biggest obstacle to city farming are high real estate values, particularly in emerging market economies where land values have skyrocketed in recent years, along with the growth of the middle class. For the poor, exclusion continues and access to land peri-urban areas is scarce. Moreover, the poor, who in developing countries are most likely to live on marginal land, are often those most engaged in urban farming. However, there are exceptions: witness Detroit, where plummeting land values and the decline of the inner city core have led to a renaissance in efforts self-sufficiency for food such as the Food Field farm. Still, it has to be acknowledged that the weight of change is on building bigger and more intensely which places pressure on vacant land. In the absence of municipal zoning and/or stronger legislative protection, urban agriculture risks remaining on the margins.

The second major trend is climate change, which will influence the growth of urban agriculture. Most affected by climate change is the hydrological cycle, which is fluctuating more than historical norms, and leading to less certainty which complicates decision making. Coupled with an increase in extremes (heat, precipitation and associated violent weather and storm surges), people's exposure to weather related hazards is on the increase. Urban agriculture has been seen to be a resilient response to externally imposed crises (conflict, economic collapse etc.). In particular, droughts in rural areas have frequently led to the migration of farmers to cities. If necessity is the mother of invention, then climate induced stress will likely increase the use of urban agriculture to improve peoples' resilience. It fits in building resilience for many migrants and city dwellers whose traditional farming livelihoods are upset by not only demographic and economic change, but also climate change.

A final trend that will dominate policy debates in the coming years relates to the exposure of commodity prices to changes in energy costs. Commodity price spikes – including agricultural goods – associated with high oil prices have led to direct impacts on markets across the globe. The 'bottom billion' often feels its impact most in disrupted food markets and high prices that take up an even greater proportion of their household income. Even those that are not alarmists concede that the era of easy-oil is done. As energy costs increase so too will the price of basic food stuffs. Price volatility makes for a strong rationale for local food production and for UA. The connection between these trends are worthy of serious consideration by economists.

The pace of growth in interest in urban agriculture has been phenomenal, yet with few easy answers, and dynamic change in the landscape of cities, more work is required. For example, urban agriculture is a promising and highly practical strategy to build resilience in cities. New business ventures, such as commercial rooftop farming, integrated production/restaurants/ markets and vertical farming are being tested by entrepreneurs worldwide with mixed results. There is, however, not shortage of excitement as the many city dwellers become increasingly connected to food production as part of a healthy and financially sensible approach to living. This energy alone – not forgetting about powerful externalities such as volatile markets and natural disasters – will drive urban agriculture forward.

CHAPTER 4

DESIGNING URBAN AGRICULTURAL FORMS: HISTORY, EDUCATION, PROPOSALS AND PROJECTS

ROBERT L. FRANCE

INTRODUCTION: EXPLORING THE FUNCTION OF FORM IN URBAN AGRICULTURE

Food production is at the core of the discussion about urban sustainability (de la Salle and Holland 2010; Hodgson et al. 2011). Urban agriculture (UA), keeping in mind that the term 'urban' can be quite elastic, also offers a potential model for rethinking urban open-spaces from the neighbourhood to the metropolitan scale. Urban agriculture has become remarkably popular in the last decade (see Introduction). Major newspapers regularly report on UA, edible schoolyards, and foraging and gleaning. Urban agriculture has been addressed in both established (Joseph 2011) and newly created (*Urban Farm;* and *Urban Agriculture*) magazines. Political leaders and royalty endorse kitchen and allotment gardens for nutrition and educational values. A panorama of UA projects involving contemporary concerns and themes has emerged over the last ten years (see Chapter 1) that reflect back to precedents and their spatial qualities and what productive gardens once meant for cities (Imbert and Fultineer 2010). Urban agriculture is about food, health, social justice, and money, and is often offered up as a panacea for urban ills, global warming, obesity, and diabetics to name but a few. At one end of the UA technology spectrum is the reclamation of road mediums with orchards, while at the other are skyscrapers of tiered gardens providing tomatoes for all.

It is significant to remember that urban gardens and farms are at their core also designed physical spaces. Landscape architecture is concerned with the importance of the visual perspective of the spaces we inhabit (Treib 2002) and is beginning to become a major player in how those UA spaces are being designed (Imbert and Fultineer 2010). Gardens can be art-filled and artful spaces. For example, before the visually stunning UA designs were published in book form (Gorgolewski et al. 2011; see also Chapter 6) they were part of the touring exhibit *Living Concrete/Carrot City*. In 2011, the Museum of Vancouver hosted an exhibit of large-scale photographs about UA (including inner-city gardens, beekeepers working atop the city's convention centre, and an industrial-scale hothouse). And established design magazines, usually concerned with showcasing high-end expressions of architecture, landscape architecture, and art, have featured articles about UA (Vitiello and Nairn 2009; Alter 2010). The purpose of the present chapter is to introduce selected built and proposed UA projects, and some historical precedents, all of which incorporate attention and detail to the design of their physical form.

HISTORY: AN ONTOGENESIS OF PRODUCTIVE URBAN LANDSCAPES

Interrelationships between city and food in production, distribution, and consumption have a long and diverse history (Steele 2009; Bjorklund 2010; see Introduction and Chapter 3). This section describes some significant signposts along one such historical pathway. As Imbert and Fultineer (2010) remind, the notion of productive landscapes combining utility with pleasure in the form of rural gardening goes back to Virgil's agrarian-themed poem *Georgics*. Further, the hybridization of what can be referred to as 'second nature' or agriculture and 'third nature' or the garden, as shown in Roman and Palladian villas, has always had an impact on the landscape imagination. The eighteenth-century concept of the ornamental farm calls to mind the gardens of the Ancients with lawns for feeding sheep and sowing crops. Such gardens were designed to be both profitable and pleasurable. The pursuit of beauty through science also shaped productive peri-urban landscapes. At Versailles, for example, ornamental gardens containing segregated areas of vegetables and orchards on a drained slough were situated to maximize microclimatic benefits to extend the typical growing season (Cockrall-King 2012).

Just as spatially compelling were the 'peach walls' located on the other side of Paris (Imbert and Fultineer 2010). Here, an intricate network of masonry walls were constructed to collect and retain heat throughout the entire day for growing fruit, vegetables, and wine (Cockrall-King 2012). The site was oriented toward the south-east, and the soil was composed of a deep layer of gypsum from wall construction mixed with clay, marl topsoil, and horse manure. Started in the seventeenth-century, cultivation peaked in the nineteenth-century with more than five hundred kilometres of walls encompassing one of the most productive growing systems ever documented (Stanhill 1977). The industry had largely disappeared by 1950 and real estate prices of the next three decades added to the demise. Today, remnant gardens exist as well as a strong collective identity with the walls. As a result, attempts are underway to revitalize this once dynamic and visually beautiful urban agricultural system.

In Amiens, France, it is possible to see the last traces of Les Hortillonnages or the 'floating gardens', which are reminiscent of those in the Xochilmilco wetlands of Mexico City (France 2011). Since the fifteenth-century, French families have intensively farmed these plots to grow radishes, carrots, onions, and leaks. This has given rise to a distinct garden economy as well as a unique and insular gardening culture (Imbert and Fultineer 2010). Families intermarried, spoke their own dialect, and guarded their horticultural knowledge. Seeds were exclusively from their own gardens, and produce was directly distributed to restaurants and markets with flat-bottomed boats. The system was undermined in the nineteenth-century by the new market economy and railroad development, as well as an opening up of the community through education and other job opportunities. By the 1970s, only a few family farms remained of the once fertile peri-urban landscape. Today, the site is championed in dozens of national and international websites as a tourist destination. The social revitalization and physical regeneration of beautiful, agricultural heritage landscapes such as Les Hortillonnages or Xochilmilco is part of a growing movement in agri-tourism (Hall et al. 2003).

Another example of the blending of garden form and function is the Westbury Court Garden, nestled in beside the church and pub in the

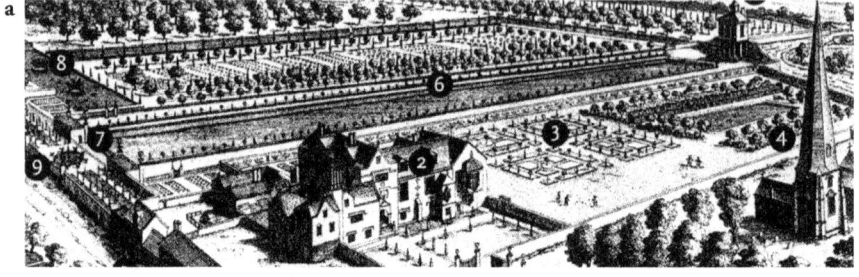

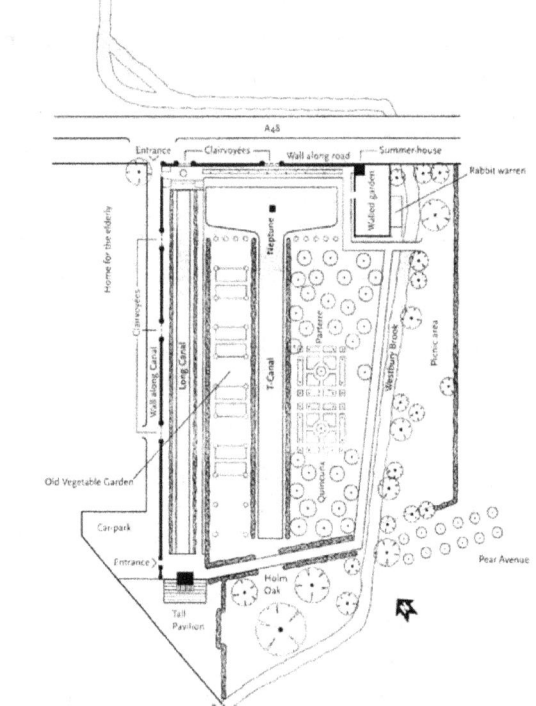

Fig. 4.1. Bird's eye view of the Westbury Court Garden in 1705-10 (a) and modern plan (b) of the restored garden showing the vegetable garden situated between the Long (#6) and Second (# 8) canals. With permission from The Natural Trust obtained from Garnett (2007).

village of Westbury-on-Severn, located near Gloucester, England. The garden, laid out at the end of the seventeenth century, is the premier surviving example in Britain of a formal Dutch water garden (Garnett 2007). Once, many dozens of such gardens existed around the country before disappearing due to the naturalistic designs popularized by the like of Capability Brown. The garden consists of several long canals flanked by a pavilion, ball and cone topiaries, and a parterre and quincunx of planting

Fig. 4.2. Images of the restored edible beds and orchard at the Westbury Court Garden.

beds and trees. Also bordering the canals and water source stream, and based in the 'productive nature of seventeenth-century gardens' (The National Trust 2004), is a surviving orchard containing old varieties of apples and a large section was set aside for strip-and-box plantings of vegetables (Figs. 4.1, 4.2).

As the city displaced food production from its centre, the relationship between living, working, and eating became more abstract. Although landscape architecture was not essential to early twentieth-century architectural debates, a small number of planners and designers sought to redress urbanization and crowded cities with sustainable, productive systems. One such was the German designer Leberecht Migge who championed food self-sufficiency in postwar Germany, through writing polemics such as *The Green Manifesto* wherein he argued for the individual production of food as a tool for land reform and to alleviate over-crowded urban conditions (Imbert and Fultineer 2010). Using 'biotechnic' principles to link home and garden, he believed that growing food was the only solution to the wasteful planning that had led to fallow streets and tenement deserts (Haney 2010). In contrast to the wasteful city, the productive garden was organized and sized according to family needs. Migge's 'garden-architectonic' approach maximized microclimatic benefits and led to intensive production. Neighbours recycled household waste in communal composting openspaces, and fruit trees were grown along walled esplanades. Migge came to look upon the productive garden as a unit of planning which could be multiplied and expanded across the region, which for Germany in the 1930s, also meant expanding into new territories.

Migge's desire to reestablish a connection with the soil, both physically and symbolically, was a recurring concern for twentieth-century landscape architects (Imbert and Fultineer 2010). In Denmark, for example, allotment gardens were part of the open-space system and designed as permanent landscape structures. For C. Sorensen, such gardens offered a cure for modern apartment dwellers severed from their connection with the earth. He believed that such elevated dwellers needed a renewed emotional intervention. In the Naerum allotment gardens outside of Copenhagen, Sorensen arranged a series of gardens each enclosed by a circular hedge built of hawthorn, sweet briar, crabapple, or lilac of a sufficient height to provide privacy (Treib 2002; Friesen 2009, Lund 2010). These ovals were very different from Migge's rational units in that they contrasted with the orthogonal order of cities and typical allotment gardens (Imbert and Fultineer 2010). Within the ovals, gardeners could operate as they pleased. The ovals, still in existence today, are arranged as a continuous curve across the slope, the ground in between serving as a buffer between units as well as a playground.

The argument for self-sufficiency embodied in the allotment garden movement rested in an economic and moral rationale (Lawson 2005). War, oil rationing, climate change, and economic downturns periodically prompted a yearning for food security, proper nutrition, and employment. To some skeptics, the current discussion of UA projects represents a stage as temporary as the 1940's victory gardens or the 1970's embrace of organic farming and self-sufficiency manuals such as *The Whole Earth Catalogue* (Imbert and Fultineer 2010). *The Whole Earth Catalogue* also represented a desire to shift environmentalism from wilderness protection toward an inclusive view of nature reconciled with modernity and technology. The 1960s also saw discussion about 'appropriate technology' that was aimed at improving living conditions in the developing world without the environmental hazards of industrialization. Imbert and Fultineeer (2010) believe that the methods and goals of UA fit the bill of appropriate technology: low investment cost, organizational simplicity, adaptability to a particular social or cultural environment, sparing use of natural resources, and high potential for employment. Further, they argue that of particular notice in today's striving for self-sufficiency and a better diet is that UA is simultaneously both off and on the grid. In short, UA is in fact a product of a top-down revolution *and* grass-root movements. The somewhat elitist desire to transform the relationship of people to food, the nostalgic relationship of people to rural agricultural ideals, the myth of Old Europe, the preservation of landscapes for agri-tourism, all are gathered in today's revolution and movement (Despommier 2010). Conversely, UA rests on models tested in the developing world (Redwood 2009): the informal, opportunistic, impromptu yet essential garden plots in the cities of Latin American and Africa contribute to a large percentage of the food supply (see Chapter 3). Likewise, the community gardens of West Philadelphia are essential for strengthening the economic base and the physical and mental health and cultural identity of the cultural community. But just as micro-loans have attracted global banks, UA has come to the attention of the business world. Evoking ecological and humanistic principles, the organization Slow Money (www.slowmoney.org) hopes to align investors with local economies to build and nurture capital industry. The ambitious aim of reviving communities based on care of the commons, diversity, and restorative practices is rather seductive but doesn't appear to have gathered the momentum. But recently corporations have returned to the production of food as part of their operating structures (Imbert and Fultineer 2010). The paternalistic control of former company towns wherein workers were provided homes and gardening plots has reemerged as workers' compensation during the recent economic downturn though boosting morale, supporting food banks, or improving the cafeteria fare (see also Chapter 8). Large companies are now testing this model by giving loans to workers to grow their own vegetables. In a similar effort, a health care provider in California seeks to improve the diet of both patients and their physicians by establishing a farmers' market on hospital grounds and cooking demonstrations as part of basic medical training. And finally, on a larger scale, the proposed 20,000-acre Hants Farm plan for Detroit has promised to rejuvenate the city by returning to its agrarian roots and putting property back on the city tax roles. A commercial venture, the project will use conventional methods to grow crops such as Christmas trees. Although advertised as a win-win proposition, the tree plantation has raised fears among some Detroit community activists that it is another land grab by the rich in a sometimes racially-charged city with a sketchy history of such undertakings (Kavanaugh 2010: Mantyk 2010).

For some, like Imbert and Fultineer (2010), the contemporary idea of UA presents a paradox. Zoning regulations, olfactory and sound control, the chickens or no chickens debate, and the triumph of the lawn, has erased almost all traces of food production within most Western cities. This contradiction between 'city' and 'country' (see Introduction) reveals the difficulty of making UA a unified system (but see Butler and Maronek 2002) and the need for landscape architects, planners, and community activists to join agriculturalists in contributing to the discipline as well as tackling policy. Furthermore, one may question whether the perception of UA as a temporary land use for disenfranchised inner city populations will, in the long run, hinder rather than promote the development of UA into a new type of open space in the sustainable cities of our future.

EDUCATION: GROWING DESIGN MINDS

The mid-twentieth-century division between ornamental and productive landscapes is a topic well worth evaluating from an educational standpoint. As heirs to both agriculture and urban traditions, landscape architects are uniquely positioned to bring third nature aesthetics back into a new urban second nature (Imbert and Fultineer 2010). In consequence, in design schools around the world UA planning and design have become to the 2010s what water sensitive and brownfield regenerative planning and design (France 2002, 2008) were to the previous decade. The idea is that inspired conceptual designs from course studio or high visibility design/build pilot projects, in which students focus on productive open-space, will lead to the acceptance of these ideas as being integral components of sustainable urbanism (Farr 2007). The following section introduces four such projects, with more are being presented in Chapter 5.

Harvard University

If there is one common element in the history of UA it is that for every successful delivered project, there are probably half-a-dozen that are still-born in conception. One such is a designed urban farm for Harvard's planned new campus across the Charles River in Allston, which was halted when the university lost interest in the idea. The site presented a spatial and social laboratory for students from the Graduate School of Design to explore ideas about UA through a series of proposals (Imbert and Fultineer 2010). The project was designed to be didactic but was also pitched as a way for mending fences characteristic of the strained relationships in such 'town-and-gown' situations. In this respect, the proposals were about reaching out, growing food, recycling waste, and living well, and fit within the developed framework of campus sustainability (France 2004). Also important, was to educate about how to consider the urban landscape in such redevelopments in terms of phasing as well as how to provide an open-space structure for the new campus that was not based on a nostalgic view of the iconic Harvard Yard model as described in Van Valkenburgh and del Tredici (2004). Through growing and experiencing food, it was thought that the university could demonstrate its commitment to sustainability and progressive development and demonstrate how its landscape architecture department, the oldest in the world, is moving into new directions. Development of such a spatial laboratory on an urban campus would offer important lessons about the need to acknowledge the challenges of urban soil, pollution, and water treatment in a highly engineered nature while at the same time providing space to sustain social, emotional, and salutary needs.

Imbert and Fultineer's students worked on conceptual designs with vegetable plots along a water course, public benches, a series of greenhouses in which to taste food and contain other activities, a system of illuminated beacons, and in homage to the nearby rail yards, the use of recycled boxcars as remedial test plots. The overarching goal was to design a space that could be used as an outdoor classroom at the same time as serving to open up the campus to the neighbourhood. In short, this was to be a productive landscape that functioned as a place to enjoy life, have a good meal, and be a base for teaching. Presently, although the University is engaged in another round of reiterations of their master plan for the new campus expansion, they have decided to ignore the urban farm proposals from the students

Fig. 4.3. The Harvard Community Garden: (a) welcoming sign; (b) wildflower border; (c) patio and tables; and (d) raised produce beds.

and instead have stated their desire to proceed with a miniature golf course in addition to, unbelievably, a McDonalds restaurant (Imbert and Fultineer 2010).

Located on a transformed patch of unused lawn in front of a student residence, the Harvard Community Garden might be looked upon at first blush as a consolation prize for the failed attempt at UA across the river for the planned Allston campus. Though this may be true, there is no denying that the more modest and realized space is a useful demonstration that form and function, beauty and productivity, can be united in UA. The garden was created in 2010 through a campus-wide collaboration involving dining services, landscaping operations, the office of sustainability, and students from the Graduate School of Design (www.garden.harvard.edu; Bast et al. 2009; Dension 2011). As the University has had a troubled history of relations with its neighbours, one major role of the project is to facilitate community outreach by creating a welcoming and inclusive social and productive space (Fig. 4.3a). Raised vegetable beds are situated behind a border of native perennials (Fig. 4.3b, d). Heirloom varieties are cultivated by students using compost gathered from across the campus, and food is donated to local charities. Another goal is to raise awareness and provide an opportunity for hands-on learning about the critical role of food in sustaining personal and environmental health. Just as important, the garden is designed to function as a social, as well as a productive, space. A patio space and tables (Fig. 4.3c) provides an outdoor classroom for food demonstrations, workshops, and lectures, as well as a unique venue for student art installations. The garden has now become recognized as a tranquil campus oasis by the students, and as 'a powerful tool in teaching Harvard undergrads about sustainable land use practices, that gives them a sense of ownership in the creation of a reimagined and valuable campus space' by faculty and management. There is no doubt that attention to the aesthetically pleasing and socially inclusive design of the garden has been a key element to its success.

University of Washington

Curricula in architecture, landscape architecture, and urban planning schools are based on lectures and design studios. Some schools also employ design/build projects (Carpenter 1997) which do not simply reiterate the content of lecture courses but offer also opportunities for students to 'explore, in an intensive and coherent manner, specific focus areas of professional practice and sustainable design' (Winterbottom 2005). Importantly, the purpose of such a pedagogic approach is to give students pragmatic, real-world experience that may be remarkably different from the hypothetical, and occasionally ungrounded world of high-end studio design. If design can be looked upon as generating an hypothetical product, then design/build can be viewed as the process of testing and experimentation. Also, students learn the benefits of collaboration and team building, and the integration of learning and understanding the materials and processes of construction, while creating a community asset. Specifically, in design/build projects at the University of Washington, landscape architecture students work on open-space renovation and community redevelopment projects based on using green technologies in garden design and watershed awareness (Winterbottom 2005). One such project was the Garden of Eatin' which was constructed at the interface of campus and community on a former trouble spot for illicit activities. Students worked to create an ecological, educational, recreational, social, and spiritual urban oasis that makes use of rainwater harvesting, permeable paving, and recycled materials, all to sustain an edible landscape of fruit bushes and flowering herbs. Another design/build project was the University Community Park and Gardens which also focused on a neglected site. Here students worked to expand the existing community gardens, educate about drought-tolerant urban plants and the construction and use of cisterns for rainwater harvesting, to develop the site as a connection between a nearby community centre and green market, and to create a park-like plaza to serve as a gathering space for cooking demonstrations and other community activities (photos of both these projects are shown in Winterbottom 2005).

Detroit Mercy University

With its thousands of hectares of abandoned lots due to financial disinvestment and a shrinking population as one-time residents flee to the suburbs, Detroit is on the front line in the how UA can be used in city-wide, post-industrial regeneration. The University of Detroit Mercy's School of Architecture has been at the forefront of exploring the interface between, and integration of, cultural and environmental factors into landscape regeneration as a means toward community redevelopment. Based on a working hypothesis that what Detroit needs is a new planning model creating 'middle landscapes' between urban centres and suburban fringes, students developed an integrative concept for the Bloody Run neighbourhood on the lower east side. The new community, referred to as Adamah, would have the following UA-related characteristics (Vogel 2008):

- Be rooted in the colonial French farming tradition and also agrarian roots from more recent immigrants from the South
- Focus on 'walk to work' job creation, including in addition to gardening and crop farming, fish and mollusk aquaculture, and artisan production
- Utilize sustainable green infrastructure and reuse of materials with a focus on the single family home and gardened lot as the basic planning unit
- Daylight Bloody Run Creek, not only for recreational and stormwater purposes, but also for crop irrigation

The Boggs Center, a local community NGO, has been working with community residents to champion and hopefully implement elements of the Adamah vision. A later studio, Adamah Redux: Urban Agri[culture] in Detroit's Lower East Side (www.margotlystra.com) further explored the ways UA and stream daylighting can be linked to activate vacant or underutilized land. These studio projects are important in demonstrating the shift from the traditional methodology of agricultural land use to a new strategy of productive landscape design as means for raising awareness and initiating conversation about community redevelopment.

Rhode Island School of Design

Design school pedagogy develops through advanced research seminars and design studio projects where the learning comes from doing the design. It is important to realize that work within the design world is just as much spatial as it is visual. Though there is good deal of writing about community gardens such as descriptions about the farming method or how many vegetables they produce or the people they employ, there is actually very little information about the physical descriptions of exactly how large and what the shape is of the areas. In consequence, projects at the Rhode Island School of Design (RISDI) used students to conduct surveys by measuring physical attributes of such gardens (Imbert and Fultineer 2010). A student project identified plant material for unconventional salad greens for a group of restaurants in Cambridge, MA that were interested in locally harvested food, whereas another project produced a conceptual design for a small growing wall containing edible plants.

Social surveys by a group of RISDI graduates revealed that vacant lots were extremely unwanted in neigbourhoods and that the best opportunities for inserting UA into the urban fabric existed in establishing temporary use of lots until such time as sites were developed, The idea, as employed elsewhere, such as the skip gardens of London (www.kingscrosscentral.com/skip), was to build a garden that could be transportable. Planting beds were constructed of roofing membrane scavenged off a job site and sewed up into containers set atop donated pallets. So when the time comes to move from the site, residents will seek someone with a tractor or forklift and shift the garden down the street to another location. Issues of possible toxins from roofing tar were not considered, however.

The city of Providence contains many backyards suitable for produce gardening. However, because many of these are in post-industrial areas of unknown soil contamination, raised planting beds are *de rigueur*. These are not neighbourhoods with nurseries where one can buy expensive bags of potting soil. As a result, soil needs to be built. Students therefore worked to develop a composter that was small and actually fun to use (Imbert and Fultineer 2010). Resembling a wheel drum with pull handles out the side, the idea is to keep the composter under the sink and when it is full to attach the handle and pull it along the street to the community composting site. There, one's private organic waste is added to the community pool and the accumulated compost in the larger bins can be spun and mixed by neighbourhood children.

Proposals: Dreaming Edible Cities

There is an established tradition in the design professions of creating envisioning projects that may be either: (a) too fantastical to ever really be seriously considered for construction (e.g. some of the truly bizarre designs for the Venice lagoon shown in Gili et al. 2008); or (b) purposely edgy or didactic so as to kick-start conversation and debate as an important and recognized step toward implementing more realistic and socially acceptable projects at some later date (e.g. the slightly outlandish but thought-provoking designs raised by artists for reclaiming Tel Aviv's Hiraya landfill as shown in Beracha Foundation (2001)).

Recently, I participated in one such envisioning exercise to reimagine the Cogswell Interchange, an elevated set of highways right on the edge of downtown Halifax, Nova Scotia, which 'since its inception [in the 1960s as part of the philosophy of urban renewal that swept across North America and whose consequences today's more enlightened urban planners and designers spend so much time trying to rectify] the interchange has been universally considered a missed opportunity…that could have (and should have) been so much more' (Strategic Urban Partnership 2013). Selected participants from around the province were invited to inform, inspire, and involve the public in their concepts for transforming the interchange. These concepts ranged from high-tech plans from professional firms, to designs from university students (Roth et al. 2013), to endearingly simple models from grade school students. My own proposal (France 2013) dealt with integrating UA with innovative stormwater management and urban biodiversity restoration, and was very successful in capturing the public's imagination, including television news coverage and a three-quarter-size front page article in the major regional newspaper. The latter began with

Fig. 4.4. Locations of conceptual plans from Lim and Liu (2010) and Gorgolewski et al. (2010): (a) Trafalgar Square, London; (b) Leadenhall Street, London; (c) Don Valley, Toronto; and (d) Gardiner Expressway, Toronto.

the following purple prose demonstrating the incredible romantic pull UA can invoke among reporters and the public alike: 'Close your eyes, Halifax, for it costs nothing to *dream*. Picture the city through the lens of an urban farmer: the scent of lavender on the salty breeze, bunches thriving in the concrete jungle, a neighbor to herbs and raspberries whose lifeblood stains your tongue and your fingertips…' (Fraser 2013).

The present section reviews selected conceptual UA designs that have been floated in books and plans, and are introduced and discussed here in sequence from the least to the most probable in terms of their elements being built in the real world.

Unlike Gorgolewski et al.'s (2011) and Vijoen et al.'s (2005) books (see these authors' further writings in Chapter 6 and its Commentary) which contain a mixture of conceptual and realized designs for UA, Lim and Liu's (2010) presents an array of designs whose outlandish, science fiction-esque nature are simply too improbable to ever really be seriously considered for implementation. One such project is The Tomato Exchange, envisioned for one of the most cherished public spaces in London: Trafalgar Square. There, across from Canada House and the National Gallery, surrounding and dwarfing the famous monuments (Fig. 4.4a), would be 16 giant glass bell-shaped tubular structures over which vines would grow and inside of which tomato-based delicacies would be highlighted. A tinted glass elevator within each bell-tower could whisk visitors, accompanied by each structure's 'custodian,' up to an eye-level view of Admiral Nelson atop his column. Tomato plants of various heirloom varieties, grown inverted and sustained through hydroponics and the microclimate of the greenhouse structures, would add to the 'visual spectacle' of the installation. Periodically, concentric planting trays suspended within the bell-towers would descend to the ground to enable harvesting by citizens. Further, Lim and Liu (2010) suggest that similar UA structures could be established in such locations as Tiananmen Square, Red Square, and the Place de la Concorde.

Despommier (2010) believes the advantages of urban farming in high-rise buildings to include: year-round, climatically controlled crop production, no crop failures due to inclement weather, no contaminated agricultural runoff, freeing up rural land for ecological restoration, no use of environmentally harmful chemicals, large reduction in water use, greatly reduced food miles, better control of food safety and security, new employment opportunities, purification of grey water to drinking water, and reuse of postharvest plant material as animal feed. Despite an endorsement by the rock musician Sting, who believes 'this visionary book provides a blueprint for securing the world's food supply and at the same time solving one of the gravest environmental crises facing us today,' scant attention is provided to issues of urban landscape regeneration. As a result, rather than discussing and presenting conceptual plans for the adaptive reuse of unattractive, derelict or under-utilized buildings such as those that now characterize Detroit, the focus instead is on showing a series of 'highly inventive, beautifully rendered,' 'futuristic' buildings with no mention made of the ecological footprint entailed in their construction. The author, whose text is chock-a-bloc full of platitudes, asks readers to suspend their 'sense of reality' for these 'fantasies.' Despommier recognizes that the designs shown in his book are 'colorful, creative objects of imagination more in the way of 'eye candy' and 'what ifs' than practical applications,' and admits that 'there are still no examples of functioning vertical farms.' The challenge therefore

History, Education, Proposals and Projects

remains how to actualize the lofty (pun intended) ideas and ideals presented in this book. Urban agriculture dreamers will have to look elsewhere since Despommier humbly concludes his chapter on the form and function of vertical farms with the statement: 'I don't claim to have enough expertise or insight to offer any higher level of description of any of the topics covered in this chapter, so I am afraid that we will all have to wait until such a team is assembled and given their marching orders to find out what happens next.'

Realistically, vertical farming is much more likely to develop through natural topography than constructed edifices. For example, Toronto is bisected by a series of ravines containing rivers that tumble down from the surrounding hills into Lake Ontario. Not only the most important urban wilds in the city, these green corridors actually define the entire metropolis (Fulford 1996) in terms of serving as neighbourhood borders, flood control systems, and transportation arteries (Fig. 4.4c). Some ravines have been completely filled in for infrastructure development. Ravine City, diagrammed in Gorgolewski et al. (2011), is an intriguing and attractively designed proposal that capitalizes on the existing gradient of ravine side-slopes by imagining a city-wide system of tiered housing units and accompanying rooftop and terraced gardens. Each dwelling would overlook the next lower down the slope, whose gardens would contain productive crops interspersed with ornamental shade trees. Food and home would thus be intimately linked together, supported by the latest developments in sustainable design, as would city and ravine through the cascading greenery. As Gorgolewski et al. (2011) explain: 'By creating living and growing space in a dense vertical format, Ravine City aims to reduce the need for sprawling suburbs, eliminating food travel distance and creating a living architecture that is part of a city ecosystem that encourages urban dwellers to take more control over their ecological footprint.' Buried admix their fantastical and improbable designs, Lim and Liu (2010) also envision a more subtle and realistic plan of compact urban land-use based on a similar stepped arrangement of homes and gardens such as Ravine City.

Located a few kilometres away from Trafalgar Square, near the iconic buildings of the City of London's financial district, and light-years away from the Tomato Exchange in terms of realism, is the site for the one-time proposed Leadenhall Street City Farm. Such building sites often remain vacant or may be temporarily used as parking lots while funding is put in place for constructing office towers (see Chapter 6). This proposal, the winner of a competition to suggest a better temporary use for the site, was based on establishing an economically viable working farm to grow vegetables, flowers, and crops in humble planters and to raise caged chickens and livestock with a budget of £125,000 (Mitchell Taylor Workshop 2009). Other design elements included public space for lunch breaks, a flower meadow, a soup kitchen using produce from the site, all surrounded by a fence made of recycled material into which a series of vegetable-shaped cut-outs would enable views (Gorgolewski et al. 2011). Sadly, the landowner decided that such a temporary use was not supportive of their positive-spin message of economic recovery following the 2008 recession. The result is that today the site is being developed to its original, office tower end-use (Fig. 4.4b). Signage on the construction fencing champions the future building's 'green code' of sustainable design (i.e. material procurement, CO_2 emissions, waste recycling, and use of public transport) but makes no mention of the missed opportunity of UA.

The land beneath and around elevated highway or railway overpasses is mostly ignored and lies derelict. Such land, however, has great potential for being transformed into dynamic public space, as for example, green infrastructure for stormwater management parks in Bellevue, Washington (Poole 2005) or as UA hubs like the Borough Farmers' Market in Southwark, London, similar to what I envisioned for Halifax (France 2013). One intriguing conceptual design, grounded in realism, is the Gardiner Urban Agriculture Hub in Toronto (Gorgolewski et al. 2011), proposed to be located below the elevated Gardiner Expressway where the Don River enters Lake Ontario (Fig. 4.4d). Agricultural hubs, through linking production to distribution, are essential for creating vibrant and sustainable UA (see Chapter 7). The proposed Gardiner hub would contain community gardens, an orchard designed with rammed-earth and living architectural structures, and a greenhouse nestled underneath the highway. The regeneration and reuse of such neglected and abandoned landscapes is one of the most promising roles that UA can play in supporting urban sustainability initiatives (Hodgson et al. 2011).

Conceptual plans exist to redesign the eight-hundred kilometre periphery of Paris as a new landscape which would perform simultaneously as open-space to break up the existing cookie-cutter form of featureless suburbs as well as an urban-rural interface with the adjourning agricultural belt lying immediately beyond the suburbs (Imbert and Fultineer 2010). The goal is to attempt to establish a physical 'dialogue' between the two worlds which presently remain unknown to each other (Pujol and Beguier 2012). Plans for the interface area are to build upon the still-visible traces of the former farming landscape, including hedges, ditches, bridleways, and infrastructure for greenhouses, together with newly constructed facilities for allotment gardens, composting, recycling and energy production, as well as sports fields, all in an attempt to design a landscape that would be attractive and available to many interest groups. Doing so would allow agriculture to re-enter the urban world as a sort of urban 'in-reach.' In such theoretical scenarios, UA offers the potential to recalibrate the social, economic, and spatial balance of the peri-urban environment (Butler and Maronek 2002). Here, it is the designer's role to underscore the importance of UA as a designed open-space having wide-ranging applications. And it is the role of politicians and planners to acknowledge UA as a new landscape system, one that is aesthetic, productive, and sustainable.

Making the valid point that there is 'a dearth of literature about urban design dedicated to the production of food under modern social circumstances,' Duany's (2011) *Garden Cities: Theory & Practice of Agrarian Urbanism* takes its inspiration from de la Salle and Holland (2010) (see Chapter 7) and proposes 'agrarian urbanism' as a professional field that involves 'food not as a means of making a living, but as a basis for making a life.' The idea is to create new villages that, due to their acknowledged reliance on the support systems that subsidize conventional suburbia, are idealized but realistic objectives rather than idolized and unattainable utopian aspirations. These new communities, focused around the civic aspects of food systems alà Lyson (2004) rather than around golf courses or lakes, offer many health, environmental, economic, and social benefits, and give value to the hitherto disparaged transition zones of the suburbs, in direct contrast to other (traditional, new, or landscape) urbanism models. Indeed, Duany is known for his axiom that 'agriculture is the new golf' with respect to designed communities. The book contains dozens of beautifully rendered illustrations showing oblique aerial views of the conceptual communities at various spatial scales. For myself, having walked more than three thousand kilometres of various pilgrimage routes throughout Europe over the last decade as well as spending time in rural regions of southeast Asia, I was struck by an inescapable feeling of 'deva vu all over again' when studying the schematics. This is because the agrarian urbanism model is very much 'once more, the wheel' as noted in the Introduction to the present book. Famous precedents of agriculture integrated into suburban American communities include Village Homes and Prairie Crossing (Thayer 1994; Philips 2013), and the movement is expanding (Ladner 2011). On the other hand, that there are so many, still functioning precedents – original ones in Europe and nouveau anachronistic ones in America – suggests that the 'back to the future' idea of agrarian urbanism could meet with success. There is one difference from a straightforward nostalgia to the past that does, however, characterize modern agrarian urbanism. Duany recognizes that some individuals who are class-conscious and uncomfortable in the presence of workers may have difficulty accepting one of the managing protocols of his model, namely that 'the great difference between Agrarian Urbanism and the moribund communes, kibbutzim, social gardens, cooperative farms, and old villages [is that] the really hard work, the demanding schedule, and the boring aspects of agriculture are handled by contract workers. The lighter, more satisfying and pleasant roster of tasks – still a good portion – would be by the willing residents in their spare time, much as they putter (and sometimes much more) in their own gardens.'

Finally, unlike the razzle-dazzle conceptual designs shown in Despommier (2010) which are preoccupied with the ego-driven construction of completely new buildings, plans of a group of Ryerson University students (supervised by J. Komisar, one of the co-authors of Chapter 6) are ethically grounded in their adaptive recycling of existing structures. The Cliffside Plaza proposal, shown in the cover feature article of the glossy design, architecture and art magazine, *Azure*, won the 2009 CitiesAlive International Student Design Challenge (www.citiesalive.org). The proposal transforms a suburban strip mall into a green oasis containing extensive plantings, food gardens, greenhouses, and a rooftop poultry farm (Alter 2010). It is worth noting that projects like this are being considered for Detroit and are similar to those already existing in London.

Projects: Landscape Design in Gardens

South Side Community Land Trust's City Farm (Providence)

Providence, Rhode Island is bisected by the elevated interstate highway and contains areas that are challenged by high unemployment, abundant vacant land and boarded up homes. The South Side Community Land Trust was started in 1981 by a group of community activists with an interest in rehabilitating different parts of the city. The purpose was to work with neighbours, many of whom were recent immigrants from South-east Asia and West Africa and whom did not have access to land. The main goals were to teach people how to grow food, to locate and secure land, and to give resources to recent immigrants. And the values that were hoped to be instilled by urban farming included social justice, sustainable small-scale agriculture, education, self-governance, and collaboration and community building (www.southsideclt.org/cityfarm). The organization's signature City Farm is located in a tough neighbourhood in which project toilets have to be locked to prevent drug use. Despite this and the very low project funding, site managers decided to use local art students and sculptors to elaborate upon the traditional chain-link fence motif (Imbert and Fultineer 2010). The resulting whimsical fence, though small in size, was designed as a cheery, welcoming gesture to the community (Fig. 4.5).

Fig. 4.5. Designed entrance fence at South Side City Farm, Providence.

BERKELEY STREET COMMUNITY GARDEN (BOSTON)

One of the largest community gardens in Boston began to be cultivated in the mid-1970s as part of an urban renewal project in a space where townhouses had been demolished. Today, the garden is composed of about 160 plots that make up a half a city block in an area that has become gentrified. Surrounded by brick townhouses, the garden began informally but in 1992 its ownership was transferred to the city and then to a local open-space land trust specifically created to preserve existing community gardens threatened by development pressures (www.berkeleygardens.org). The gardens were originally built for food production to help augment the budgets of the low-to-moderate income urban families.

Today, the garden land trust continues to favor that original use but people are allowed to grow flowers. The result is a patch work of food and ornamental gardens, the latter being attractive enough (Fig. 4.6a, b) to lure happenstance passersby off the street. In this respect, the garden is particularly interesting as it has evolved in an extremely exposed site alongside several streets. This necessitated attention paid to the recently completed bordering fence. The finely detailed fence (Fig. 4.6c), costing half a million dollars, has made walking down the street a completely different experience. The artfully designed fence is important in that it helps to celebrate the garden as a valued place instead being a marginal space surrounded by a common chain-link fence whose message would be one of exclusion. As well, the new fence also helps denote the sharp gradient change and presence of garden retaining walls (Fig. 4.6d). User access to the garden is by a series of paths and there are communal spaces for seating (Fig. 4.6e) and storing equipment in sheds. Of special note are the water troughs that empty into small, tool-washing basins inscribed with poems generated by snippets of conversation overheard in the garden over a series of time (Fig. 4.6f, g).

Throughout the garden, people are encouraged to customize entries to their plots by adding their own fences which are frequently constructed of humble chicken-wire and pressurized lumber. Community gardens are also important for allowing an intermingling of cultures to forge a dialogue on the land about what and how things are grown (Imbert and Fultineer 2010). One of the most fascinating things about the Berkeley Street Garden is how different ethnicities cultivate their plots. For example, Chinese-Americans often garden vertically, using wooden structures to enable climbing vines. One lesson here is for UA garden design is to enable diversity

HISTORY, EDUCATION, PROPOSALS AND PROJECTS

Fig. 4.6. Berkeley Street Community Garden, Boston: (a, b) produce and ornamental plots; (c-e) designed fence and seats; and (f, g) inscribed water troughs.

in the physical framework of the garden so as to encourage a diversity of growing approaches side-by-side. It is not a one-size/style fits all model, and the challenge is to how to allow the physical design to reflect the cultural dynamics of the wider community.

NEW YORK RESTORATION PROJECT'S CURTIS '50-CENT' JACKSON GARDEN (QUEENS, NYC)

The New York Restoration Project was started in 1995 by Bette Midler who had been disgusted by the sorry state of the city's parks (Ravor 2008). So began a privately funded initiative to clean up the parks. In 1999, the year Mayor Guliani took back many gardens temporarily established on city land (von Hassel 2002), the Restoration Project stepped in and made it possible to purchase and save some of them. The idea was to use the gardens to reboot a community sense of ownership, to generate media attention in order to attract more funding and enthusiasm from the public, to help people see and form new ideas, to use the gardens to create a unified identify among sites that had long been degraded and scattered across the city, and to bring a new level of beauty and function to the idea of UA (Imbert and Fultineer 2010). Specifically, the Restoration Project asked the question about what design does for the gardens? Although it was easy to obtain funding for gardens in Manhattan, it was much more difficult to do so for other areas such as Brooklyn or the Bronx. Hence partnerships had to sought.

One such successful partnership led to the Curtis '50-Cent' Jackson Garden on a vacant lot next to commuter rail in the working-class neighbourhood of Jamaica, an area of Queens characterized by a lack of publically accessible open-space. Raised beds at different heights to allow all ages of the community to garden. Far from being randomly assorted, the raised beds have a formal geometry in their arrangement in lines parallel to the rail line running along one border (Alexander 2013). Edible plants are mixed with ornamental plants into blocks of colour, thereby erasing the distinction between the two vegetative typologies (Gorgolewski et al. 2011). In further homage to the past, a metal shipping container is reused as the toolshed. As in all Restoration Project gardens, rainwater is collected and used in a visual manner, in this case through a series of 6 playfully-shaped, 4-metre high, brightly coloured water towers that funnel water into two underground cisterns where it is stored for irrigation. A series of small fences or screens double as growing structures. One major element of this garden is how its visual presence stands up juxtaposed against the transportation infrastructure and surrounding roads (Imbert and Fultineer 2010). The bordering fence is set one-metre inside the property and contains an attractive trellis structure that provides shade for people waiting outside for the bus as well as serving as a lure to pull people into the garden, thus making the site part of the community.

The joyful and attractive design of the garden is used for many different types of gatherings. Although a few critical voices have been raised emphasizing their belief that parks and gardens are diametric opposites that can never be reconciled, the site has received considerable praise:

> 'Inspired by the Kitchen Gardens of Villandry, France, the formal geometry in the [Curtis '50 Cent' Jackson Community Gardens] essentially provides the framework for the landscape's design, creating playful spaces for children and adults alike. The curvilinear shaped parterres in conjunction with the orthogonal raised beds create artful experiences throughout the garden. Vegetation planted by the community introduce a new layer of complexity that reinforces ownership in the garden.' (Alexander 2013)

And:

> '[The garden] demonstrates that a plant can be appreciated for its form as well as its nutritional content and, conversely, that a functional shed, pump, bench or water collector can be considered a beautiful detail instead of an obstacle to beauty.' (Gorgowlewski et al. 2011).

Conclusion: Moving Urban Agriculture from Last Resort to Lasting Resource

The survey of proposals and projects in this chapter highlights the power of expressing consciousness of design through the visible form. A valid question concerns what it is that design can contribute to UA. Imbert and Fultineer (2010) believe that designers approach UA quite differently from those in other disciplines. Although designers can study growing and system flows, they are above all concerned with the form of how things are made, a viewpoint that can be a critically important resource to consider in

UA. Designers bring an entirely different engagement between the community and the garden. They instigate a high level of communication within the community and a self-examination of what it is that the neighbourhood may actually be trying to achieve. Designers therefore become catalysts themselves for the promulgation and acceptance of UA. By working at all of the aesthetic, productive and social scales, achieving a balance between formal, ordered design and more naturalistic forms, landscape architecture has the potential to transform UA by increasing its widespread acceptance in not only periurban or suburban areas but also in downtown urban cores. Again, a precedent is the way in which landscape design has completely revolutionized stormwater management in the last few decades (Bays et al. 2002; France 2002, 2008). There can be an unflattering perception of community gardens being an admission of failure in lieu of something else being developed. By making productive landscapes in urban settings (*sensu* Viljoen et al. 2005) more recognizable as systems for public enjoyment in addition to simply producing food, landscape architecture removes feelings that UA is only the last resort rather than being a treasured resource to the community (Imbert and Fultineer 2010).

Landscape design contributes to the physical elements that make gardens a success (Imbert and Fultineer 2010). The smallest designed element, even if very modest, can contribute to the beautification of urban food production, as for example the edgy architecture of contemporary beehives in urban Buffalo (Rochon 2013). Gates and fences are used to create a clear boundary that not only regulates access but at the same time allows the garden to establish its presence by giving more credibility to the area. By using attractively designed vegetative elements and accompanying structures, such as those shown in the photographs in this chapter and in Johnson (2010), Gorgolweski et al. (2011) and Philips (2013), the visual message that such spaces convey is both of the pride of community and a statement of about the permanence of UA.

REFERENCES

Alexander, D. 2013. Curtis '50 Cent' Jackson community garden. www.foodurbanism.org.

Alter, L. 2010. The urban farm. Azure. May issue: 58-63.

Bast, E. and others. 2009. The Mount Auburn Street garden. Sustainable Allston Project Group of the Harvard College Environmental Action Committee.

Bays, J. and others. 2002. Moving from single-purpose treatment wetlands toward multifunction designed wetland parks. p. 357-358 *in* France, R.L. (Ed.) Handbook of water sensitive planning and design. Lewis Publ.

Beracha Foundation, The. 2001. Towards Ayalon Park (Containing examples from the Hiriya Exhibition at the Tel Aviv Museum of Art, Nov. 1999-April 2000). The Beracha Foundation.

Bjorklund, A. 2010. Historical urban agriculture. Coronet Books.

Butler, A. and B. Maronek. 2002. Urban and *a*gricultural communities: Opportunities for common ground. U.S. Coun. Agri. Sci. and Tech.

Carpenter, W.J. 1997. Learning by building, design and construction in architectural education. Van Nostrand Reinhold.

Cockrall-King, J. 2012. Food and the city: Urban agriculture and the new food revolution. Prometheus Books.

Denison, L. 2011. Proposal of the Harvard College garden project. Harvard Faculty Arts and Sciences.

Despommier, D. 2010. The vertical farm: Feeding the world in the 21st century. Thomas Dunn Books.

Duany, A. 2011. Garden cities: Theory & practice of agrarian urbanism. The Prince's Found. Built Environ.

Farr, D. 2007. Sustainable urbanism: Urban design with nature. Wiley.

France, R.L. (Ed.) 2002. Handbook of water sensitive planning and design. Lewis.

France, R.L. 2004. Developing ecological design principles for water, air, soil, and food for the new Allston campus. Internal document prepared for the Harvard Sustainability Planning Committee.

France, R.L. (Ed.) 2008. Handbook regenerative landscape design. CRC Press.

France, R.L. 2011. Preservation, rehabilitation, and management of heritage wetlands in Mexico. p. 173-210 *In* France, R. and Contributors. Restorative redevelopment of devastated ecocultural landscapes. CRC Press.

France, R. 2013. The 'Little Dig': Form and function in Halifax's inexpensive alternative to Boston's Big Dig (the most expensive public works project in history). Presentation at the Cogswell Shake-Up Envisioning Session, May 2013.

Fraser, L. 2013. City of dreams: No more 'Road to Nowhere': Urban planners envision a downtown Halifax of redesigned streets, tree-lined boulevards, urban gardens. The Chronicle Herald, May 16, 2103.

Friesen, C. 2009. Form, function and fairytales: The design and mystery of allotment gardens in Landskrona and Naerum. Landscape Arch. Gardens.

Fulford, R. 1996. Accidental city: The transformation of Toronto. Houghton Mifflin.

Garnett, O. 2007. Westbury Court Garden. The National Trust.

Gili, M., M. Puente and A. Puyuelo. (Eds.) 2008. Concurso 2G competition: Venice Lagoon Park. 2G Dossier.

Gorgolewski, M., J. Komisar and J. Nasr. 2011. Carrot city: Creating places for urban agriculture. The Monacelli Press.

Hall, M., L. Sharples, R. Mitchell, N. Macionis and B. Cambourne. (Eds.) 2003. Food tourism around the world: Development, management and markets. Butterworth-Heinemann.

Haney, D. 2010. When modern was green: Life and work of landscape architect Leberecht Migge. Routledge.

Hodgson, K., M. C. Campbell and M. Bailkey. 2011. Urban Agriculture: Growing healthy, sustainable places. Amer. Planning Assoc.

Imbert, D. and S. Fultineer. 2010. Agri-urban food forms: Systems, ecology and design. Paper presented at the Planning Urban Agricultural Systems for the 21st Century conference. NSAC, Truro, NS, Sept.

Johnson, J. 2010. Designs on food. Azure. May issue: 65-75.

Kavanaugh, K. 2010. John Hantz: The man has a plan, but does Detroit have a farming future? www.modelmedia.com.

Ladner, P. 2011. The urban food revolution: Changing the way we feed cities. New Society.

Lawson, L. 2005. City bountiful: A century of community gardening in America. Univ. Calif. Press.

Lim, C.J. and E. Lu. 2010. Smartcities + ecowarriors. Routledge.

Lund, A. 2010. Denmark's oval community gardens. The City Farmer News. www.cityfarmer.info

Mantyk, E. 2010. World's largest urban farm slated for Detroit. www.theepochtimes.com.

Mitchell Taylor Workshop. 2009, Leadenhall City Farm proposal – London, England. Accessed on www.cityfarmer.info.

National Trust, The. 2004. Westbury Court Garden. The National Trust.

Philips, A. 2013. Designing urban agriculture: A complete guide to the planning, design, construction, maintenance, and management of edible landscapes. Wiley.

Poole, K. 2005. Watershed management as urban design: The civic hydrology of Bellevue, Washington. p. 337-349 *in* France, R.L. (Ed.) Facilitating watershed awareness: Fostering awareness and stewardship. Rowman & Littlefield.

Pujol, D and M. Beguier. 2012. Paris' near urban agriculture. www.ruaf.org

Ravor, A. 2008. Healthy spaces, for people and the Earth. The New York Times, Nov. 5, 2008

Redwood, M. 2009. Agriculture in urban planning: Generating livelihoods and food security. Earthscan.

Rochon, L. 2013. City space: Building sweet buzz in an urban wasteland. The Globe and Mail, June 20, 2012.

Roth, N., B. Rokosh and D. Tiniakos-Doran. 2013. Cogswell redesign. Dalhousie Univ.

Stanhill, G. 1977. An urban agro-ecosystem: The example of Nineteenth-century Paris. Agro-Ecosystems 3:269-

Steele, C. 2009. Hungry city: How food shapes our lives. Vintage Books.

Thayer, R. 1994. Gray world, green heart: Technology, nature, and sustainable landscapes. Wiley.

Treib, M. 2002. The architecture of landscape, 1940-1960. Scholarly Book Serv. Inc.

Van Valkenburgh, M. and P. del Tredici. 2004. Restoring the Harvard Yard landscape. Arnoldia 3-11.

Viljoen, A., K. Bohn and J. Howe. (Eds.) 2005. Continuous productive urban landscapes: Designing urban agriculture for sustainable cities. Elsevier.

Vitielo, D. and M. Nairn. 2009. Everyday urban agriculture: From community gardening to community security. Harvard Design Magazine 30: 25-31.

Vogel, S. 2008. Detroit (re)turns to nature. p. 189-204 in France, R.L. (Ed.) Handbook of regenerative landscape design. CRC Press.

von Hassel, M. 2002. The struggle for Eden: Community gardens in New York City. Praeger.

Winterbottom, D. 2005. Applying the theory: Design/build models for water harvesting and watershed awareness. p. 231-251 *In* France, R.L. (Ed.) Facilitating watershed management: Fostering awareness and stewardship. Rowman & Littlefield.

Commentary – Missing the Gardener

Laura Lawson

My commentary starts with a heretical statement: if landscape architecture is to contribute to the design potential of urban agriculture, the landscape architect must also be gardener. If not an actual gardener, then at least he or she needs to empathize with the desires and needs of a gardener or farmer. Evocative Photoshop images may garner public interest and support, and they may win design awards, but images do not make a garden: gardeners do. Beyond the design and technical skills of landscape architecture, successful design for urban agriculture requires understanding the requirements of cultivation and the labor and commitment involved with building productivity and sustaining the garden.

As Robert France points out, there are many historical precedents for urban agriculture that reveal beauty in the blending of form (the garden) and function (gardening). To this historical review, however, I would like to add the enabler – the gardener. Historically, the gardener might be groundkeeper, farmer, staff, homeowner, servant, or slave. As a productive garden is never designed just once but changes with each seasonal planting, multiple gardeners have shaped the form and function. Behind the beautifully tended and human-scaled spaces, such as cloister gardens or castle kitchen garden, are gardeners who reveled in the utility of warm walls to protect fruit-bearing trees, dedicated themselves to crisply edging planting beds to allow for intensive successional planting, and endlessly trekked the path from water source to planting bed to assure plant growth. Remnant urban farms such as Robert France cites were the work of farmers who had cultural and economic ties to their land's productivity, and were sometimes labeled as holdouts to progress and at other times opportunistic survivors shifting their product to meet urban demands for particular delicacies. Social concerns also infused the intended function of urban agriculture, with allotment gardens, war and victory gardens, school gardens, and community gardens all emerging to address a range of social, economic, and educational needs. Gardeners in these contexts often took advantage of underutilized land that required substantial investment in sweat-equity to make it productive. Today's urban agriculture tends to be propositional, often ignoring past precedents and opting for technically sophisticated models that lend themselves to professional design development – green walls, green roofs, integrated wastewater systems, etc. – yet as the models from the past reveal, attending to the gardener is also critical to understanding the form and function of the garden.

Only very recently has the professional designer – landscape architect, architect, and planner – been involved in the creation of urban agriculture (Lawson 2004). For over a hundred years, the profession of landscape architecture has sought to distance itself from gardening and the act of 'landscaping.' In the United States, the exceptions were the early women's landscape gardening educational opportunities, such as Lowthorpe School of Landscape Architecture and Horticulture or the Pennsylvania School of Horticulture for Women, that sought to prepare women for varied careers – as designers but also as possible school garden coordinators and as philanthropic leaders in civic gardening (Lawson 2012). A review of *Landscape Architecture Magazine* during World Wars I and II reveals the profession's ambivalence to the national call to grow food, cautioning against the destruction of established gardens for the sake of a potato patch. Some attention to urban agriculture emerged in the 70s and 80s, with landscape architects like Karl Linn, Mark Francis, Randy Hester, and others promoting the participatory nature of community gardening as grassroots action to address urban decay and as community open space (Francis et al., 1984; Hester 1984; Linn 2007). In the last forty years or so, myriad landscape architects have provided pro-bono services to community gardens and school gardens, yet much of this work has remained tangential to the discipline and profession. Only in the past few years has attention grown, as witnessed by the number of presentations on urban agriculture at universities and professional conferences, the number of books and articles on the topic, and the demand by students to study urban agriculture. This new interest redresses the missed opportunities of the past to engage the profession with production – rural and urban – but also reveals foresight to the expanding integration of green systems necessary for more resilient communities. Food is a basic resource that is tied to the land, and as landscape architects it now seems obvious that it is part of our field's scope.

Robert France points out the efforts to engage landscape architectural education with urban agriculture. He cites valuable examples at public and private universities – some applied and some theoretical. As my first statement suggests, I would like to develop this idea of urban gardening experiential education a bit more. Adding urban agriculture to design pedagogy not only introduces a new type of space but also a more engaged relationship between the space and its participants. Whereas many other designed spaces – parks, home gardens, plazas, streets, etc. – are designed based on desired visual qualities, play or activity enabled by the space, or the experience of moving through the space, urban gardening is also designed based on the ongoing care of the garden. Experienced gardeners reviewing a garden plan are very aware of the time and labor implications of a garden design that has too many wide paths that have to be mulched and weeded, too many un-claimed planting areas that won't be watered or weeded, or inconvenient compost area. Planting design for urban gardening requires an ever-changing palette that has capacity for successive changes. New material comes in regularly and material is taken out regularly. There are different time frames for gardening: the everyday tending and watering of newly planted beds, the frequent weeding around plants, harvest time for fruiting plants, end-of-season clean-up, etc.

Just as many landscape architecture curricula are adding design-*build* studios and construction courses to appreciate the relationship between material qualities, construction, and design, so too we need a design-*garden* studios in which students design and then tend a garden over the course of a year. The design of a raised bed may seem simplistic until one's back hurts from leaning over a bed that is too high or wide. The seasonal and daily routines of gardening – planting, watering, weeding, harvesting, replanting, sharing ideas with other gardeners, learning from mistakes, realizing an unexpected surprise – these are experiences that will train future landscape architects to empathize and celebrate the urban gardener.

This past summer, I supervised four landscape architecture students who were tasked to provide design assistance to several community gardens in town. On their own, the students did two unexpected things: they developed a blog to share their work with others and they signed up for a plot at one of the gardens. Two of the students – both excellent designers – had never gardened before and were guided by the other two students plus a couple of supportive gardeners. On that first day, they weeded their raised garden bed and the paths around it. They struggled with tough weeds that were anchored at the base of their bed and wished for a string edger trimmer that would make quick work of the project, but the garden didn't have such equipment. They then mulched their paths in hopes that no new weeds would grow (they did, of course). The students returned to studio to develop a planting design for their 4x 8 bed. Later in the week, equipped with seeds, new gloves, and some hand tools, they planted their bed. Green plants started to come up, but most were weeds that probably came from the compost material they used. While weeding, a gardener pointed out purslane, a delicious weed that the students wisely kept in their plot. Throughout May and June, a student or two would go every day or so to water and to observe how the garden functioned. This and their ongoing conversations with the other gardeners helped in their overall design project. One of their first design ideas was to remove some of the raised beds to make a space for benches; they realized quickly, however, that those beds were already occupied, and so they shifted the benches to an underutilized edge of the garden that incidentally could not be cultivated because of shade (and that shade came in handy to a weary gardener). By July, the students were less enthusiastic about having to go water at the garden. They noticed that gardeners came early in the day or in the evening. They rejoiced in an afternoon thunderstorm that meant they could stay in studio and wouldn't have to go water. The work of gardening became evident, though enthusiasm for their flowers, peppers, and tomatoes remained strong. The blog tracked their experience, both in the garden and in their design work. I believe that the critical elements – experience, community interaction, and reflection – helped make this summer project successful for both the community who benefited from the new seating area and other improvements and the students who came away with new skills, maybe a little humbleness, and increased sensitivity about design that worked for the gardeners.

I return to my statement: if landscape architecture is to contribute to the design potential of urban agriculture, the landscape architect must be gardener or approach the project with an understanding of the gardener's perspective. I do not mean to suggest that landscape architects take on the vocation of gardening and urban farming, although I know several students who are interested in just that. My comment is more about the avocation of gardening – being engaged with gardening as an activity so that one is aware of the risk, labor, and love associated with growing food (and eating it). Landscape architects don't necessarily have to love gardening, but they do have to appreciate it as a learned skill and a laborious task that must be worthwhile if people are going to ultimately care for the garden. A gardener looking at a landscape architect's plan is also imagining what they can make of it – should the beds be planted in potatoes or peppers, can the hose reach all the plants without knocking them over, where will the weed pile be, how long until the orchard bears fruit? A landscape architect that understands the way gardeners think will be the one to expand our profession into sustainable urban agriculture.

REFERENCES

Francis, Mark, Lisa Cashdan, and Lynn Paxson. *Community Open Spaces: Greening Neighborhoods Through Community Action and Land Conservation.* Washington, D.C.: Island Press, 1984.

Hester, Randolph T. *Planning Neighborhood Space for People,* Second edition. New York: Van Nostrand Reinhold, 1984.

Lawson, Laura. 'Women and the Civic Garden Campaigns of the Progressive Era: 'A Woman has a feeling about dirt which men only pretend to have…' *Women in Landscape Architecture: Essays on History and Practice.* Edited by Louise Mozingo and Linda Jewell. North Carolina: McFarland and Company, 2012.

Lawson, Laura. 'The Planner in the Garden: A Historical View into the Relationship between Planning and Community Gardens.' *Journal of Planning History* 3, 2 (May 2004): 151-176.

Linn, Karl. *Building Commons and Community.* New York: New Village Press, 2007.

CHAPTER 5

Urban Agriculture Linkages: Patterns, Planning, and Education

Karen Landman, PhD

Introduction

The Conference Board of Canada recently released a report entitled 'Valuing Food: The Economic Contribution of Canada's Food Sector' (Grant et al. 2011). The report states that,

> [T]oday, more Canadians think about all aspects of food (from how it is produced and what is in it, to where and when they eat it) than ever before. Basic food security is now less of a concern to most Canadians than obesity, nutrition, and the environmental and social impacts of food. How can we better educate and engage consumers to promote and achieve improved health outcomes (Grant et al. 2011, p. 55)?

The report also notes that there is an increased consumer interest in food, the Canadian population is more than ten times ethnically diverse than a century ago, and this population is increasingly urban. Where else but in the urban environment is there a strong opportunity to link people to their food system, in order to gain the improved health outcomes that will benefit all Canadians?

This chapter is based on my 2009 urban agriculture road tour, which covered approximately 30,000 kilometers through Canada and the United States. While this distance in no way captures all of Canada and the United States, I saw enough urban agriculture project to observe emerging patterns.

These patterns are outlined and briefly described in this chapter, and are: academic research, urban planning and design, urban farms (both non-profit and for-profit), student farms, community gardens, and urban agriculture for children and youth.

SECTION 1: ACADEMIC RESEARCH

Urban agriculture has become a focus of interest for university faculty and students in many academic disciplines, with research areas including the nutritional contributions of community gardens; the community development space that community garden sites offer; the potential to reduce food deserts in the urban core; alternative food production systems such as aquaponics; and the recycling of organic wastes from industry (e.g. brewery waste) into compost for urban arable soil enrichment. Landscape architects, both within practice and the discipline, have long been involved in designing community gardens in our cities; the change we are seeing within this design profession now is to move beyond the site and into systems thinking in general. Indeed, the terms 'agricultural urbanism' (de la Salle and Holland 2010; see Chapter 7), 'food urbanism' and CPUL (continuous productive urban landscapes) (Viljoen and Bohn 2009; see Commentary for Chapter 6) are becoming commonplace in design schools. The impetus for food systems thinking as an urban system issue, however, is coming from city planning research. City planning education encourages students to adopt a comprehensive approach to urban planning, with specializations that may include urban design, real estate development, land use planning, economic development, housing and transportation, to name a few; no planning textbooks to date have included food systems planning as a professional focus. Within the purview of those who physically shape cities, American planning professors Kameshwari Pothukuchi and Jerome Kaufman have been North American leaders in bringing the discussion on food systems to the planning and design professions; included in this discussion is the role of urban agriculture in planning for and shaping sustainable cities.

Planning is concerned with the public good and with community development. Planners are trained to understand community development from a system and process perspective: inventory, analyze, implement, monitor and evaluate. In their article 'The Food System: A Stranger to the Planning Field', Pothukuchi and Kaufman (2000) presented their research on the presence, or lack thereof, of the food system in planning literature and in the daily work of planners. These researchers found a dearth of information and discussion on food systems in the literature, as well as in the thinking of planners in their daily work. Pothukuchi and Kaufman essentially asked the questions:

> 'Why have planners paid so little attention to the food system?
>
> Why should the food system become important as a focus of planners' attention?
>
> What constructive role can planners play in the food system?' (2000:113).

These questions arose as a result of working with graduate-level planning students on community food system research over time. Upon completion of a class report entitled 'Fertile Ground: Planning for the Madison/Dane County Food System' (University of Wisconsin-Madison 1997), the planning professors and students aimed to answer the above questions through the analysis of leading planning journals and textbooks and a survey of 22 U.S. city planning agencies. They found that discussion of community food issues had been rare to that point in the major journals. Some work had been done by feminist planners on elements such as food co-ops, community kitchens, and community gardens (Franck & Ahrentzen 1989), but this provides only a limited view of food systems (Pothukuchi and Kaufman 2000). For the 1997-1998 survey, the authors targeted cities that had, for the most part, food policy councils or other types of active food-focused organizations. They discovered that these city planning agencies were minimally or not at all involved in food systems. Where planning agencies were involved, 'their role is reactive rather than proactive and piecemeal rather than comprehensive' (Pothukuchi and Kaufman 2000:114).

Why were planners so limited in their work on food systems? Pothukuchi and Kaufman (2000) categorized the responses into seven categories, which are abbreviated here but explained more extensively in their research report. Briefly, the responses were: it's not our turf; it's not an urban issue; the food system is driven primarily by the private market; planning agencies aren't funded to do food system planning; if it ain't broke why fix it?; we don't know enough about the food system to make a greater contribution (Pothukuchi and Kaufman 2000:115). When asked if planners should be more involved in food system planning, given the range of possible responses, only 25% said 'no'.

Since this research, special planning journal issues devoted entirely to food planning have included the *Journal of Planning Education and Research* (Summer 2004) and *Progressive Planning* (Winter 2004). The American Planning Association issued the 'Policy Guide on Community and Regional Food Planning' (2007), based on research by Pothukuchi, Kaufman and others; the Policy Guide states that converging factors that explain the heightened awareness among planners, among a number, are:

> Recognition that food system activities take up a significant amount of urban and regional land
>
> Understanding that farmland in metropolitan areas, and therefore the capacity to produce for local and regional markets, is being lost at a strong pace
>
> Awareness that access to healthy food in low-income areas is an increasing problem for which urban agriculture can offer an important solution (American Planning Association 2007: 2)

The Policy Guide offers seven General Policies and 26 Specific Policies, providing comprehensive and detailed suggestions for how planners can monitor and contribute to sustainable food systems for the communities in which they work. This document has been enormously influential in raising the awareness of planning students throughout North America on the role they can play in their future professions, and has given rise to graduate student food systems research from many disciplines that has influenced the municipalities that have been the focus of their research.

My own work with landscape architecture students at the University of Guelph has resulted in a number of research projects at the graduate and undergraduate level. Tracey Tomlik (2009) looked to the Transition Town movement, based on Hopkins (2008), to use 'an ethical design system applicable to food production and land use, as well as community building' (King 2008, p. 118) for the development of a permaculture land use plan for the City of Guelph. Upon reading the City's Official Plan (OP) – the document which is relied on for guiding the development of the municipality – Tomlik found that there were no real barriers for her idea of a permaculture land use plan, but there was also nothing in the OP, at the time, that fostered urban food production in the City. Tomlik argues that urban open space has the potential to provide a source of energy in the form of local food production that will be vital to the future sustainability of communities. However, while the City of Guelph is planning to increase its population in the next ten years without increasing its boundaries, a call for more urban food production will create yet another land use for the limited open space in the City, competing with other green space requirements such as natural areas, sports fields, the urban forest, and parks. The challenge in developing urban food production as a legitimate land use will be in convincing planners and citizens of the importance of a land use designation for urban food production (Tomlik 2009).

Kelsey Cramer (2009), another University of Guelph Landscape Architecture student, developed a GIS sieve mapping technique to assess the food production potential at the landscape scale in Nanaimo, British Columbia, based, partly, on the research of Mendes et al.'s (2008) work on landscape assessment of Portland, Oregon, and Vancouver, British Columbia; Kaethler's (2006) study of urban agriculture potential in Vancouver; and the PhD research of Bhattarya (2005), who developed a strategy for identifying and evaluating urban agriculture sites in Gainesville, Florida. Cramer (2009) found that, even with Nanaimo's rugged landscape, close to half the land parcels in the city had some potential. She suggests that her work is a starting point for planners to consider where and what type of urban agriculture could be integrated into the Nanaimo landscape, and refers municipalities to the document entitled 'Urban Agriculture Guide: Urban Agriculture in the Netherlands under the Magnifying Glass' (Wageningen University 2007) for a step-by-step approach to planning at the municipal scale.

Cramer (2009) makes the distinction between socially-oriented urban agriculture and economically-oriented urban agriculture. She points out that many municipalities across Canada have programs in place that permit the integration of community gardens into the public green space, but few mechanisms exist that promote economically-oriented approaches to urban food production. She concludes her research by suggesting that urban agriculture be given proactive scrutiny during the development of Nanaimo's comprehensive green infrastructure plan. Nasr et al. (2010) echo this approach in their report 'Scaling Up Urban Agriculture in Toronto', with a call to extend growing/production strategies to an entire city, rather than a piecemeal site-by-site approach that has been the norm. As well, Nasr et al. (2010) argue that there should be an increased development of profit-based food production to allow for a stronger association amongst growers, processors, distributors and retailers, while maintaining a balance with socially-oriented urban agriculture.

Integration requires more than appropriate physical infrastructure; developing supportive policy allows for planners and other municipal staff to actively give their attention to the creation of urban agriculture in their landscapes. As an example, a team of students (Hazen, Dietrich O'Connor and Hayhurst 2011), partnered with the Institute of Community Engaged Scholarship at the University of Guelph, worked with the Guelph Wellington Food Roundtable to influence policy in the City of Guelph's Official Plan (OP) review process. Through a participatory action research model and by inserting food system thinking into the OP, Hazen et al. (2011) worked with city policy planners, city councillors and other stakeholders to find a way to integrate urban agriculture and other elements of our food system in a way that responds to the needs of the City and the surrounding rural landscape. For example, the OP currently states:

> 'Amendments to the Plan: When considering an application to amend the Official Plan, Council shall consider the following matters:
>
> viii) the impact of the proposed use on sewage, water and solid waste management systems, the transportation system, community facilities and the Natural Heritage System;' (Guelph OP)

Hazen et al. (2011) proposed that this be changed to:

> viii) the impact of the proposed use on sewage, water and solid waste management systems, the transportation system, food systems, community facilities and the Natural Heritage System;

This might appear to be a simple 'fix' in raising awareness about the food system within the City, but could have a remarkable impact over the long term by requiring planners to consider food systems in all impact assessments. Apart from this individual change, Hazen et al. (2011) developed 95 proposed additions to the OP – additions that ranged from further

Fig. 5.1 Farming the front garden in Guelph, Ontario (Source: Author)

developing the Strategic Goals for the City under the headings of Economy, Community Infrastructure, Sustainability and Housing, to food system details under Environmental Impact Studies, Contaminated Properties, Field to Table to Field Energy Accounting, Climate Change, Cultural Heritage Resources, Community Facilities and so on. The room for integrating urban agriculture in particular (Fig. 5.1), and food systems thinking in general, is immense, as demonstrated by these imaginative young people. In response, the City planners have demonstrated a sincere interest in the proposal from Hazen et al. (2011). At the time of this writing, the revised OP has been submitted to the provincial Ministry of Municipal Affairs and Housing for final approval; one of the revisions to be approved includes the newly-added 'Strategic Goal: Planning a Complete and Healthy Community 1.g) To foster sustainable local food systems'; and 'Section 9.1.3 Urban Agriculture Objectives a) To encourage urban agriculture throughout the City in appropriate locations, b) To support a local food system including the cultivation of food within the urban environment' (City of Guelph 2012). This participatory action research demonstrated the effectiveness of linking knowledgeable students to a municipal policy project in order to assist time-pressed planners in writing policy that can enable more food production in our urban landscapes (Hayhurst, Dietrich-O'Connor, Hazen and Landman 2013).

Policy is an important piece, but so too is the need for revisioning built form that can elegantly accommodate urban agriculture in our cities. The discussion in North America has moved beyond whether urban agriculture should (re-)exist at all, to what sort of interesting and imaginative (if, at times, overly romantic) prototypes will be created to accommodate food production in a functional and aesthetic way. Gorgolewski et al. (2011) have provided a fascinating collection of built and proposed urban agriculture projects for a revisioning of the contemporary city in their charmingly entitled book, *Carrot City: Creating Places for Urban Agriculture*. Their book covers the range of scales that designers work at, from city-wide to neighbourhoods, to the home, and to details such as rooftop production, composting and greenhouses (see Chapter 6). While some of the work presented in *Carrot City* may be overly fanciful and could perhaps benefit from collaborative consultation with farmers, who know how to grow food, the book offers a resource to the education of architects, landscape architects, planners and engineers who have not fully grasped the potential for urban agriculture as a mainstream design and land-use consideration.

Perhaps one of the most interesting research projects on urban agriculture in the past decade, with regard to its potential for design and planning, is that of Viljoen's (2005) concept of 'Continuous Productive Urban Landscapes' (CPULs), which offers both 'a vision and a strategy' (Jac Smit in Viljoen 2005, Foreword) for shaping and living in urban landscapes. CPULs are open urban spaces that are strategically linked, combining agricultural and other landscape elements throughout the city landscape (Viljoen 2005). A productive urban landscape is 'open urban space planted and managed in such as way as to be environmentally and economically productive, for example, providing food from urban agriculture, pollution absorption, the cooling effect of trees or increased biodiversity from wildlife corridors' (Viljoen 2005; p. xviii). CPULs are also expected to contribute to social productivity by offering lifestyle advantages, particularly through well-connected walkable landscapes that are designed primarily for pedestrians and bicycles. Particularly important for CPULs is connecting urban agriculture, not only as we see it now through city farms, market gardens, residential gardens and community gardens, but also through the introduction of agricultural fields into the contemporary city. These spaces would also have high ecological value while hosting individual design strategies that reflect local history and sense of place (see commentary on Chapter 6).

Viljoen and Bohn (2009) furthered the research on CPULs by investigating the integration of urban agriculture in Cuba. The authors base their thinking on the notions of infrastructural urbanism, ecological footprint, and open space contributions to sustainable contemporary cities. Viljoen and Bohn selected ten urban agriculture sites for detailed investigation related to spatial qualities, function and perception, in order to develop design strategies in a more conscious way; urban agriculture had developed in Cuba in a very pragmatic way – sites were chosen largely for efficiency. The researchers found that the most important spatial and use variations were related to physical characteristics and to patterns of use and occupation; these included 'enclosure', 'multiple use', 'shared visual facility', 'linking device', 'sculptural quality', and 'incremental occupation' (Viljoen and Bohn 2009, p. 55) . The authors ask a very important question: [h]ow is urban agriculture perceived visually? Since urban agriculture, in North America especially, requires a cultural shift for general acceptance of urban agriculture as just another form of urban greening that needs to be developed, along with the very real commercial development it can offer. Viljoen and Bohn encourage more research on changing the cultural perception of urban agriculture as a 'non-urban land-use and of lesser beauty' (2009, p. 60).

Section 2: Urban Planning and Design

McPherson (2011), interested in the linkages between urban agriculture and sustainability for his landscape architecture graduate research project, developed a set of Urban Agriculture Design Principles with the aim of enhancing the environmental, social and economic potential of sites at both the site and community level. Aesthetics were especially of interest in his work, given that this is a value-added piece that landscape architects can bring to any design work (see Chapter 4). Due to the high level of public scrutiny, urban agriculture needs to be well designed and appropriately located in order to gain public acceptance and loyalty. McPherson (2011) makes the case that it is the role of both designers and planners to successfully integrate food production space and design elements with strong aesthetic considerations. Many landscape architecture firms are incorporating urban agriculture into their design agenda and are gaining recognition for their work from a design perspective; an example is Hoerr Schaudt Landscape Architects, who received an American Society of Landscape

Architecture Honor Award in 2010 for Rooftop Haven for Urban Agriculture, an innovative greenroof site for vegetable production and youth education. Others are using urban agriculture as a planning and design framework for communities, such as de la Salle and Holland's (2010) *Agricultural Urbanism: Handbook for Building Sustainable Food & Agriculture Systems in 21st Century Cities*. Mougeot (see Chapter 3) argues that urban agriculture must be critically interwoven with urban dynamics if it is to prosper in the city; integration, he tells us, is key, whether through physical planning and design, economic development or multi-functionality. Nordahl (see Chapter 2) demonstrates how this can be done through the creation of edible municipal gardens, street trees that provide orchard fruit, and the re-introduction of victory gardens. McPherson (2011) takes the subject of integration to a more detailed level through his encouragement to create learning centres, community kitchens, retrofitted industrial sites, and stormwater collection and nutrient cycling, to name a few strategies. Imbert (2010) urges designers to see the growing interest in North American urban agriculture as an opportunity to think about urban design in a new way. Indeed, while many view urban agriculture as a sustainable food-supply opportunity that aims to improve community health in many ways, others view these sites as unkempt weed patches (mis) managed by latter-day hippies, squatters and freeloaders. One powerful tool at the disposal of designers in building acceptance for and integration of food production sites is the ability to create beauty on these sites (see Chapter 4). McPherson (2011) suggests a number of possibilities in creating beautiful urban agriculture sites, including harmonizing site elements and the site with the surrounding context; creating pleasing views into and out of the site; creating a sense of order and readability on the site; and establishing attractive border plantings and entrances.

Integrating urban agriculture into our cities in a meaningful and sustainable way is a new challenge for North American urban municipalities, but there are some examples of planning for urban agriculture at the city-scale. The Kamloops Food Policy Council in British Columbia (BC) commissioned and subsequently released a 'Best Practices in Urban Agriculture' report (True Consulting Group, 2007) in preparation for the development of an urban agriculture strategy for the city (Fig. 5.2). The report draws from Canadian examples – from Vancouver, elsewhere in BC, Montreal, Ottawa, Toronto, Waterloo – and from outside Canada to

Fig. 5.2 Community garden, Kamloops BC (Source: Author)

provide a best practices summary on infrastructure, economic development, departmental and sector coordination, and land-use planning. The report recommends pursuing opportunities to expand current policies for urban agriculture purposes, including economic and social planning perspectives.

On April 15, 2011, the City of Minneapolis adopted the 'Urban Agriculture Policy Plan: A Land Use and Development Plan for a Healthy, Sustainable Local Food System', developed by the City's Community Planning and Economic Development Department as part of their sustainable growth plan, and a city-wide consultation process that began in December 2008. The newly-adopted plan has a series of recommendations that incorporate urban agriculture into 'Land Use and Zoning, Land Availability and Economic Development' (City of Minneapolis 2011).

The Urban Agriculture Policy Plan also provides suggested future efforts that include a re-assessment of the community garden program; marketing and branding opportunities for urban produce; the creation of an organization that can work on building partnerships between growers, processors and restaurants, and compost generation and growers; landbanking opportunities for property management and permanency; planning and education for healthy eating; linking growers to designers; and more coordinated composting.

Once supportive policy is in place, it will be necessary for municipal staff to have an inventory of soil conditions – not only for better understanding where the arable land is, but also for knowing of any contamination issues. The City of Minneapolis plan provides very limited information on this problem, apart from stating that 'transforming poor soils into areas fit for growing... can remediate past damage...' (2011, p. 53); and a recommendation on the called-for review of City-owned land to assure that 'soil testing has taken place on all City-owned lots used for community gardens' (2011, p. 60). However, the document does state that all existing community garden sites have had soil tests through the City's Groundwork Assessment Program (GAP), which 'facilitates environmental assessment for reuse of properties that benefit the community through greenspace, open space reuses and natural areas; affordable housing; recreational, education, community centers, day care centers; and other nonprofit facilities' and 'provides additional resources and technical assistance for nonprofit organizations to use for investigation and cleanup of contaminated sites' (GAP 2012). While other federal Groundwork initiatives began in 2002, Minneapolis's GAP claims to be unique in that it works with neighbourhood groups to meet neighbourhood needs.

Healthy, arable soil is fundamental to urban agriculture, at least if the project requires soil for production. Toronto's Public Health office has developed an urban soil testing protocol for the purpose of urban food production, in conjunction with the City's Parks, Forestry and Recreation Department and in consultation with the Toronto Environment Office. The goal for the Guide, as outlined in Soil Assessment Guide for New City Allotment and Community Gardens-Summary (Toronto Public Health 2011), is to encourage urban food production while minimizing unnecessary soil assessment and exposure-reduction measures, and to provide a flexible tool that is relatively inexpensive to use. The Guide aims to protect human health; to provide guidance on soil sampling, analysis and interpretation from an urban food production perspective; and to be flexible, easy and relatively inexpensive to implement. There are four steps: 1) establish the level of concern; 2) sample and test the soil if needed, 3) interpret the soil tests using soil screening values, and finally 4) mitigate the risks. Three levels of concern are established based on a site visit and site history research, as well as a three-tier system for reducing exposure to any possible contaminants. For the City of Toronto, brownfields are regulated by Ontario

Regulation 153/04 (updated in 2009, O. Reg. 511/09), under Part XV.1 of the Environmental Protection Act. During Step 1 of the Guide, it is recommended that the site should be assessed for whether there are any requirements for the site under these regulations. In addition to any provincial requirements, the Guide is intended to be used for all lands that the City may consider for gardening and food production.

Food Planning in Ontario

To raise awareness about the issues concerning urban agriculture, and food systems in general, the Ontario Professional Planning Institute (OPPI) held a symposium in 2010, entitled 'Healthy Communities and Planning for Food – a Harvest of Ideas,' which brought together a record number of urban and rural planners to discuss issues associated with creating and fostering healthy food systems. Before the symposium, the OPPI commissioned a survey of their 3,000 members on food systems, with the aim of reporting on the results at the symposium. The goal of the survey was to understand whether and how Ontario planners play a role in building healthy communities through community and regional food planning. Actual levels of involvement were reported at significantly lower than desired levels. For example, only 15% of respondents reported 'significant involvement' (12%) or 'top priority' (3%) given to community and regional food system issues; this contrasts sharply with the 61% who stated that they would like to have a high level of involvement. A shortage of resources, trained staff, lack of one's organization's intersection with food issues and political support were reported to be the primary reasons for low levels of involvement (InfoFeedback Survey Services Inc., 2010).

Both the symposium and the survey highlighted the fact that many planners are already involved in some form of planning for food systems but also that many more wish to be involved. After the symposium, the OPPI developed a 'call to action' for their membership, which included planning policy considerations for food systems in Community Sustainability Plans, Official Plans, secondary plans, zoning by-laws, and public health reports. OPPI asks planners to review local documents with a food systems lens, particularly planners who work at the provincial or municipal level. OPPI also identified a need for on-going research into agriculture and food systems to better understand complexity, interrelationships and processes (OPPI 2011).

Fig. 5.3 Fresh City Farms, tilling soil in Toronto (Source: Author)

Historically, food issues have been 'silo-ed' within ministries and departments; to a considerable extent, they still are. In Canada, formal policy for food and agriculture is typically dealt with at the federal and, more explicitly, provincial levels, but increasingly cities are developing strategies not only for access to fresh nutritious food but also to arable soils for the purpose of food production (Fig. 5.3). Toronto is considered to be a North American leader in effective policy creation, governance models, food access projects and capacity building for urban agriculture. In 2007, Toronto's Public Health department released a report entitled The State of Toronto's Food, which identified the complexity of food systems through a number of activities: production, processing, distribution, marketing, consumption, disposal and back to production. The report warned of a significant increase in food-related problems that include hunger, obesity, and chronic disease, and called for a coordinated and strategic approach. In June, 2008, the Toronto Board of Health directed the Medical Officer of Health to convene a panel of community food experts and senior City staff to develop a Toronto Food Strategy. Within the City, community organizations, city staff, councilors, private businesses and academics are working together to make these strategies a reality. In August 2012, an Urban Agriculture Summit was held in Toronto, with the aim of expanding already considerable networks, developing alliances, increasing political commitment and sharing experiences. There are many grassroots urban agriculture projects in the City; these networking events go a long way in creating a common vision and sharing resources. Toronto Public Health points to the opportunities for redesigning neighbourhoods; Toronto's Tower Renewal project, for example, sets out to modernize 1960s high rises while creating a stronger sense of community. There is an opportunity throughout this project for ground-floor food businesses, community gardens and farmers' markets. Community gardens are an especially useful way for creating more social cohesion while offering gardeners, especially new immigrants, access to a patch of arable soil to grow familiar vegetables and to meet neighbours.

TORONTO URBAN FARM

With the responsibility of managing conservation lands, Ontario's Conservation Authorities are looking for ways to make their urban lands relevant and accessible for adjacent neighbourhoods. The Greater Toronto Area is the most culturally and ethnically diverse region in all of Canada, with more than 50% of the population born in countries outside of Canada. In response to this demographic, the Toronto and Region Conservation Authority (TRCA) has developed a number of programs to engage this diverse population and to foster a stewardship ethic towards and love for Toronto's natural areas.

Fig. 5.4 Okra production on TRCA lands (Source: Author)

One TRCA program, the Living City (www.thelivingcity.org/), created the concept of a Toronto Urban Farm in 2002 through a partnership with the City of Toronto. The Farm sits on 3.2 hectares (8 acres) of TRCA-owned land which is located, arguably, in one of Toronto's most vulnerable and stigmatized communities. Farm programs engage youth and the broader community in organic farming, leadership development, environmental stewardship and health promotion. Services are provided through collaboration with the surrounding neighbourhood and with organizations from various sectors, such as social agencies, schools, faith groups, and businesses. Once the Farm concept was established, the TRCA turned over the land parcel to the City of Toronto's Community Gardens Program (CGP) within the Parks, Forestry and Recreation Division under a Management Agreement. The Toronto Urban Farm operates as an extension of the CGP's Rockcliffe Demonstration and Teaching Garden, which offers multiple services that support community gardening and urban agriculture city-wide, such as the demonstration of management practices in urban agriculture, heirloom vegetable seedling production, youth and adult training in organic food production, and children's gardening (Fig. 5.4).

The objectives of the Farm help to fulfill Toronto City Council's mandate to promote urban agriculture and create local food production pilot projects. It also fulfills TRCA's commitment to the Sustainability Round Table under its Living City vision by means of:

> Increasing participants' knowledge and skills concerning food production
>
> Providing youth employment and leadership training
>
> Building community capacity to address local food security issues
>
> Promoting healthy nutrition and active lifestyles

Like many other historic urban farms, which were usually rural until surrounded by urban development, the Toronto Urban Farm also has some heritage features that have survived. Braeburn House is a heritage stone house, built by John Grubb in 1853. The house was moved to the current site in 1962, stone by stone, when threatened by demolition, and is now used as a training facility with offices and storage space, which allows for continued use of the building while maintaining its architectural heritage value for the community.

SECTION 3: URBAN FARMS

Urban farms are either non-profit or for-profit operations, with some hybridity between the two types. In improving their own practices, urban farmers are also increasingly networking across cities, regionally and internationally. In May 2011, an internationally-focused conference, Urban Agriculture for Resilient Cities: Lessons Learned in Policy, Research and Practice, was held in Almere, Netherlands, to mark the 10th anniversary of the RUAF Foundation (Resource Centres on Urban Agriculture and Food Security). The conference presentations were largely focused on research in developing countries, where urban agriculture is widely practiced and on which researchers have published a great deal of analysis. The pattern in North America for urban agriculture conferences tends to first draw from NGOs and entrepreneurs who are working from the ground up, with a smattering of researchers. In August 2012, the Toronto Urban Agriculture Summit brought together NGOs and entrepreneurs to learn from each other through workshops, demonstrations and tours; the theme of the conference was 'building capacity for action', and was an opportunity for those working on the frontline of urban agriculture to share knowledge, skills and experience.

One of the most productive North American NGOs in building capacity is Growing Power (Fig. 5.5), a national organization headquartered on Silver Spring Drive in Milwaukee that is dedicated to supporting the development and sustainability of community-based food systems; its stated goal is 'to grow food, to grow minds, and to grow community.' The founder, Will Allen, was recognized in *Time Magazine*'s '100 most influential people' list in 2010, and in 2008 was awarded the prestigious McArthur Foundation 'genius award.' Allen is under such demand for explaining and disseminating his vision that the Growing Power website has a press kit as a first stop for the many people interested in emulating Growing Power's goal. But even Growing Power needs help with funding; Allen admits that '[to] survive as a nonprofit these days, we have to grow some of our own money, instead of just writing for grants' (McNally 2010). Growing Power attempts to do this through workshops, lectures, sales of soil and compost, wholesale and retail sales of fish and produce, and publications. Sales of delicate salad greens to city restaurants is especially profitable.

Research on small-scale agriculture has shown that the production of, especially, fresh fruits and vegetables to the local market can create

Fig. 5.5 Growing Power, Milwaukee WI (Source: Author)

significant job growth and local economic improvements (O'Hara 2011), while food-miles-related emissions on various agriculture and food commodities is believed to be highest for fruits and vegetables (Kissinger 2012). In an investigation of the job creation potential for urban agriculture in Greater Boston, the Conservation Law Foundation (2012) estimates that at least 130 to 200 direct farming jobs could be generated through 50 acres of urban agriculture; with an estimate of potentially 800 arable acres of land in Greater Boston, if put into production this could create at least 2,080 on-farm jobs and an additional 1,200 jobs in supporting businesses. Nasr et al. (2010) found that the supply of land is not an insurmountable barrier to urban agriculture, at least in Toronto. However, a number of less-evident barriers impact this supply of land: 'taxation systems and government structures based on the assumption that agriculture is a rural activity only; the need for knowledge sharing among those involved in urban agriculture; and the dearth of incentives to attract landowners and foundations to provide financial or in-kind support' (Nasr et al. 2010, p.7). While cautioning that the share of production for urban agriculture is currently very low, Zezza and Tasciotti (2010) have found, in a sample of developing countries, that there is a positive correlation between engagement in urban agriculture and dietary adequacy indicators. Profit, then, is not the only motivator; improved levels of public health is a productive contribution to society as well.

In comparing the pros and cons of non-profit versus for-profit urban agriculture, the Rodale Institute interviewed representatives from both types of urban farm (www.rodaleinstitute.org). For success, relationships and performance (i.e. quality and price) are seen as the foundation in a for-profit context, while community development and engagement was the measure of success used in the non-profit context. Both farm types need soil, seeds and water, and motivated and hard-working staff, as well as markets, however.

Greensgrow Farms in Philadelphia is a for-profit farm and winner of the Greater Philadelphia Chamber of Commerce's 2011 Sustainable Business of the Year award, and winner of the 2012 Sustainable Agriculture Leadership Award from The Pennsylvania Association for Sustainable Agriculture. Today, Greensgrow Farms is made up of a plant nursery, a farm stand and a 600-member Community Supported Agriculture program, located on one acre in Philadelphia's Kensington neighborhood, the former site of a galvanized steel plant. In 2009, Greensgrow reported over $1 million income, and currently employs 20 people. Greensgrow began in 1997, and continues to develop its for-profit mission, which today includes lessons in composting, hydroponic growing and beekeeping. Since 2007, they have generated their own biodiesel from restaurant waste oil (www.greensgrow.org).

Greensgrow is an excellent example of the potential for urban agriculture to reactivate dormant brownfield spaces in our cities. A newer urban farm venture, Stone's Throw Urban Farm has leased 18 vacant lots in Minneapolis and St Paul, having recently signed lease agreements with the landowners. Their goal is to make enough profit so that full-time employees can make a living. They are currently providing vegetables to 100 CSA shareholders. Stone's Throw successfully launched a Kickstarter campaign to raise investment funding for an additional 10 lots. But not every urban farmer needs to target brownfields for production; small plot intensive (SPIN) farming is another example of creative land-access. Wally Satzewich and Gail Vandersteen, owners of Wally's Urban Market Garden, started farming on a 20-acre farm outside of Saskatoon, Saskatchewan (Fig. 5.6). They experienced a number of challenges: late spring and early fall frosts, wildlife browsing, fluctuating water supply during dry spells, and labour shortages. They decided to move into the city, gaining access to residential backyards with fertile soil through an agreement with the owners. Their growing area

Fig. 5.6 SPIN farm plot, Saskatoon SK (Source: Author)

totaled just over a half acre, what Wally calls 'sub-acre' farming (http://spinfarming.com). They gained an extended growing season due to the urban heat effect, access to municipal water supply, greatly reduced damage from wildlife, and a ready market at the Saskatoon Farmers' Market. Wally and Gail have meticulously documented how to intensively manage a sub-acre farm in order to gain the highest returns possible and, with their skills in marketing, have proven that one can make a reasonable living. Very low investment upfront (no land or large-scale equipment to buy), minimal mechanization (their work is largely hand labour) and maximum fiscal discipline and planning have led Wally and Gail to world-wide renown for their SPIN techniques. They also provide learning guides on SPIN farming basics, work-flow practices, marketing and the development of specialized crops, leading to the creation of other SPIN farmers across North America. Green City Acres is spin-off SPIN enterprise in Kelowna, BC, where Curtis Stone farms 0.75 acres over 8 plots throughout central Kelowna. In exchange for their land, the homeowners receive a weekly box of vegetables during the growing season. Green City Acres is entirely pedal powered; bicycles and custom built trailers serve all transportation needs, including fresh produce deliveries to restaurants and the farmers market, as well as the transport of compost and equipment (www.greencityacres.com). In the second year of production, Green City Acres achieved over $65,000 in sales (EcoFriendly Sask).

A much more technologically-intensive example, Lufa Farms in Montreal has taken a lofty approach by developing a 31,000 square foot controlled-environment greenhouse on the roof an office building, in which they produce over 25 varieties of vegetables. Billed as an urban agriculture prototype, Lufa Farms offers several weekly-basket options and deliver to a group drop-off location; for seniors or the disabled, home deliveries are a possibility for a small fee. Founded by Mohamed Hage, the prototype design was developed through the input of engineers, architects, plant scientists, and farming experts. The goals of Lufa Farms are to demonstrate that urban rooftop agriculture is more than a possibility, to build more rooftop farms, and to evolve research and development. Their claim is that these rooftop farms will bring land lost to urban development back to farming; help reduce the urban heat island effect; minimize the distance, time and handling of food between the producer and the consumer; and engage the consumer in a relationship with a local farm (https://lufa.com/en).

Visser Farms in Edmonton (Fig. 5.7) offers a more traditional model of what one might expect a farm to be. Arguably the best farm in Alberta for microclimate and soil quality, Visser Farms is surrounded by development and experiences all the pressures that any farm might in that context. The family has been growing potatoes, particularly seed potatoes, for three generations. Located along the North Saskatchewan River, which provides the farm with a climate-tempering effect, the Visser family is able to achieve a high yield and quality as a result of what is referred to as 'northern vigour'. Potato crops grown from northern seed produce more vigorous plants, resulting in even crop development, higher yield, and superior grades (www4.agr.gc.ca). Visser Farms is an example of a farm in an urban context that produces a high quality product that has not only local but export market significance; indeed, they export their potato seed as far away as Thailand. In order to draw attention to the importance of this and other valuable agricultural lands under threat of development, the Greater Edmonton Alliance (GEA), an advocacy group, organized a Great Potato Giveaway in September, 2009, with the Edmonton Potato Growers and the Visser family. The giveaway offered 23 kilograms of free potatoes for the picking, to anyone who showed up to glean potatoes that were newly surfaced by a mechanical harvester. On the day of the harvest, the demand was so strong that gleaners formed a two-hour and kilometers-long traffic

Fig. 5.7 Visser Farms, Edmonton AB (Source: Author)

jam, exceeding the greatest hopes of the GEA and the Visser family. The GEA had made proposed amendments to the city's development plan, including an assessment of the impact on local food production in all development decisions (Drake and Sands 2009). Since the potato giveaway, this and other efforts have brought Edmonton to the fore in developing a city-wide food and agriculture strategy by collaborating with citizens, community organizations, businesses and other stakeholders. The City now maintains a Food and Agriculture Blog, has conducted a series of focus groups on this subject, and has hosted a May 2012 Food in the City Conference (City of Edmonton 2012).

Zenger Farms in Portland, Oregon, (Fig. 5.8) is another farm that has survived despite the pressures of urban development. The land was originally settled by Jacob Johnson in the 19th century as part of a 320-acre homestead; Johnson's sawmill business supplied much of the lumber for Portland's homes at the time. Eventually, the land was purchased by Ulrich Zenger in 1913, who operated a dairy farm. Zenger's son, Ulrich Zenger Jr., inherited the farm in 1954. Zenger Jr. wished to leave the land in agriculture and explored ways to do that. In 1994, five years after Zenger Jr.'s death, the land was purchased by the City of Portland's Bureau of Environmental Services (BES); the farm was strategically located for the purpose of BES work on environmental stewardship, conservation and storm water

Fig. 5.8 Zenger Farm, Portland OR (Source: Author)

management for Johnson Creek. In 1995, Urban Bounty Farm leased the farmland for cultivation purposes but also for educational and community events, forming partnerships with the Environmental Middle School and the Portland State University Capstone Program, among others, to offer the farm as an open-air classroom on organic agriculture and land stewardship for urban students and nearby residents. This expanded role led to the establishment of the Friends of Zenger Farm, an organization that developed the Zenger Farm Master Plan, and partnered with the BES to secure a 50-year lease. Friends of Zenger Farm in now a non-profit farm and wetland that promotes sustainable food systems, environmental stewardship and local economic development through a working urban farm (www.zengerfarm.org).

In Ontario, Canada, FarmStart is a not-for-profit organization that is focused on the creation of new farmers, for whom land tenure is also an issue. In response to the dwindling numbers of farmers in the province, FarmStart, founded by the dynamic Christie Young, was formed in 2005 to support and encourage a new generation of farmers to develop locally-based, ecologically-sound, and economically-viable agricultural enterprises (http://www.trca.on.ca/the-living-city). In 2008, the Toronto Region Conservation Authority (TRCA) leased 15 hectares to FarmStart on a renewable-lease basis at the McVean Farm; the farm now hosts The McVean

Incubator Farm project, which provides prospective farmers access to land, equipment, infrastructure and mentorship during the first five years of their farm business start-up (Fig. 5.9). Many of the farmers who come to try their luck and skill are new immigrants, with as many as 17 countries represented at the site at any time. The TRCA offers infrastructure support by providing fencing, irrigation and storage facilities, as well as access to the heritage-designated barn. The project is modeled on the successful Intervale Farms Program in Burlington, Vermont and FarmStart's first incubator farm project at the Ignatius Farm in Guelph, Ontario (www.farmstart.ca/). FarmStart takes care of acquiring the land, provides critical on-site infrastructure and equipment, and supports the farmers in their business planning, production and marketing. Through one-on-one consultation, courses and workshops they provide access to mentors, business development and production advice and resources, technical training and farm succession support. The farmers cooperate by sharing equipment and markets as well as growing techniques and experiences, all of which contribute to their learning and success in farming (www.farmstart.ca/).

Based on the 2007 census, about half of Greater Toronto's population

Fig. 5.9 Open house tour of McVean Farm, Toronto ON (Source: Author)

(2.3 million people) was born outside of Canada, creating a large market opportunity for so-called ethno-cultural foods. Although the Ontario agricultural community is beginning to make local connections to some of these ethno-cultural markets, it has been suggested that any current peri-urban farmers do not have knowledge or understanding of these market demands, and there are often financial, structural and cultural factors that affect a farmer's ability to diversify and take risks on new products. For farmers who may be interested in trying new crops that are clearly in high demand, the microclimate and intensive cultivation for South Asian, African and Latin American vegetables that are sought by the residents of the Greater Toronto Area often pose many challenges. However, as seen with the SPIN farm model, microclimate advantage and intensive-cultivation opportunities are certainly to be found in the urban landscape.

Ontario's FarmStart recently launched the Landmark Start-Up Farm near Hamilton, which is a landmark for FarmStart and the Start-Up Farm concept in many ways; this is the first time a Start-Up Farm will be established on privately owned farmland. It is also the first Start-Up Farm in Ontario outside of the Greater Toronto Area and is surrounded by working farmland. The Landmark Farm is 50 acres, will have two farm enterprises initiating their operations, and will serve aspiring new farmers from the Hamilton, Ancaster, Burlington and Flamborough regions (www.farmstart.ca). A particularly-innovative organization, FarmStart was chosen in 2011 as one of Tides Canada's Top Ten; Tides Canada selects and honors organizations which build innovative solutions to complex social and environmental issues.

Section 4: Student Farms

Being successful in farming requires a great deal of knowledge and experience, and a complex set of skills. One may romanticize about going back to the land and becoming a farmer, but it takes years of learning and apprenticeship to be successful at it. Given that less than 2% of the population is actively farming, how do we train and educate young people who want to take up this profession? Fortunately, in North America there is a long tradition of student farms that can provide the necessary learning environment.

BEREA COLLEGE – THE GARDENS AND GREENHOUSE

Berea College, Kentucky, is one of the oldest continually-operating student farms in the United States, founded by abolitionists in 1855. The College's website provides a brief history of the student farms, with the first garden established in 1871. By 1927, twenty-five students were employed by the farm in fruit and vegetable production. By 1998, the horticultural cultivation component of the College, referred to as the Gardens and Greenhouse, transitioned to organic management and began composting food waste from the College food service. Currently, the agricultural and horticultural efforts at Berea are comprised of about five hundred acres; approximately 90% is used for livestock and crop production, with twelve acres in horticultural crops. The Gardens and Greenhouse enterprises include the production and sales of salad greens, herbs, perennials, annuals, honey, and mushrooms. The greens are sold locally during the fall and spring through wholesale and retail marketing, while the other products are sold through direct marketing with local delivery and seasonal farmers markets (Berea College, 2012).

UNIVERSITY OF GUELPH – THE GUELPH CENTRE FOR URBAN ORGANIC FARMING

The University of Guelph has its roots in agricultural training for Ontario's farmers. In 1874, the Ontario School of Agriculture first opened its doors and by 1880 the name of the institution was changed to the Ontario Agricultural College (OAC) and Experimental Farm. At the time it was part of the University of Toronto. In 1965 an act passed by the Government of Ontario brought together OAC and two other colleges - the Macdonald Institute (a school for home economists and nutritionists) and the Ontario Veterinary College – to create the University of Guelph, which has now grown to seven colleges. The University has three regional campuses – two in eastern Ontario and one in southwestern Ontario; all teach agriculture and conduct applied research throughout the province. The city has grown around the main campus, resulting in food production and trial fields being pushed out into the rural landscape. However, the recent establishment of a BSc degree in Organic Agriculture led to the need for undergraduate students to gain practical skills in vegetable production on

Fig. 5.10 Guelph Centre for Urban Organic Farming, University of Guelph
(Source: Author)

the main campus, resulting in the Guelph Centre for Urban Organic Farming (GCUOF) which was established in 2008 at a 2.5 hectare site at The Arboretum for the purpose of organic vegetable production training (Fig. 5.10). As with other student farms of this nature (as opposed to the large-scale experimental farms), the GCUOF is an outdoor classroom for students who take vegetable production and soil science courses, but it is linked to many community groups. Young children from the on-campus Childcare and Learning Centre make regular visits throughout the season and enjoy seeding, planting and harvesting quick-growing crops such as radishes and lettuce. The University's School of Hospitality, Tourism and Management provides a Garden2Table program to a local primary school, giving students the opportunity to plant, sample, harvest, cook and eat from GCUOF's vegetable beds. In the first summer, GCUOF benefited from 4,000 volunteer hours from people in the city of Guelph. In 2011, eight University of Southern Mississippi students paid a visit to the GCUOF as part of a group of students participating in a sustainability-themed exchange program with the University of Guelph. Martha Gay Scroggins, the GCUOF's co-ordinator, states that the attention and participation from the University, the city and beyond is 'the real growth factor' at work on this student farm (www.uoguelph.ca/gcuof/).

The last decade has seen an increase in the 'old pedagogical idea of finding ways to combine liberal arts undergraduate education with hands-on, practical farming and gardening experience' (Sayre, in Sayre and Clark, 2011: 1). Frederick Kirschenmann – Leopold Center Distinguished Fellow, Professor in Philosophy and Religious Studies at Iowa State University, and farmer – argues that we need to begin to imagine new farming systems that are more knowledge-intensive and that are managed by farmers who are educated in resilient, interactive ecological operations. And we need consumers who understand the challenges and full cost of growing food. Farmers who have the skills to deal with expensive, declining energy; ecological degradation; unpredictable and widely varying climate; and decreasing water supplies will be needed in great supply. Kirschenmann argues that student farms 'can play a major role in supplying the intellectual capital for this revolution in agriculture' (in Sayre and Clark, 2001, p. xvi).

UNIVERSITY OF CALIFORNIA, DAVIS – STUDENT FARM

Davis is located approximately 110 kilometers northeast of San Francisco, in the Sacramento Valley, the northern portion of the Central Valley, with a population of about 66,000. The University of California, Davis, is a teaching and research institution, established in 1905; the campus is the largest within the University of California system with the third largest enrollment. UC Davis is ranked as one of the top 10 public universities in the United States, and has very high research activity. The campus was originally established as the University Farm, part of the agricultural extension of UC Berkeley. The location has a Mediterranean climate of dry, hot summers and cool, rainy, winters typical of the Central Valley.

The Student Farm has its origins in the student movements of the 1960s and early 70s that were focused on environmental, social and political issues. Several students worked with supportive faculty and others to address these issues, organizing a conference in 1973 to critique land-grant university research priorities and their social impacts. By 1975, students offered a course entitled 'Seminar on Alternatives in Agriculture', and by 1976 pressure was increasing for significant program changes. A group of

Fig. 5.11 University of California, Davis – Student Farm (Source: Author)

students developed a proposal to create the Agricultural Alternatives Development Program and a Student Experimental Farm (SEF). The Dean approved the proposal and assigned more than twenty acres of university farmland to the SEF, and gave the proposed program a budget and some operating funds (Van Horn, in Sayre and Clark 2012). The site had useful buildings, greenhouses, irrigation, and remnants of olive, fig and almond orchards. It was less than a ten-minute bike ride from the centre of campus and next to a six acre community garden (Fig. 5.11).

Van Horn (in Sayre and Clark 2012) has written a detailed and interesting history of the student farm, chronicling the research, collaboration and learning that has been accommodated at the SEF since the 1970s. While work at the SEF was discouraged or ignored by some faculty, the work of students, under rigorous guidance of participating faculty, has resulted in improved farming practices for organic and ecologically-oriented farmers. A significant effort to develop a program major focused on sustainable agriculture began in 2004. The major is based on seven principles which focus on: 'interdisciplinary breadth, systems thinking, skill development, experiential learning, linking the real world with the classroom, community building and adaptive curriculum management' (Van Horn, in Sayre and Clark 2012). The SEF, now named the Student

Farm (SF) continues to play an important role as a field-based laboratory and for other class activities in at least three of the core courses, and as a site for internships and research projects.

UNIVERSITY OF OREGON – THE URBAN FARM

Eugene is home to the University of Oregon and has a population of approximately 160,000. Lying in the Willamette Valley, it has a Marine West Coast climate with warm, dry summers and mild, wet winters. Spring and fall are drizzly moist seasons, and winter offers only sporadic snowfall. Eugene is known for its community activism. Student protests in the 1970s led to the University of Oregon's participatory planning process, known as 'The Oregon Experiment' (1975) – devised by Christopher Alexander and collaborators. The process is still used by the University in a modified form, and played a somewhat pivotal role for the Urban Farm on campus. The University is built on what was once farmland; in 1974 Richard Britz, an instructor in landscape architecture, named a student garden plot on Class 1 soil The Urban Farm, rather a visionary name for the 1970s. Britz believed that growing food was a first step to building sustainable communities (Bettman, in Sayre and Clark, 2012), and he taught an urban farm class in addition to his regular teaching responsibilities. After Britz left the University in 1981, the Urban Farm languished for a while.

Fig. 5.12 University of Oregon Urban Farm (Source: Author)

In 1983, landscape architecture professor Ann Bettman took up the cause. She attributes the relative lack of enthusiasm from students and faculty at the time to the pro-business Reagan era and found that she spent much of the 1980s defending the farm from becoming a building site. But it was not long before more of the site was built upon, piece by piece, which is typically how we lose our prime farmland – incrementally, over time, until the cumulative effect is so overwhelming that no-one seems capable of saving the last remnants.

However, the 1990s saw a resurgence of student interest in food and the environment. The 0.6 hectare site (Fig. 5.12) became the focus of a master plan class project for landscape architecture students. Bettman worked as director and the Urban Farm became an outdoor classroom for 80 students and six team leaders. In the fall of 2007, Harper Keeler took over the directorship. Currently, the facilities include 100 raised beds, a greenhouse/toolshed, 60 semi-dwarf fruit trees, a composting area, some beehives and a plastic hoophouse. Bettman (in Sayre and Clark 2012) states that it is necessary from time-to-time to remind administrators that the farm is a classroom and requires investment and repair as with any other university facility.

The Urban Farm class is offered through the Department of Landscape Architecture, the only landscape architecture faculty in North America that has a farm specifically for teaching design. Students attending class are from programs across campus, however. The class also takes tours of nearby farms and participates in planting and harvesting at some of them. The Urban Farm also promotes school gardens in the greater community, and participates in the training of teachers who are interested in having a school garden. In 2008, the Department received an endowment which will provide stable funding for the Urban Farm into the foreseeable future.

The University of Oregon's Urban Farm is beautiful and it is clear role that the landscape architecture faculty and students play in making it that way. Space is given for solitary contemplation and for large group gatherings. There are sunny spots and shady spots, and the planting design was thoughtful and charming. It is an inspiration for how lovely a place of food production and learning can be.

Evergreen State College Organic Farm

Evergreen is a progressive, public liberal arts and sciences college, founded in the late 1960s as an experimental and non-traditional college. Known for

Fig. 5.13 Evergreen State College Farm Composting Facility (Source: Author)

its innovative interdisciplinary, collaborative and team-taught academic programs, the focus is on teaching rather than research; there are approximately 4800 students. Evergreen is in the small city of Olympia, the capital of the state of Washington. Located at the southern end of Puget Sound, the climate of Olympia and its environs is characterized as Marine West Coast. Most of this part of Washington's weather is brought in by weather systems that form near the Aleutian Islands in Alaska, resulting in considerable rain, cloud and fog.

From the main campus, one finds the farm by following a path for a fifteen-minute walk through the lush west coast woody growth – Douglas fir, western red cedar, and fir, with salal and huge sword ferns as undergrowth. The farmstead has the feeling of a quiet clearing in the green, green forest, but it is clearly a busy site, with compost piles, outbuildings, hoophouses, tidy rows of vegetables, a permaculture garden and equipment sheds (Fig. 5.13).

The organic farm was founded in 1972, inspired by the back-to-the-land movement of the time. A derelict farmstead on Lewis Road, on the periphery of the campus, was the focus of environmental design students' efforts in creating a farm proposal for the Board of Regents. The old farmstead is now a five-acre farm that serves the students and faculty as a site for learning both theory and praxis.

The structure of the programs taught at the farm are modeled on Evergreen's learning contracts, where students propose an independent study that is then overseen by faculty; the original farm-development plan was organized as a group learning contract overseen by a faculty member. There are currently three agriculture and food system programs that make use of the farm as a learning grounds. The Practice of Sustainable Agriculture (PSA) program integrates theoretical and applied aspects of small-scale organic farming. Each week there are eight hours of classroom instruction and twenty hours of hands-on work at Evergreen's Organic Farm. It is the PSA program students who do the bulk of the work at the farm; one faculty member works with the farm manager, several paid student employees and approximately twenty-five student farmers. Ecological Agriculture is a nine-month, team-taught program that looks beyond the site to the ecological scale. Emphasis is on 'hands-on activities including field trips, labs and field experiments, as well as systems thinking, expository and scientific report writing, library research and quantitative reasoning skills' (www.ifoam.org). Finally, the Food, Health and Sustainability program looks broadly at food systems, but also at the biological molecular level in order to gain an understanding of food quality, nutrition and health. Students conduct experiments in the lab and in the farm kitchen to learn the scientific principles of food preparation. Graduating students go on to create their own farms, work in agricultural policy, or contribute in other ways to food systems in western Washington.

The Evergreen Organic Farm employs a farm manager, and faculty oversee program delivery. Maintenance of the farm's buildings, partial payment of utilities, and staff and faculty time are paid for by the College. Day-to-day production derives funding from farm sales to campus cafeterias, a student-run cafe, a campus farm stand, the twenty-share CSA, and on-farm sales. Regular contributions are made to the local food bank. The farm also has a one-day Harvest Festival in October that features tours, music, children's activities and educational exhibits.

University of British Columbia – UBC Farm

Vancouver is on Canada's west coast. It's a city of approximately 600,000 people, but the metropolitan area has about 2.3 million. The summer months are typically dry, with precipitation occurring only one in five days during July and August. However, it rains and sometimes snows during

Fig. 5.14 University of British Columbia Student Farm (Source: Author)

nearly half the days from November through March, with a Marine West Coast climate.

The University of British Columbia (UBC) was founded in 1908. The main campus is only 30 minutes from downtown Vancouver and currently has an enrollment of 46,000 students. UBC founders believed the future for the province was in agriculture and, after a province-wide survey, they selected Point Grey as the site of the university farm, seven miles to the west of downtown Vancouver (www.library.ubc.ca/archives). By 1922, agricultural fields had been cleared and cultivated, and extensive research was underway. By the end of WWII, the university was moving into its largest expansion to accommodate the growing student body. The farmland was greatly reduced due to parking lots, playing fields and student residences, and agricultural research was relegated to the outer parts of the south campus. Since much of the south campus was treed at the time, each discipline carved out research space in the forest. The soils required substantial preparation, as much of it was acidic, nutrient-poor, gravelly glacial till. The Department of Plant Science worked on improving the growing conditions through drainage tile, irrigation, rock-picking and cover-cropping. However, by 1969 UBC moved from training farmers to training scientists, and agricultural research funding was directed to federal experimental stations.

By 1997, the University's Official Community Plan designated the farm buildings as 'housing reserve', and the fields as 'future housing reserve'. That same year a new Dean of Agricultural Sciences – Professor Moura Quayle from the Landscape Architecture Program – was appointed and the Faculty was reorganized as a non-departmentalized Faculty, eventually becoming the Faculty of Land and Food Systems (www.landfood.ubc.ca/about/faculty-history). In the process, there was a renewed interest in maintaining an agricultural element in an increasingly-developing urban matrix. Students, faculty and staff developed a vision paper, entitled 'Re-Inventing the UBC Farm: Urban Agriculture and Forestry on the Point Grey Campus'. Students and faculty engaged in the long-term planning process for UBC in order to hold their ground. A Friends of the Farm was formed, which focused its energy on outreach, building support for the Farm beyond the campus. A visioning workshop drew together UBC alumni, and others, and resulted in the production of plans, sketches, and objectives. On April 7, 2009, UBC's president unveiled a new permanent sign at the farm gates.

Today, the 24-hectare UBC Farm (Figs. 5.14, 5.13) is operated as an academic facility under the management of the Centre for Sustainable Food Systems, a subunit within the Faculty of Land and Food Systems. The Center is currently run by a program coordinator. In-house staff at UBC Farm includes three full-time and two part-time staff, five contract

Fig. 5.15 UBC Student Farm Children's Garden (Source: Author)

employees and seventeen seasonally-paid student employees. There are many researchers, apprentices, course-based students, children, volunteers and visitors. On the day I arrived at the UBC Farm, staff were busily harvesting and preparing vegetables for the farmgate sales that were to take place the next morning. Day-camp children were excitedly setting a table under the trees to dine al fresco on the pizza they had just baked in the outdoor oven, after harvesting vegetables and herbs from their pizza garden. Chickens had just been released on a fully harvested bed, and were madly digging up and enjoying what insects and worms they could find.

The UBC Farm has adopted the motto 'no one thing does just one thing'. In 2008, students in 50 courses, coming from eight faculties, used the Farm in 2008 for integrative and co-curricular learning. Class topics include climate change, community health, food security and ecosystem services. On-site research includes biofuels, animal welfare, soil conservation, and immunology of bees. In 2009, the UBC Board of Governors received a new academic plan for the south campus, entitled 'Cultivating Place: An Academic Plan for Applied Sustainability on South Campus and Beyond'. Given the vulnerability of student farms to development pressure, particularly from their home institutions, the plan is an optimistic but determined vision for the future of the UBC Farm.

SECTION 5: COMMUNITY GARDENS

Community gardens have their roots in the allotment garden movement in Europe. In England, the 16th-18th century closing of common lands, the movement of labour into the cities during the Industrial Revolution, and the need for both food and respite from urban life led to the creation of these gardens. In 1887, an Act of Parliament obliged municipalities to provide access to allotment grounds where there was a demand. In 1908, Parliament passed the Small Holdings and Allotments Act, which is still in force (Taylor, 2006). The National Society of Allotment & Leisure Gardeners Limited was established as a co-operative in 1901; is owned, managed and funded by its members to protect, promote and preserve allotments for future generations to enjoy; and employs a full time in-house legal consultant in order to represent the rights of allotment gardeners in the UK. This co-operative is recognized by the government during any official consultation process relating to the possible disposal of statutory allotment land.

In the Netherlands, the Bond van Volkstuinders (the Federation of Allotment Gardeners) is an association of 29 parks with 6000 allotment gardens in and around Amsterdam. These sites are seen as active recreation parks, and are all about the work and pleasure of gardening. The group declares on its website that 'the work is not only limited to your own garden, but extends to the entire area of the garden park', making it very clear that the volkstuin (people's garden) is a communal as well as individual venture. While the Bond van Volkstuinders opposes removal or relocation of allotments, there is also a stated sense of obligation to the greater good beyond their membership, in that these spaces may be required for other purposes.

While not always as well developed or as historical as allotment gardens in Europe, community gardens are found throughout North America on public or private lands, in the urban core to the peri-urban landscape. The North American community garden has its origins in the beginning of the 20th century, and escalated in numbers as the Victory gardens of the First World War were developed. However, the American Community Garden Association, a bi-national non-profit, was founded as late as 1979. The Mission of the ACGA, as stated on their website, is 'to build community by increasing and enhancing community gardening and greening across the United States and Canada' (www.communitygarden.org/).

Community gardens across the United States and Canada may be tended communally but are more typically divided into smaller plots for individual use. The fruits, vegetables and flowers grown are usually for home consumption and for sharing with extended family and friends. Occasionally, there may even be some income generated in community gardens, to supplement the cost of communal needs, such as tools, irrigation supplies and seeds, or the income may be for personal gain, such as through the sale of herbs or flowers. Increasingly these gardens contribute to nearby food banks through the Grow-a-Row program, which had its beginnings in Winnipeg in 1986 (www.growarow.org).

There is a large body of literature that examines the role of community gardens and allotments in providing a meaningful measure of food security and improved nutrition, particularly in developing countries (see Chapter 3). Cuba is often used as an example of the benefits that accrue when urban gardeners are given space for self-provision gardens; it is estimated that Havana had over 26,000 such gardens during the 'special period' – the time when Soviet aid and trade were radically curtailed in 1989 (Moskow 1999); the pressure for increased local food production in Havana generated meaningful innovation in turning green space into production space.

There is also a developing body of literature on developed countries that connects community gardens to urban sustainability (Holland 2004), to community development (Hancock 2001; Saldivar-Tanaka and Krasny 2004; Glover et al. 2005) and to increased health for urban citizens (Dickinson et al. 2003; Wakefield et al. 2007). There is an expanding network of community gardens in North America, with various goals and strategies; many gardens have been developed as a response to poverty, food deserts, and the lack of culturally-familiar foods; environmental degradation; concerns with food safety (Holland 2004); and the need for 'participatory landscapes' (Saldivar-Tanaka and Krasny 2004), where citizens can meet, engage with each other, and organize for a common social or cultural goal (Glover et al. 2005) (Fig. 5.16).

Holland (2004) researched the contribution to local sustainability made by community gardens and city farms in the UK; the two forms of urban agriculture were lumped together since both are eligible for membership in the Federation of City Farms and Community Gardens Association, an

Fig. 5.16 Seattle P-Patch Community Garden – Work Bee Planning (Source: Author)

organization that requires common management strategies, regardless of type. Holland examined the city farms and gardens as they pertained to the local approach to policy integration as framed in Local Agenda 21 (1992), which encouraged us all to 'think globally, act locally'. Holland asked: 'Can the model of community gardens inform the development, progress and expansion of local sustainability?' (2004: 291). The hypothesis was that community gardening may provide an example of sustainability already at work at the local level and an opportunity to reveal practices from which we can learn and that we can translate to other aspects of our lives. Holland found that the 'locality' effect is an important element, in that the nature of the diversity and connections that form due to participation in a community garden is dependent on local conditions and influences and 'insider knowledge is vital if the scheme is to be a success in terms of access and participation' (2004: 303). Holland's results demonstrated that there were many purposes for the community gardens that relate more to their function in community development than strictly food production. The weakest pillar of sustainability was that of economic development; Holland urges communities to consider carefully the economic benefits that community gardening can deliver.

Hancock (2001) has made the case that community gardens do deliver social and natural capital and can deliver on economic development if the approach taken is that of primarily generating human capital, which, he argues, will then lead to increased economic, natural, and social capital. Hancock defines human capital as 'healthy, well educated, skilled, innovative and creative people who are engaged in their communities and participate in governance' (2001: 275). Glover et al. (2005) set out to examine the democratizing effect of participation in community gardens by 'community-garden leaders' as opposed to just 'community-garden gardeners'. While the study resulted in a call for longitudinal studies that could convincingly track the relationship between participation in community gardens and democratic involvement over time, there was an evident relationship in some of the findings between community garden engagement and other general civic engagement.

The potential for increased civic engagement by community garden participants is, ironically, sometimes a barrier to the creation of more community gardens due to the nature of land ownership. Armstrong (2000) found that lack of access to land was a common reason for participating in community gardens. Indeed, perhaps the greatest challenge for community gardens, apart from the general community valuing their existence, is the issue of land tenure. For a landowner (often a developer) who has a property that might be suited to a temporary community garden until the site can be developed, there is always a risk that the garden participants will resist any future efforts to convert the garden to the possible development. Glover et al. (2005) have made the case that voluntary associations can spur individuals to act collectively to exert pressure and create change; this collective action can then be used against the landowner in resisting the demise or relocation of a community garden. In the United States, there is a history of the conversion of vacant lots owned by absentee landlords into community gardens during the 1960s and early 1970s (Schmelzkopf 1995). Land tenure can be equally insecure when the land is owned by the city, as seen most prominently, perhaps, when New York City Mayor Giuliani proposed selling city-owned lands where community gardens were leased by community groups in order to reduce municipal debt (Nemore 1998, in Saldivar-Tanaka and Krasny 2004). In my own experience, developers are often willing to temporarily allow access to their properties for community garden purposes, but only with a well-thought-out legal agreement that guarantees the sites will be released for development at an opportune time for the developers.

Wakefield et al. (2007) also argue that community gardens are sites where communication with people from other cultures can begin, using food and shared experience as a starting point for understanding, bringing people out of isolation, and serving as a starting point for broader discussions for the purpose of community development. In examining the role of Latino community gardens in community development, Saldivar-Tanaka and Krasny (2004) found that the most important role of the gardens was in community development, secondly as open space, and, to a lesser degree, as spaces of food production; they call for more research on the economic benefits and contributions to quality of life to fully understand the importance of community gardens for those who use them.

An improvement in quality of life, particularly in the area of positive health benefits, has long been claimed as an outcome of community garden involvement. Dickinson et al. (2003) found in an examination of California community gardeners that there was improved access to more food, more nutritious food, and increased physical activity. Based on both rural and

Fig. 5.17 Troy Farms Community Garden, Madison WI (Source: Author)

urban upstate New York community gardens research, Armstrong (2000) revealed there was not only increased physical activity for participants but also improved mental health opportunities; access to nature, supplementary food for low-income households, and benefits to mental health were cited more frequently in urban areas than in rural areas. Health promotion programs often have a narrow focus; community gardens, Armstrong (2000) argues, may provide a more integrated perspective to health promotion through, for example, healthy food, improved mental health, and the creation of pleasing green spaces and neighbourhood aesthetics (Fig. 5.17). In Toronto, Wakefield et al. (2007) used participant observation, focus groups and in-depth interviews to reveal that community garden participants believed that their activities provided real health benefits. However, the authors argue that these perceived benefits exist against a 'backdrop of insecure land tenure and access, bureaucratic resistance, concerns about soil contamination and a lack of awareness and understanding between community members and decision-makers' (Wakefield et al. 2007: 1). There is a need for more empirical evidence to demonstrate to decision-makers that there are long-term health benefits to be gained through the careful and purposeful creation of community gardens.

There are communities with considerable history in community garden creation and that continue to provide leadership in the development of policy and implementation. The City of Portland, Oregon, has had a formal community gardens program since 1974, resulting in an extensive community garden system throughout the city, with approximately 3,000 gardeners working these plots. Oregon is consistently ranked among the top 10 US states for hunger (Oregon Food Bank, 2012); community gardens throughout the state participate in the Produce for People program, making fresh local food available through food banks. As in many other communities, Portland has a volunteer-based nonprofit organization – the Friends of Portland Community Gardens – whose mission is 'to support community gardening opportunities for all Portland-area residents to grow healthy food and build community' (FPCG, 2012). These grassroots groups fill a need by supporting a city's efforts and bringing a great deal of energy, skills and can-do attitude to what can be a challenging undertaking for city staff, given limited resources.

The formal beginnings of community gardens in Seattle, Washington, date back to 1973, when the first P-Patch garden was established. The land was acquired from the Picardo family who ran a truck farm in the early 1900s; the 'P' in Picardo was used in the garden name to honour the family. The Seattle Department of Neighbourhoods runs the P-Patch Community Gardening Program in conjunction with a nonprofit organization, The P-Patch Trust. This partnership oversees 75 P-Patch gardens distributed throughout the city, equaling approximately 23 acres and serving over 4,400 gardeners (Fig. 5.18). In recent years the demand for space in P-Patch community gardens has grown and the citizenry has responded. In 2008, citizens passed the Parks and Green Space Levy from which $2 million has been dedicated to the development of new P-Patch community gardens. This funding has been further leveraged to build and plan for 15 new gardens. The P-Patch Program is experimenting with different models of community gardening, including large tracts for substantial food production, collective gardens that do not have individual garden plots, giving gardens, and rooftop gardens. In addition to community gardening, the P-Patch Program facilitates and partners on other programming such as market gardening, youth gardening and community food security. These programs serve all citizens of Seattle but with an emphasis on low-income, immigrant populations and youth (City of Seattle, 2012).

To the north of Seattle, the Canadian city of Vancouver has created a tourism opportunity out of their extensive community garden system (Fig.

Fig. 5.18 P-Patch Community Garden, Seattle (Source: Author)

5.19), with Community Garden Walking and Cycling Tours of eight neighbourhoods. The tour maps are found on the City's website and offer an opportunity for urban agriculture tourists to visit new gardens, such as the one in front of City Hall that was created as part of an Olympic Games project, and old ones, such as the Arbutus Gardens that were established as war-time Victory Gardens. While many of Vancouver's community garden initiatives are newer than those in Portland and Seattle, they have been working hard to catch up. Many of the newer gardens can trace their lineage to 1990, when nutritionists in the Vancouver Health Department discussed the need for a food policy that would cover issues such as local food security, the production and supply of adequate quality foods, and the opportunity for access to healthy food for all. By networking beyond their own department, the nutritionists included agricultural land sustainability, the Buy BC First program, food support programs and nutrition education programs in the discussion. In 1993, the Vancouver Food Policy Coalition was formed; members included FarmFolk/CityFolk, Vancouver Health Department, City of Vancouver Social Planning Department, B.C. Ministry of Agriculture, Reach Community Health Centre, Chinese Cultural Centre, B.C. Dieticians and Nutritionists Association, the Greater Vancouver Food Bank Society and the Council of Marketing Boards for

B.C. (City of Vancouver, 2012). Eventually, another iteration, the Lower Mainland Food Coalition (formerly the Vancouver Food Policy Coalition and Lower Mainland Food Council) emerged in late 2002. The LMFC created a mandate for what they hoped to achieve, and released a briefing document entitled Closer to Home: A Recipe for a Community-Based Food Organization. In July of 2003, Vancouver City Council passed a motion to create a just and sustainable food system for Vancouver and subsequently created the Food Policy Task Force. From there, a Food Action Plan was developed and community gardens are listed as one of five action items. Vancouver's food policy development was largely instigated by public health nutritionists, a group that is often the source for support for urban agriculture because it combines nutrition with healthy activity.

Fig. 5.19 Vancouver Victory Garden (Source: Author)

While earlier community gardens in North America existed as part of the Victory Garden campaign, and then later as part of the 1970s environmental movement, they are only relatively recently experiencing considerable scrutiny from the academic world. Community gardens are seen as a means to community development, and are increasingly being 'appropriated by various statutory and voluntary agencies as an intervention to aid urban regeneration, social cohesion and related health problems' (Firth et al. 2011, p. 555, citing Kingsley and Townsend 2006). Research on the real benefits of community gardens to the 'community' is in demand as cash-strapped and resource-poor communities decide on how to allocate less and less funding for real community benefits. In order to better assess the community-building capacity of these gardens, Firth et al. (2011) propose the use of a social capital framework, based on Putnam's (2000) use of the term 'social capital', meaning the connections between individuals and groups, and the benefits and trust that are generated from these connections.

Firth et al. (2011) found that it is possible, and useful, to distinguish between 'place-based' and 'interest-based' communities when examining social capital in the community gardens they studied. Place-based gardens are 'internally driven', as they are created and managed by people within the neighbourhood in which they are found; these gardens reflect the values and motivations of the neighbourhood participants. While there is strength in a place-based approach, it is important to guard against insularity and exclusivity, and to maintain links with other community organizations and institutions (Firth et al. 2011). Interest-based gardens are more clearly led by individuals or groups from outside the neighbourhood, with social capital benefits going to broader organizations and institutions, while not necessarily denying benefits to the local neighbourhood. Although their research is based on a limited case-study approach, Firth et al. (2011) highlight the generation of social capital from community gardens through the creation of 1) a strong sense of collective ownership and pride; 2) a meeting place; 3) an inclusive space that is open to a range of social backgrounds; and 4) partnerships with institutions and authorities that allow for access to resources while maintaining a level of local control. The authors encourage other researchers to take a social capital framework approach, and to use both qualitative and quantitative methodologies in order to better understand the benefits that are provided from the creation and maintenance of community gardens.

While academics can provide useful information on the community-building possibilities of community gardens, designers and planners can make a contribution at the local and city-wide scale by developing best practices for the physical siting and building of these gardens. Often the first stumbling block for the establishment of a community garden is knowing if the soil on-site is appropriate, or even safe, for the growing of fruits and vegetables. Creating an urban soils testing-protocol, and guidance on soil sampling and on what to test for (heavy metals, in particular) would be an extremely beneficial first step in assisting neighbourhood champions and groups, who are unlikely to have soil science knowledge. Once the soils are tested and it is clear that the site is safe for gardening, or a plan for rehabilitation is possible, there can be a more detailed assessment on the suitability for a proposed food production site.

Research has shown that community gardens can contribute to social capital, human health and food security, ecological health and biodiversity, as well as an increase in local education, skills and training (Wakefield et al. 2007). Other research has demonstrated the positive community-building outcomes of these gardens (Firth et al. 2011). Some have expressed concern that not all community garden initiatives benefit the local community to the degree that might be claimed (DeLind 2003). While community gardens can respond to people's desire to reconnect with food, nature and community (Firth et al. 2011), it behoves those involved in the development of community gardens to ensure safe soil and safe sites, community engagement fair access to resources, and improved personal health for participants.

SECTION 6: URBAN AGRICULTURE FOR CHILDREN AND YOUTH

Increasingly, children are the focus of public health concerns with regard to obesity, diabetes, malnutrition, and sedentary behaviour. Coupled with this concern is the connection people are making with lowered public health; the increasing industrialization of the modern food system with an associated fear of food contamination (Blay-Palmer 2008); and the resulting distancing that the industrial system has created between the production of food and the consumption of food (Bagdonis et al. 2009). Overweight children are seen to have a much higher likelihood of excess weight in adulthood (Pyle 2006); with excess weight comes associated health problems. The Standing Committee on Health of the Canadian House of

Commons noted in a 2007 report that Canada has one of the highest rates of childhood obesity in the developed world, ranking fifth out of 34 OECD countries. Recent data reveal that 26% of young Canadians aged 2-17 years are overweight or obese (Center for Science in the Public Interest 2007, cited in Winson 2008). More detailed data on the diets of children and youth in the US context reveal that only 2% of youth meet Food Guide recommendations for the five major food groups, while 84% of schoolchildren eat too much fat (Winson 2008; see Chapter 2). Much of the exposure to food for school-aged children and youth is in the school environment; it is in this environment, it is argued, that these poor health trends can be reversed (Briggs et al. 2003).

Added to these public health concerns is another modern phenomenon known as Nature-Deficit Disorder, as outlined by California-based Richard Louv in his book *Last Child in the Woods: Saving Our Children from Nature-Deficit Disorder* (2005). Louv (2005, p. 34) uses the term to describe 'the human costs of alienation from nature, among them: diminished use of the senses, attention difficulties, and higher rates of physical and emotional illnesses.' With lives increasingly lived through computer and TV screen-interaction, and with less and less freedom due to the modern phenomenon of 'helicopter parents', perceptions of 'stranger danger' and heightened and often-exaggerated concerns about safety and risk, it appears we are raising a generation of couch-potato children, leading ultimately to the diminishment of childhood experience and the near-guarantee of a lifetime of poor health, both mental and physical (Louv 2005). While outdoor learning is crucial for children to develop meaningful connections between the outside world and their 'interior, hidden, affective world' (Robin Moore, cited in Louv, 2005, p. 65), parents – even those who have purportedly expressed interest in feeding their children only animals that have experienced free-range lives – are denying their children the freedom to roam in nature.

The opportunity for improved lives through exposure to nature is considerable. Sigman (2007) found that children exposed to nature learned more and learned better, but also that they learned differently. Children experienced improvements in four significant ways: 'cognitively (greater knowledge and understanding); affectively (attitudes, values, beliefs and self-perceptions); interpersonally and socially (communication skills, leadership, and teamwork); and physically and behaviourally (fitness, personal behaviours and social actions)'. Sigman (2007) refers to this as the 'countryside effect'.

One of the ways by which concerns about child obesity trends, disconnections with and fears about how our food is produced, and children's lack of connection with nature is being addressed is through farm-to-school (FTS) initiatives. Some FTS programs go beyond local food provisioning to include farm field trips, school gardens, and classes on culinary skills, nutrition and food systems. In research on FTS, Bagdonis et al. (2009) suggest that a useful method for understanding how FTS programs are shaped is in understanding how a problem is framed. There are three types of framing: diagnostic framing, prognostic framing and motivational framing.

Diagnostic framing refers to the task of identifying and defining a problem, and then directing blame or responsibility for the problem. Prognostic framing involves articulation of an approach for addressing the problematic situation. Motivational framing, the final core task of framing, provides the rationale for action that will remedy the defined social problem (Bagdonis et al. 2009, p. 110).

Understanding how problems are framed can result in understanding how collective action can vary, and how diverse stakeholders may be working within multiple and possibly contradictory motivational frames (Bagdonis et al. 2009). Bagdonis et al. (2009) caution, however, that if one group concentrates solely on nutrition education – having framed the problem in this particular way – while another group focuses on the use of school gardens to teach about nature, broader efforts to improve public health and connect children and youth to food systems may be undermined due to a lack of unified policy. At the same time, differing community contexts will result in different responses, and this difference needs to be respected within the development of policy. Benford and Snow (2000, p. 624 as cited in Bagdonis et al. 2009, p. 117) recommend 'frame bridging' in order to link 'two or more ideologically congruent but structurally unconnected frames regarding a particular issue or problem.'

School Gardens

Bagdonis et al. (2009) argued for the importance of local 'champions' in the FTS initiatives they studied. Champions bring inspiration, energy, personal passion, commitment, and a network of contacts and resources to these initiatives; champions can be either individuals or non-governmental organizations, or both. One long-standing champion of both schoolground education and improved local food systems is restaurateur Alice Waters of Chez Panisse fame, who arguably launched the local food movement in her Berkeley, California, restaurant in 1971. In a 2011 interview (Nowness, August 24, 2011), in anticipation of celebrating the 40-year anniversary of the restaurant, Waters explained that her menu changes depending on what is perfect that day, arriving from 85 farmers, fishermen, foragers and ranchers. Waters helped launch The Edible Schoolyard in 1995 at the Martin Luther King Middle School, also in Berkeley, which resulted in the transformation of a vacant lot into a productive garden (Fig. 5.20) that combines education in horticulture and gastronomy; the children cook the food they have grown, either in the beautiful catering kitchen or in the outdoor oven. Waters believes that if children are involved in the growing and preparing of food, they will also want to eat it. 'I think this is the way to turn around this crisis in the nation's health. If children have the chance, they all fall in love with real food, and through the Edible Schoolyard project they learn lifelong lessons about nutrition. I am just hopeful we can bring this experience to every child' (Waters as cited in Nowness, August 24, 2011).

Gardens like the Edible Schoolyard are often the only interaction some urban children have with nature, and with food production (O'Brien 2004; see Chapter 2). Students can also learn about biology, ecology, agriculture, nutrition and healthy eating habits in these gardens. Another Berkeley school garden, Willard Middle School, started in 1991, offers every sixth-grade student gardening, cooking and nutrition classes. The garden teacher, Matt Tsang, oversees 3,500 square feet of crops such as carrots, potatoes, greens, strawberries, sunflowers, and more. Tsang states that 'maybe a kid who's not doing well in a mainstream class can come out here and be a success' (O'Brien 2004, p. 14). Another garden at Thomas Jefferson Elementary School in Burbank has fifth-grade students tending a vegetable garden as well as a citrus orchard. The students have a harvest party every year, take some of the produce home, and donate to local homeless shelters. The school gardens are a response to children's poor nutrition. The physical outdoor experience is an important piece in the learning. Travis Smith, program supervisor for the Berkeley School District's Nutritional Network, sees school gardens as an antidote to the children's disconnect with good food. He says, 'just talking about the food pyramid doesn't grab these kids' (in O'Brien 2004, p. 15).

Fig. 5.20 The Edible Schoolyard Berkeley CA (Source: Author)

In 2005, the Food and Agriculture Organization (FAO) of the United Nations, launched the publication *Setting up and running a school garden: A Manual for Teachers, Parents and Communities*. For the FAO, the keys to the development of children and their future livelihoods are adequate nutrition and education. Children who are hungry cannot learn well. The FAO believes that schools can make a real contribution in overcoming hunger and malnutrition, and that school gardens are a 'platform for learning' – not as a primary source for food but rather as a way to better nutrition and education (FAO 2005). The FAO states that nutrition concerns link the developed and the developing countries, which are increasingly sharing dietary problems. This kind of frame bridging might not seem credible at first glance, but the need to change perceptions of healthy foods and to learn 'how they are best grown, prepared and eaten is common in many communities, rich and poor, and may be critical in building community health in both' (FAO 2005, Foreword).

An example of a NGO that is championing school gardens in Ottawa is a charity organization called Nutrients for Life, which launched a school garden network on May 1, 2012, in order to provide teachers with case studies, lesson guides and even rabbit-proofing advice. Their website also offers solutions to the most common problems for school gardens, such as how to get the plants successfully through the summer if students are away. Maurice DiGiuseppe, a professor at the University of Ontario Institute of

Technology's faculty of education, believes that school gardens are shifting from aesthetic and/or environmental purposes to gardening for educational and social purposes (Hammer 2012). Opportunities to be in the garden also provide experience-based learning, which is a way to make teaching more authentic (Atwill-Bradbury in Hammer 2012).

In British Columbia, the Richmond Schoolyard Society, another non-profit community-based project, links children and youth with gardens, food and community. Their work is based on three concepts: learn, grow and nourish. Children are linked with adult volunteers from the community to grow, harvest and eat food. The activities are linked with the provincial school curriculum, helping to link food and gardening to classroom concepts. The Society is also partnered with the University of British Columbia in its Community Learning Initiative, wherein university students gain an understanding of how their course work relates to critical social issues through community service-learning experience; students generate journal writings, small group discussion, analytical papers and reflective essays. In 2008, university students from Food, Nutrition and Health, and Biology: Human Ecology, worked with the Society on three projects; one project was a Childrens' Food Security Project, where the students help Grade 5, 6 and 7 children prepare a presentation to Richmond City Council about food security. The Society lists five principles that guide its work: child focused and community-based; collaborative and participatory; intergenerational cooperation and mutual respect; social and personal responsibility; and stewardship of the land and its resources (www.kidsinthegarden.org).

CULINARY SKILLS

Increasingly linked to classroom gardening are schoolchildren's connections to food preparation and culinary skills (Fig. 5.21). In Vancouver, Growing Chefs! Chefs for Children's Urban Agriculture runs a program for primary schools to excite children about growing, cooking and eating delicious, healthy food. Chef volunteers are paired with Grades 1–3 students from March to June, visiting the classroom every two weeks to help students tend to indoor vegetable gardens and to teach the children how to cook delicious meals with what they have grown. Established as a non-profit organization in 2005, Growing Chefs! has two main goals: to support and

Fig. 5.21 UBC Student Farm, Day Camp children prepare a meal (Source: Author)

encourage the development and growth of urban agriculture, and to provide an avenue for chefs and growers to engage in the community and to support food sustainability. By 2010, 65 chef volunteers had visited with 17 classrooms in the city, and began pilots beyond Vancouver into Richmond and Burnaby. Teachers are provided with a Teacher's Kit that outlines the program, and provides copies of handouts and extension lessons. Each lesson uses a combination of games, activities and discussion points to cover themes such as urban agriculture, vegetable exploration, cooking, nutrition, garden crafts, and foods around the world. The lessons are helpfully integrated with the provincial curriculum for a variety of subjects, including math, science and art (http://growingchefs.ca/).

At the University of Guelph, Ontario, students from the School of Hospitality and Tourism Management (HTM) work with the Grade 4 class at Jean Little Public School to plant, harvest and prepare organically grown vegetables through the Garden2Table program. Professor Bruce McAdams works with the HTM Student Association, several HTM student volunteers and the Guelph Centre for Urban Organic Farming (GCUOF) to organize several trips to the university-based GCUOF to learn about organic food production and to the HTM kitchen to prepare the vegetables the children had helped grow, and then to sit down as a group and enjoy the harvest meals. The children also helped harvest vegetables for a GCUOF fundraising dinner, raising $5,000 to help create a well to supply GCUOF with running water.

In Stratford, Ontario, good food champion and Chef Paul Finklestein oversees the Screaming Avocado Cafe at the Stratford Northwestern Secondary School. The goal of the program is to 'connect youth to good, clean and fair local food and develop their ability to prepare healthy meals from scratch' (www.screamingavocado). Students' assignments are to bring the recipes home and prepare them for their families; the students are seen as the cross-generational tool for change, altering their families' perceptions and consumption of food one meal at a time. In the school cafe, students use locally sourced ingredients and feed up to 300 patrons every lunch hour. The menu mixes common pasta and pizza with lesser known meals such as duck confit and sushi. Over 200 students per year participate in the program, managing a large kitchen classroom, 3,000 square feet of organic garden, an organic greenhouse, a 6-acre school farm initiative, a culinary club with national and international experiences (recently hosting Inuit children from Canada's Arctic), outreach programs to elementary schoolchildren, and culinary club dinners.

In Fergus, Ontario, at the Centre Wellington District High School, Chef Chris Jess, another good food champion, has developed a culinary arts program, The Food School, where he teaches 300 secondary school students every year in how to become confident in the kitchen, skill building and exposure to foundational knowledge about cooking is the focus of the program (http://foodschool.ca/). The Grade 11 students participate in an all-day, off-site program where students grow an acre of organic vegetables that are then used in the school kitchen. The vegetable production is part of the four-credit agricultural curriculum. In addition, the students maintain an English-style kitchen garden and an heirloom fruit orchard at the school. The students generate value-added products which supply 'The Pantry', where anyone can buy preserves, pickles, artisan breads and fresh pasta. Students also maintain an online journal called 'The Cookbook'. The Grade 12 students work directly with the Centre Wellington Community Food Bank, assessing donated produce and running workshops for food bank patrons on how best to prepare donated foods; these workshops help students build confidence as they assume a teaching role. Indeed, some of the students live on their own, and have their own problems. The food skills Chris Jess teaches helps students to be independent and self-confident and to develop the ability to feed themselves and others. Finally, students compost kitchen waste, looping it all back to the vegetable garden production. Jess's next project will be the development of 'The Farm School', next door to the high school, in order to more closely link food production skills with food processing skills for the students (Jess 2012).

FARM CAMPS AND CLUBS

With an increasing interest in growing urban food, there is a parallel interest in less formal training environments than schools and universities. Day camps that teach children vegetable production and even animal husbandry are on the rise. In Fort Worth, Texas, Elizabeth Samudio runs Elizabeth Anna's Farm School, where children learn about permaculture, edible and ornamental gardening, farm to fork cuisine, and basic animal husbandry. Education moves beyond food and into what might be termed 'lifestyle', offering also flower arranging, observing nature, yoga stretches, journaling, and expressive art (www.elizabethanna.net/farm-school/). According to the American Camp Association, 84% of camps offer gardening activities and 12% have added farm or ranch components to their activities.

A traditionally farm-focused club, and one of North America's longest-running youth organizations, a 4-H club is where young people 'learn to do by doing.' In urban Canada, the Calgary 4-H Southpaws club have brought food and husbandry skills into the city, with 'Horse' and 'Rabbit' projects. In 2011, the province of Ontario's 4-H clubs had 16% urban child-and-youth membership and 11% urban adult-volunteer members (www.4-hontario.ca). In January, 2011, a family in Seattle created an urban 4-H club in the Wallingford neighbourhood, which the founders named Cooped Up in Seattle. The Wallingford neighbourhood, and indeed much of Seattle, is known for embracing the community garden and urban agriculture movement. The focus of the Cooped Up in Seattle club is what 4-H refers to as the 'farm arts'; in particular, for the Wallingford neighbourhood, this includes raising urban livestock and growing vegetables (www.mywallingford.com). University of Minnesota Extension has an Urban Youth Development Office, which is an Urban 4-H program and includes a 'Perfect Poultry' program (UME 2012).

Vancouver's Environmental Youth Alliance (EYA) is a youth-driven non-profit organization 'dedicated to the health of our urban environment, our planet, and the well-being of its people' (www.eya.ca). In 2011, the City gave EYA a $5,000 grant for their Lawns to Loaves project, wherein they trained and supplied about 25 growers of wheat and conducted workshops for nearly 200 young people. The project aims to educate urban youth about the processes involved in growing grain, milling it to flour and then baking bread, albeit on a micro-level. About 75 loaves of bread were produced from backyards, churchyards and schoolyards. While the City did not repeat the grant, the project is still running on a smaller scale. The EYA also hosts seed swaps, sends out pollinator assessment squads to gauge the health of local pollinators, runs a four-month apprenticeship program for youth to learn about beekeeping, and organizes work parties for their Means of Production garden.

Urban Livestock

Most North American cities have bylaws that allow or, more commonly, do not allow urban livestock (see commentary on Chapter 2). While urban dogs may have the run of parks at times, and urban cats seem largely free to reduce the songbird population, urban livestock gets little respect in many city bylaws. A few exceptions exist, however. The City of Guelph, Ontario, has long had a chicken bylaw; it is not unusual to hear the low clucking of backyard hens (but no roosters) when one walks through the city. Indeed, one can also keep pigeons, ducks and geese as long as they are properly housed and kept 15 meters from the neighbours' houses. Rachel, a mother of three young children, recently tested the tolerance of the bylaw officer by adding four goats to her long-established five chickens, small orchard and large vegetable garden. For Rachel, the goats are family pets that happen to provide her children with milk (Seto 2012). The City's manager of permits and zoning states that while goats for agricultural purposes are not allowed in residential areas, they are allowed for the purpose of family pets – the number and purpose is what establishes the appropriateness of the animal(s) in the neighbourhood. Rachel's greatest concern was what to do with the goat manure that would be generated. Manure, however, is a resource that is sought out by urban farming projects, and the University's Guelph Centre for Urban Organic Farming and a private urban farming business, Backyard Bounty, were both very happy to remove the extra product from Rachel's backyard to enhance the fertility of

Fig. 5.22 Growing Power's goats provide milk (Source: Author)

their plots. The same could not be said about the dog and cat byproducts in the neighbours' yards. While some urban agriculture goals are modest, the opportunity to have chickens or other small livestock such as goats can provide children an opportunity to learn to care for an animal and reap the benefits of home-produced food (Fig. 5.22).

Bees are another form of urban livestock; the regulations restricting or allowing beekeeping across North America vary greatly. In Ontario, the Bees Act requires all bees to be registered with the Provincial Apiarist. Historically, the Act did not allow beehives to be kept within 100 feet of a property line, but this was rarely policed unless there was a problem. In 2009 the Ontario Bees Act was amended and regulations that limited urban beekeeping were written out of the new Act (www.justfood.ca). The Canadian Honey Council (www.honeycouncil.ca) tracks beekeeping regulations, and directs potential beekeepers to courses offered across the country. In BC, the Vancouver Convention Centre's greenroof is home for four beehives, making a contribution to the ecological services that the roof offers through the more than 400,000 indigenous plants and grasses from 25 different species of the Pacific Northwest (www.vancouverconvention-centre.com). The wildflower honey is distributed through promotional use. The White House vegetable garden has two beehives, owned and managed by a White House employee (www.thedailygreen.com). Urban areas offer excellent habitat for bees – there is more plant species diversity than in the typically monoculture agricultural landscape, and often there is less use of pesticides. Paris, France, is well known for its beekeeping tradition. Henri Clement, president of the French National Union of French Beekeepers, says that, 'in Paris, each beehive produces a minimum of 50 to 60 kilograms (110 to 130 pounds) of honey per harvest, and the death rate of the colonies is 3 to 5 percent. But in the countryside, one beehive only gives you 10 to 20 kilograms (about 20 to 40 pounds) of honey, and the death rate is 30 to 40 percent. It is a sign of alarm' (www.huffingtonpost.com). New York City was among the few jurisdictions in the US that deemed beekeeping illegal, lumping the honeybee together with hyenas, tarantulas, cobras, dingoes and other animals considered too dangerous or venomous for city life. NYC beekeepers worked to win the right to husband bees in the City; in 2010, honeybees were removed from the City's Health Code register of venomous insects and other prohibited animals following a unanimous vote by the Board of Health. The New York City Beekeepers Association encourages beekeepers to take courses, register their hives and follow best management practices for safe urban beekeeping (www.nyc-bees.org).

The Food and Agriculture Organization (FAO) of the United Nations works to alleviate hunger around the world, in both developed and developing countries. The FAO provides information and guidance on the keeping of urban livestock. In the entitled Livestock Keeping in Urban Areas (www.fao.org), the FAO reminds us that urban agriculture has existed in various forms and places for a long time, and goes back to the Aztec and Mayan civilizations and prehistoric Jericho. Livestock have often been part of urban agriculture but, until recently, were often regarded as problematic, backward and a sign of poverty. As with all branches of urban agriculture, however, livestock keeping now seems to be gaining recognition for the role that it can play in improving urban living conditions (FAO, 2000).

So What's Next?

This chapter has provided an overview of what I experienced on my North American urban agriculture road tour, which began in the summer of 2009. Since returning home from that 30,000 km odyssey, urban agriculture has evolved exponentially, both horizontally across city landscapes and vertically from grassroots initiatives to municipal policies and infrastructure. Researchers are investigating how urban agriculture can be used in a strategic way to create more sustainable, livable cities in ways that improve our quality of life. Farmers are hosting workshops to share skills in growing, such as in developing urban micro-orchards, and in marketing, such as through pop-up markets strategically located based on public transit routes and patterns. Organizations are creating community kitchens, and cities are negotiating access to public lands for the purpose of food production.

Urban agriculture is not just about growing and eating food in the city. It is also about our re-envisioning our city infrastructure and about community engagement at all levels. Often, it is about social linkages, urban agriculture and, always, it is about human and ecological health. It offers up diverse and distinctive initiatives that are also networked through neighbourhoods, municipalities, across the country, and internationally. A generation from now, I expect we will find urban agriculture to be a perfectly normal, everyday part of life in the city.

References

Agriculture Sustainability Institute, University of California-Davis. Accessed July 22, 2012. www.sarep.ucdavis.edu/programs

American Community Garden Association Accessed July 10, 2012. http://www.communitygarden.org/

American Planning Association. 2007. Policy Guide on Community and Regional Food Planning. http://www.planning.org/policy/guides/adopted/food.htm

Armstrong, D. 2000. 'A survey of community gardens in upstate new York: implications for health promotion and community development.' Health and Place 6, 319-327.

Bagdonis, J.M., C.C. Hinrichs, K.A. Schafft. 2009. 'The emergence and framing of farm-to-school initiatives: civic engagement, health and local agriculture.' Agriculture and Human Values 26, 107-119.

Berea College. Accessed July 23, 2012. www.berea.edu/

Bhattarya, S. 2005 'A strategy for identifying and evaluating sites for urban agriculture: A case study of Gainesville, Florida.' University of Florida, PhD Dissertation.

Blay-Palmer, A. 2008. Food fears: From industrial to sustainable food systems. Aldershot, UK: Ashgate.

Briggs, M., S. Safaii, and D. L. Beall. 2003. 'Nutrition services: An essential component of comprehensive school health programs.' Journal of the

American Dietetic Association 103: 4, 505-514.

City of Edmonton. Accessed July 5, 2012. www.edmonton.ca/

City of Guelph. 2012. Official Plan Amendment No. 48. Report 12-59.

City of Minneapolis. 2011. Urban Agriculture Policy Plan: A Land Use and Development Plan for a Healthy, Sustainable Local Food System. Developed by the Minneapolis Community Planning and Economic Development Department.

Conservation Law Foundation. 2012. The Promise of Urban Agriculture: New Growing Green Report. Boston.

Cramer, K. 2009. 'Urban agriculture and greenspace in the City of Nanaimo, British Columbia.' University of Guelph, MLA Dissertation.

De La Salle, J. and M. Holland. 2010. Agricultural Urbanism: Handbook for Building Sustainable Food & Agriculture Systems in 21st Century Cities. Winnipeg, MB: Green Frigate Books.

DeLind, L. 2003. 'Considerably more than vegetables, a lot less community: the dilemmas of community supported agriculture.' in J. Adams, ed. Fighting for the farm: rural American transformed. Philadelphia: University of Pennsylvania Press, 192-206.

Dickinson, J., S. Duma, H. Paulsen, L. Rilveria, J. Twiss and T. Weinman. 2003 'Community gardens: lessons learned from California healthy cities and communities.' American Journal of Public Health 93, 1435-1438.

Drake, L. and A. Sands. 2009. 'Thousands dig in for free potatoes: Environmental giveaway brings out crowds hours early, prompts traffic jam in northeast.' Edmonton Journal. September 27, 2009.

Elizabeth Anna Farm School. Accessed June 23, 2012. www.elizabethanna.net/permaculture/farm-school/

Environmental Youth Alliance. Accessed June 30, 2012 http://www.eya.ca/splash.php

FAO, K. Tontisirin, M. Solh. 2005. Setting up and running a school garden: A Manual for Teachers, Parents and Communities. Rome: United Nations.

FarmStart. Accessed June 23, 2012. http://www.farmstart.ca/

Firth, C., D. Maye and D. Pearson. 2011. 'Developing 'community' in community gardens.' Local Environment. 16:6, 555-568.

Flanagan, C. 2010. 'Cultivating Failure: How school gardens are cheating our most vulnerable students.' The Atlantic. January/February 2010.

The Food School. Accessed July 5, 2012. http://foodschool.ca/

Fort Worth Star-Telegram. Accessed June 24, 2012. http://www.star-telegram.com

4-H Ontario. Accessed June 24, 2012. http://www.4-hontario.ca/

Franck, K.A. and Ahrentzen, S. (Eds.) 1989. New Households, New Housing. New York: Van Nostrand Reinhold.

Glover, T.D., K.J. Shinew and D. C. Parry. 2005. 'Association, Sociability, and Civic Culture: The Democratic Effect of Community Gardening.' Leisure Sciences 27:1, 75-92.

Gorgolewski, M., J. Komisar and J. Nasr. 2011. Carrot City: Creating Places for Urban Agriculture. New York: The Monacelli Press, Random House.

Grant, M., M. Bassett, M. Stewart, and J. Adès . 2011. Valuing Food: The Economic Contribution of Canada's Food Sector. Canada: Conference Board of Canada,

Green City Acres. Accessed June 22, 2012. www.greencityacres.com/

Greensgrow Farms. Accessed June 22, 2012. www.greensgrow.org/farm/overview/history.html

Groundwork Assessment Program (GAP). City of Minneapolis. http://www.groundworkminneapolis.org/gap.htm

Grow-a-Row. Accessed July 18, 2012. http://www.growarow.org/

Guelph Centre for Urban Organic Farming. Accessed July 22, 2012. http://www.uoguelph.ca/gcuof/

Hammer, K. 2012. 'Kids and dirt behind school garden trend.' The Globe and Mail. May 4, 2012.

Hancock, T. 2001. 'People, partnerships and human progress: building community capital.' Health Promotion International 16:3, 275-280.

Hazen, S., F. Dietrich-O'Connor and R. Hayhurst 2011. A Framework for Sustainable Food Systems: Comprehensive Scan Recommendations Policy Workshop – in collaboration with the Guelph Wellington Food Round Table & City of Guelph Official Plan Update.

Hayhurst, R., F. Dietrich-O'Connor, S. Hazen and K. Landman. 2013. Community-based research for food system development in the City of Guelph, Ontario. Local Environment: The International Journal of Justice and Sustainability. 18:5, 606-619.

Hodgson, K., M.C. Caton and M. Bailkey. 2011. Urban Agriculture: Growing Healthy, Sustainable Places. American Planning Association Planning Advisory Service.

Holland, L. 2004. 'Diversity and connections in community gardens: a contribution to local sustainability.' Local Environment 9:3, 285-305.

Hopkins, R. 2008. The Transition Handbook: from oil dependency to local resilience. White River Junction, VT: Chelsea Green Publishing.

Imbert, D. 2010. 'Let them eat kale: The growing interest in urban agriculture means we need to think about the city in a whole new way.' Architecture Boston. Aug 4.

InfoFeedback Survey Services Inc., 2010. Ontario Professional Planners Institute: Healthy Communities and Planning for Food. Prepared for the Ontario

Professional Planners Institute.

Jess, C. 2012. Teacher – Centre Wellington District High School. Personal communication.

Kaethler, T. 2006. 'Growing space: The potential for urban agriculture in the City of Vancouver.' University of British Columbia: School of Community and Regional Planning, MSc Dissertation.

King, C. 2008. 'Community resilience and contemporary agri-ecological systems: Reconnecting people and food, and people with people.' Systems Research and Behavioral Science. 25, 111-124.

Kingsley, J.Y and M. Townsend. 2006. "Dig In" to social capital: community gardens as mechanisms for growing urban social connectedness. Urban Policy Research. 24:4, 525-537.

Kissinger, M. 2012. 'International trade related food miles – The case of Canada.' Food Policy 37, 171-178.

Louv, R., 2005. Last Child in the Woods: Saving Our Children from Nature-Deficit Disorder. Chapel Hill: Algonquin Books.

Lufa Farms. Accessed July 20, 2012. https://lufa.com/

McNally, J. 2010. How is this man changing the way the world grows food? Milwaukee Magazine April 2010.

McPherson, B. 2011. 'Urban Agriculture: Design Principles for Enhancing Sustainability.' University of Guelph: MLA Dissertation

Mendes, W, K. Balmer, T. Kaethler and A. Rhoads. 2008. 'Using land inventories to plan for urban agriculture: Experiences from Portland and Vancouver.' Journal of the American Planning Association. 74:4, 435-449.

Metcalf, S.S., and M.J. Widener. 2011. 'Growing Buffalo's capacity for local food: A systems framework for sustainable agriculture.' Applied Geography , 1-10.

Moskow, A. 1999. 'Havana's self-provision gardens.' Environment & Urbanization 11:2, 127-133.

My Wallingford. http://www.mywallingford.com/ Accessed July 12, 2012.

Nasr, J, R. MacRae, J. Kuhns, M. Danyluk, P. Kaill-Vinish, M. Michalak and A. Snider. 2010. Scaling Up Urban Agriculture in Toronto: Building the Infrastructure. Toronto: Metcalf Foundation.

O'Brien, B. 2004. 'School Gardens Nurture Knowledge and Healthy Habits.' California Coast & Ocean. 2(July), 14.

O'Hara, J.K. 2011. Market Forces: Creating Jobs Through Public Investment in Local and Regional Foodsystems. Prepared for the Union of Concerned Scientists.

Ontario Professional Planners Institute (OPPI). 2011. Healthy Communities and Planning for Food: Planning for Food Systems in Ontario. A Call to Action.

Pothukuchi, K. and Kaufman, J.L. 2000. The food system: A stranger to the planning field. Journal of the American Planning Association 66:2, 112-124.

Pothukuchi, K. & Kaufman, J.L. 1999. 'Placing the food system on the urban agenda: The role of municipal institutions in food systems planning.' Agriculture and Human Values 213-244.

Praktijkonderzoek Plant and Omgeving. 2007. (From kelsey cramer).

Putnam, R. 2000. Bowling alone: the collapse and revival of American community. New York: Simon Shuster.

Pyle, S. 2006. 'Fighting the epidemic: The role of schools in reducing childhood obesity.' Psychology in the Schools 43:3, 361-376.

Richmond Schoolyard Society http://www.kidsinthegarden.org/ Accessed July 20, 2012.

Rodale Institute. www.rodaleinstitute.org (Accessed July 3, 2012) Urban Farm Models: For-profit versus nonprofit. By J.N. Smith.

Saldivar-Tanaka, L. and M. Krasny. 2004. 'Culturing community development, neighbourhood open space, and civic agriculture: The case of Latino community gardens in New York City.' Agriculture and Human Values 21, 399-412.

Sayre, L. and S. Clark. Eds. 2011. Fields of Learning: The Student Farm Movement in North America. Lexington, KY: The University Press of Kentucky.

Schmelzkopf, K. 1995. 'Urban community gardens as contested space.' Geographical Review, 85, 364-381.

Screaming Avocado Cafe http://screamingavocado.blogspot.ca/ Accessed July 20, 2012.

Seto, C. 2012. 'Urban farms take root in Guelph.' Guelph Mercury. June 18, 2012.

Sigman, A. 2007. Agricultural literacy: Giving concrete children food for thought. www.face-online.org/uk/resources/news/Agricultural%20Literacy.pdf

Soil Born Farms. Accessed June 12, 2012. www.soilborn.org/

SPIN Farming. Accessed June 21, 2012. http://spinfarming.com/

Taylor, P. (Ed.) The Oxford Companion to the Garden. New York, Oxford: Oxford University Press.

Tomlik, T. 2009. The Integration of Permaculture into a Land Use Plan for the City of Guelph, Ontario. University of Guelph: Unpublished MLA Thesis.

Toronto Public Health, 2011. Soil Assessment Guide for New City Allotment and Community Gardens- Summary. Prepared by Toronto Public Health, in collaboration with City of Toronto Parks, Forestry and Recreation and in consultation with the Toronto Environment Office.

Toronto Public Health. 2007 The State of Toronto's Food. Discussion Paper for a Toronto Food Strategy.
Toronto and Region Conservation Authority (TRCA). The Living City. http://www.trca.on.ca
True Consulting Group. 2007. Best Practices in Urban Agriculture. Prepared for The Kamloops Food Policy Council. BC.
University of Minnesota Extension – Urban Youth Development Office. 2012. Minnesota Urban 4-H Youth Development. http://z.umn.edu/urbanyd
University of Wisconsin-Madison. 1997. Fertile Ground: Planning for the Madison/Dane County Food System. Prepared by a UW-Madison Department of Urban and Regional Planning workshop.
Viljoen, A. (Ed.) 2005. CPULs: Continuous Productive Urban Landscapes. Designing Urban Agriculture for Sustainable Cities. Burlington, MA: Elsevier Architectural Press.
Viljoen, A. and K. Bohn. 2009. 'Continuous Productive Urban Landscape (CPUL): Essential Infrastructure and Edible Ornament.' Open House International 34 (2), 50-60.
Wageningen University. 2007. Urban Agriculture Guide: UA in the Netherlands under the Magnifying Glass. Lelystad, NL: Praktijondersoek Plant and Omgeving.
Wakefield, S., F. Yeudall, C. Taron, J. Reynolds and A. Skinner. 2007. 'Growing urban health: Community gardening in South-East Toronto.' Health Promotion International, 1-10.
Waters, A. August 24, 2011. 'Alice Waters: Edible Education.' Nowness. http://www.nowness.com/
Wiecinski, S. The Success of Garden2Table. Accessed July 19, 2012. http://www.uoguelph.ca/hornblower/2010/school-news/garden-to-table-guelph.html
Winson, A. 2008. 'School food environments and the obesity issue: content, structural determinants, and agency in Canadian high schools.' Agriculture and Human Values, 25, 499-511.
Zenger Farm. Accessed June 19, 2012. www.soilborn.org/
Zezza, A. and L. Tasciotti. 2010. 'Urban agriculture, poverty, and food security: Empirical evidence from a sample of developing countries.' Food Policy 35: 265-273.

Commentary – The Globalization of a Good Food Idea: Tracking the Spread of a CSA from West to East

Sarah Elton

Ten years ago in North America, the term 'urban agriculture' would have been considered by most to be an oxymoron – the urban space having been 'cleansed' of anything farm-related by municipal by-laws and efforts to modernize and industrialize, separating agriculture from the city. How quickly things have changed. A decade later, the sustainable food movement has turned 'urban agriculture' into a common term, as well as a career path for a new generation; I frequently meet university aged students who tell me they want to work in this burgeoning field. Karen Landman's chapter profiles the explosion of North American urban agriculture projects that civil society is undertaking in cities big and small, from educational kitchen gardens in schools and on university campuses, to city farms where food is grown on public land, to the slow creep of urban livestock back into acceptance. As the author notes, much of this activity has been done without the involvement of urban planners, however, she does write that this field is beginning to consider food production in urban design.

Landman catalogues and categorizes the innovative solutions civil society has found to urban problems that she researched while on a 30,000 km road trip across the continent. While researching my book *Consumed: Food for a Finite Planet* (University of Chicago Press, 2013), I too embarked on food-production focused travels in North America as well as in China, India, and France. While I visited many rural farms dedicated to sustainable production, I also travelled along the food chain to cities where I was continuously aware of the presence of urban agriculture.

As Landman notes, citing the Food and Agriculture Organization, urban agriculture (particularly livestock rearing) has been part of city life since prehistoric times. This historical connection between agriculture and the city was most obvious to me in China, where, in areas that hadn't fully modernized, I observed various modes food production in spare patches of soil, on vacant corners of pavement, or even on rooftops. In Beijing, I was taken by a food activist on an urban agriculture tour of a traditional hutong neighbourhood, characterized by narrow streets and old homes built around closed courtyards. This neighbourhood stood in stark contrast to the modern apartment complexes that are replacing the hutongs in the city. Despite many changes, it was obvious that people still found room for food. There were edible plants growing in pots on sunny doorsteps. A squash vine grew up a tree from a thin patch of soil and fruited from its boughs. And people had placed recently-harvested cabbages on the metal rooftops to dry in the late autumn sun, as preparation for salting and preserving.

In addition to such long-standing city food producing habits, just as in North American where the social movement that Landman describes is exploring different forms of urban agriculture, similar innovative food-growing endeavors exist in Beijing, as well as in other parts of China and Hong Kong. The global networks of the worldwide sustainable food movement have disseminated the ideas and innovations that Landman describes and, like pollen in the wind, they have fertilized creative minds far away. Electronic information networks, combined with in-person meetings, exchanges and conferences, are quickly spreading these ideas around the globe as is witnessed by the case of Little Donkey Farm, on the outskirts of Beijing.

Little Donkey Farm

Little Donkey Farm is a 15 hectare parcel of land on the north western edge of Beijing, in an area where farmland is quickly being swallowed by the growing metropolis. The farm was founded in 2008 as a demonstration project in peri-urban agriculture, in partnership with the Haidian District Agriculture and Forestry Ministry and Renmin University. At that time, a third of the population of the local village had traded their land rights for cash, making way for more development in the area. Because of its location on the liminal space between city and farm, Little Donkey offered a different vision for peri-urban agricultural land – at least symbolically.

In 2010 when I visited, the farm provided 120 allotment plots to locals as well as volunteer opportunities for interested parties. I was told that some of the people who came regularly to work there had previously farmed nearby but when they relinquished their rights to the land in exchange for money, they were relocated to a group of apartment towers where they no longer had access to growing space. The farm also runs a Community

Supported Agriculture program with more than 250 members, in addition to 120 working shareholders – that is, people who work on the farm in exchange for food.

Little Donkey Farm is China's first CSA and is the product of an exchange of ideas between the United States and China[1]. The founding farmer, Shi Yan who was a rural development graduate of Renmin University, was sent to a small vegetable farm in Minnesota after she finished her studies. The trip was organized by her professor, Wen Tiejun, who is a scholar at Renmin University and a well-connected proponent of sustainable agriculture in the country. She spent six months working in the United States, learning not only how to grow food but how to run a CSA. When she returned to China, she got to work creating the demonstration farm in the image of what she'd seen in the United States. And while there are many similarities between a North American CSA and Little Donkey Farm, they have also incorporated elements that Shi described as being inspired by past Chinese farming practices such as the use of human manure[2].

Little Donkey Farm's CSA has been so popular that they have several hundred people on the waiting list. There is a deep desire for the organic food that they grow because repeated food safety scandals in the country have raised the public's awareness about the state of the conventional system and has also seeded mistrust in foods that are certified organic. 'If there is a[n organic] label on it, more likely than not it's fake,' said Chang Tianle, who used to work for an American agriculture and trade institute in Beijing and left to run a local food organization in the city . The CSA model helps to overcome this mistrust because members are able to come to Little Donkey Farm to see for themselves how their food is grown. Members are invited to visit throughout the season to volunteer, weeding the fields and providing other labour, as well as to celebrate harvests and special events.

The farm not only provides members with locally grown organic food that they can trust, it also reconnects urban dwellers with the natural cycles of food production – a goal of the urban agriculture movement that Landman describes. When Shy put together seasonally appropriate food boxes for her members, not everyone was happy. 'The people in Beijing don't have any idea of the season. They get angry!' she said. 'I tell them in June you can't receive tomatoes and cucumbers – and not because we won't give you the expensive vegetables.'

In conclusion, Little Donkey Farm is an offshoot of the sustainable food movement in North America and is an example of how projects such as the ones Landman documents are being adopted by people in other countries and adapted to local cultures and contexts. Just as urban agriculture has gone viral in North America, the ideas and philosophy behind this movement are going viral around the world and are giving rise to projects such as Little Donkey Farm.

NOTES

1   It should be noted that the North American CSA is an offshoot of a producer-consumer partnership first developed in Japan in the 1960s called the Teikei system.
2   Shi referred to R.H. King's documentation of the human manure collection system of Shanghai from his book *Farmers of Forty Centuries* (1911).

CHAPTER 6

RESILIENT CITY = CARROT CITY: URBAN AGRICULTURE THEORIES AND DESIGNS

MARK GORGOLEWSKI,
JUNE KOMISAR & JOE NASR

INTRODUCTION

Humanity finds itself in an unprecedented situation – the scale and pace of change and uncertainty around us is astonishing, and yet there seems to be no clear idea of which direction we should be going. Climate change, peak oil, poverty, pollution, water availability, financial instability, terrorism, population movements, food insecurity...etc. are all causing major disruptions, with consequences that are difficult to predict, and with little agreement about how to address each one let alone the interactions between them. Increasingly, scholars, thinkers and writers are speculating that a dramatic shift is imminent, and are questioning the blind conviction that the global market economy and technological innovation generating further economic growth will lead us out of trouble. Climate scientists give ever more bleak projections about the impact of rises in global temperature, and warn that we are far off track from reducing our greenhouse gas emissions to anything close to what is required. Some commentators such as James Lovelock, the co-originator of the Gaia theory, have projected that global climate change, exacerbated by various other factors, may lead to a huge reduction of human population by the end of the century (Lovelock 2009). In the 2004 Massey lectures in Canada, Ronald Wright, agreed that without suitable economic replacements for fossil fuels the earth may soon not be able to support more than 1 billion people (Wright 2004). Edward O. Wilson warns of massive biodiversity loss threatening many of the natural cycles on which we rely (Wilson 2002), while Wade Davis laments the loss of much of our cultural diversity, the very stuff from which we may find the solutions to live in harmony with a changing world (Davis 2009).

Commentators on urban issues have observed that due to the huge population movements towards cities in developing countries, many 21st-century cities '...*rather than being made out of glass and steel as envisioned by earlier generations of urbanists, are instead largely constructed out of crude brick, straw, recycled plastic, cement blocks, and scrap wood. Instead of cities of light soaring toward heaven, much of the twenty-first-century urban world squats in squalor, surrounded by pollution, excrement, and decay*' (Davis 2006). Even the highly respected urbanist Jane Jacobs devoted her final book to the very real possibility of our civilization sinking into a dark age (Jacobs 2004).

The work of Thomas Homer-Dixon (2006) explores the growing body of evidence indicating that modern societies are failing to find the appropriate responses to major contemporary challenges. He highlights '*population imbalances, energy shortages, environmental damage, climate change, and income gaps*' as key threats to contemporary society. Homer-Dixon suggests that the interaction of these threats may cause major shocks to our current economic, socio-political and environmental systems, which some people believe we are beginning to see. How we respond may provide opportunities for radical shifts in global politics, lifestyles and attitudes that may allow humanity to reorganize into more robust and resilient forms. Bill McKibben has theorized that so much has already changed and the old familiar planet Earth is so transformed that it is effectively gone and we should now think of our planet as a wholly different, strange new world, he proposes the name *Eaarth* for this changed environment, where natural systems are unlikely to be as favourable to our survival as they were on the old planet (McKibben 2010).

Wicked Problems

Thus, it is increasingly becoming clear that many of the above problems cannot be successfully addressed through the lens of traditional problem solving. As far back as 1973, Rittel and Webber, observed that there is a whole realm of social planning problems that cannot be successfully treated with traditional linear, analytical approaches. They called these *wicked problems*. In contrast to *tame problems*, wicked problems consist of complex, interacting issues that keep evolving in a dynamic social context (Rittel & Webber, 1973). They are ill-defined, have innumerable causes, and do not have a right answer. Since the definition of the 'problem' is strongly stakeholder dependent, there is often little consensus about what the problem is, let alone how to resolve it. Furthermore, conventional processes fail to tackle wicked problems, and they may exacerbate the problem by generating undesirable consequences.

Wicked problems do not really have a solution as '… *any solution, after being implemented, will generate waves of consequences over an extended – virtually an unbounded – period of time*' (Richey 2005). Moreover, every solution is a '*one-shot operation*' because there is no opportunity to learn by trial-and-error, every attempt will alter the situation leading to further, possibly greater, problems. Thus, solutions to wicked problems are not right or wrong, but better or worse, especially as different stakeholders may favour different solutions. Problems such as climate change, and food insecurity are regarded as 'super wicked' as they have the added complexity that those seeking to solve the problems are also causing them, time is running out but the effects are long term, and there is no central authority to deal with them.

Much of the debate over how we should respond to these changes has become polarized in recent years. Some believe that progress as it is commonly understood in the modern era will be sufficient to solve the pressing socio-political, socio-economic and socio-environmental problems of the coming decades. This group generally view the growth of cities and industry as a process of continual evolution and have focused the sustainability debate on seeking technical fixes to environmental, social or economic problems (Glaeser 2011 or Friedman 2008). However, many such 'big pipe solutions' lead to additional complexity and often address one problem but lead to others, and prevent more small scale, locally appropriate approaches to be implemented. Others believe that it is impossible for societies and current consumption patterns to continue to expand on a finite planet and that significant realignment is necessary (McKibben 2007). There are various views about how this realignment may progress but many argue for community scale, localized, solutions. Rather than trying to 'solve' major problems, this approach recognizes their wicked nature and suggests that it is more appropriate to look at small scale incremental ways to ameliorate and reduce the wickedness of the problem.

Food Supply as a Wicked Problem

The concept of wickedness helps explain the difficulties communities have with addressing food issues which include food literacy, energy impact of food miles, obesity, food insecurity and food safety. Furthermore, the separation of cities from their food sources is directly linked to many of the most pressing problems in the world today – climate change, energy supply, water availability, pollution, and global poverty, and can be thought of as one of many interlinked wicked problems. Cheap energy supplies have a huge impact on food supply given the energy intensity of current food production methods, and the use of fertilizers based on fossil fuels. The World Wildlife Fund estimates that the total food supply chain contributes about 30% of the total UK greenhouse gas emissions (Audsley et al. 2009). With a world population having reached 7 billion in 2011 and predicted to grow to 9 billion by 2050, what we eat, how we produce it, and where it comes from, become key factors in the battle with climate change. Moreover, cooking from basic, fresh ingredients is likely to be less carbon intensive than using highly processed foods. In the UK it has been suggested that carbon dioxide emissions could be reduced by about 22% if food were produced organically, consumed locally, and only when in season (Audsley et al. 2009).

Movements such as community-supported agriculture, farmers' markets, the 100-mile diet and Slow Food put the food supply at the heart of localized approaches towards urban sustainability, reconnecting cities to their local food systems, and reducing transport distances. In addition to potentially reducing food's climate change impacts, a focus on local food supply including growing, processing, selling, cooking, recycling, composting, can also act as a focus for community participation and engagement, empowering people through learning about their food system and its health and cultural dimensions.

Resilient Cities

Newman et al. (2009) have speculated that there are four potential future scenarios for our cities: Collapse – where increased complexity leads to more 'wicked' characteristics and requires increasing amounts of food and other resources that are in short supply leading to a drastic decrease in human population size and/or political/economic/social complexity; Rural City – where resource shortages lead to reduced population density necessary to supply resources (particularly food) locally; Divided City – where the rich exclude themselves in protected self-sufficient neighbourhoods with all the most desirable resources, and the poor are left to make do with whatever is left (envisaged by Margaret Atwood in her novel *The Year of The Flood*); and Resilient City – which can effectively operate and provide services under conditions of distress, such as when global supply chains begin to break down due to oil shortages. Resilient cities can better absorb various shocks and stresses to which they may be exposed, including world food supply problems.

According to Newman et al. the Resilient City model offers most hope for a secure and prosperous future, and the concept of resilience may be a useful way to conceptualize the nature of urban environments that we need to create. This can help to minimize the negative impacts of an uncertain world and to address the 'wicked' nature of the problems we face. In science the concept of resilience is defined as the property of a material or system to withstand shock without permanent deformation or rupture (as in the power of resuming an original shape or position after compression, bending, etc). The Oxford English Dictionary discusses resilience in terms of being able to resist, recover, rebound or spring back quickly or easily from a misfortune, shock, illness, etc. A resilient person or system is regarded as adaptable, robust, or hardy. In an urban context, the ResilientCity.org web site defines a resilient city as: *'one that has developed capacities to help absorb future shocks and stresses to its social, economic, and technical systems and infrastructures so as to still be able to maintain essentially the same functions, structures, systems, and identity.'*

The process of moving to more resilient systems will require cities to transform from highly dependent systems relying on resources from widely distributed, but often uncertain sources towards more localized, low-carbon intensity models, and new models focusing more on local supply systems. The challenge is to identify new paradigms that build on local context and local community infrastructure to increase the resilience capacities of the city. The following design principles have been suggested by ResilientCity.org:
- Carbon Dependency Reduction
- Systems Diversity

- Systems Redundancy
- Infrastructure Durability
- System Feed-back Sensitivity
- Local Self-Sufficiency
- Responsive to Natural Systems
- Waste = Food

These principles provide a framework to assess the potential of various proposals to move cities towards more resilient forms.

Resilient City = Productive City

Growing food in or close to cities can be seen as a central aspect of resilience, reducing dependency on distant food supplies which can easily be affected by disrupted transport, armed conflicts, droughts or flooding and increasing food prices. Apart from enhancing food security and reducing the urban ecological footprint, local food systems can also play a role in city greening, air quality and water management (controlling storm water flows). However, the food systems need to integrate with other components of a resilient infrastructure to contribute to system diversity, durability and redundancy. Mougeot (2006) imagines a city as an ecosystem, and lists four key aspects of resilience: urban agriculture integrated into urban management (requiring governmental recognition); self-reliance through local food systems (local markets and food security through cooperation of local producers; available green spaces that provides ecological and social benefits to both the rich and the poor; and well-established resource recovery, in which waste is reused as bio-compost.

Cities and Food

In the past, when transport options were limited and the technology of preserving food was less developed, there existed a very close link between the forms of cities and their regional food supply. The invention of agriculture supported the development of cities and a dramatic increase in human population. The design of buildings was also influenced by the needs of processing, preserving and storing food. However, since the industrial revolution, growing fruit and vegetables within or close to urban areas has been largely eroded, particularly in western nations. Large-scale industrialized agriculture has become a specialized rural activity, and the distances to market have become long and reliant on cheap transport and preservation techniques.

Even quite recently questions of urban food supply were accorded great importance by some of the early theorizers of modern urbanism. Ebenezer Howard's Garden City proposals from 1902, Frank Lloyd Wright's Broadacre City of the 1920s and even Le Corbusier's 1922 Contemporary City proposal all addressed food production, albeit in very different ways. Patrick Geddes, explored food as part of his concept of the transect (a section through a region that describes the land use along its length)[1], establishing specificities of productive uses connected to location, relative to city centers (Geddes, 1915). Others such as innovative German landscape designers Leberecht Migge in the early 20th century went as far as proposing that Germany's social and economic problems could be addressed through family food self-sufficiency, returning a degree of social and economic autonomy to the individual by providing small, intensive vegetable gardens where everyone could grow their own food (Haney 2010; see Chapter 4). Migge's vision, influenced by the writings of Peter Kropotkin and Raoul France, included forward-looking policies for regional and national resource management based on France's biotechnic principles. Migge's work in a variety of *Siedlung* settlement plans attempted to integrate the functions of the dwelling and garden. In particular, he was interested in household waste as a resource, and proposed a variety of systems at various scales of the home and the community that enabled household sewage and green waste to be recycled into fertiliser to grow foodstuffs.

Despite these leading thinkers, conventional planning throughout the twentieth century has frowned upon mixing agricultural uses with housing. Modern agriculture is regarded as an industrial process, generating noise, odours, pollution, manure and other wastes, and using heavy machinery that should be kept away from homes. Conversely trespass and vandalism can be a problem to farmers. But to successfully create resilience, and in particular food system resilience, in our urban environment requires a careful consideration of the impact of food on our urban spaces. There are many demands on space within the city with local energy harvesting systems, water collection and treatment, etc, and this will likely increase as we build resiliency. So, after many years where food was largely ignored by city authorities, city planners and designers are beginning to consider how food systems can be integrated with other (old and new) functions of the city and its infrastructure and develop productive green urban infrastructure for the city. Alternatives to industrial agriculture using smaller scale, organic approaches to food production, less reliant on chemical fertilisers, insecticides and herbicides may be more suitable for integration with urban and suburban environments. Reports suggest that intensive growing methods employing bio-intensive production methods suited to urban spaces can significantly improve yields compared to conventional production techniques (Ackerman 2009). Suitable techniques for small, underused or neglected urban sites in urban areas may include intercropping, intensive soil management, or hydroponic cultivation. As a result, some cities are beginning to examine strategies for integrating food into urban planning and design.

In Rotterdam, Netherlands, work to develop a food strategy stresses the need for urban agriculture to be economically viable, spatially integrated into the city, and to be woven into the social fabric (Graaf & van der Schans 2009). Such spatial integration addresses the need to find appropriate locations within the city for food production, which may include opportunistic interventions such as the use of niches and overlooked spaces, and planned interventions such as integrating food production into the design of new buildings. Technical integration addresses opportunities to make connections between available resources such as waste heat, water, nutrients available in waste, etc. for the benefit of productive gardens. Social integration addresses such issues as health, community engagement, and education about gardening and nutrition.

A recent report by Columbia University's Urban Design Lab (Ackerman 2009) concludes that '*Urban agriculture can play a critical role as productive green urban infrastructure. There is significant potential for urban agriculture to provide critical environmental services to the city through storm-water run-off mitigation, soil remediation, and energy use reduction.*' The study identifies vacant land, schools, open space, social housing providers, surface parking, green streets, privately owned public spaces, yard space, and rooftops as potential locations for urban agriculture.

In Vancouver, the work carried out at the early planning stages of the Southeast False Creek (SEFC) project (site of the 2010 Vancouver Olympic Village) demonstrates how planning at the neighbourhood scale can facilitate the introduction of agriculture into high-density, high-rise urban areas. Holland Barrs Planning Group (now HB Lanarc) prepared a report for the City in 2007 that identifies '*viable UA (urban agriculture) opportunities to enhance the sustainability strategies of high-density developments*'

(Holland Barrs 2007; see Chapter 7). This report proposes design guidelines, technical solutions, and management strategies, which are intended to facilitate urban agriculture in the neighbourhood. It highlights the perspectives and needs of the designer and the gardener, and categorizes a range of opportunities for urban food production in private spaces such as: rooftops, balconies, around buildings, in courtyards, and inside buildings; as well as more public spaces such as: plazas, parks, streets, schools and community centres. The report discusses each of these in some detail to identify particular approaches and considerations. It is a useful document for other neighbourhoods considering integration of food production.

The approach proposed at SEFC, which has been expanded in the book *Agricultural Urbanism* (de la Salle & Holland 2010), is opportunistic – creating multi-use spaces so that growing food does not displace other activities. Also, it proposes that urban agriculture should enhance the design concept for the neighbourhood or building, becoming part of the marketing strategy for the residential projects and a creative driver for a variety of community activities. The intent is for urban agriculture to be visible and therefore its appearance should be tidy and attractive, and showcase a wide range of food related opportunities.

SEFC taps into the growing wave of interest in urban agriculture in Vancouver, and elsewhere, as people become more aware of the environmental and social benefits of producing and buying local food. It demonstrates the potential of municipal policy to initiate urban agriculture, illustrating how neighbourhood planning can stimulate new design ideas that accommodate food growth in dense urban areas. The City of Vancouver now has a mandate to consider urban agriculture as part of a full spectrum of food systems.

Resilient City = Carrot City

Carrot City (Gorgolewski et al. 2011) is an initiative at Ryerson University in Toronto that explores the relationship of design and urban food systems as well as the impact that agricultural issues have on the creation of urban spaces and buildings as society addresses the issues of more resilient cities[2]. The Carrot City initiative has studied examples of how cities may adapt to embrace food systems, and what potential this offers to create unique urban spaces. A variety of city zones have been identified that encompass very

differing and distinctive characteristics which offer a variety of opportunities for urban agriculture. For example:
- City centres often feature dense development due to the high cost of land. In such areas, land is scarce but buildings can be designed with integrated food production components.
- Traditional urban residential areas feature a fairly dense urban fabric with small yards and limited public green space. Here focus can be on strategies that incorporate planters and raised beds, rooftop gardens on new buildings, and farmers' markets.
- Old industrial areas, many of which are in transition offer significant land opportunities for urban agriculture. However, prior land contamination often makes greenhouses, food preparation businesses, raised-bed gardening, rooftop gardening and small agricultural businesses most suitable for these areas.
- Older suburbs tend to have enough land to offer opportunities for growing in community spaces as well as in front and back yards.
- Newer, low-density suburbs have considerable public land available for food production as well as large front and back yards of private homes.
- Commercial areas and business parks at the edge of cities and government complexes often have large parking lots and lawns that can be used for horticulture.
- Peri-urban agricultural land close to the city edge can be used for extensive food production as well as providing opportunities for integrating recreation and education with agricultural activities.
- Infrastructure – highway, rail, power line corridors, etc. often has considerable waste land affording opportunities to integrate food production with the spaces provided for energy and transportation infrastructure.
- City solid waste and wastewater and storm-water may be treated and reused as nutrient sources.
- Areas in transition such as sites awaiting development may provide short-term opportunities for community engaged food activity.

Within these zones contemporary cities are full of spaces that offer potential to build resilience around food, and to create a new type of urban environment. Below several examples are discussed (Gorgolewski et al. 2011).

JUNK SPACE

The flight of heavy industries from many North American cities have created landscapes that are often left unused due to complex social and economic pressures that make the land undesirable for any use. Such spaces, sometimes described as 'junk spaces' (Kunstler, 1993) or 'drosscapes' (Berger 2006), are often condemned as urban scars and lead to localized social and economic poverty. Although the post industrial spaces of cities such as Detroit are perhaps most well known for this phenomenon, a recent Brookings Foundation study reported that 70 major American cities averaged 15% vacant land area, with higher vacancy rates in the south (Brookings Foundation 2000). Even in thriving cities such as New York the Columbia University study quoted above suggests that there are 5,000 acres of vacant land (the equivalent of six times the area of Central Park) likely to be suitable for farming. In many cities around the world there is an ongoing debate about what is an appropriate response to such waste spaces and specifically how to reduce the impact of essential infrastructure on local neighbourhoods, particularly as the environmental justice movement has highlighted that the worst land uses tend to occur in the most impoverished parts of cities.

Yet these spaces often have great potential to contribute to more resilient localized solutions to city needs by building local capacity in food supply, energy independence, etc. while also improving the quality of the environment. Abandoned industrial zones, riverbanks, ravines, rail corridors, space below raised highways, and many other spaces can be seen as idle sites that are ready to be transformed into food producing zones (Smit et al. 2001). Land contamination can be a significant issue requiring creative responses, but increasingly designers are looking at the potential for such spaces to become an asset and a catalyst for community-based food production. For example, Stacey Murphy's proposal 'Park N Farm – Terraforming the Strip Mall Parking Lot' is a strategy to transform oversized US strip mall parking lots into food producing areas. Several recent projects in Vancouver have implemented some of these ideas, including an urban farm on unused ground level car parking space by Solefoods, and a hydroponic urban farm on part of an underused multi-storey parking structure created by Alterrus Systems Ltd.

The winning entry of the Cities Alive 2009 student design competition, entitled 'Cliffside Plaza, the post carbon strip mall' focuses on the untapped potential of extensive urban surfaces associated with automobiles (Fig. 6.1). The design team sought to offer *'a viable solution for the revitalization of dilapidated commercial strips throughout North America'*. The proposal recommends *'the insertion of green and interactive spaces into the fabric of the*

Fig. 6.1. Cliffside Village is a proposal for a post carbon strip mall by Ryerson University students.

site [to promote] new and diverse activities, including farmers' markets, playgrounds, urban farming, cycling etc...' (Feinmesser et al. 2009). Food production spaces thus would be used as part of the strategy for reclaiming older car-oriented developments from the dominance of the car. These projects show that undervalued infrastructure spaces in the city have considerable potential for community food production.

In the UK, What If Projects has mapped neglected spaces that surround the inner city housing estates in Shoreditch, London. They have identified, as Jane Jacobs in North America had suggested, that gaps within the urban fabric can detach and isolate communities. They have been developing a strategy for how such unloved spaces can accommodate the needs of the local population, including for growing food. In Toronto, the Tower Renewal initiative[3] links the potential for local food production with a neighbourhood's social and physical renewal.

TEMPORARILY VACANT LAND

In successful cities another particular type of waste space are the prominent city centre sites that often stand empty, boarded up or used as temporary parking lots for years while they await development. These locations offer opportunities for short or medium term urban agriculture projects that can begin to introduce people to a more resilient approach to food. In 2009,

Mitchell Taylor Workshop won a competition to propose a use for up to 5 years, for an empty site at Leadenhall Street in the City of London, where a proposal for a 47-storey commercial building was mothballed due to the reduced demand for office space (see Chapter 4). The 'City Farm' project proposal, shown in Fig. 6.2, is full of innovative ideas about how urban agriculture and the commercial world of finance can interact and co-exist alongside one another. There is even a subversive element to the project: after experiencing this landscape, people revolt against the typical barren landscape they are exposed to and demand a new urban environment more closely integrated with the natural cycles and systems around them. Although this project was never implemented, the proposal has stimulated discussion about how other vacant sites can start to engage the public realm and developers have been encouraged to carry out temporary makeovers of recession-hit sites to ensure that they do not blight the area.

Pubic Farm 1 by WORK Architecture Company in 2008 was also a short term demonstration of how creative proposals around food can temporarily utilize urban space. This installation at New York's PS1 Contemporary Art

Fig. 6.2. The City Farm proposal by Mitchell Taylor Workshop in the centre of London's financial district opened up a discussion about the use of temporarily vacant sides

Fig. 6.3. Riverpark Farm on Manhattan's east side in New York is set up on a construction site that has been halted for economic reasons. The planters use portable milk crates that can be easily removed when construction is restarted.

Center, exemplifies an artistic approach to local food provision and was inspired by recent developments in organic and biodynamic farming and the potential to integrate these into urban environments. It uses cheap cardboard construction tubes to create a sculptural intervention within an urban courtyard that illustrates how a bold, creative approach can celebrate densification and at the same time bring the systems and infrastructure that sustain a city from the periphery to its core. The aim was to demonstrate a self-sustaining, self-regulating, and multi-dimensional productive urban garden, and the result demonstrates many of the principles of urban resilience. Riverpark Farm in New York, shown in Fig. 6.3, uses thousands of ubiquitous plastic milk crates to create a temporary farm that was initially located on a building site where construction was halted but was later moved to another nearby site after the developer wished to restart construction.

In 2007, What If Projects used polypropylene bags that are often used in the construction industry to move building materials and waste to and from site, to create temporary gardens in a rundown area of Shoreditch in London. Seventy 11-sq ft (1m²) bags, each filled with half a ton of soil, are used as 'plots' for local residents to grow food on an unused paved area that has been dubbed Vacant Lot[4]. Since the success of the polypropylene bags on the original Vacant Lot site, the approach is being expanded for food production in vacant spaces on inner-city housing estates in other neighbourhoods in London.

THE URBAN LAWN

Another ubiquitous waste space that can be repurposed by urban agriculture into a resource that contributes to resilience is the front lawn. Grounded in history, nowhere is the front lawn prized as much as in the United States suburbs. Statistically, Americans plant more grass than any other crop, thus making lawns the largest agricultural sector in the United States. Americans spend over $30 billion a year on lawns that cover more than 30 million acres of their country.

Recently, there is a growing movement against the front lawn, and what it has come to represent. As Michael Pollan puts it *'the front lawn is a symbol of, and a metaphor for, our skewed relationship to the land'* (Pollan 2006). Architect, designer and educator Fritz Haeg sees the front lawn as a representation of wasted potential. As a response to what he regards as the unhealthy addiction that Americans have with the front lawn, Haeg started the project Edible Estates: Attack on the Front Lawn. Through a series of 'Regional Prototype Gardens' planted across the US and Europe, he contrasts the monoculture of the traditional domestic front lawn with a lush, aesthetically pleasing, climate-appropriate edible landscape. The act of converting suburban lawns into edible estates has the potential to increase awareness of the connectivity of our planet, our climate, our government, our city, our street, our neighbours, our house, our soil, and our food. Started as more of an art project, Edible Estates has become a movement that questions our relationships with our neighbours, the source of our food, and our connection to the natural environment. It aims to make our private land a public model for the world in which we would like to live.

Romses Architects' Harvest Green 02 proposal, which was a winning entry to the FormShift ideas competition for the City of Vancouver in 2009, challenged the use of rear lawns by allocating a rear portion of

Fig. 6.4. The Harvest Green proposals by Romses Architects for Vancouver explored the potential for the use of backyards for food, energy and water harvesting and other community uses

Vancouver's lots for a variety of productive new uses (Fig. 6.4). In this way the backyards of the city can become far more of a resource for the city. Harvest Green 02 proposes the gradual introduction of a new web of food and local energy production overlaying existing residential neighbourhoods.

In the UK, Katrin Bohn and Andre Viljoen's work on Continuous Productive Urban Landscapes has also challenged planners to conceive green urban spaces to become continuous linked spaces of cultivation (Viljoen et al. 2005). They proposed that urban green space should not be grass but become a coherent network of connected productive spaces, where food is produced. Their 2004 proposal for a 'sustainable landscape strategy' for the Thames Gateway, a large redevelopment area of East London, proposed that such a landscape infrastructure would need to consider both the spaces between existing and proposed developments, as well as the land within the development sites.

These projects replace the ubiquitous urban lawns that rely on heavy maintenance and chemicals for their existence with unique spaces that potentially comprise of a wealth of biodiversity. Reactions to this radical intervention include both interest and curiosity about this transformation.

Productive Rooftops

For years the roof has been a largely wasted part of the building, underused, rarely considered as a resource, and left to keep out the rain and snow as economically as possible and for as long as possible until the leaks spring up and maintenance is required. However, with the need for resilience in urban design roof-scapes are increasingly becoming a resource, and a contested space. Urban roofs are in demand due to their significant potential for creative uses such as generating energy, collecting water, as well as growing nourishment and providing amenity space. Roofs are increasingly seen as valuable, and some building owners are now looking to lease their precious roof space to organizations that can use them productively.

Recently, rooftop food production has expanded with several larger scale initiatives that aim to demonstrate the commercial feasibility of significant rooftop farming. Several such projects in New York are now providing vegetables to the local community, such as Brooklyn Grange and Eagle Street rooftop farms. These projects have been initiated by urban farming enthusiasts who would like to expand to cover multiple acres of New York City's unused rooftops with vegetables, providing local communities with access to fresh, seasonal produce.

In other cases hotels, restaurants and shops are producing food on their roofs for sale or for use in their kitchens. Eli Zabar's Vinegar Factory Markets rooftop farm in New York has been producing food commercially for sale in the market below since 1995. Seattle Urban Farm Company grows vegetables in a garden on top of the Bastille restaurant in Seattle. The 'Rocket' restaurant in Portland Oregon provides staples for its menu from its roof where 39 wading pools 45' in diameter provided about 12 square feet each of growing space. In Toronto, the Chef of the Parts and Labour haute cuisine restaurant harvests some of his ingredients from the rooftop, and the Carrot Common building is introducing a garden to produce vegetables on the roof of a health-food store below. In this case the need to replace the roof provided an opportunity to propose a community garden facility on the roof. The Fairmont Hotel chain uses the roofs of several of their hotels for herb and vegetable production that is used in their kitchens.

Thanks to Chicago's Green Roof Grant Program, the city is home to over 200 green roofs, covering 2.5 million square feet, including on City Hall but not many of them produce food. However, some interesting productive green roofs are sprouting up around the city, both for community and

Fig. 6.5. A simple productive green roof on True Nature Foods store in Chicago, demonstrates a low-tech approach to rooftop farming.

commercial projects. Several restaurants such as Carnivale in the warehouse district and Browntrout in the north centre now grow produce on their rooftops. The productive roofs at Uncommon Ground restaurant and True Nature Foods store (Fig. 6.5) are two interesting small commercial examples, both of which supply vegetables and herbs to the commercial activity beneath. The Gary Comer Youth Center Located on an infill site in a disadvantaged neighbourhood of Chicago's south side has provided an outdoor class space and a safe haven for children and seniors from the community to enjoy and learn about plants and food. The garden is designed as a series of long strips of plant beds that hold from 18" to 24" depth of soil and allow a variety of organic food crops to be cultivated by the community. In an area of little biodiversity, the garden has become an oasis not only for children and seniors but also birds, bees, worms caterpillars, and other wildlife that was seldom seen in the area. This green roof is a great model for exploiting traditionally under-utilized space for the benefit of the community. It is a unique space of respite from the environment below, introducing children to the wonder of growing plants for food while teaching them about nutrition and the value of fresh food.

Farming Subdivisions

The consumption of farm land at the edge of urban conurbations is well documented, and of continuing concern. One response to this in North America has been the adoption of 'Conservation Subdivisions' that aim to accommodate the pressure for residential development allowed under zoning regulations, while protecting agricultural land and natural resources. A proportion of the land is set aside for uses such as food production, forestry, waste water disposal, or outdoor recreation. The number of residential units may not decrease, rather the lots are usually smaller leading to the same overall density, but arranged in clusters of greater density with open space between. This reduces the need for infrastructure such as streets, sewer lines, and services, and provides financial and environmental benefits for the developer and the municipality. Other elements such as wells and septic systems can be shared, reducing the costs of construction, operation, and maintenance. This allows some of the land to be used towards meeting the resource demands of the city.

'Farming Subdivisions' have evolved in recent years as a particular type of conservation subdivision where residential uses are mixed with working agricultural land used for orchards, vineyards, annual and perennial crops, and livestock (see Chapter 7). Typically such subdivisions are protected through a conservation easement or land donation which limits what type of development is allowed, but does not always ensure the land will continue to be farmed. Usually long-term agreements with farmers in the community encourage adoption of organic and small-scale farming practices to minimize the impacts on residents and provide jobs within the community. The Agritopia Project in the Town of Gilbert near Phoenix, Arizona is a 210-acre mixed-use community centred on a local farm. The speciality crops, grown using organic methods, are sold at the Farm Stand and are used at a local restaurant. In addition to gardens, stores, educational facilities, restaurants, and community buildings, the zoning codes permit more than one dwelling unit on a lot. This provides for flexibility in the use of the lots as family needs change, including, family gardens, second units, or small business facilities. Community farm lots in raised beds are also available for community members to rent.

Colorado-based consultant Quint Redmond has proposed the 'Agriburbia' concept for suburban housing developments with food production facilities interspersing the homes. The intention is to put residences into closer contact with the source of their food by providing fresh, local food for homes and restaurants, while providing economic benefit for the community. His proposals include a calculation of the calorific needs of the community and a design that can meet at least 50% of these needs from the site. Agriburbia projects have been proposed for many sites in the USA, often integrated with New Urbanism planning principles for the building components. For example, the Platte River Village is a proposal for a 618-acre development in Milliken, Denver for 944 planned homes surrounded by 108 acres of backyard farms and 152 acres of drip-irrigated community farms.

Although such communities may reduce 'food miles' travelled if the food which they produce is consumed locally, this has to be balanced by the potential of additional car transport and other environmental damage they generate. Many farm subdivisions are aimed at affluent homeowners and focus on speciality agriculture such as vineyards rather than local food needs. They also continue to fuel the development of exurbia, bringing people to the edge of cities, and exacerbating sprawl. Many of these developments have limited community diversity, and consist of large family houses located in places which are poorly served by public transport and require the residents to rely on cars for transport. However, some are beginning to integrate more diversity and agriculture targeted at the local community, and if designed as mixed use communities with employment potential and close to public transport they can reduce the environmental footprint of their residents and help build resilience. Prairie Crossing is an example of a farm subdivision that addresses a variety of resilience and community issues, including transport, education and diversity of residents. Quint Redmond has developed a tool to compare how a community addresses the carbon intensity of three key aspects of future resilience: transport, shelter and food (Redmond 2010). Farming subdivisions can score well in the food category if they provide locally appropriate food, but perform less well in the transport and shelter categories as they are in locations where cars are necessary for transport, and the large, single-family houses are usually energy intensive (per occupant).

Conclusion

One of the most compelling reasons for integrating agriculture and urban settlements goes beyond the provision of food sources alone – it is based on the fundamental place of the food system in a resilient community and its urban nutrient cycles. 'A complete or ecologically sustainable design for a city would be a closed loop, with all the wastes from one process used as an input to another process. The city would be in balance. Because food and fuel are a major industry in a city, urban agriculture has a large role to play in closing open, polluting loops in the nutrient cycle' (Smit et al. 2001).

Urban resilience requires us to think in cyclical ways and to connect systems that have in recent years become separated and specialized, whether this is energy, water, food or materials systems. It also demands that people are empowered and mobilize their available resources. In addition to any contribution to the city's food supply, it is important to recognize that just as important is the potential for urban agriculture to promote other community goals such as improved health, reductions in obesity, increased physical activity, youth education, storm water management, biodiversity, as well as economic benefits from job creation and local economic stimulation.

Some designers have started to recognize the potential this offers for a new type of urbanism and architecture. They have begun to address this reality by proposing built-environment patterns that seek solutions to the food cycle while tying it to the problems in urban resource and nutrient cycles. Thus, food production, processing of food wastes, transformation of urban solid and liquid wastes, energy generation and conservation, and other goals of resilient communities are combined in highly creative ways with the conception of environments for living, working, playing, growing and mobility. However, the wider adoption and success of urban agriculture and the creation of appropriate urban spaces relies on appropriate municipal policies. Partly through increasing awareness by planners and partly through pressures from citizens, some cities are beginning to assist through zoning policies, land allocations, strategy development, and even funding. For example, Seattle's comprehensive plan of 2005 requires at least one community garden for every 2,500 households in a neighbourhood. However, local policies are often still based on outdated planning and community health attitudes and can present significant barriers to food production. As architects, landscape architects and other designers are finally moving from reimagining productive cities to designing such cities it is important that planners and municipal leaders contribute their part to implementing these designs.

References

Ackerman, K. 2009. The Potential for Urban Agriculture in New York City. NY, Columbia University Urban Design Lab.

Audsley, E. et al. 2009. How Low Can We Go: An assessment of greenhouse gas emissions from the UK food system and the scope for reduction by 2050. WWF-UK and Food Climate Research Network, UK 2009, downloaded from http://assets.wwf.org.uk/downloads/how_low_report_1.pdf.

Berger, A. 2006. Drosscape: Wasting Land in Urban America. New York: Princeton Architectural Press.

Brookings Foundation. 2000. Vacant Land in Cities: An Urban Resource.

Davis, M. 2006. Planet of Slums. London & New York: Verso.

Davis, W 2009. Wayfinders: Why Ancient Wisdom Matters in the Modern World. Toronto: House of Anansi Press.

De Graaf, P. & van der Schans, J.W. 2009. Integrated urban agriculture in industrialised countries – Design principles for locally organised food cycles in the Dutch context. SASBE09 Conference, Delft, The Netherlands.

de la Salle, J. & Holland, M. 2010. Agricultural urbanism: Handbook for Building Sustainable Food Systems in 21st Century Cities. Winnipeg: Green Frigate Books.

Feinmesser, D., Hendershott, A., Mitt, K., Tso, T., and advisor Komisar, J. 2009. Cliffside Plaza, the post carbon strip mall. Entry to Cities Alive 2009 competition. www.greenroofs.org/index.php/mediaresource/grhc-news-releases/transforming-the-face-of-buildings.

Friedman, T. 2008. Hot flat and crowded. New York: Farrar, Straus and Giroux.

Geddes, P. 1915. Cities in Evolution. London: Williams and Norgate.

Glaeser, E. 2011. Triumph of the City. New York: Penguin Press.

Gorgolewski, M., Komisar, J. & Nasr, J. 2011. Carrot City – creating places for urban agriculture. New York: Monacelli Press.

Haney, D. 2010. When Modern Was Green: Life and Work of Landscape Architect Leberecht Migge. London: Routledge.

Holland Barrs. 2007. Designing Urban Agriculture Opportunities for Southeast False Creek. http://www.hblanarc.ca/projects/project_details.asp?ProjectID=93

Homer-Dixon, T. 2006. The Up Side of Down: Catastrophe, creativity and the renewal of civilization. Washington, DC: Island Press/Shearwater Books.

Jacobs, J. 2004. Dark Age Ahead: Caution. New York: Random House.

Kunstler, J.H. 1993. The Geography of Nowhere: The Rise and Decline of America's Man-Made Landscape. New York: Touchstone.

Lovelock, J. 2009. The Vanishing Face of Gaia: A Final Warning. New York: Basic Books.

McKibben, B. 2007. Deep Economy – The wealth of communities and the durable future. New York: Times Books.

McKibben, B. 2010. Eaarth. USA: St. Martin's Griffin.

Mougeot, L. 2006. Growing Better Cities, Ottawa. International Development Research Centre (IDRC).

Newman, P., Beatley, T., and Boyer, H. 2009. Resilient Cities: Responding to Peak Oil and Climate Change. Washington, DC: Island Press.

Pollan, M. 2006. The omnivore's dilemma: a natural history of four meals. New York: Penguin Press.

Redmond, M.Q. 2010. Feeding the Future: A New View of 'Providing Lands'. Building Metropolitan Atlanta: Past, Present & Future – 18th Congress for the New Urbanism, pp. 74-77.

Richey, T. 2005. Wicked Problems, Structuring Social Messes with Morphological Analysis. Swedish Morphological Society, http://www.swemorph.com/.

Rittel, H. & Webber, M. 1973. Dilemmas in a General Theory of Planning. Policy Sciences, Vol. 4 pp155-169, Amsterdam: Elsevier Scientific Publishing Company.

Smit,J., Nasr, J. & Ratta, A. 2001. Urban Agriculture: Food Jobs and Sustainable Cities. New York: United Nations Development Programme.

Viljoen, A., Bohn, K. & Howe, J. 2005. Continuous Productive Urban Landscapes: Designing urban agriculture for sustainable cities. Oxford: Architectural Press.

Wilson, E.O. 2002. The Future of Life. New York: Alfred A. Knopf.

Wright, R. 2004. A Short History of Progress. Toronto: House of Anansi Press.

Notes

1. Geddes classic Valley Section can be found at http://www.transect.org/natural_img.html. For the adaptation of the transect by the RPAA, see the drawings prepared by Henry Wright for the New York State Commission of Housing and Regional Planning, especially the Regional Transect with Sectors & Communities, found at http://www.transect.org/regional_img.html.
2. See also www.carrotcity.org
3. www.toronto.ca/tower_renewal/
4. See www.what-if.info/VACANT_LOT.html

COMMENTARY – URBAN AGRICULTURE AND DESIRE

ANDRE VILJOEN AND KATRIN BOHN

Mark Gorgolewski, June Komisar and Joe Nasr implicitly ask us if we see the global resource glass half-full or half-empty. This is a 'wicked' question, and our individual responses will colour the way we imagine the future and – in relation to the theme of this book and chapter – the evolution of economically-viable urban agriculture.

In pessimistic future scenarios of extreme resource shortages and a possible return to a society that looks something like 'neo-liberal feudalism', the prospects for urban agriculture may be fairly straightforward. In this scenario of real scarcity with extremes of wealth and poverty, urban agriculture is likely to become established out of necessity, as a survival strategy for most, while alongside it, another 'luxury' version may co-exist serving a privileged niche community.

To an extent and with regionally differing characteristics, this division can already be found in the more affluent cities of the Global North and South. Most of the food-producing examples Gorgolewski *et al.* quote in their chapter can be located in or connected to such privileged niches, either selling expensive products to a few or being thought up by affluent urbanites to 'better' less-lucky neighbourhoods. Or both. The glass question is 'wickedly' intertwined with our society's omnipotent economical system whose uppermost aim to maximise commercial viability – for an individual or a neighbourhood – rules it out that alternative food systems may succeed. Mind you, this is taking the pessimistic view: the food resource glass is half-empty, and all efforts to remediate this are drops in the ocean leading to the glass getting even emptier.

Contrary to the above, a deeper investigation of the mentioned – as well as other urban agriculture projects trying to operate commercially – has, in our experience, revealed motivations that are not primarily driven by the aim to maximise profits. Rather the desire is to provide for better, i.e. more ecologically-sound and health-enabling urban food systems supplying tastier and more varied foods. The reality of most small-scale producers is that, in order to survive, they rely on niche markets for basic income, and this fact comments more on how poorly we value food production, than evidences a desire to 'cash in'. In any respect, urban – as much as any non-highly-industrialised – farming requires too much hard work to make it an easy option for income generation! Most economically-viable urban agriculture projects experiment at the same time with wider questions of urban space production, food sovereignty, biodiversity and ecological literacy clearly confronting the current urban food system. Now, the glass is half-full.

However, even if we see the glass half-full, the challenge is to avoid it becoming half-empty. The key question in a time with fundamental problems as described by Gorgolewski et al. so vividly, seems to be *how* to transition to a food system that is reliable, equitable and attractive to both, producers and consumers. On the face of it, the comfortable and easy access to food that most of us in the Global North experience, interwoven in a complex web of interdependencies and opportunities, personal and corporate interests, helps to isolate us from the perception of a direct need to change.

Wicked Problems Require Wicked Solutions

Mark Gorgolewski, June Komisar and Joe Nasr rightly characterise the process of shifting to a more equitable and sustainable food system a 'super wicked problem'.

The wicked problems related to food, such as one-way resource flows, income discrepancies between producers and consumers and embedded public health consequences will require wicked solutions, if change is to be managed, beneficial and evolutionary.

Rationally, it is possible to see how urban agriculture can close resource loops and provide jobs in cities and also contribute positively to urban life qualities. However, whilst some recent 'evolutionary' solutions, such as mobile phones, have spread like wildfire, clearly meeting a new demand, urban agriculture, as part of a solution to the pending food crisis, has not. Practice and discourse of the latter are developing at speed, but do not yet impact in a way that is comparable to, for example, that of the 'virtual world'.

While questions of yield and technique continue to drive the applied and technical development of urban agriculture, we argue that an equal emphasis must be placed on uncovering the desires that will drive people to support urban agriculture as a contribution to an optimistic future, rather than only as a response to either food poverty or 'dilettante indulgence'.

Urban agriculture, in comparison to other desires, such as the above mentioned mobile telecommunications, is fundamentally different, being both new, i.e. in terms of process, but also familiar with respect to memories, i.e. of farming and landscape. It reintroduces to cities a positive version of the rural that, even if it did not ever exist in their realities, probably occupies a place in residents' imagined past. The array of existing and emerging urban agriculture projects already found across the world – and as documented within the *Carrot City* project by Gorgolewski et al. – demonstrates that there is no shortage of fascination, experimentation and innovation in the desire to find viable solutions to urban food production.

Two of the most direct and perhaps ideologically neutral areas for exploring desires in this context are *food culture* and *public open space*. The media attention given to food culture is one of those areas where shifts in public perception can clearly be seen, and, although it can be argued that this still veers more towards 'privileged niche markets' than consciousness raising about sustainable urban food systems, there is nonetheless sufficient focus on the origins and qualities of food to enable the urban agriculture movement to creatively and critically capitalise on this growing public awareness.

Especially within the design and planning professions, a much discussed consequence of urban agriculture is its impact on public open space, and on public desires for green space within and on buildings in general. Although the privatisation of public space is anything but ideologically neutral, and although the use priorities of green space can be much contested, there is generally common consent about the value and significance of open urban space within cities.

The potential contribution of urban agriculture to public and open space as part of a new productive urban landscape is one of the aspects of urban agriculture that we have been exploring since the late 1990s. Coming from a position that the global resource glass is half-full and aiming to improve on this, we contend that urban agriculture – here in its spatial sense: as fields, growing surfaces, productive spaces – can contribute positively to cities in a number of different ways. Looking at issues of access as an example, food-productive space can range from publicly accessible, 'edible landscapes', such as those being integrated into cities in the Netherlands by the Social Design Lab for Urban Agriculture, to the now seminal, private-enterprise, often larger organoponicos found in Cuba. Both types of production contribute to the public realm, publicly accessible edible landscapes do so directly, in such a way that participation and harvesting by all is encouraged, and commercial operations do so by providing a visually shared landscape, much as rural farming landscapes are enjoyed by visitors to the countryside. But more than accommodating a distant 'gaze', commercial urban agriculture often adds a new type of urban space for relaxation alongside the edges of fields, or by providing spaces and venues for celebrations, such as weddings and parties. Projects such as New York's much publicised Brooklyn Grange Rooftop Farm, do this explicitly, but equally interesting with respect to desire are projects such as New York's even more highly publicised elevated linear park, the High Line. The High Line's similarity with the landscape of urban agriculture arises from its seasonal planting scheme designed by Piet Oudolf, following his practice of the so called 'New Perennial Movement', which celebrates the processes of growth, blossoming, die back and germination, rather than the more familiar ornamental aesthetic of the municipal park. Furthermore the pedestrian routes on the highline although adjacent to planting, are often separated from the plants, so that as in agricultural landscapes, while the public may pass and enjoy the landscape, often they are not encouraged to enter it, except in designated areas. The High Line presents a highly managed and artificial landscape, similar to an agricultural field with pathways and public destinations set within it. The popularity and evident desire for such landscapes within densely built cities is demonstrated by the large number of visitors attracted to the High Line, and the increase in property value of buildings alongside it. This very evidence of the desire evoked by the High Line, is often the reason why community gardeners object to it as a symbol of expensive vanity that has encouraged gentrification. An alternative reading of the High Line, it that it demonstrates an unfulfilled desire for multifunctional productive landscapes, which could as well be met by the coherent introduction of urban agriculture into cities.

Gorgolewski, Komisar and Nasr conclude that resilient cities provide a key response to the super wicked problems associated with current urban food systems. Their *Carrot City* project case studies and reflections on urban agriculture design and practise show us the 'how-to-get-there': via contextualised, state-of-the-art, visionary and economically-viable possibilities of acting for more equitable, sustainable and high-quality food systems. And exactly because food and space are so wickedly intertwined with any other aspect of urban life, these new food systems will ultimately lead to more resilient cities in a broader sense. Our own *CPUL City* design concept, for example, is one of the early cases within the *Carrot City* case study collection, and, in turn, has been used as an example of how spatial design and urban food production can come together in support of urban biodiversity by the United Nations' University Institute for Advanced Studies, which concluded that concepts like Continuous Productive Urban Landscapes (CPULs) can provide *'powerful design instruments to better the chances for biodiversity, sustainability and resilience'*.

If resilient cities that include food-productive landscapes are the wicked solution in strategic terms, how do we move towards them practically? As Gorgolewski, Komisar and Nasr write, several notable architects, landscape architects and urbanists have – and do – advocate urban agriculture, and an environmental case can be made for consequential reductions in greenhouse gas emissions. However, why did Howard's or Migge's plans not really take off? Was it because neither did address the fundamentals of desire? Does this desire exist at all, and if yes, how can it be better directed so as to create durable spaces for durable food production? If people in houses with gardens wanted to grow food they could, but without the necessity, everyone is not a farmer, but that does not mean that they would not value a working productive urban landscape. Moreover, the mass self-growing of food in the current cultural and economic climate is unlikely to become a primary source of food, but then, it may have other benefits. Recent, as yet unpublished, work by Mikey Tomkins has shown how community food gardening in London for many is about (re) claiming the public realm and public space and about realising that urban space is made, and not (a) given. Although community food gardening is unlikely to feed cities, it may raise awareness and generate a desire for more resilient urban food systems – run by professional urban farmers.

The wicked solution will need to act on several fronts, engaging policy makers, food and farming practitioners, spatial designers and the public. With this in mind, we have extended the *CPUL City* design concept by developing a toolkit of *CPUL City Actions* to provide a comprehensive and multi-scale strategic framework of actions for the practical and planned implementation of productive urban landscapes and urban agriculture. Four distinct 'actions' categorise the various tools most relevant to the architectural, urban design and planning professions. They acknowledge the complex interdependencies within food systems planning, but also help to define particular tasks within the competency of an individual. We visualise them as the 'CPUL City Clover', a unity of four actions which must happen jointly, but can take on different size and shape depending on their particular context.

The four actions are:

Action **U+D** = *Bottom Up + Top Down*

Infrastructural, as well as individual food-productive projects need parallel top-down and bottom-up initiatives and integrative design and planning.

An urban agriculture project will have the best chance of long-term success, when it can rely on a strong base of local supporters, active and passive, and when they are steadily engaged in negotiation processes with those entities that govern their lives, for example local councils or food distribution systems. The larger, i.e. more infrastructural a project is, such as a CPUL, the more interdependencies it needs and creates.

Action **VIS** = *Visualising Consequences*

The qualities and aims of urban agriculture and productive urban landscapes, such as CPULs, need visualising to convince decision makers and raise public awareness.

Visualising ideas and concepts is one of the primary skills of architects, planners and designers. Usually, this is done through the design and/or prototyping of the idea in question thereby predicting and discussing its potential – i.e. spatial, user, environmental or financial – results. In the case of productive urban landscapes, this action widens to include a range of urban agriculture experts and practitioners in the process. It encompasses the public and visually descriptive dissemination of ideas, data and best-practice examples, mostly in form of exhibitions, installations, prototypes and online/paper/live presentations. Here, the design professional becomes the 'agent of change', carrying on a long, and at times problematic, tradition of the architectural manifesto as a herald of future change and challenges.

Action **IUC** = *Inventory of Urban Capacity*

An inventory is necessary for each location, especially of spatial, resource, stakeholder and managerial capacities in order to best respond to local opportunities.

At the beginning of the relatively short history of the urban agriculture movement in the Global North, (planning) emphasis was given to identifying (i.e. location, state of use, availability/ownership) and mapping (i.e. sun direction, soil quality, pollution, water, exposure to wind, adjacency to markets and compost) open urban space. In recent years, it has become clear that stakeholder and managerial/maintenance capacity around a site and in a food growing project are as important. Moreover, available resources need to be recorded and systematically integrated into the planning and execution of productive urban landscape projects.

Action **R** = *Researching for Change*

Constant research, development and consolidation of productive urban landscape projects and concepts is needed to respond to changing circumstances.

Social and environmental conditions can change rapidly – locally, regionally, nationally and globally. To keep pace with such developments, but also to scrutinise the achievements of concepts such as *CPUL City*, urban agriculture projects have to undergo repeated evaluation and evolution. Theory and practice need to be able to accommodate change, to anticipate the future by having understood the past. The main partners for this action are the multi-disciplinary experts and researchers in universities or other research institutions on the one side and the practising urban farmers on the other.

The actions proposed here form the start of a process. Remember, the glass is just half-full. If these actions can be harnessed to produce future infrastructure, then we may soon see urban agriculture take its place within cities as an essential and desired element of urban infrastructure… ultimately providing *more experience with less consumption.*

CHAPTER 7

AGRICULTURAL URBANISM: BUILDING SUSTAINABLE URBAN AND REGIONAL FOOD SYSTEMS FOR 21ST CENTURY CITIES

MARK HOLLAND & JANINE DE LA SALLE

INTRODUCTION

Everybody eats. Food is a part of our landscapes, our social lives, our economies, our cultures, and our well-being. Food is connected to us on both a personal and a planetary scale. The way food is grown, shipped around the world, bought, sold, and eventually consumed is all a part of a complex interconnected web. This web is made up of various public and private players whom operate within an environmental and political economy which consists of multiple layers of rules and regulations. Interestingly, while so essential, few other aspects of our lives so crucial to the health and wealth of our communities are as opaque and confusing as our food system.

This level of food awareness can clearly be reflected through observation of the past 50 years of city planning where food has been thought of much like sleep: it's necessary, it's good for us, but it's largely unconscious. Certainly, in the past little thought has been put towards just how food is connected to the way our towns and cities grow and function. This outmoded way of thinking however, has recently shifted, and a new dimension of food and agricultural planning has emerged as a powerful strategy for creating sustainable community health and wealth.

Today, the discussion surrounding sustainable food systems has become visibly embedded within political and ideological perspectives – often being framed as a battle of good versus evil. And, just like eating, this archetypal framework too is part of the human condition. However, when food and agriculture are examined through the lens of a systems perspective, much common ground can be established between divergent perspectives – especially in the areas of community health and wealth.

This chapter will explore this common ground, map out Sustainable Urban and Regional Food Systems (SURFOS), as well as discuss an approach to integrating food and urban systems (Agricultural Urbanism) as a key strategy. Leading examples from the field of food and agriculture systems planning will then be presented and discussed.

A Framework and Starting Point

The topic of food and agriculture is traditionally unfamiliar territory for many municipal governments who have typically relied on other levels of government, universities and the non-profit sector to take-on food and agriculture issues and planning. City-planners and decision makers have tended to focus on more familiar concerns such as roads, infrastructure, water, solid waste, and managing land and development. As a result, food and agriculture have often been viewed as extraneous issues for many municipal governments and are often perceived to be one more budget item, often fraught with political battles, with far reaching and possibly uncertain implications. However, the pressing concerns of sustainability and resiliency are encouraging local governments to think more creatively about how they can address issues of community resilience and liveability and food and agriculture are consistently showing up as providing some of most interesting opportunities. Additionally, many local governments in Canada are experiencing smaller budgets and greater responsibilities, especially around the sustainability agenda.

Although the last ten years has seen steady growth in the body of knowledge within food and agriculture sustainability practices, resources, and publications, there are rarely any precedents or even templates for what food system planning is or how it can connect to other dimensions of local government. Taken together, these challenges indicate that there is a need to collectively build food and agriculture frameworks, as well as to establish starting points for furthering the sophistication and effectiveness of planning.

The concepts of Sustainable Urban and Regional Food Systems (SURFOS) and Agricultural Urbanism (de la Salle and Holland 2010) are, amongst others that are emerging, beginning to provide frameworks and strategies for integrating food and agriculture into neighbourhoods, communities, and regional planning systems – one of which is based on integrating key elements of the food system and integrating them with the many aspects of city planning.

Food production, processing, distribution, education, consumption and waste management/recovery are directly related to many issues which municipalities grapple with such as land use, urban design, transportation, economic development, waste management, cost of living, and health. Food systems both impact and are impacted by these concerns, allowing for local governments across the continent to start recognizing the enormous opportunity provided by a more thoughtful consideration of food and its relationship to local community development. This in turn highlights an opportunity to increase the sustainability, prosperity, and quality-of-life of their communities which can be a critical lever for achieving other planning goals and strategies.

Sustainable Urban and Regional Food Systems (SURFOS)

Much has been written on the need to reinvent the global food system in order to better reflect the realities and challenges of the 21st century in order to achieve sustainability, economic diversity, and higher levels of health and equity. Even more has been written on the many small actions which a person or community can take in order to support a more sustainable food system. What is largely lacking from the discourse, is a systems analysis and strategy for food and agriculture that integrates policy, planning, design, and implementation with community food system objectives. While the challenges associated with local to global food systems are relatively easy to identify, creating and implementing a new vision of sustainable local and regional food systems within any given community is more complex, and will eventually lead to a restructuring of regional food sectors over time.

In envisioning what this system might look like, we first need to explore the principles that would form the foundation for a Sustainable Urban and Regional Food System (SURFOS). Since an increasing majority of people now live in relatively urban regions, and elements of food systems now include a wide diversity of land uses – from massive agricultural fields to industrial centres to urban retail environments – we believe that more sustainable food systems should be considered simultaneously at the regional and urban scales.

In most cases, regional and urban food system scales will not yield food self-sufficiency as global trade in food has become an integral part of our industrialized society. However, a food system which delivers higher health, higher economic value, and lower environmental impact will necessarily mean reduced transportation distances over the next century, leading to the creation of a more regionalized food system which also directly integrates the opportunities of denser, urban environments.

The following principles draw from many perspectives and are based on – and respond directly to – the problems which have been identified with the overly global, and arguably unsustainable, food system we possess today in most industrialized countries. These principles are framed as public policy guidelines or actions in accordance with the pragmatic philosophy of sustainable urban and regional food systems.

Principle 1 – Develop a sustainable regional food strategy reaching to 2050

Consciously planning food systems is not typically done in a conventional capitalist economy. Instead, most aspects of the food system are driven by the private sector and managed by a constellation of various government departments, marketing boards, commissions, and others. While this fragmentation is inevitable, in order to create a more strategic system, an overall goal-oriented view of a sustainable regional food system needs to be brought to the table – one in which each smaller player can find their strategic role. There are many elements, considerations and unique, region-specific factors to be considered when developing a SURFOS, and these in turn need to be organized under an overall, defensible, comprehensive, and supportable strategy.

It is important that this strategy extend its view out to 2050. The food system has many moving parts, all them continuously evolving. Changes over the next several decades will include the price of energy, controls on emissions, trade agreements, technology, population, urbanization, taste culture and many more. A food system strategy needs to not only include the many factors and opportunities in a region's food system, but also to outline a decade-by-decade policy path to achieve its goals taking into consideration foreseeable social, economic, environmental and technological changes.

This strategy is best developed as a joint effort across the public and private sectors, as both play central roles in the food system. That being said, community organizations and/or post-secondary institutions are also capable of leading this project. Since no individual entity has jurisdiction over all players in a food system, who leads the strategy is less important than ensuring that all stakeholder perspectives and concerns are represented in its development.

Principle 2 – Shift the focus from agriculture to food and develop a value-added food economy

Other than ensuring appropriate health standards, the majority of attention in government on the food system has been focused on supporting and managing 'agriculture' – the part of the food system which produces raw ingredients. Of both interest and concern to many farming advocates is the reality that the food-to-dollar percentage which a consumer pays that ultimately reaches the farmer is relatively small and appears to be declining (Canning, USDA, 2011). By many accounts, the majority of the food-to-dollar percentage is spent up in the multiple layers of food processing, packaging, storage, transportation, and the companies involved in turning a raw ingredients into something to be purchased by the consumer. While farming advocates decry this inequity, from an alternative perspective these differentials show that the majority of the economic, cultural, and environmental impacts associated with the food we eat occur post-field.

Furthermore, as the era of increasing fuel costs and emissions controls continues to unfold, the price of elements in a global food system previously reliant on inexpensive energy will also change. The current global food economy has its base in regions that rely upon thin margins of comparative advantage for agricultural production and processing. As fuel costs go up, these regions will necessarily adapt and evolve. These pressures will predictably both drive technological innovation in process, storage and transportation as well as encourage local alternatives to inputs from more distant regions – especially for more perishable food stuffs.

A more sustainable food system strategy should strategically focus more on 'food' than on agriculture alone. This is not to say that agriculture doesn't remain central to the equation. In fact, the preservation of food producing land in urbanizing regions is of utmost importance in the future. However, agriculture is only one of many elements in the system that creates the food on which we rely. Future economic and cultural advantage will lie in a sustainable regional food system model that is based upon a value-added food economy beyond the conventional focus on agriculture.

Principle 3 – Restructure the Inputs to the Food System

The production of food requires a wide range of 'inputs' including nutrients, materials, water, energy, expertise, labour, finance, amongst others. The current and conventional model of the food economy is predicated on a paradigm that is largely blind to the limits of the earth's capacity to supply endless amounts of material, energy, water, and nutrients, as well as the assumption that the earth can absorb significant waste, toxins, and pollution. In light of concepts such as ecological economics and 'ecological footprint' analysis, this paradigm is slowly evolving. However, the core economic system underpinning the global food production system still remains largely conventional. Not only are the continuing policies and actions under this 20th century paradigm damaging ecosystems around the world, they are causing many missed economic opportunities that could achieve efficiencies and reclamation of wastes, as well as unused streams of resources.

A SURFOS strategy offers significant opportunities to capitalize on synergies that exist between a food system and many other urban and regional infrastructure, social and economic systems – including tapping into new flows of water, nutrients, energy, and finance. A comprehensive SURFOS strategy should also examine potential regional sources for nutrients, water and reclaimed wastewater, electricity, managed storm-water, heat and reclaimed waste heat, as well as alternative utility models of financing.

One of the most visible examples of this type of innovative infrastructure thinking is the City of Vancouver's landfill gas reclamation project that captures methane gas from the landfill in order to power a cogeneration system which generates electricity for thousands of homes. The remaining, otherwise wasted, CO^2 and heat is then sent into a nearby commercial greenhouse – thereby not only reclaiming wastes but using a much longer-term utility model of financing to change the costs of food system inputs.

Principle 4 – Integrate health centrally into food system consciousness

Some of the largest and fastest growing areas of healthcare costs in North America are those associated with preventable chronic diseases – primarily those linked to lifestyle, and in particular, food and exercise (CDC, 2014; see Chapter 2). The recent rise in attention to 'health' in planning has begun stimulating a new focus on pedestrian-oriented design and increasing discussions on ensuring access to healthy food in neighbourhoods – including interest in the 'organics' industry in response to concerns about the impact of pesticides on health. With the baby boomer demographic approaching retirement age, facing a growing list of health issues associated with aging, as well as having more disposable income than ever before the profile of health is expected to continue to rise.

Connecting with health issues and opportunities is an important leverage point for promoting healthy regional food systems. A primary area of consideration regarding health includes the promotion of both industrial and organic (or near-organic) farming methods. A successful system will also ensure that: there are no food-deserts in the community; everyone has access to food stores which offer a wide range of raw ingredients; and there is support for farmers' markets. Another area of consideration is the need to have community gardens throughout the community in order to provide an opportunity for residents to both learn about and grow food. Additionally, over time one of the most important aspects is to include a healthy food education and festival presence so as to build up and maintain a 'culture of healthy food' in the community.

Principle 5 – Strategically support local food production

Each community has a unique geographical, cultural, and economic profile and as such each individual community will need to be strategic in what aspects and products it chooses to focus on for its food economy. In reality, the market will determine the bulk of what is produced; however, community initiatives, government policy, as well as overall community vision and brand identity will also contribute strongly to the local food economy in many ways.

The first strategic goal for a community is to produce as much regional commodity and specialty food as possible. Any policy, program, incentive, or initiative that promotes the creation of food for the local economy has value.

The second strategic goal is to develop specific areas of significant market expertise in the food economy. These can be based on existing areas of comparative advantage, or on strategically selected and promoted areas or food product types. Trade in food is important, and significant economic benefit can be achieved by excelling in various food products.

The third strategic goal is to produce as many of the short-term perishable food items to be consumed in a community as possible. A significant amount of energy and emissions are consumed and released when moving highly perishable food items around the world every day. This practice also encourages the harvesting of produce before it has fully ripened, which results in the extensive use of food chemicals to keep the food from ripening and or spoiling too soon. (CNN, 2011) Most communities can support their own greenhouses and local food production companies, where local distributors and wholesalers support such practices.

Another strategic opportunity is the reality of 'alcohol.' Due to their weight and volume, alcohol and other beverages have significantly high energy and emissions profiles in the contemporary food system. (Garnett, 2007) There are few areas in the food system where government regulation enforces such a monopoly of energy and emission-intensive food stuffs production and transportation than in liquor regulation. Acting to help counterbalance the high emissions profile of alcohol is the rise of local microbreweries across North America. Since beer can be produced anywhere that grain can be shipped to, this provides strong testament to the value of a local brewing culture. Likewise, spirits can also be produced anywhere that public policy and regulations do not prohibit them – and where this is the case, both the rise and quality of micro-distillers showcases a dynamic economic opportunity. Wine can be produced across much of North America as well, including in areas beyond those currently in serious cultivation. Since the overall price and value of alcohol is a well-known major piece of the food economy, significant economic development is possible in regions where localized brewing is taken advantage of.

Principle 6 – Develop a Vibrant Local Food Culture

While there are many more principles that could be explored, the final one to be recommended here is the coordination of participants in a regional food system. Participants in a capitalist economy rarely self-coordinate around sustainability issues, however significant benefit can be found for most all players if someone steps up to proactively coordinate stakeholders around a goal. By coordinating food system participants to work together, the profile and depth of the region's food culture and identity can be grown exponentially. Since food is so closely linked with community identity, a positive food reputation in a region for great food can bring many benefits, not the least of which is tourism (Hild, 2009). Food can also be a strong force in regional identity and pride, which can prove to be a critical factor in attracting and keeping an educated workforce, innovative entrepreneurs and an affluent retirement economy.

A vibrant food culture will almost certainly entail a greater level of health as it involves local cooking, cultural recipes, artisan techniques, as well as the celebration of chefs and the skills of cooking. Combined, all of these can begin to shift the balance of food consumption away from highly processed and preserved foods.

Scale, Growth, and an Agricultural Urbanism

When considering how to operationalize the above principles, any experienced policy analyst will immediately identify the fact that each principle will require many actors to work in tandem – particularly actors who typically have interests or jurisdictions at different scales, thus bringing up the question of scale.

Boundaries for Local

Sustainable Urban and Regional Food Systems (SURFOS) are inherently focused on 'local' strategies. Given the complex nature of food systems, it is crucial to identify what exactly the boundaries of 'local' means for a given region or community as a basis for strategy and/or policy development.

Unlike political boundaries, defining the area for what constitutes 'local,' or is a local food economy, is no simple task as there is no one definition of 'local' which is widely accepted. For the purposes of providing a starting point, local will be presented along a spectrum of most to least local. There are several elements that must be considered together in order to determine what is and is not considered local. Factors that influence the shades of local include:

- **Ownership** and/or location of headquarters for food and agriculture related businesses;
- **Residency of labour force** where the majority of jobs are concentrated;
- **Location** of primary production; and
- **Location of** processing and distribution
- **Jurisdictional boundaries** of municipalities, regions, provinces and countries.

The outside threshold for what is not considered local is based on the 600 km definition of 'local' as adopted by the US Congress in the 2008 Farm Act. That is, everything within a 600 km radius of a town or city is considered local. The rationale here being that within the 600 km most cities in Canada and the United States have access to a wide range of bio-regions which produce, process, distribute, sell, and serve a wide enough range of food goods to make up the average food basket. While many of the shades of local extend beyond the boundaries of a municipality, opportunities for how local government may impact the local food economy must also be identified (Fig. 7.1).

The shades of local spectrum presented here is not meant to be viewed as a rule, but more as a guideline to help communities identify for themselves what counts as local. By clearly identifying what is meant by local, a crucial

Fig. 7.1. Shades of Local

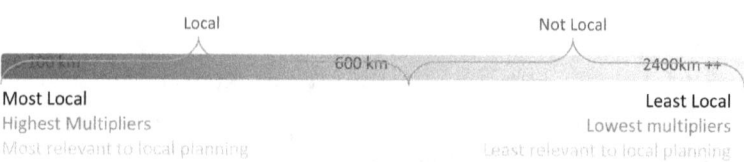

starting point for policy development and strategy development/implementation is provided.

SECURE FOOD SYSTEM-SUPPORTIVE LAND USE PATTERNS AT ALL SCALES

A focus on SURFOS may be perceived by some as arbitrary, exclusive of, or in contradiction to the many other scales of food and agriculture. While this may be the case in certain instances, a SURFOS is primarily compatible or non-interactive with larger systems. Below, Figure 7.2 depicts some of the major scales of food and agriculture systems and where they overlap. While these larger systems of food and agriculture economies are powerful economic drivers, local governments are limited in their ability to influence areas which fall outside of their prevue. Therefore, there is a compelling logic to starting at the local level.

Regional and urban planning policies traditionally focus on 'land' – preserving agricultural land and ensuring sufficient land for industrial, residential, and commercial uses for future growth. In a growing region, increased sustainable food system performance necessarily starts with planning in order to enhance food-related land use capacity in the future. As such, regional and urban planning, as well as development patterns both need to have more explicit food programs.

Fig. 7.2. Intersecting scales of food systems

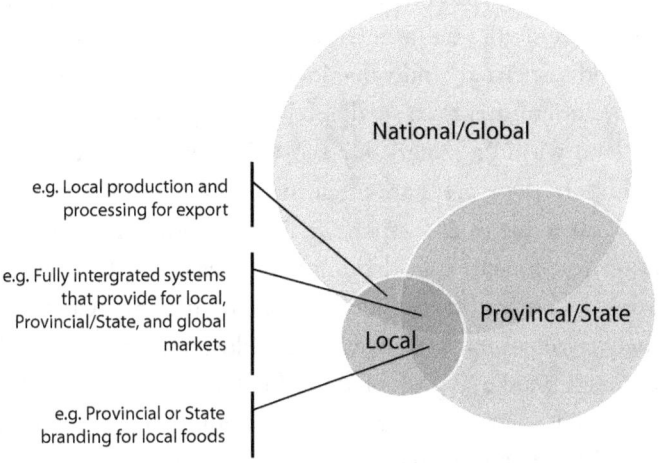

THE REGIONAL SCALE

The first scale of land use planning to consider is the regional pattern of development and food systems. Much has been written supporting, smart-growth, compact development and preserving farmland. While these are important goals, a growing region has never been able to reasonably accommodate all of its growth over many decades solely within existing city boundaries, however the need to minimize impact on land from development remains.

With respect to development on the edges of urban areas and in between cities, this needs to be done within transit-oriented corridors of mixed-use villages that connect nearby cities in a hub-and-spoke model. These 'spokes,' roughly 1 km wide, should centre on a major transit line in order to ensure easy access to transit from most residential areas to all major centers of jobs and education – a pattern that can be structured and maintained through growth along boundaries and zoning changes. This approach will also allow for both infill and greenfield development and the associated balance of land and housing costs, but does so in a manner which permits the preservation of farmland throughout the region – and within areas easily accessed by many residents to support vertically-integrated, artisan agriculture economies and experiences.

In order to keep its value down, areas of high quality soils appropriate for large-scale, industrial field agriculture must be zoned and regulated to solely support agriculture and thereby be kept from land speculation. For example, in British Columbia, Provincial legislation protects agricultural land through its designation as Agricultural Land Reserve, which limits non-agricultural activities on farm land. This legislation significantly limits speculation and associated land value increases, maintaining low cost land for large-scale agriculture. Even small levels of speculation can drive farmers off of their land within a remarkably short time due to rapid rises in land taxes. In addition, these areas are often inappropriate to locate adjacent to where families live due to dust, sprays, noise, and other negative impacts.

In addition to protecting field production, regional planning needs to also ensure that there is sufficient land for the food industry. Conventionally, a municipality will often not favour one industry over another through zoning and rather take a position that food processing should go into existing industrial zones. However, attention should be paid in a community to the possibility of integrating food related industries into lower quality field agriculture areas where existing industrial land is too scarce or too expensive to support an economically challenged food industry sector. The controls on these lands would need to unlike conventional industrial zoning which allows a broad range of industrial uses. Instead, such zoning would need to be carefully focus solely on the food industry to achieve its goals. Some will no doubt challenge a practice of allowing industrial uses – even if zoned solely for food-industry related activities – on any field land.

However, there is a second type of non-urban agriculture that should be identified – that of 'Artisan Agriculture' (de la Salle and Holland 2010). Artisan Agriculture is a term used to describe farm types that are vertically integrated and are characterized by a farmer not only growing food ingredients in fields and barns, but also engaging in the additional processing, packaging, retailing, and selling of the farm food-experiences within the same farm area. Unlike industrial agriculture which sees urban populations as a nuisance and a threat, artisan agriculture sees urban populations as an enormous customer base located within a short drive of their farm.

An artisan agriculture zone can be created by a municipality to support the diversity of food-related uses that are included in this concept and this zoning can then be used as an interface area between more urban areas and industrial agriculture areas. It can also be structured to support an effective access pattern by urbanites seeking farm experiences – thereby adding more closely connecting urban consumers with their food sources, as well as bringing additional prosperity to farmers. While there are developers in many areas integrating food-related uses consciously into their projects, there are few municipalities developing comprehensive food system strategies that include artisan agriculture concept zones. It is hoped that this concept becomes more prevalent in municipal economic development planning.

When planned strategically, the regional dimension of a sustainable food system will include an industrial food component including protected industrial agriculture lands, food processing, industrial areas for warehousing and distributions systems as well as innovative infrastructure systems that connect and circulate nutrients, energy, and water. In addition, an artisan and experiential dimension of food will offer artisan agriculture lands, value-added food activity, agro-tourism, farmer direct sales, and other uses that enhance the profile and experience of the regional food culture.

The Importance of the Regional Scale

The above discussion endeavours to present an overview of some the principles to be used as a framework when considering actions on how to increase the vibrancy, economic prosperity, and sustainability of the food system. The regional level is an appropriate scale of food system planning for the 21st century as it combines an effective geographical scale (that creates a high level of diversity, ecological performance, and prosperity in the food system) with the public, private, and non-profit sectors working and interacting together in meaningful ways.

It is critical that food system planning not focus solely on the production of a narrow range of food stuffs perceived to be those that the region has comparative advantage in – although these too should be pursued. In addition to this 'export mentality,' the local health, culture, and identity of communities in the region should also be supported, and should form a basis for policy and initiatives. In order to claim the opportunities these offer it is important to address all aspects of the food system, and not simply those of agricultural production.

The above discussion of the regional and urban systems perspective on food is all well and good however, in daily practice the processes of building and operating a city are pragmatic and concrete rather than theoretical. Moreover, in a growing region that is constrained by various political or geographical boundaries, the competition for land becomes a zero sum game – in which it is uncertain whether or not any given acre will be used for natural, residential, industrial, commercial, or agricultural uses. And thus we come to the discussion on how to work at a planning and development scale in order to begin to create change within a regional food system so as to meet sustainability goals.

Agricultural Urbanism

For the past 10 years of our professional practice in consulting to local governments, developers, and non-profit agencies, we have been working to change the narrative of food – to show how strong local food and agriculture systems can co-exist with both other scales of food systems and, more importantly, with urban systems. In any constrained region, the future requires that we better integrate agriculture with urban development to meet our sustainable community objectives on both fronts.

With collaboration from the many organizations, a framework called

Agricultural Urbanism (AU) has emerged with perspectives and tools for unpacking key strategies for building resilient food systems at both local and regional levels, and then integrating them successfully into urban systems (de la Salle and Holland 2010).

We define Agricultural Urbanism as a:

> '...planning, policy and design framework for developing a wide range of food and agriculture system elements into multiple community scales: neighbourhood, city/town, and region. AU refocuses community health and wealth around food and agriculture'.
>
> (de la Salle and Holland 2010)

Any region in North America which is currently growing is increasingly faced with an ongoing struggle between expanding urbanized areas interacting with an older non-urbanized environments – and often with a growing suburban context in between the two. To continue to see the food

Fig. 7.3. Urban to Rural Context for Food and Agriculture Planning. Drawing by Joanna Clark, HB Lanarc Golder

system as a disparate and uncoordinated element within regional planning and economic development strategies is to miss out on major economic and cultural opportunities, as well as to lock ourselves into unnecessarily high ecological impacts for our food supply in the future. As such, we are arguing that we need to break down the out-of-date perspectives of agriculture being synonymous with food planning, as well as the view that agricultural and urban systems are mutually exclusive. Instead, we are arguing for an integration of the two and a shift towards a whole regional food system consciousness into an 'agricultural urbanism' as the way forward to achieve sustainable urban and regional food systems.

A key dimension of AU is the urban-to-rural context that shapes the opportunities for resilient food and agriculture systems. Through considering the food system across the range of downtown, mature, mixed-used neighbourhoods, industrial, institutional, to rural residential and agricultural lands a comprehensive approach begins to take shape. Combining the elements of the food system into an urban context (Fig. 7.3) begins to offer a planning framework from the urban-to-rural context in which a wide variety of strategies for SURFOS are possible.

Planning Framework for Agricultural Urbanism

The first part of the framework for Agricultural Urbanism (AU) is the framework of the food and agriculture system – the process and various stages which a raw food product goes through to reach its final state as waste. A systems perspective provides a tool in which to check that the opportunities being explored are comprehensive and mutually supportive. Traditionally, local governments mostly focused on the land around food production, but more recently have begun to look at the social, environmental, and economic opportunities in the other stages of the food and agriculture system. Figure 7.4 depicts the key dimensions of the food system.

The Urban and Neighbourhood Scales

While the regional scale is critical for the overall planning and public policy which shapes economic and agricultural activity, the scales at which most communities can begin to act are those on the urban or neighbourhood

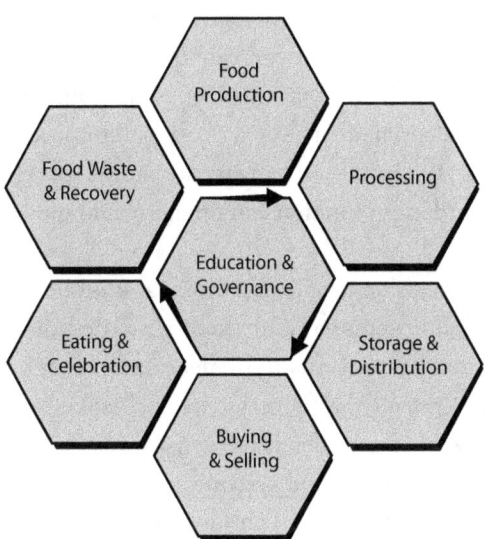

Fig. 7.4. Key Dimensions of a Food and Agriculture System

level – and thus these which have been favourites of urban agriculture advocates for some time. Here, the attention to the food systems needs to focus on urban food production infrastructure, industrial and artisan food processing, a network of food retail (including farmers' markets), celebration of food culture, and the opportunity to create food hubs. At these levels, agricultural urbanism begins to become operable–and from there down to the backyard.

Neighbourhood Elements of an Agricultural Urbanism

The foundation of an agricultural urbanism framework or strategy involves addressing each element of the food system and then working to maximize the vitality and health of each element at a neighbourhood scale (de la Salle and Holland 2010).

The first food system element to consider in AU is the ***urban production of raw food products (urban agriculture)***. Supporting urban agriculture from a city planning point of view includes providing extensive public lands for community gardens through parks and greenways in areas with multi-family housing. Due to urban density issues, it is often difficult to find adequate open space with sufficient sun to grow food. Single family areas however, often have back and front yards that can support growing food.

Cities also need to establish policies that manage semi-commercial agricultural production in residential areas so as to avoid unnecessary conflicts between neighbours. In most cases these are not a problem, however occasionally serious garden production can offend neighbours and cause zoning disputes.

This book has a predominant focus on urban agriculture as it is one of the leading trends in sustainable food systems work in the past two decades. An AU perspective strongly embraces all that this movement has put forward, however, it also argues that the rest of the food system is of equal importance and therefore it must be likewise considered and consciously integrated into the planning of any regional or local food system.

The second element of the food system to consider in an agricultural urbanism framework is *food processing*. Industrial (large-scale) and artisan (small-scale) food processing capacity needs to be supported in policy and strategies and integrated into as many neighbourhoods across the city as possible to create jobs, enhance food culture, and to increase the profile of food within every neighbourhood. Increased regional food processing infrastructure also enables greater food recovery within the highly wasteful food wholesale, retail, and consumer sectors. In particular, an analysis could be useful in identifying areas where existing industrial or commercial activities create flows of heat, water, or nutrients that could then potentially support an urban greenhouse facility.

The third element to consider is food ***warehousing and distribution***. Due to the scale of warehousing and easy access to major highways, much of food warehousing and distribution is centralized in low-cost industrial areas – often many miles from the urban centres where the food will be consumed. This fact has recently become sensationalized through the concept of 'food miles' – or how far the food you eat has to travel from the field or farm to your table. In some cases, the lack of appropriate warehousing and distribution facilities can limit the viability of commercial agriculture and food production in a region. As such, to ensure the maximum value in a regional food system, communities need to actively monitor and promote food warehousing and distribution.

The fourth element to consider is ***food retail and food services***. Every neighbourhood requires convenient access to food, grocery stores, and restaurants. Managing this need takes a conscious monitoring of neighbourhoods, as well as possible public policy or incentive interventions where market forces tend to centralize large grocery stores in only a few areas, leaving 'food deserts' in other areas. Establishing long term secure contracts for farmers' markets across cities will help the markets establish themselves and thrive over time. This in turn ensures a more stable supply of food in neighbourhoods, as well as provides business incubation and direct marketing opportunities for medium- to small-scale producers.

The fifth element to consider is *food education*. The knowledge of growing, preserving, and cooking food has ebbed in the past decades as processed food became a major part of our North American diet – as a result we have lost much of the legacy of knowledge that comes with centuries of growing and raising food (see Chapter 2). A strong sense of community will promote food education on a wide spectrum – from basic nutrition to advanced gourmet 'foodie' culture. All in all, an increased knowledge of food will support healthier lifestyles and increase the diversity of local and regional food economies. There are many venues to increase knowledge of food in a community including schools, workplaces, municipal initiatives and others. These can often be best coordinated through the development and implementation of a regional food strategy.

The sixth element in an agricultural urbanism strategy is the *celebration of food*. Celebration of food is often spoken of and written about in a family setting and some experience it at a church or other group setting as well. Significant cultural and economic benefits can accrue to communities that promote a wide range of food and beverage festivals. A short internet search on food festivals will uncover a festival for just about any food type or ingredient all across North America – offering up many ideas and opportunities for any community to draw inspiration from.

The seventh element to consider is *food security*. Food 'insecurity' has gained significant attention over the past few years as food banks have reported significant increases in demands due to economic pressures. Concurrently, we also see vast quantities of food wasted in restaurants, grocery stories, and in the home daily (Bloom, 2011). A coordinated strategy to divert food waste and increase support for food banks in order to address the surprising issue of malnutrition or hunger in our North American cities has many benefits – especially for children from low-income families. One additional and different perspective on food security in North America is the drive to reduce dependence upon other countries on anything – including food, energy, and others. This perspective returns to other elements noted in the food system above, particular through regional food production, processing, warehousing, and distribution.

The above framework of food system elements provides a foundation for building an effective sustainable urban food system in any community. It also forms a foundation for urban planners, designers, and developers to use to enhance the development program for any project or neighbourhood so as to increase the social, economic, and environmental performance of its food system.

Food Hubs

One of the most interesting trends emerging in urban food system strategies is the creation of 'food hubs.' Food hubs are a concentration of as many food system elements in one location as possible. These locations become centres for the food economy and culture and assist in the viability and profile of local food systems. Each food hub is unique based on its own program and location. They can include local processing, warehousing, distribution, retail, restaurants, food education, and food security support – to name a few. All are located in one location and are often managed in a cooperative or centralized manner. They typically also become a vibrant hub of food knowledge, exchange, and energy – and, in some cases even becoming an experiential destination in a city context.

Food hubs often become an important magnet for the potent emerging sector of small to medium scale local ownership and/or leadership programs in the food and agriculture industry. This emerging sector includes community organizations, farmers' market organizations, pre-and post-secondary education institutions, restaurants, grocery stores, entrepreneurs, food trucks, grocery stores, urban and peri-urban farmers, small-scale processors, community supported agriculture fresh-box programs, and business associations among others. All of which are creating opportunities within the local food sector. While these small energetic enterprises can get lost in a larger industrial or commercial context, within a smaller regional context they can form important relationships and attain disproportionate profile in a community by being part of a food hub. Several successful food hub projects are examined in the final section of this chapter.

Implementing Agricultural Urbanism

The major players in developing and implementing sustainable food system strategies to create agricultural urbanism include the local government, private sector developers, community groups, and academics. Because the implementation of elements in a food system most typically involves real land and development, the two major stakeholders in this process are local government and developers.

Local Government Roles

Local government can capitalize on efficiencies made possible by an integrated planning approach, which brings together different systems (e.g. infrastructure, energy, buildings, etc.) that perform different but synergistic functions to meet the vision and goals of a sustainable food system.

Key leverage points for local governments to utilize for creating more sustainable food systems include:

- Growth management (e.g. urban containment boundaries, densification, farm/urban edge integration)
- Land use (e.g. zoning and protections for food lands)
- Transportation (e.g. food distribution, walkable and transit oriented food amenities)
- Parks and open space (e.g. food festivals, farmers' markets, urban agriculture, demonstration and education)
- Infrastructure (e.g. value-added processing and distribution centres, pipe sizing for irrigation)
- Waste system (e.g. infrastructure for food waste reduction)
- Housing (e.g. community amenity around food and agriculture, and unit designs for cooking and growing food)
- Corporate operations (e.g. food procurement, demonstration kitchens, and gardens)
- Education and community resources (e.g. workshops, partnerships)

Increasingly, local governments are also beginning to identify local food and agriculture opportunities and aligning policy and plans with community objectives around health and wealth.

Engaging Developers in Agricultural Urbanism

While communities and local governments often take the initiative to envision and create agricultural or sustainable food systems plans, in most cases it is the private sector which drives the planning, design, and development. Therefore, it is critical that food systems planning evolve to have an easy fit with the reality of those who actually develop the buildings and neighbourhoods in which we live and work in.

Each development project has a unique scale, target market and structure of land uses, and as such, there is no single recipe for how food should be integrated. In some cases, it may be strategic planning to preserve farmland on the edge of a city, and in others, it may be creating rooftop gardens in a densely populated urban environment in order to support hotel chefs. Because of their many elements, it is most effective if a simple food strategy can be completed for each project by the developer in response to a public sector food strategy to outline the optimum way to integrate food into its project.

Developers need to connect the value of including as many elements of the food system in their projects to their marketing and financial plans. Often this involves highlighting elements that will increase the desirability and differentiation of their projects in a competitive marketplace. In some cases, 'food' can become a key brand element in the project and form an important part of marketing. In the same way that golf courses can make some neighbourhood more attractive to golfers, visible food system elements can have an impact in the market. Food carries strong positive emotions for most of us and a project that carries a 'food brand' and offers unique food-related amenities and experiences can be especially attractive in a competitive market to 'lifestyle' driven home buyers – especially those that are already food aware.

There are a growing number of examples of these, including two profiled later in this chapter – Southlands and New Monaco. For lower income projects, the ability to grow food and potentially even create additional income from processing food is valuable. Conversely, for higher income projects, the value of artisan food is already well-known and appreciated as a general rule that can increase the value of a project.

Examples and Lessons from the Field

This section provides examples of agricultural urbanism in practice, including observations on our own experiences in the field. These examples are drawn from projects in the public, private, and non-profit sectors and represent a small sample of the broad range of innovations and strategies for using agricultural urbanism approaches.

Southeast False Creek Neighbourhood, Vancouver, BC, Canada

One of the first urban development projects we were involved in developing a food strategy for was the Southeast False Creek (SEFC) neighbourhood on the waterfront in Vancouver – a neighbourhood which temporarily became the Athletes Village for the 2010 Winter Olympics. (de la Salle and Holland 2010)

This project was a classic urban agriculture plan but one which focused on a very high-density project. The site itself is 32.4 ha (80 acres) and is situated in an old industrial downtown waterfront which is being redeveloped as a mixed-use neighbourhood to house 13,000 people.

Two studies were completed that focused on urban agriculture and a number of related food system elements. The first study was undertaken by a multi-disciplinary team of consultants in 2002 and set the foundation for subsequent planning work (http://vancouver.ca/commsvcs/southeast/documents/pdf/urbanagr.pdf).

In 2007, a second study focused on specific design elements in order to maximize the opportunity for urban agriculture. The study took an innovative path by focusing on four intensive workshops as well as their subsequent documentation and design guideline development. At the time of the second study, many buildings were under development under a variety of owners and design teams. The intensive workshops honed in on different issues and areas of the site and were multi-hour, multi-stakeholder design charrettes that had the architects and landscape architects who were doing the work on the site involved in its design. Following presentations on the issues and opportunities, several hours of work were done focusing on designing opportunities for urban agriculture to be worked into the actual building and site plans. The workshop approach utilised a wide array of design professionals in the city and resulted in a rapid dissemination of ideas and creative techniques of high-density urban agriculture across the site (http://vancouver.ca/commsvcs/southeast/documents/pdf/designingUA.pdf).

Highlights of the plan included:
- Strategies for growing, processing, and distributing food, as well as food security, cultural appropriateness, community kitchens, celebration of food, and food education;
- A significant demonstration garden in the central public park aimed at showcasing techniques for growing food in high-density environments;
- Balcony designs that would support individual micro-gardens;
- Rooftop garden designs (Fig. 7.15);
- Productive edible landscaping strategies;
- A farmers' market location; and
- Food stores

The neighbourhood's core was built rapidly in order to be ready to house athletes for the 2010 Olympics. As a result, there was a very tight budget for construction, which was then followed by an oversupply of condominiums on the market post-Olympics. The combination of these two elements

Fig. 7.5. Section of a rooftop landscape plan for Southeast False Creek, Vancouver B.C. Source: Courtesy of Durante Kreuk Landscape Architects

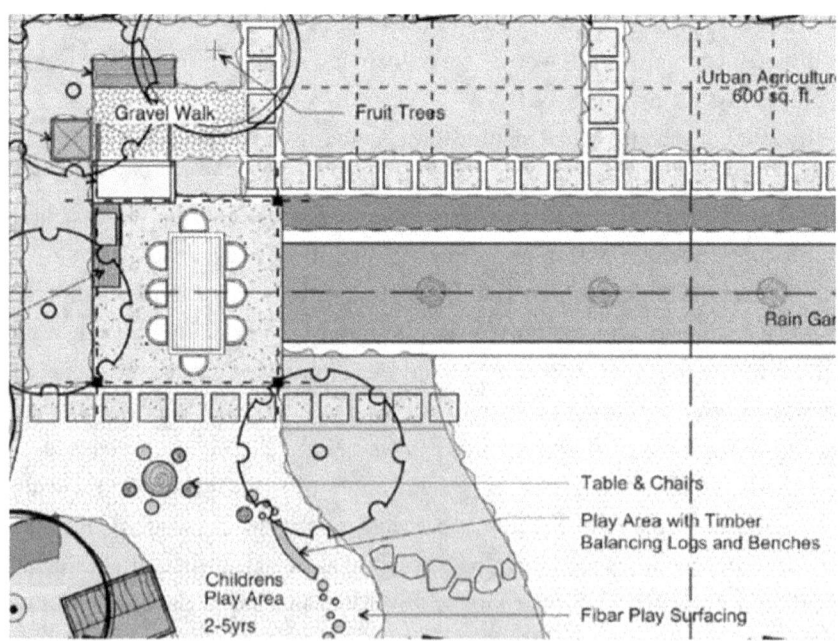

meant that a significant majority of any planned urban agriculture elements in SEFC have been postponed to a later phase – particularly those that involve public parkland. However, SEFC's urban agriculture plan remains the most comprehensive of any created for a neighbourhood in the City of Vancouver, and its reports have been distributed across North America to other teams who are also grappling with how best to claim opportunities for urban agriculture in high-density urban settings. Furthermore, SEFC urban agriculture studies have laid the foundation of urban food system strategies and associated thinking, that ultimately led to the creation of the concept of agricultural urbanism – which has been expounded upon in subsequent projects which we have undertaken.

SOUTHLANDS, TSAWWASSEN, BC

During the 1980s an epic drama began over a piece of land in Tsawwassen, a small town on the southeastern tip of the Lower Mainland in BC, when political manoeuvring resulted in the removal of a 202.4 ha (500 acre) parcel of agricultural land from BC's powerful provincial Agricultural Land Reserve (ALR). The project owner brought forward a proposal to develop 2,000 single-family homes on the site and the resulting battle in the community led to the public hearing on this development proposal – acquiring the dubious record of being the longest public hearing in Canadian history. In the end, the proposal for single family home development plan was defeated.

A number of years later, the land was sold to another developer – one who had a longstanding and esteemed history within the community. He started by keeping the existing agricultural uses on the land, and ultimately moved his family onto the site into a renovated farmhouse.

Fast-forward several decades to a time when although the economics of agriculture on the site are in decline, the community has evolved into one of the most expensive in the Lower Mainland. Once again, the developer approached the community for a comprehensive public consultation and planning process to determine what would be the best use for the parcel of land. This time however, a group of community members were able to work together in order to develop a vision for the site without any interference from the developer, and a compelling vision for its future began to emerge – one which included agriculture, development, and ecosystem preservation.

The developer then hired a team of consultants to work with the community group in order to take their vision and translate it into the necessary professional work so as to be effective in a formal approvals and development process. It was at this time that we became involved, and were asked to help formalize both a sustainability plan for the project as well as a food system strategy – all building upon the community's previous work.

The developer had hired the well-known American firm DPZ (Duany Plater-Zyberk), who had an illustrious reputation as creators of the major intellectual movements of New Urbanism and Neo-Traditional Town Planning. The principles of New Urbanism today are widely recognized as a strong foundation on which to build great neighbourhoods (www.cnu.org). New Urbanism is based on a conceptual transect of development gradients, from rural to high-density, with several types of neighbourhoods along that continuum. As the Southlands food system strategy took shape it became apparent that its vision was not entirely consistent with conventional interpretations of the transect and that innovation would be required in order to ensure that the agricultural capacity of the site was maintained while development was integrated.

On a rainy day, as we were driving back from a project strategy meeting the word 'Agricultural Urbanism' emerged in a conversation between us – and it felt immediately like a powerful concept, albeit undefined. During the following months, we worked closely with the community and the developer to develop this concept further – including setting up a website in order to deploy the ideas to the larger community.

The hallmark of the DPZ planning method was a week-long community planning and design charrette where the community, DPZ's team, and other project consultants worked together to develop a powerful concept and plan for the site, as well as a wide range of policies, design guidelines, and typologies for the project.

The concept and framework of AU was presented for the first time in its entirety to the DPZ team and the Tsawwassen community at the start of the charrette, where it instantly connected with all involved and went on to significantly influence the vision for the site. We had prepared a design brief to inform the many involved in the project on the principles and design strategies to consider for AU.

The developer had renovated a large barn so that the charrette could occur on site. In this barn and at the end of the week of hard work, a large revival tent was erected outside and the entire community was invited to come for the final presentation.

The designers, consultants, and community worked together for an entire week in the charrette in order to create something that no one had seen before: a highly urban neighbourhood plan that through development, actually enhanced the viability and prosperity of the food system far more than could have been achieved through conventional approaches.

The plan which ultimately resulted stands today (Fig. 7.7) as one of the most interesting integrations of urbanity and sustainable food systems yet to be conceived. The plan included:

- A maximum development footprint of about 30% of the site;
- A sustainability-driven mixed-use neighbourhood with green development guidelines, and a diversity of housing at a density that will greatly enhance the overall sustainability and transit performance of the entire community;
- The creation of an Agricultural Trust to hold title to about 40% of the site under the management of a local post-secondary institution (Kwantlen Polytechnic University) that had a strong sustainable horticulture and agriculture program;
- A full agricultural education program with facilities, curriculum, teaching, and mentoring farming areas, as well as full enterprise farming plots, including housing for the farmers and farm labourers;
- A vertically integrated strategy for food processing and retail, direct from the farmer to visitors and residents through farmers' stalls along the high street, as well as a year-round farmers' market and other elements;
- An integrated green infrastructure program which treats urban runoff for use as agricultural irrigation, as well as creates energy from agricultural waste and other innovative systems; and
- A comprehensive habitat enhancement strategy which integrates protected areas into urban habitat development that is carefully managed alongside urban and agriculturally productive areas.

Several months later, the developer took the report from the charrette and began a development application process to develop the site in accordance to the vision which came from the community via the charrette.

This charrette, the development application, and the subsequent publishing of the book *Agricultural Urbanism* (de la Salle and Holland 2010), launched a widespread debate within the Tsawwassen community, across the region, and out into other areas of the Province about not only the project site itself, but about the entire concept of AU.

The anti-development forces in Tsawwassen gained momentum the following year, causing the Delta Council, facing an election, to quash any proposal and start a process to put the land back in the Agricultural Land Reserve (a provincial land use designation used in British Columbia Canada to preserve farm land) – thereby prohibiting development of any kind on the site. The significant percentage of the community whom supported the project's concepts then worked together to communicate the tangible benefits for the community, farming, and surrounding ecosystem.

Later in 2011 Delta's City Council indicated that they would negotiate with the developer for a modified version of the results of the charrette – which had become politically tainted from the storm of emotion and lobbying that had taken place during the preceding two years. Presently, the developer is negotiating with the local government for a modified concept that still includes agriculture, development, and ecosystem preservation, but abandons many of the more detailed and creative innovations of the charrette plan. Some basic elements such as locating the neighbourhood on the lower quality soils, leaving the highest quality soils for field production, remains a key aspect of the discussion.

After the developer and the municipality came to an agreement about the project and the City supported the appropriate changes to the Official Community Plan, in 2014, Metro Vancouver, the regional regulatory body, also supported the project by excluding it from a protected designation in the Regional Growth Strategy.

The experience of working with the community to create the concepts of Agricultural Urbanism and then riding through the storm which ensued around the project and its core concepts demonstrated a number of things, including:

- The historical drama and polemic of development on agricultural land has become so emotionally charged that creative solutions are difficult to put on the table – and even more difficult for politicians to deal with. At this point, so many fall prey to thinking that the only thing required for a sustainable food system is raw agricultural land. It appeared that few could accept the value that Southlands offered in proposing to fill a major gap in the regional food system of training and nurturing the next generation of farmers and food producers by creating a place where a value-added model of farm production could help ensure reasonable incomes for farm families;
- Many in a community want to preserve agricultural land for its pastoral and romantic visible character but are reticent to also accept the serious

Fig. 7.7. The 'Canal Plan', one of three site concepts resulting from the Southlands Charrette. Source: Courtesy of Century Group, drawing by Duany Plater-Zyberk

implications to an adjacent residential area of major industrial agriculture, and will therefore use various means of claiming pro-agricultural positions in order to largely freeze the land for their viewing enjoyment – regardless the impact on a landowner or farmers. While this stand-point effectively sterilizes land from an agriculture and development perspective, the land does remain theoretically available for future farming or other uses (unlike farmland that has been converted to developed land); and
- The opportunities for merging both urban and agricultural food systems are exciting and offer enormous win/wins for those willing to tackle them.

In spite of the conflict over this piece of land and its underlying concepts, the work to begin to refocus attention from solely agricultural land to the more important issues of sustainable urban and regional food systems has started, and will undoubtedly continue to grow and evolve the discussion surrounding the project over upcoming years – a process which never could have begun in BC without the leadership of the Southlands project developer.

New Monaco, Okanagan Valley, BC

The New Monaco project is a 50.6 ha (125 acre) master-planned community in BC's Okanagan Valley in the small town of Peachland (www.newmonaco.ca). Presently this project is partway through its approvals process, but nevertheless offers an interesting insight into how a progressive developer can integrate a food systems strategy into a development project (District of Peachland, 2011).

In June 2011, Peachland's Mayor and Council unanimously approved the proposal to develop the New Monaco community with 2800 housing units and 250,000 sq. ft. of commercial/retail space along with a hotel. The vision for the community includes:

- A mixed-use village and residential area structured as a transit- and pedestrian-oriented neighbourhood;
- A comprehensive strategy for green buildings and innovative infrastructure;
- A diversity of multi-family housing including affordable housing as well as a sequence of assisted housing to support aging-in-place;
- A multi-faceted local economy built on several elements including: a health and medical cluster, a high-tech cluster, an educational cluster, as well as a food, hospitality and recreation cluster; and
- An extensive system of parks and trails.

As consultants we worked with the landowner in order to develop a conceptual sustainable food systems strategy early on in the project – a process which was highly productive as the landowner had a history as a successful restaurateur. The Okanagan Valley has a deep history of food and wine culture, including historically being one of the best fruit-producing regions in Canada. It also has over 200 wineries within roughly an hour's drive of the New Monaco site, and is known as the best wine region north of Napa Valley.

Food strategy elements that emerged at New Monaco include:
- A comprehensive urban agricultural strategy including: community gardens, productive landscaping, and chef's gardens throughout the built area;

- Vineyards and a winery located on the site's south-facing arid and rocky slopes, possibly managed in a partnership with a local college;
- An artisan food processing agenda – connected to the market and planned food festivals;
- A significant food and wine market in the heart of the village centre, along with other food retail integrated throughout the community;
- A major wine destination facility, brew pubs, and others;
- A major cluster of cafés and restaurants;
- Food festivals throughout the year;
- A chef's lodge (residency, industrial kitchen, restaurant space) developed for Chef Emmanuel David, a seven-time international culinary gold medal winner for Canada who is a personal friend of the project's managing partner; and
- A major destination training facility for cuisine and hospitality, intended as a partnership with a local college.

The developer hired a team of local filmmakers who are just finishing up a TV program on the food, wine, and lifestyle of the Okanagan (http://fitforaking.co/) to lead the work on the project's promotional video. This was done so as to ensure maximum incorporation of images and information from the Valley's food culture.

The Okanagan Valley, for all its reputation for food and wine, is still struggling to reach a critical mass of a food culture – the first formal events

Fig. 7.8. New Monaco Site Plan for Approved Area Structure Plan – June 2011, District of Peachland, BC.

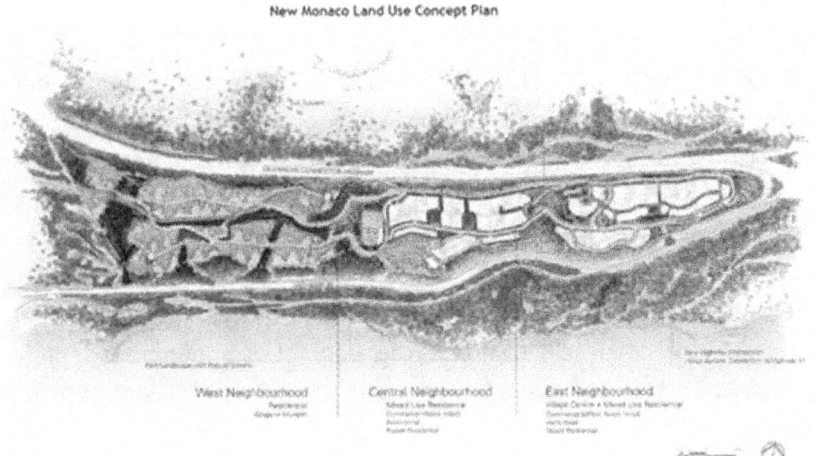

to connect producers and local chefs occurred in 2013. While it is seen as a key food and wine destination, the reality is that the food culture and their leaders are scattered all over the Valley. New Monaco has taken it upon itself to program and design its village centre to become a hub for the experience of food and wine culture in the Valley.

The New Monaco project points to the potential advantage which a conscious integration of food into a project can offer a developer in terms of positioning, reputation, and network connections for the project's success in the community.

CITY OF EDMONTON: CITY-WIDE FOOD AND URBAN AGRICULTURE STRATEGY

The City of Edmonton is amongst the leading municipalities in North America who are undertaking comprehensive planning to identify local opportunities for sustainability in food and agriculture systems. Although other metropolitan centres such as Toronto, Calgary, and Vancouver have undertaken food system strategies, Edmonton is unique in how it has linked a significant discussion around land use, growth management, and over 7,000 ha of farmland into the planning process in addition to many other opportunity areas.

In 2010, the City of Edmonton adopted *The Way We Grow*, the Municipal Development Plan (MDP) for the City. The MDP contains three key recommendations: 1) Establish an Edmonton Food Council, 2) Develop a city-wide food and agriculture strategy, and the twist 3) No new area plans for the urban growth areas could be approved until the CWFAS was completed.

Since November of 2011, a dedicated Project Advisory Committee has been meeting to discuss and debate the scope and scale of the Strategy as well as the recommendations it contains. The advisory committee is comprised of a range of stakeholder groups representing multiple perspectives and bring a range of backgrounds from farming, agriculture and business consulting, and developers to community organizations, senior levels of government, universities, and local businesses. This group, along with the dedicated staff team at the City of Edmonton and project consultants, developed a Strategy to create a more resilient food system in Edmonton.

The development of the Strategy over 2011 and 2012 involved a substantial consultation process including pubic surveys, citizen panels[1], stakeholder group meetings, an agriculture inventory and assessment, and a report on opportunities for the local food economy.

Project Vision, Goals and Key Directions

The following vision statement provides the basis for the MDP food and agriculture section as well as the vision for the Strategy (City of Edmonton, 2012).

> Edmonton has a resilient food and agriculture system that contributes to the local economy and the overall cultural, financial, social and environmental sustainability of the city.

Establishing a vision as part of the statutory plan provided an essential starting point for the development of the strategy. Much of the process involved understanding what this vision meant from the multiple, and sometimes conflicting, perspectives of the stakeholders and larger community.

The discussion around the vision for the Strategy generated five key goals regarding further guidance on providing a comprehensive set of recommendations based upon the values of the stakeholders and community. The five goals of the Strategy are:

1. A stronger, more vibrant local economy

Food and agriculture in Edmonton contribute more significantly to the creation of community wealth. There are more jobs and business opportunities in the local food and agriculture sectors. As a result, Edmontonians have more opportunities to buy, share, and enjoy local and regional food.

2. A healthier, more food secure community

Everyone in Edmonton has access to enough nutritious, safe, and culturally-appropriate food. People have more opportunities to learn about and participate in the local food system by growing, buying, and celebrating. Local food is more accessible to everyone – individuals, families, and communities are encouraged to grow, prepare, preserve, and purchase local food.

3. Healthier ecosystems
Food and agriculture systems positively contribute to the overall health and ecosystem services that green spaces provide. Areas of high biodiversity, environmental sensitivity, and ecological significance are protected. Food and agricultural areas are managed to support wildlife habitat, conserve water use, and are environmentally benign or restorative.

4. Less energy, emissions, and waste
The food and agriculture systems are highly energy efficient and generate little waste. These systems reuse waste-heat, agricultural by-products, and food wastes to create alternative renewable energy sources as an advantage for local organizations and businesses. Less solid waste and air pollution are generated during the producing, transporting, distributing, marketing, packaging, eating, and recycling of food.

5. More vibrant, attractive, and unique places
Food and agriculture both create and contribute to vibrant, attractive, and unique places for Edmontonians and visitors alike. Public and private spaces are designed to use food and agriculture as a way to enhance the local food culture, celebrate food, as well as animate and enliven shared spaces. Visitors to Edmonton appreciate and experience the local food culture. Food growing, processing, buying, selling, and eating places are considered at the neighbourhood level.

As the consultation progressed, nine key directions were distilled out of a multi-tiered process. The key directions then provided the scope for the recommendations – the specific actions that are being recommended to the City Council.
- Establish the Edmonton Food Council
- Provide Food Skill Education and Information
- Integrate Land Use for Agriculture
- Expand Urban Agriculture
- Support Farmers and Ecological Approaches to Farming
- Develop Local Food Infrastructure Capacity
- Increase Local Food Demand and Link with Supply
- Enliven the Public Realm Through a Diversity of Food Activities
- Treat Food Waste as a Resource

It should be noted that there was substantial debate within the Project Advisory Committee about every aspect of the Strategy. In the end, not everyone agreed upon everything, and some members did not support the Strategy in whole or in part. For full project details, resources, and documents please visit the City of Edmonton's website at (www.edmonton.ca/FoodandAg).

It has yet to be determined how the Strategy will affect land use decisions for Edmonton. Like other communities who commendably undertake food and agriculture system strategies, the CWFAS itself is only a starting point to help Edmonton move towards more resilient food systems. Edmonton has hosted a community-wide forum for the discussion around the exciting opportunities and real challenges for achieving a community vision for food and agriculture. Not all of the tough questions will have been answered through the Strategy, although frameworks and starting points are provided to integrate the multiple perspectives from within the community into recommendations for how the City of Edmonton should make decisions. This outcome is in and of itself significant and puts Edmonton on the path to leading and inspiring municipalities all across North America to think and plan for food and agriculture.

Food Hubs[2]

As the planning profession begins to embrace food and agriculture as important opportunities for sustainable cities and towns, planners have begun searching for ideas that can be implemented at the local level. Food hubs are gaining popularity throughout Canada and the US as a way to build strong local food systems and healthy communities.

As we struggle with the challenges of the 21st century and set targets to curb our bad habits, food and agriculture have surfaced as one of the most significant sustainability opportunities. The planning and design profession has found itself at the forefront of managing many of the fundamental aspects of the food and agriculture system such as land use, infrastructure, long range planning, community development, and green building – among many others.

One of the key barriers to a strong local food system is the lack of infrastructure linking rural supply with urban demand – namely, processing, storage, distribution, and sales points. There is wide agreement in the industry that these infrastructure gaps have the most effect on small and medium-sized producers and buyers which are not served by the current high-volume production and wholesale system established for primarily export VEDC (2009).

Food hubs, in their many iterations, provide an entry point for multi-sector investment in local food systems. In Canada and the US, many cities are building food hubs as a way of supporting both communities and local farming by filling the local food infrastructure gap.

Opportunity in Synergy

Within our food value chain, small and medium-sized farms, processors, and distributors have the best opportunity for augmenting and securing local food supply. Their marketplace flexibility, higher product quality, traceability, and capacity permits them to build the brand and value of local food through longer, stronger buyer relationships. Studies have demonstrated that locally-produced foods, sold directly to local buyers, generate higher margins and up to three-times the spin-off economic impact and returns on investment compared with traditional supermarkets (Barney & Worth, 2008).

Food hubs not only provide local food economy support, but also result in a range of benefits. For example, food hubs enable institutional procurement of local food by providing aggregation and distribution at a scale that may accommodate large purchasers. Food hubs also provide the necessary infrastructure to spark new entrepreneurial business by providing commercial kitchens and much needed cold, dry, and frozen storage. For instance, in Metro Vancouver, over 50% of produce that is grown is wasted *pre-consumer* (VEDC 2009). A regional food hub would provide the opportunity for entrepreneurs to test out products by using this wasted produce to make sauces, juices, and other value-added products, and to possibly start a business that has an immediate competitive edge due to inexpensive raw product costs. In addition to supporting small food-related businesses, food hubs also assist existing ventures by helping to scale-up and streamline their operations through providing warehousing and cold storage suitable for small-scale and medium producers.

Other benefits of food hubs include increasing access to local foods at the neighbourhood level, as well as supporting regional farming and farmers by increasing access to large urban markets – regardless of the size of the farm. Food hubs are also a place for the community to learn about food, farming, and healthy eating and food hubs may also contribute to the reduction of GHG emissions associated with long distance travel required to import products that are grown or produced locally.

Working Definition of Food Hubs

A food hub is a place that integrates a wide spectrum of land uses, design strategies, and programs focused on food with a view to increased access, visibility, and the experience of growing food within the city. The USDA defines a food hub as 'a centrally located facility with a business management structure facilitating the aggregation, storage, processing, distribution, and/or marketing of locally/regionally produced food products' (USDA, 2010). While this definition lacks the richness of the food experience, as well as the social and community dimensions of food, it does provide a base-description of what food hubs are.

Food hubs are designed to meet specific needs in a given region or municipality and they differ from place to place. The central theme of all food hubs however, is that many operations are close to each other. This proximity creates opportunities and synergies centred around local food connections, a strong farm sector, and healthy communities. Based on examples from across North America, food hub performance areas include:

- *Aggregation, distribution, and storage*: By providing the access, warehousing, and coordination required to bringing products from many farms to one location; increases in market access for local producers and; supply in the quantity, quality and the consistency which large purchasers such as restaurants and institutions demand.
- *Processing and commercial kitchens*: Access to processing facilities, such as commercial kitchens offer opportunities for small businesses to test products, food cart vendors to prepare healthy items, and entrepreneurs to process foods. This in turn allows produce that would otherwise be wasted to be transformed into value-added items. Communities permitted this access are then able to learn about food preparation in a professional setting.
- *Teaching and learning spaces*: Classrooms, food labs, demonstration sites, and educational greenhouses provide important food and agriculture learning opportunities.
- *Community gathering spaces*: Food hubs may have many different structures such as a farmers' market hall that could be used as lecture halls or rented out for celebratory events when not in use.

- *Direct-marketing*: Often, food hubs feature a farmers' marketplace or may provide other direct marketing functions. This business sector is critical to increasing capacity for existing farmers' markets and increasing the availability of local food to consumers.
- *Front-line services*: Some food hubs will be more focused on a community outreach model that could involve front-line services, like providing affordable healthy food to low-income families.
- *Food retail*: Permanent food retail facilities, operated by local individuals, can provide a country market-like atmosphere that will add to the enjoyment of frequenting food hubs.
- *Green design and quality public realm*: Welcoming the public into these multi-functional areas requires that other factors need to be considered. While public safety is a first consideration, dining facilities must be provided, and areas where children can play would encourage their parents to bring them along. A food hub would be the ideal place to incorporate green building design standards and should also include on-site compost collection facilities to complete the circle.
- *Office space*: Office space for community groups, businesses, and others endeavours would also add to the value of the business model.

Leading Examples of Food Hubs

There are many examples of the various food hub models across North America. In fact, there has been so much interest in establishing food hubs that funders and partners have been unable to keep up with the demand. The following examples each illustrate one of the food hub models described.

The Stop: A Community Model: The Stop Community Food Centre or 'The Stop' is located in Davenport West – one of Toronto's lowest income neighbourhoods. It was opened in the mid-1970s as a food bank, where it provided emergency food relief to the community. Since then, The Stop has evolved into a Community Food Centre that complements its emergency food service activities with skill-building and educational programs centred on food and food security (Sharf et al, 2010).

Recent influences of The Stop include (The Stop 2008):
- Each week approximately 600 people now shop at The Green Barn Market, a key facility within the Stop;
- 176 community kitchen sessions welcomed the participation of 1,664 people who were able to learn about food preparation;
- 290 children participated in a food systems educational program which included learning about poverty, cooking, food security, and farming issues;

- The Green Barn Farmer's Market featured 50 vendors selling farm produce worth approximately $1.25 million; and
- The purchase of local farm production valued at approximately $30,000 as well as $40,000 of locally produced organic food.(The Stop, 2008)

The Food District Model, Detroit Eastern Market: Established in 1891, the Eastern Market District is considered the largest public market in the United States (Sieniewicz, 2008). Located on 43-acres of land approximately one mile northeast of Detroit's downtown core, facilities consist of five large warehouses over six blocks that are used year-round for a wholesale farmers' market. It operates at night throughout the week and on Saturday mornings the 'AM Market' is open to the public. Surrounding these warehouses there are permanent buildings which are occupied by privately-owned shops, restaurants, and offices – most of which are in involved in food-related businesses like wholesale food distribution. In total, there are over 250 independent vendors and merchants in the Eastern Market, mostly involved in food processing, wholesaling and retailing, with the market alone generating around $25 million annually.

Local Food Business Model, Calgary Farmers' Market: The Calgary farmers' market is an indoor venue open four days a week with annual revenues of approximately $60 million. The market is planning to build a processing kitchen on site and open a chefs' market. The Calgary Farmers' Market is a New Generation Co-operative with no support from government or additional grants.

New City Market, a work in progress: The New City Market initiative in Vancouver, currently in its pre-development planning phase (Fig 7.9), has envisioned and tested the feasibility of a 50,000 sq. ft. facility that will feature a market hall, a distribution centre for aggregation and distribution support, and a commercial kitchen. Office space and restaurants are also part of the overall business plan, as is the capability to hold special events. Design and planning for the New City Market is based upon the local food business model of the food hub.

In short, food hubs in their many incarnations are an emerging and innovative strategy for local governments and communities. While impact and success must be continually monitored and reported on widely, the investment in and development of multi-sector food hubs is sure to provide returns.

Fig 7.9. Illustrative Concept for New City Market, Vancouver BC.
Source: citylab http://thecitylab.net

Conclusion

As global, national, and local food systems continue to show their vulnerabilities and shortcomings such as food shortages, cost of food, obesity, starvation, desertification of land, as well as the exporting of jobs and other value in the food system to other countries, the visibility of the food system and its complex workings will continue to increase. Governments, universities, non-profits, and the private sector will thus increasingly be drawn into thinking about how food and agriculture can be addressed in regional and urban contexts to increase the resilience and social and economic value of the community.

As communities face the new challenges of the 21st century and embrace the change that leads to opportunity, harnessing the latent potential of sustainable regional food and agriculture systems (SURFOS) will be essential.

Agricultural Urbanism (AU) provides a framework and approach for planning and design professionals to proactively harness the economic, social, and environmental value of food and agriculture systems. AU poses an interesting challenge to the conventional views surrounding land use, urban design, development, and policy. Under the pressure of growth, many communities in North America are grappling with how to address irreplaceable farmland and ecosystems. Without a practical framework for identifying the value and opportunity of taking action in many ways on food systems, the building blocks for SURFOS can be ill defined or poorly connected to decisions, communities risk continuing to experience negative trends in economic development and health. However, with a framework like AU, planners and designers are better able to proactively approach conflicting land uses, economic development, community health, and environmental restoration.

New tools, policies, and designs are needed to achieve higher performance in food and agriculture systems that bring more benefits including health and wealth to communities. While there are barriers to implementing AU it is crucial to continue to develop new innovative solutions for communities while also tracking their impact and progress. Communities, governments, businesses and universities across North America are inspiring others to identify and take advantage of sustainable food system opportunities.

This chapter has discussed how planning for food and agriculture systems at the local level provides powerful strategies for creating more community and regional health and wealth. It has also presented AU as one such strategy for reconsidering how our communities grow. These ideas have been offered here not as a definitive work on food and cities but rather perspectives and starting points that contribute to a growing focus on food and agriculture at the local level.

References

Barney & Worth. 2008. 'Growing Portland's Farmers' Markets. Direct-Market Economic Analysis'.

Bloom, Johnathan. 2010. How America Throws Away Nearly Half of Its Food (and What We Can Do About It). Da Capo Press, Philadelphia PA.

Canning, Patrick. 2011. 'A Revised and Expanded Food Dollar Series – A Better Understanding of Our Food Costs.' USDA Economic Research Service, Economic Research Report Number 114, February 2011.

Centre for Disease Control and Prevention. 2014. Chronic Disease and Health Promotion. Accessed Nov 22, 2014. http://www.cdc.gov/chronicdisease/overview/

CNN. 2011. How the Modern Day Tomato Came To Be. Retrieved Nov 22, 2014. http://eatocracy.cnn.com/2011/09/08/how-the-modern-day-tomato-came-to-be/

de la Salle, Janine, Mark Holland. 2010. Agricultural Urbanism: Building Sustainable Food Systems for 21st Century Cities. Green Frigate Books.

District of Peachland. 2011. 'New Monaco Area Structure Plan'. http://www.peachland.ca/cms.asp?wpID=316.

Garnett, Tara. 2007. 'The Alcohol we drink and its contribution to the UK's greenhouse gas emissions: A discussion paper.' Food Climate Research Network, University of Surrey.

Hild, Chris (2009). 'The Economy of Local Food in Vancouver'. Vancouver Economic Development Commission.

Sharf, Kathryn, Levkoe, Charles Z., Saul, Nick. 2010. 'In Every Community A Place for Food: The Role of the Community Food Centre in Building a Local, Sustainable, and Just Food System'. Prepared by the Metcalf Foundation, Toronto Ont.

Sieniewicz, Krieger Chan. 2008. 'Eastern Market Corporation. Eastern Market District Economic Development Strategy'. Cambridge, MA.

Siwa Msangi, Rosegrant, Mark. 2009. *World Agriculture in a Dramatically Changing Environment.* Food and Agriculture Organization. http://www.fao.org/docrep/014/i2280e/i2280e02.pdf

The Stop. 2008. 'The Stop Community Food Centre Growing Together Annual Report 2007/2008.'

VEDC. 2009. 'The Economy of Local Food in Vancouver'. Vancouver Economic Development Commission.

USDA. 2010. Blog post, Dec 14, 2010. Accessed April 2011, URL: http://blogs.usda.gov/2010/12/14/getting-to-scale-with-regional-food-hubs/

Notes

1 Please visit the Centre for Public Involvement at the University of Alberta for more information on the Citizen Panel Process.

2 Excerpts from an article first published in Plan Canada Fall 2011. Fall Reference: de la Salle, Janine (2011). Local Food Hubs: A New Strategy in the Field of Food System Planning. Plan Canada, Fall 2011.

Commentary – Food Regions, Values and Equity

Betsy Donald

Mark Holland and Janine de la Salle's Chapter on *Agriculture Urbanism: building sustainable urban and regional food systems for 21st Century cities*, is a stimulating read, providing a wealth of information on the latest thinking in this field. I like their term 'agricultural urbanism' because it brings us back to a key issue in food system planning: namely, the importance of preserving prime-farm land in the face of rapid urbanization and development pressures. Their solutions are innovative because they emphasize the fundamental connection between agricultural preservation and value-added local food development. Few authors have done this in such a systematic study and Holland and de la Salle are to be commended for this. Their planning case of Southlands, Tsawwassen, BC is a wonderful vision of how agricultural preservation and value-added food production could co-exist alongside a new housing and commercial development. It is too bad the plan was stalled at the political level. We can only hope that local governments and other social actors will seriously consider and eventually implement these kinds of visionary plans.

I want to respond to three themes that they discuss in their paper: (1) the concept of a regional food planning system, (2) the importance of adding value through a food- not-just agricultural approach to planning; and (3) their nascent conversation about food deserts and equity in the food system.

First, I agree with their focus on a regional food system, in which they argue that the regional scale is an appropriate scale to examine sustainable food systems. As I have reported elsewhere, there are two types of regionalization: the trend towards local food production and the consumption of 'regional foods'; and the emergence of new regional food networks (Kneafsey 2010; Donald et al. 2010). Holland and de la Salle explore both but focus on the importance of a network perspective as it reflects a curiosity about the complex ways in which food is produced, distributed, consumed and discarded. They also acknowledge that regional food systems often defy strict categorization of being completely 'local' or 'global', 'alternative' or 'conventional'. The network perspective is useful because it provides a conceptual terminology for a system that deals with *relationships* rather than just monolithic structures of systems (see Kneafsey 2010, 179). As they point out, relationship building is key when implementing on the ground sustainable food plans. In developing a regional food system, however, they suggest that 'who leads the strategy is less important than ensuring that all stakeholder perspectives and concerns are represented in its development.' I agree that it doesn't matter whether it is a public, private or non-profit actor, but I would emphasize the point that a strong civic leader is a necessary condition. A review of any successfully implemented regional food system reveals the importance of a civic actor or leader that takes charge and moves things forward. Wayne Roberts, former manager of Toronto's Food Policy Council (2000-2010), is an example of the kind of visionary leader who was able to build relationships among disparate actors and get things done (Blay-Palmer 2009).

Second, I strongly agree with Holland and de la Salle's thesis that any successful agricultural preservation program must have a value-added food processing component. This is something I found in my own research on the 'creative food economy' where several years ago we spent a considerable amount of time interviewing food firms that had different innovative pathways than more traditional food manufacturing firms (Blay-Palmer and Donald 2006; Donald and Blay-Palmer 2006). Two companies in particular stood out as examples of companies that had transitioned from a more traditional food production approach to one that was more innovative in terms of addressing the principles of agricultural urbanism. The first example is Thomas' Utopia Brand certified hand-packed organic tomatoes that are canned locally and sold across Canada. A third generation tomato growing farm located in Maidstone, Ontario the company states on its website that it is 'no longer about maximizing productivity and yield', but 'rather about addressing the demand for environmental accountability and integrity through sustainable field and factory practices'. Their company also demonstrates how links can be rebuilt between the rural and the urban and how sophisticated urban demands can offer opportunities for rural development (Blay-Palmer and Donald 2006: 387).

Another example of value-added agricultural urbanism is Mapleton's Organic Dairy, a 600 acre dairy and grain farm in Southern Ontario on the outskirts of a rapidly developing urban region. This company also transitioned from a conventional dairy farm to an organic farm with a CSA offering meat, milk, frozen yogurt and ice cream. Innovations for Mapleton, like many other small organic and local farms, also include the development of new distribution channels (on-farm, trade shows, music festivals, and a community-shared agricultural buying group) as a way to build product recognition and get their products to consumers (Donald 2009:11). One of the challenges this and other small companies face concerns distribution and the wish to retain the ownership and pricing of their product.

A few years ago Mapleton's ice cream was in huge demand and the company made the decision to refuse Walmart's interest to stock their product 'for ethical and business reasons' but decided to go with Sobey's instead. As reported in the paper, from *Kraft to Craft*: 'In making these decisions, Mapleton sits in the complicated space of opposing yet complementary markets: through its efforts to construct alternatives to the conventional market by going local and organic and building closer social ties between farmers and consumers, Mapleton is also de-commodifying food. On the other hand, Mapleton is responding to consumer demand for local, fresh and sustainable products through the place-based marketing and distribution of its product in a more conventional manner (Donald 2009: 12).

This distribution dilemma faced by artisanal value-added food companies can be addressed in part through the planning of 'food hubs', smaller retail shops and closer connections between urban and rural development as Holland and de la Salle document. Nevertheless food access and retail distribution questions also raise a third issue which I want to touch upon: food deserts and the difficulty of achieving equity and justice in the food system.

Local and alternative food movements for years have been accused of ignoring issues of justice, equity and access in constructing alternative food systems (Allen 2010). Is local food simply food for the urban elite or is there a social inclusion opportunity? (Donald and Blay-Palmer 2006). Fortunately, there is more and more research pointing to the later, but it is still a challenging issue that must be addressed. Part of any solution to the food desert problem must address the broader issues of affordability and need and the particular structural realities of growing inequality in our cities. A recent paper by Alan Walks (2013) found that income inequality and polarization have been growing much faster in our big cities like Toronto, Vancouver and Calgary, than in Canada overall. We now see wealthier neighbourhoods with farmer's markets, fancy supermarkets, healthier residents and safer streets abutting poorer neighbourhoods with food deserts, more health problems and substandard infrastructure. Fortunately, there are many people and charities committed to developing innovative food delivery and access programs for those living in poverty. Yet, as others have argued, this is not enough: fundamentally many of those living in poverty need financial access in the form of better welfare and other social development policies, for example, to adequately access good quality food through any food retail channel (Bedore 2010). Certainty, this is a topic that still requires a great deal of reflection given the profoundly unequal societies we are creating that leave far too many people hungry and without adequate access to good food. Indeed, we should all push the concept of agricultural urbanism further in this direction.

References

Allen, P. 2010. Realizing justice in local food systems. Cambridge Journal of Regions, Economy and Society, 3(2), 295-308.

Bedore, M. 2010. Just urban food systems: A new direction for food access and urban social justice. Geography Compass, 4(9), 1418-1432.

Blay-Palmer, A. 2009. The Canadian pioneer: The genesis of urban food policy in Toronto. International Planning Studies, 14(4), 401-416.

Donald, B., & Blay-Palmer, A. 2006. The urban creative-food economy: producing food for the urban elite or social inclusion opportunity?. Environment and planning A, 38(10), 1901.

Blay-Palmer, A., & Donald, B. 2006. A tale of three tomatoes: The new food economy in Toronto, Canada. Economic Geography, 82(4), 383-399.

Donald, B. 2008. Food systems planning and sustainable cities and regions: the role of the firm in sustainable food capitalism. Regional Studies, 42(9), 1251-1262.

Donald, B. 2009. From Kraft to Craft: innovation and creativity in Ontario's Food Economy. Martin Prosperity Institute.

Donald, B., Gertler, M., Gray, M., & Lobao, L. 2010. Re-regionalizing the food system?. Cambridge Journal of Regions, Economy and Society, 3(2), 171-175.

Kneafsey, M. 2010. The region in food—important or irrelevant?. Cambridge Journal of Regions, Economy and Society, 3(2), 177-190.

Walks, A. 2013. Income inequality and polarization in Canada's Cities: an examination and new form of measurement, Working Paper, University of Toronto's Cities Centre, Research Paper 227, August 2013, accessed March 16, 2014.

Chapter 8

Urban Agriculture as a Response to the Great Recession

Nevin Cohen

Introduction

Historically, economic downturns have prompted cities to support urban agriculture to enable people to supplement their diets and to provide low-cost stewardship of vacant spaces (Lawson 2005). As in previous periods of economic crisis, the global financial meltdown of 2007 and the ensuing 'great recession' have also contributed to the recent growth in urban agriculture activity and the implementation of supportive municipal policies. A number of cities have revised zoning ordinances to accommodate agriculture, adopted local laws and regulations to make it easier to farm, and have made organizational changes within government to integrate urban agriculture more fully into agency procedures and the city's physical landscape (Cohen 2012). One of the key questions for policymakers is whether the burst of interest in urban agriculture will endure, or whether the attention to the issue will wane when the economy rebounds. This chapter argues that the urban agriculture policies, governance structures, and physical changes created in response to and shaped by the financial crisis make it likely that urban agriculture will remain as much a part of the city's political and physical landscape as conventional systems of water and sewage, sanitation, transportation, parks, and housing.[1]

Economic Drivers of Urban Agriculture

The recent economic crisis, beginning in 2007, resulted in a loss of nearly $20 trillion worth of assets owned by US households due to collapsing housing prices and financial markets, along with a decline in median household wealth of approximately 40% (Beachy 2012). The crisis caused industrial production to fall, with the resulting loss of some 8.8 million US jobs and, by 2009, a drop in average household income of $5,800 in the US and a resulting 2% fall in the world's production of goods and services (Beachy 2012). Compounding the effects of the Great Recession, global commodity markets had been highly volatile, with food prices reaching their highest levels in 30 years during the summer of 2008, falling the following winter, and then rising again soon thereafter. Food price volatility and overall price increases are likely to increase as climate change results in more frequent extreme weather events, food production expands to marginal lands to keep up with rising demand, and water scarcity and soil depletion make growing food more challenging (Food and Agriculture Organization 2012). These economic challenges have led to three important drivers of urban agriculture policy:

- Rising food insecurity and diet related diseases;
- Declining municipal revenues coupled with increased costs; and
- Cultural changes that have made alternative food systems increasingly popular.

The policy responses to these drivers have included various strategies to support urban agriculture.

Food Insecurity and Obesity

A significant consequence of the great recession and food price spikes has been increased food insecurity and malnourishment, even in relatively well-off cities in the global North. For example, enrollment in the US Supplemental Nutrition Assistance Program (SNAP) grew 20% between fiscal year 2009 and 2010 as household incomes fell (USDA 2011). Between 2010 and 2011, 29 cities surveyed by the US Conference of Mayors reported an average increase of 15.5% in emergency food assistance requests (United States Conference of Mayors 2011). Rising food insecurity, and reliance on inexpensive diets high in carbohydrates and fats, has led to an increase in the number of people who are overweight and obese, resulting in high public health costs (see Chapter 2). In the US, some 73 million adults and

12 million children and adolescents are obese, requiring 21% of the nation's annual medical expenditures for treatment of obesity-related diseases and causing 122,000 deaths per year (Institute of Medicine 2012; Finkelstein et al. 2009).

While the great recession has exacerbated food insecurity, it has also prompted municipal support for urban agriculture. In the US, for example, the American Recovery and Reinvestment Act of 2009 (Recovery Act) provided $372 million in grants to municipalities under its Communities Putting Prevention to Work (CPPW) program that supports initiatives to reduce obesity and improve public health, in part an attempt to rein in the costs of health care. The CPPW grants have enabled a number of cities to engage in food systems planning and program development, including plans that identify opportunities to expand urban agriculture.1 Chicago, for example, used CPPW funds to develop an urban agriculture policy for the city that allows produce sales at community gardens and encourages aquaculture (integrated fish and produce farming), and enabled the city to convene a workshop to develop a citywide food plan to address urban agriculture. Portland's Multnomah County used its CPPW grant to work with faith-based organizations to establish community gardens and farm stands. Minneapolis developed four Local Food Resource Hubs with its CPPW money to help residents to grow, preserve, cook and compost their own produce.[2]

In addition to the work carried out under the CPPW grants, community activists and urban agriculture practitioners, in many cases with the support of government agencies, religious institutions, NGOs and philanthropic organizations, have created gardens and farms to help people grow their own food and operate related ventures, such as farmers' markets, to supply surrounding communities with fresh produce. The goals of these gardens and farms include educating residents about food, nutrition, and food system inequities in addition to producing food. Some activists have even gone further, recognizing that food production merely alleviates the symptoms of deeper inequities that have underpinned the economic crisis, and have organized agricultural projects to promote social, economic, environmental, and food justice by addressing racial oppression, gender inequality, and economic disparities through the process of food cultivation (Reynolds and Cohen, forthcoming).

Economic Development and Job Creation

Cities have faced significant economic repercussions from the Great Recession, including declining local tax bases, rising municipal costs, and reduced federal aid, which have pressured them to roll back services and delay infrastructure projects (Pagano et al., 2012). Urban agriculture has been advanced as a strategy to transform the urban environment into one that businesses and middle class residents find clean, attractive, and healthier, while opening up new land for investment through remediation, rezoning, and redevelopment and augmenting tax revenue by increasing real estate values. Often urban agriculture policies are folded into broader sustainability initiatives, a form of 'sustainability fix' that attempts to use cost-effective environmental initiatives to support development (While et al. 2004). Urban agriculture also has the potential to reduce municipal costs as farmers and gardeners clean up vacant sites, remediate contaminated soil, manage formerly vacant public spaces, and program their sites with educational, youth development and job readiness training programs, activities for seniors, and food retail distribution businesses like farmers' markets and Community Supported Agriculture (CSA) shares (Cohen et al. 2012). Farms and gardens also provide ecosystem services, helping to contain storm water potentially at a lower cost than conventional infrastructure built and managed by cities (Cohen & Ackerman 2011). Cities have also supported agriculture to facilitate entrepreneurship and economic development, including the creation of for-profit farms, urban agriculture suppliers, farmers' markets, and food processing businesses (see chapter 7). In extreme cases, like the city of Detroit, which faces a fiscal crisis so grave it is nearly in receivership, urban agriculture has been a strategy for getting some of its 40 square miles of vacant land back onto the tax roles and maintained by private businesses.

Cultural Changes

The economic crisis and resulting high unemployment and lower earning potential in conventional jobs has made craft-based occupations, including farming and small-scale food production, attractive employment and small business opportunities (Beachy 2012). This has been accompanied by a cultural shift as well. Research by Conill et al. (2012) in Spain found that in the aftermath of the economic crisis people have increasingly sought out a range of creative activities, including urban agriculture, not only to earn subsistence income but also to explore new opportunities for social interaction based on ecological values. As McClintock (2010) argues, the heightened interest in urban agriculture is also the result of a reaction against the increasing alienation from the environment and food production that urban residents experience. Interest in creating alternative food systems has also been spurred by a desire to counter other looming global crises affecting food, from climate change to concerns about peak oil, water, and soil.

Policy Responses

The financial crisis and the great recession have shaped the nature of urban agriculture policymaking and program development in several key respects. The increasing level of food insecurity and malnourishment, and resulting human and public health costs, have led cities to focus on supporting urban agriculture as a means to augment the existing food retail system and to improve food access and nutrition. Job losses, declining real estate values and the need for cities, even those faring well in the recession, to remain economically competitive have spurred policies to support entrepreneurial urban agriculture that create jobs, and farm and garden projects that augment or replace municipal services. Cultural changes have required cities to respond to new food production, processing, and distribution ventures. These impacts and policy responses have required the development of new governance structures to integrate urban agriculture more effectively throughout city government, and in doing so have helped to institutionalize the practice of urban agriculture.

Opening up new urban agriculture spaces

Cities have instituted policies to make it easier for urban agriculture projects to be located in different zones, atop roofs, and in marginal spaces. These have taken the form of zoning amendments, new local laws, and regulatory changes.

Zoning for urban agriculture

The growth in the number of community gardens, neighborhood farms, and for-profit urban agriculture projects has required cities to address the legal status of food production. Cities have attempted to facilitate urban agriculture by recognizing it as a permissible activity throughout the city.

Over the past few years a number of cities have revised their zoning ordinances to add urban farms and gardens as approved land uses, along with appropriate ancillary infrastructure like compost bins and farm stands (Hodgson et al. 2011). The details vary about where different types of activities can take place and the size and other standards for farms and gardens, but cities have generally allowed community gardens in all parts of the city and larger farms in commercial and manufacturing zones. In many cases, the decision to permit and encourage urban agriculture has been framed as an economic development strategy. For example, in announcing a zoning ordinance change that permits urban farms and gardens in Chicago, the Mayor emphasized that they would lead to job generation and increased tax revenue, as well as greater access to healthy produce.[3]

LAND TENURE FOR URBAN FARMS

As the recession has relieved development pressures, and there is less demand for the land community gardens and farms occupy, cities have taken the opportunity to revisit land tenure policies for urban agriculture. Many cities have policies by which gardens and farms operate on city property with annual licenses, but to build permanency into urban agriculture some cities have adopted longer-term or renewable license and lease arrangements. Longer-term tenure enables farmers and gardeners to make more substantial investments in their site's infrastructure, and may make it easier for them to obtain external funding for their projects. For example, the NYC Parks Department has entered into a long-term lease with the urban agriculture NGO Added Value to enable the group to continue farming the Red Hook ball field it has occupied since 2003. Other cities have adopted different land tenure terms for gardens and farms. For instance, Baltimore[4] and Boston[5] issued requests for qualifications and proposals for urban farms that would be given five-year renewable leases, while the City of Oakland leases land to City Slicker Farms for 10 years. Another mechanism to provide long-term protection for urban agriculture sites is the use of a non-profit land trust, which typically holds land in perpetuity for community gardens or farms.

DISPOSAL OF VACANT, UNDEVELOPABLE, CITY PROPERTIES

The dearth of space for growing food is one of the biggest constraints on the expansion of urban agriculture (Cohen et al. 2012). One strategy employed by cities is conducting land assessments to identify vacant parcels suitable for and worth allocating to urban agriculture. Portland, Vancouver, Oakland and San Francisco, among other cities, have conducted such assessments (Mendes et al. 2008), and New York City is in the process of doing so. In San Francisco, a Mayoral Directive required all city agencies with jurisdiction over property to identify parcels suitable for or actively used for food-producing gardens.[6,7] To do so, a group of agency representatives from the Mayor's Director of Greening, City Planning, the Department of Public Health, and the Department of the Environment developed evaluative criteria (from adequate site access to the absence of plans for development). Individual agencies reviewed 120 sites and uncovered a total of 13 new parcels that were deemed available for gardening. Detroit, with 40 square miles of vacant properties, recently sold 140 acres of city-owned property for $520,000 to the Hantz Group for the creation of a tree farm, motivated by the desire to reduce its portfolio of vacant land, to turn vacant properties into tax-paying parcels, and to shift the burden of maintenance from the city to a private owner.[8]

Greening Stalled Development Sites

The recession has halted the completion of many development projects that were slated for construction, leaving stalled development sites throughout cities. In New York City, for example, there are more than 600 stalled sites (Cohen et al. 2012:9). One strategy for creatively integrating food production into densely developed cities is to provide incentives for mobile or temporary farms and gardens on such temporarily available land. In San Francisco, for example, city officials created a program called the Green Developer Agreement (GDA) to encourage temporary green uses of stalled development sites (San Francisco Planning Department 2010). This agreement allows developers to preserve their development approvals for a 5-8 year period as long as the site is used for a 'green' purpose, including urban agriculture. In 2010 Hayes Valley Farm was able to open an interim-use urban farm project in San Francisco on a vacant parcel whose owner entered into a GDA with the city.[9]

Encouraging edible green roofs

Cities are supporting rooftop agriculture for a number of reasons: putting what are potentially thousands of acres of unused space to productive use, creating jobs and economic value; providing roof insulation and thereby reducing energy consumption; and capturing rainwater and therefore alleviating combined sewer overflow pollution. In New York City, for example, the potential for expanding the number of rooftop agriculture projects is substantial. New York has an estimated 3,000 acres of flat rooftops on buildings likely to be able to support the weight of rooftop farms without major structural improvements (Ackerman, 2011). Housing developers (e.g., Blue Sea Development) are building rooftop greenhouses into their residential projects;[10] entrepreneurs have started commercial rooftop farms (e.g., Eagle Street Rooftop Farm; Brooklyn Grange); and grocers (e.g., Eli Zabar's) and restaurants (e.g., Bell, Book and Candle) are growing food on their roofs. Two recently adopted policies make it easier for buildings in New York to accommodate rooftop greenhouses: Local Law 49 of 2011 amends the building code by adding greenhouses to the list of rooftop structures (such as water tanks and ventilation equipment) that do not count towards building height limits, provided that the greenhouses occupy less than one-third of a roof's area.[11] An amendment to New York City's zoning text excludes rooftop greenhouses atop commercial buildings from the lot's floor area and height limits.[12]

USING MARGINAL SPACES FOR FOOD PRODUCTION

Relatively small spaces can be used for food production (see chapter 2). Some practitioners have found ways to aggregate dispersed garden plots, like backyards, to grow enough produce to run a CSA.[13] Small public spaces such as median strips can be used to grow food as well. In Seattle, for example, residents are allowed to grow edible plants in what are known as 'parking strips,' the space between the curb and sidewalk found in residential neighborhoods.[14] Portland's Bureau of Transportation also allows edible landscaping in parking strips.

CONNECTING URBAN AGRICULTURE TO ECONOMIC DEVELOPMENT

In addition to finding new spaces for food production, cities are adopting policies to use urban agriculture and related food businesses as an economic development strategy. This takes the form of programs to encourage the development of food businesses, planning for food-related community development, the capture of ecosystem services provided by farms and gardens, and the use of urban agriculture as a means to improve the health and wellbeing of community residents.

SUPPORT FOR SMALL FOOD BUSINESSES

Cultural shifts and economic necessity have led to an increased number of entrepreneurs starting small food businesses, from food trucks and pushcarts selling fresh produce to cottage food production using local ingredients. The growth of craft or specialty food businesses mirrors a national growth in sales of specialty foods by 19.1% between 2009 and 2011 (National Association for Specialty Food Trade 2012). To accommodate and spur the growth of this sector, more than 30 states have enacted cottage food laws easing restrictions on the sale of homemade food.[15] The need to increase access to fresh foods has also been an impetus to the development of policies allowing mobile vending by small food businesses. For example, New York City's Green Carts program, run by the Department of Health and Mental Hygiene, issues 1,000 additional licenses to mobile food vendors who agree to sell only in specific under-served communities.[16] The city is exploring the possibility of helping these vendors source some of their produce from urban farms.

FOOD AS A COMMUNITY DEVELOPMENT STRATEGY

In October 2012, Chicago released a draft food systems plan,[17] called *A Recipe for Healthy Places,* which recommends changes to the city's food environment to reduce obesity and strategies to improve education about food, nutrition and healthy eating habits. The plan includes two interesting initiatives to support urban food production at the neighborhood scale. The Green Healthy Neighborhoods project involves residents and NGOs in several South Side neighborhoods (Englewood, West Englewood, Washington Park, Woodlawn and parts of New City and Greater Grand Crossing) in developing a land-use strategy to create urban agriculture districts. The plan also calls for the creation of farms and gardens with the City joint venturing with an NGO or land trust to develop city owned vacant land into urban agriculture sites, including amalgamated scattered farm sites.

On July 12, 2011, the City of Boston's Department of Neighborhood Development and Boston Redevelopment Authority issued an RFP seeking community groups to create organic farms on three city-owned sites in

Dorchester. Boston will issue five-year leases on the sites at the cost of $500/acre with the option to extend the leases for an additional ten years.[18] A major objective is to foster community development, so applicants must provide a plan for community participation and engagement in the farm operations and business activities, including how farm neighbors will be involved indecision making about the farm and its activities. In addition applicants must have a plan to provide 'community benefits and outcomes sought by the community,' including but not limited to: making some of the produce available to local residents at an affordable price; providing job training and internships to local residents, particularly youth; making a portion of the produce available to local schools; donating a percentage of produce to food pantries; and making a portion of the produce available to local stores.

Urban Agriculture as a Means to Healthier Communities

Cities are strategically integrating urban agriculture into the built landscape at multiple scales by creating incentives for developers to provide growing spaces in their projects. Health concerns and economic development opportunities have been the major drivers. In New York City, a 202-apartment affordable housing project in the Bronx called Via Verde, created by the city's Housing Preservation and Development Department and developed by the Jonathan Rose Companies, includes a small apple orchard and rooftop community gardens. Via Verde was selected from a competitive Request for Proposals process that required respondents to consider incorporating access to nutritious food, a fitness theme, and places for social gathering into the development (City of NY 2006). In December 2010, the New York City Housing Authority sold a parcel of land at a public housing project to another developer (Blue Sea Development, mentioned above) to build 124 units of affordable housing. The developer secured funds from the city to incorporate a 10,000-square-foot hydroponic rooftop greenhouse to grow produce on a commercial basis for the surrounding community (HUD 2011).

Urban Agriculture as Green Infrastructure

Cities are recognizing that urban farms and gardens function as 'green infrastructure' that provide ecosystem services and reduce municipal costs, a key need in the current recession. For example, New York City's Department of Environmental Protection (DEP), the agency in charge of water and sewer infrastructure, negotiated a consent order with state and federal officials allowing it to use low-tech, landscape design techniques ('green infrastructure') to reduce the quantity of stormwater that reaches the sewer system and is discharged untreated into waterways by slowing its flow and allowing it to absorb into the ground.[19] To implement this plan, DEP has committed to investing $187 million in such green infrastructure over the next four years, and over $2.4 billion by 2030, a much smaller sum than required to build conventional infrastructure to achieve the same degree of stormwater management. As part of this program, DEP funded three new urban agriculture projects: a rooftop garden at a non-profit that provides social services, a vegetable garden near the Gowanus Canal, which has been declared a toxic site under the federal Superfund program, and a commercial rooftop farm atop an industrial building in Brooklyn. By including urban farm and garden sites in this program, the City is simultaneously tackling the problem of sewage discharges and providing other multidimensional benefits associated with urban agriculture (Cohen and Ackerman, 2012).

URBAN AGRICULTURE GOVERNANCE IN AN ERA OF ECONOMIC AUSTERITY

The Great Recession has influenced the shape of urban agriculture governance in three ways:
- First, the continued fiscal constraints on municipal government has made it unlikely that cities will create new bureaucracies to manage urban agriculture and food policy, requiring organizational solutions that integrate the work of existing agencies and staff.
- Second, engaging citizens in policy development and program operation offers the potential for reducing conflict and costs of program delivery, creating an incentive for cities to start food policy councils and otherwise engage citizens in governance.
- Third, establishing laws and regulations to legalize, protect, and signal municipal commitment to urban agriculture has the potential to attract private capital, philanthropic dollars, and federal grants to urban agriculture projects, and ensures that food businesses will have the regulatory support and clear and consistent rules to enable them to succeed.

FOSTERING INTER-AGENCY COLLABORATION TO MAXIMIZE ADMINISTRATIVE EFFICIENCY

Urban agriculture is a boundary-spanning issue in cities that were developed with governance strategies that reflect 'mid-twentieth century institutional design' with divided, functional programs (e.g., in health, education, sanitation) that have their own policy communities developed around these different sectors (Healey 2012). Advancing urban agriculture depends on the support of multiple agencies, which requires breaking down silos between government agencies and fostering collaboration between government and non-governmental actors.

In some cities planning departments are involved in urban agriculture policy, yet they have mainly focused on zoning and physical planning, not integrative policy planning. In other cities, agencies involved in sustainability planning or strategic planning have begun to weave together policies related to urban agriculture, and in a small but growing number of cities food policy coordinators have been hired to encourage coordination across different silos of government. Governance forums like food policy councils are also being invented in the spaces between government and civil society (Healey 2012).

Cities have opportunities to incorporate food production into various aspects of their operations or physical development by encouraging agency staff to consider how urban agriculture can help them to address diverse programmatic issues, from support for residents in affordable housing projects to the management of the putrescible portion of the waste stream. Many city agencies have responsibilities that directly or indirectly affect urban agriculture. For example, sanitation departments process organic waste that could be composted and returned to farms and gardens. Numerous city agencies, especially schools, procure food, some of which could come from urban farms thus spurring the market for urban produce. The city's water and sewer agency is responsible for providing sustainable sources of irrigation water and managing stormwater discharges, which could be stemmed through rainwater harvesting and farms built on impermeable surfaces. Housing agencies produce buildings that could be built with garden sites. Parks departments typically have underused parkland that could be farmed. Plans and policies that encourage agency staff to identify ways in which urban agriculture can address their core mission, and governance structures that create opportunities for staff to collaborate across agency boundaries and provide incentives for them to do so result in food production being integrated into a wide range of city functions.

In Seattle, for example, an effort to integrate urban agriculture into the missions of different city agencies has led to the creation of a Food Interdepartmental Team (IDT), a working group of senior staff members from different agencies who collaborate on various food policy issues (City of Seattle 2012). The IDT has been successful at coordinating food policy work across different agencies that has led to the creation of a Food Action Plan. The plan calls for integrating urban agriculture into the city's Comprehensive Plan, and recommends integrating supportive policies into additional plans and efforts, such as incentive programs to encourage green development. One such program, the Green Factor, requires developers of new projects to increase the use of landscaping, providing a bonus for incorporating productive (vegetated) landscapes into new development. A second program, Priority Green, allows expedited permitting for projects that meet Seattle's sustainability goals, which includes the design of on-site food production into new projects.

A number of US and Canadian cities have food policy coordinators or directors to guide food systems policy and program development, often with input from food policy councils composed of various government and non-governmental stakeholders (Hatfield 2012). Because food policy directors are not the head of a city agency, they typically develop policy-making authority by working closely with city officials that possess power through their control of land (e.g., parks, housing) or by virtue of their regulatory authority (e.g., health). Connection to and support of elected officials also provides power to get local legislation and programmatic initiatives adopted.

Given the importance of interdepartmental coordination for a cross-cutting issue like food policy, one of the key tasks of food policy coordinators is to ensure that agency programs and policies are coordinated and working towards the same citywide goals. But when city agencies do not see it as part of their mission to support sustainable food systems, any effort on the part of related agencies to contribute to the food system is often based on the interest and willingness of the agency head to do so. Creating structural change so that agency directors see improving the food system as part of their mission, and one they will be evaluated on, is key. Overall, this coordination has the potential to reduce city administrative and operating costs, and thus is consistent with the overall goals of city governments in this period of economic recession to shrink bureaucracies and improve efficiencies.

ENGAGING CITIZENS IN POLICY DEVELOPMENT

Nearly 200 communities in North America have food policy councils[20] (Scherb et al. 2012). These councils are groups of stakeholders who evaluate food systems issues for a municipality, county or state, identify problems that can be addressed through public policy, and recommend actions that governments should take to develop plans and policy platforms for integrating urban agriculture into agency activities and related governmental processes. Food policy councils can serve as a formal mechanism to meld the ideas and opinions of a wide range of stakeholders, both government officials and non-governmental actors. Most also educate the public about food policy issues through public programs, outreach, and through the process of encouraging public participation in the development of policy plans. Councils may develop specific policy proposals, lobby for specific legislation, and participate in regulatory processes. Some food policy councils are involved in long-range food systems planning while others focus on narrower issues related to food access. Engaging citizens in food planning and policy development uses the expertise of a wide range of individuals and has the potential to enable programs to be launched and operated efficiently, thus potentially reducing municipal costs.

INSTITUTIONALIZING A CITY'S COMMITMENT TO URBAN AGRICULTURE

URBAN AGRICULTURE POLICY

An urban agriculture policy demonstrates that food production is an important element in the city's sustainable food system by outlining goals (e.g., supporting urban agriculture as an open space amenity in underserved neighborhoods, making school gardens a year-round community resource, or promoting economic development opportunities for low-income residents at urban farms and gardens), establishing objectives (e.g., creating a certain number of new farms and gardens, or creating a certain number of new urban agriculture jobs), and specifying the roles and responsibilities of city agencies in achieving these goals and objectives. A policy commitment has several effects. It empowers commissioners to initiate new programs, institute supportive agency practices, lobby for expanded budgets to run programs, and introduce regulations to advance urban agriculture. It also legitimizes the work of agency staff in support of urban agriculture, especially in those agencies not directly responsible for gardens and farms. It signals to entrepreneurs, the philanthropic community, educational institutions, and businesses that urban agriculture has a future, thus encouraging private investment in new and expanding food production and social enterprise ventures; and helps advocates within and outside of government maintain budgets for urban agriculture, even if priorities change from one mayoral administration to the next.

Municipal food and agriculture plans

Increasingly, cities are developing plans to address the complex and interconnected dimensions of the food system. For example, Minneapolis adopted an Urban Agriculture Policy Plan that makes a number of recommendations to support urban agriculture, including a recommendation that the city 'prioritize local food production and distribution' when deciding on the use of city-owned and private property, including new development projects 'that could potentially affect existing local food resources' and incentives for developers to include space for food production, distribution, and composting in new projects. Such policies include allowing urban agriculture to count toward green space set-aside requirements and green building requirements. The Minneapolis plan also calls for the creation of an 'overarching policy framework' to support urban agriculture (see chapter 5). These policies include an inventory of land for agriculture and food distribution, support for ownership or long-term tenure for growers and farmers markets, reducing liability and property taxes for urban farms and distribution facilities, and making vacant and foreclosed properties more accessible for food growing and distribution.

An urban agriculture plan would improve governance structures, practices, and programs to broaden participation in urban agriculture policy-making and provide more equitable access to material and financial resources. Specifically, it would be a process through which a city determines its goals and objectives for expanding urban agriculture, including potentially recognizing the limits and capacity for urban food production, the costs of expanding production, opportunity costs for using farmable land, and the potential for urban agriculture to meet the needs of different communities. A plan is a vehicle for assessing the land and rooftop space needs for a variety of urban agriculture scenarios over the next decade, including identifying opportunities for emerging forms of urban agriculture, such as rooftop spaces that could be used for food production. It also is a process for determining the long-term capital and annual operating budgets required to adequately support the city's urban agriculture program.

URBAN AGRICULTURE INFRASTRUCTURE

Support for the construction of physical infrastructure for urban agriculture is another clear signal of a city's policy commitment to the sector. Many cities are developing policies to promote the conversion of vacant spaces into farms and the development of the storage, processing and distribution infrastructure that can make urban agriculture more efficient and, in some cases, commercially viable. But in an economic recession few cities are investing public money in these infrastructure improvements, relying instead on foundation dollars and private investments.

A city's farmers and gardeners could benefit from shared large-scale infrastructure and centralized facilities, which could help reduce the cost of food distribution and spur business development. Other municipalities have created facilities known as 'food hubs' that combine the following: Shared trucks for farms and gardens to pick up material like soil and compost, and to deliver produce to farmers' markets, vendors, or other retail outlets; Refrigeration equipment to reduce the waste of unsold produce at farmers' markets and to enable weekly harvests to be sold on more than one market day; Processing facilities to add value to and preserve the produce grown on farms and in gardens; Warehouses to aggregate produce from multiple gardens and farms, and potentially serve as a distribution point to multiple markets (see chapter 7).

Toronto's The Stop Community Food Resource Center, for example, is a community-based food hub facility that includes an 8,000-square-foot garden, a greenhouse, a 'global roots' garden to demonstrate culturally specific foods, and many other food-related projects. For example, The Stop runs a feeding program, a farmers market, a café, and a food share program that buys and redistributes produce through farm stands located across the city. The organization also has facilities to teach cooking and nutrition, an after-school program and summer camp, and other educational programs. Detroit's Eastern Market is the city's wholesale food distribution facility, with a six-block farmers market for 250 local vendors surrounded by food distributors and other food establishments. Eastern Market has a demonstration urban farm, an after-hours wholesale market, and special food-related public programming to draw customers to the market.

Conclusions

The economic crisis, and economic constraints facing cities, coupled with cultural shifts and an underlying political milieu favoring strategies of government rollback and increasing reliance on private sector initiatives has opened a window of opportunity for the implementation of new policies and programs to support urban agriculture (Cohen 2012; Neuner et al. 2012). This political environment has created opportunities for innovative strategies to maximize the efficiency of food systems governance, through interdepartmental collaboration, cross-departmental coordination by food policy directors, public participation processes that engage citizens in food planning, and support for programs, policies, and infrastructure that aim to increase administrative efficiency and reduce costs, create jobs, and spur economic development. All of these techniques are consistent with a neoliberal political ideology of limited government and an effort to move responsibility from city agencies to the private and NGO sectors. Yet policy entrepreneurs working in government, advocacy organizations, philanthropies and farms have taken advantage of the crisis and renewed interest in local food and farming to invent, copy, and push for various kinds of urban agriculture policies and programs.

The kinds of urban agriculture programs that have been developed reflect the impacts of the recession on municipal budgets: innovative uses of marginal urban land; support for entrepreneurial projects including for-profit farming ventures; and projects that include programming to achieve community development, job creation, and cost reduction goals. Cities in the US strapped for planning dollars have taken advantage of Recovery Act funds, which focus on obesity prevention, to do food system planning, resulting in a focus on using agriculture as a strategy for addressing the costly health consequences of malnourishment. Limited fiscal resources have also made public private partnerships and public participation an important strategy for gaining input and acceptance of food policies, including policies around urban agriculture. The development of urban agriculture has required new governance structures too, and in a period of austerity these also reflect the focus on cost-effective administration of farming and gardening activities. Cities are developing creative means to integrate the work of multiple agencies that can contribute to urban agriculture projects and are incorporating a wide range of stakeholders in the process, including involving citizens in the process of policy analysis and development. Cities are also committing to urban agriculture through land use and program plans, policies, and the dedication of land to food production in public and private development projects and on city property.

One impact of these policies forged in the great recession is a shift in the perception of urban agriculture from one of a community-based activity to one with job creation, economic development, cost-reduction, and entrepreneurship potential. For this reason, it is likely that urban agriculture planning and policy will be treated as a valuable element of city planning and long-range development. Urban agriculture is now perceived by many cities to be an asset that has the potential to green vacant spaces, improve real estate values, generate media attention and serve as a marketing tool, and attract 'agricultural creatives,' young farmers and gardeners who can expand the food culture in a city. Cities are also paying more attention to the ecosystem services function of urban farms and gardens, recognizing that agriculture can provide municipal benefits such as stormwater management and waste reduction at a lower cost than conventional infrastructure and municipal services. Therefore, policies that will facilitate urban agriculture over the long run, like changes to the zoning ordinance or capital projects to build farms and gardens as green infrastructure, enable the proliferation of commercial urban farms and gardens, rooftop agriculture, and related infrastructure like food hubs, commercial kitchens, and markets.

The current activity in support of urban agriculture is distinct from previous periods in which urban agriculture was promoted. Once viewed as an expedient means to help families grow subsistence crops, or for residents of neighborhoods faced with disinvestment and abandoned lots to turn those spaces into community assets, it is now a more significant part of city planning. One difference has to do with the type of urban agriculture projects that are being supported: larger scale community farms run by

NGOs, private farms established as for-profit ventures, and urban agriculture projects that provide multiple economic and community development benefits. Urban agriculture is also being designed into the physical landscape of the city in a more integrated fashion than before, with cities like Chicago planning for food production on a neighborhood scale, and cities like New York, Vancouver, Toronto, and Seattle creating incentives to build food production spaces into new development projects. Governance processes, from citizen-based food policy councils to food policy directors to interdepartmental teams that foster cross-agency collaboration, help to institutionalize the practice of urban agriculture in city government. Finally, cities are making longer term commitments to urban farms and gardens in the form of renewable licenses and longer term leases for urban agriculture projects, support for related infrastructure like food hubs, and formal policies that commit municipal government to supporting urban farms and gardens. None of these changes guarantee that urban agriculture will continue to get the same level of attention and support that exists at the moment, but they reflect a more significant commitment to urban agriculture that suggests urban food production will continue to grow.

References

Ackerman, K. 2011. The Potential for Urban Agriculture in New York City: Growing Capacity, Food Security, & Green Infrastructure. NY: Columbia University.

Beachy, Ben. 2012. 'A Financial Crisis Manual: Causes, Consequences, and Lessons of the Financial Crisis.' Medford, MA: Tufts University. http://www.ase.tufts.edu/gdae/publications/working_papers/index.html.

City of New York. Department of Housing Preservation and Development. 2006. New Housing New York Legacy Project Request for Proposals. Issue Date: June 12, 2006. Accessed at http://www.aiany.org/NHNY/rfp/index.php on January 20, 2012.

City of Seattle. 2012. Food Action Plan. Accessed at http://www.seattle.gov/environment/food_plan.htm

Cohen, N. 2012. 'Planning for urban agriculture: problem recognition, policy formation, and politics.' In Sustainable Food Planning: evolving theory and practice, A. Viljoen and J.S.C. Wiskerke. Wageningen: Wageningen Academic Publishers.

Cohen, N. and K. Ackerman. 2011. Breaking New Ground. The New York Times. http://bittman.blogs.nytimes.com/2011/11/21/breaking-new-ground/

Cohen, N., Kristin Reynolds and Rupal Sanghvi. 2012. Five Borough Farm: Seeding the Growth of Urban Agriculture in New York. NY: The Design Trust for Public Space.

Conill, Joana, Manuel Castells, Amalia Cardenas, Lisa Servon. 2012. 'Beyond the Crisis: The Emergence of Alternative Economic Practices.' In Aftermath: The Cultures of the Economic Crisis, ed. M. Castells, J. Caraca and G. Cardoso. Oxford: Oxford University Press.

Finkelstein, Erica, Justin G Trogdon, Joel W Cohen, and William Dietz. 2009. 'Annual Medical Spending Attributable to Obesity: Payer-and Service-specific Estimates.' Health Affairs (Project Hope) 28 (5): w822–31.

FAO, WFP and IFAD. 2012. The State of Food Insecurity in the World 2012. Economic growth is necessary but not sufficient to accelerate reduction of hunger and malnutrition. Rome, FAO.

Hatfield, Molly M. 2012. 'City Food Policy and Programs: Lessons Harvested from an Emerging Field.' Portland: City of Portland, Oregon Bureau of Planning and Sustainability.

Healey, Patsy. 2012. 'Re-enchanting Democracy as a Mode of Governance.' Critical Policy Studies 6 (1): 19–39.

Hodgson, K., M. C. Campbell, and M. Bailkey. 2011. Urban agriculture: growing healthy, sustainable places. Chicago: APA Planning Advisory Service No. 563.

IOM (Institute of Medicine). 2012. 'Accelerating Progress in Obesity Prevention: Solving the Weight of the Nation.' Washington, DC: The National Academies Press. Pg. 18.

Lawson, Laura. 2004. 'The Planner in the Garden: A Historical View into the Relationship Between Planning and Community Gardens.' Journal of Planning History 3 (2) (May): 151–176.

McClintock, N. 2010. 'Why farm the city? Theorizing urban agriculture through a lens of metabolic rift.' Journal of Regions, Economy and Society 3 (2): 191-207.

Mendes, Wendy, Kevin Balmer, Terra Kaethler, and Amanda Rhoads. 2008. 'Using Land Inventories to Plan for Urban Agriculture: Experiences From Portland and Vancouver.' Journal of the American Planning Association 74 (4) (September): 435–449.

National Association for Specialty Food Trade. 2012. The State of the Specialty Food Industry 2012. NY: NASFT.

Neuner, K., S. Kelly and S. Raja. 2012. Planning to eat?: innovative local government plans and policies to build healthy food systems in the United States. Buffalo, NY.

Pagano, M. A., Christopher W. Hoene & Christiana McFarland. 2012. Research Brief on America's Cities: City Fiscal Conditions 2012. Washington, DC:

National League of Cities. Accessed at http://www.nlc.org/Documents/Find%20City%20Solutions/Research%20Innovation/Finance/city-fiscal-conditions-research-brief-rpt-sep12.pdf

San Francisco Planning Department. 2010. 'Executive Summary: Draft Green Development Agreement Legislation.'

Scherb, Allyson, Anne Palmer, Shannon Frattaroli, and Keshia Pollack. 2012. 'Exploring Food System Policy: A Survey of Food Policy Councils in the United States.' Journal of Agriculture, Food Systems, and Community Development 2(4), 3-14.

US Department of Agriculture (USDA) (2011). Annual Summary of Food and Nutrition Service Programs. Accessed at http://www.fns.usda.gov/pd/annual.htm.

U.S. Department of Housing and Urban Development Office of Public and Indian Housing (HUD). 2011. 'Final PHA Plan. Annual Plan for Fiscal Year 2012.' New York City Housing Authority. October 18, 2011. pg. 7.

While, Aidan, AEG Jonas, and David Gibbs. 2004. 'The Environment and the Entrepreneurial City: Searching for the Urban Sustainability Fix in Manchester and Leeds.' International Journal of Urban and Regional Research 28 (May 2003): 549–569.

NOTES

1. http://www.dhhs.gov/news/press/2010pres/03/20100319a.html
2. http://www.minneapolismn.gov/health/cppw/dhfs_hubs
3. https://www.cityofchicago.org/city/en/depts/mayor/press_room/press_releases/2011/july_2011/mayor_emanuel_announcesplantocreatejobsspureconomicdevelopmentan.html
4. Request For Qualifications: Urban Agriculture in the City of Baltimore. RFQ Issued: March 25, 2011. Issued by: Baltimore City Department of Planning and Department of Housing and Community Development. Accessed at http://cleanergreener.highrockhosting2.com/uploads/files/Urban%20Agriculture%20RFQ%203.25.11.pdf on January 30, 2012.
5. http://www.cityofboston.gov/news/default.aspx?id=5188
6. City of San Francisco. Executive Directive on Healthy and Sustainable Food 09-03. Summary Report. December 2010. pg. 7 and appendix F.
7. Other cities that have gone through the process of searching for new land suitable for urban agriculture include Portland, Vancouver, and Oakland. See Mendes, W., Balmer, K., Kaethler, T., & Rhoads, A. (2008). Using Land Inventories to Plan for Urban Agriculture: Experiences from Portland and Vancouver. *Journal of the American Planning Association.* 74(4), 435-449.

8 http://www.crainsdetroit.com/article/20121211/NEWS/121219972/detroit-city-council-oks-land-sale-to-hantz-woodlands
9 http://www.hayesvalleyfarm.com/
10 http://www.prlog.org/11833817-oldcastle-precast-helps-construct-green-affordable-housing-for-families-in-need.html
11 http://www.nyc.gov/html/dob/downloads/pdf/ll49of2011.pdf
12 http://www.nyc.gov/html/dcp/html/greenbuildings/index.shtml
13 BK Farmyards:: http://bkfarmyards.blogspot.com/p/foxtrot-farmyard.html
14 Seattle, City of, Department of Transportation. (2011) 'Department of Transportation Client Assistance Memo 2305: Gardening in Planting Strips.' January 1. Available at: www.seattle.gov/transportation/stuse_garden.htm (last accessed April 26, 2011). (Clarifies that residents may plant raised-bed gardens in the strip of the public right-of-way between the sidewalk and the curb.)
15 See http://www.theselc.org/cottage-food-laws/
16 http://www.nyc.gov/html/doh/html/cdp/cdp_pan_green_carts.shtml
17 http://www.healthyplaceschicago.org/food/food-plan-overview.lasso
18 http://www.cityofboston.gov/news/default.aspx?id=5188
19 http://www.nyc.gov/html/dep/html/stormwater/using_green_infra_to_manage_stormwater.shtml
20 http://www.markwinne.com/wp-content/uploads/2012/09/fp-councils-may-2012.pdf

Notes

1 The chapter is based on: structured interviews of 31 individuals with unique knowledge about aspects of urban agriculture in New York City conducted for a project of The Design Trust for Public Space; semi-structured interviews of 30 urban agriculture experts in six North American cities; a review of urban agriculture policy documents and reports; and participation by the author in New York City food policymaking processes.

Commentary – Will It Last? Questions Regarding the Staying Power of Urban Agriculture

Jennifer Cockrall-King

Will It Last?

The fact that urban agriculture is so readily adaptable in so many different environments, it seems like it can pop up overnight (and does, in the case of acts of guerrilla gardening). However, it can also disappear just as easily (as when a municipal bylaw demands the removal of a hive of urban bees or a flock of urban laying hens.) It's inherently shovel-ready, but also controversial. Not everyone is a fan of an urban farm in a residential neighbourhood.

Over the past few years, we've seen a rush of enthusiasm for experimenting with urban food production. Lawns are being overturned and rooftops farmed. Ground is being broken for vertical farms and parkland is being turned into urban orchards and food forests. As Nevin Cohen explains in this chapter, the economic recession proved to be the impetus for the recent investment of so much energy into urban agriculture. Driven mainly by the initiatives of individuals and groups working at the production-level of urban agriculture, increased access to growing spaces, policy changes and basic municipal supports are now in place that were not there a decade ago. However, these gains in favour of urban agriculture activities have been generally ad hoc reactions and many barriers still exist across communities.

The question moving forward, optimistically into recovery from the economic crisis, or less optimistically as we adjust to the 'new normal', is whether urban agriculture has staying power. Will we finally loosen our grip on the global food engine enough to allow some seasonal variety to our 'endless summer' diets of fresh strawberries baby arugula twelve months a year? Have we done enough to truly ensure a long-term shift away from an urban environment that is only designed for the consumption of food? Are the supports in place to encourage hyper-local production and distribution? Will we continue to reinforce structures and policies that enable and foster urban agriculture in future municipal development blueprints?

Cohen provides a thorough exposition of the landscape surrounding these questions. He acknowledges the ebb and flow of urban agriculture throughout the years has been in reaction to negative economic stimulus. When times are tough, the tough get gardening. When the economy improves, we turn our backs on urban agriculture, as if we've permanently moved onwards and upwards from such difficult and laborious work. How do we avoid repeating this history? This is the next big hurdle.

Currently, urban agriculture is still trendy and it has a generally positive image, despite the many barriers in its way. But it's far from mainstream. A lot of sweat equity is required to grow your own food, and in some communities it's illegal. It's a commitment for households to sign up for a Community Supported Agriculture box of fresh vegetables grown on an urban farm. Urban farmers have to compete with more better-funded businesses and residences for urban space. And it's less convenient to support urban food producers who don't have access to the 24/7-supermarket distribution chain. These are not insignificant challenges in our time-stressed world. But we have seen the consequences of the other option. And to continue to outsource our food production and selectively grow and consume food that travels over thousands of kilometres and can endure weeks or months in shipping containers means we'll continue to pay the health consequences of a food system that values cheapness and shelf-life, not flavour, nutrition and freshness.

I've spent the last few years obsessed with the question of whether urban agriculture will endure beyond the economic recession and the initial groundswell? In a way, my book *Food and the City: Urban Agriculture and the New Food Revolution* (Prometheus Books, 2012) is the long-form response. In it, I write about my own my journey from big box shopper in the 1990s to rediscovering my food-growing roots, however rudimentary, as an adult looking to rediscover food that had nutrition, flavour and freshness. Little by little, taking back some control of the food that I ate, by growing it myself or buying it directly from people who were growing and harvesting it the way I felt good about, was incremental, effective and addictive. It was a journey that led me to take a serious look at the fragilities of the industrial global food system, and to investigate the role that urban agriculture was playing in re-establishing healthier, tastier, local food economies in places like Paris, Los Angeles, London, Vancouver, Toronto, Milwaukee, Detroit, Chicago and on the island of Cuba.

Cuba, in particular, opened my eyes to the realities and practical potential of urban agriculture on my first trip there in 2007. After seeing organic urban farms as commonplace in residential communities as our supermarket chains and warehouse supercenters are in Canada and the United States, I began to recognize potential in every possible urban space for food production everywhere I looked. I returned in 2010, to further figure out how Cuba has emerged as a leader in urban agriculture, permaculture and high-yield organic urban and peri-urban food production with a very low carbon footprint. (Hint: Cuba had no choice. It was the only way to make it through a sustained simultaneous food and fuel shock in the early 1990s as 85 percent of its foreign trade went away almost overnight. The collapse of the Soviet Union was devastating for Cuba as it relied on foreign imports for two-thirds of its food supply, all of its fuel, and 80 percent of its farming equipment from just one trading partner.[1] With 11 million citizens to feed, Cubans turned to urban agriculture. Without access to chemical fertilizers, chemical pesticides and fungicides, and energy to transport and refrigerate food, ubiquitous urban organic farm cooperatives emerged as a cornerstone of Cuba's post-industrial food system. By the early 2000s, it was reported that organic urban and peri-urban farms were supplying Havana with 90 percent of its fresh produce.[2])

While my own personal trips to Cuba in 2007 and 2010 were extreme eye-opening experiences, I found rumblings of dissent from the industrial food model in almost every city I looked. Paris, which has an impressive history of urban agriculture just before the Industrial Revolution, is now rediscovering its food production potential through community gardens and urban beekeeping. I saw impressive municipal supports in London through its Capital Growth governmental campaign and its bid to create 2012 new growing spaces by 2012, the year when London hosted the summer Olympic games.[3] I went to Los Angeles to see where issues of race and a lack of public land are stumbling blocks to food security in communities that could otherwise grow their own fresh food. I met with young urban farmers making a strong economic case for commercial farms in cities like Vancouver and Kelowna, British Columbia.[4] I saw how community gardens were helping immigrant communities feel at home in Toronto. I heard urban agriculture pioneer, Will Allen, discuss how his 2.5-acre urban agriculture not only provided fresh food to 10,000 residents in Milwaukee[5], but how he also used it as a haphazard crime-fighting tool.[6] I met with the president of Hanz Farms, Mike Score, the man charged with shepherding a 40-acre urban farm into being in blighted, empty, inner city Detroit.[7] And I also spent time with John Edel, an industrial rehabilitator experimenting with vertical farming in Chicago where millions of square feet of unused manufacturing and food production space lie vacant.[8] What I saw wherever I looked, in fact, was the beginning of a broad movement where groups of people were using the highly adaptable tool of urban agriculture as an attempt to overcome way to address specific vulnerabilities in their communities, improve their lives, their environments and their health. While most projects I saw had to cope with the idiosyncrasies of outdated and cumbersome bylaws, they were nonetheless moving forward.

Imagine now what possibilities will emerge in cities. As Cohen proposes, governance structures, municipal policies and even physical structures within cities are now being put into place to promote, enable and support urban agricultural initiatives. If structure enables behavior, we can only assume that urban agriculture will continue long after the initial impetus has faded.

While Cohen focuses primarily on the more concrete responses to urban agriculture, I'd like to stress the importance of the shifts in social values that have also taken place. Just to touch on a few of these, urban agriculture has empowered citizens to become 'city builders' and to engage in community activism and municipal politics in an impressive way. Citizen groups are demanding seats at policy development and urban planning tables in municipal politics in the past few years in ways that previously only property developers would. School food gardens are teaching culinary literacy to our next generations, filling in a gap of knowledge that are otherwise being exploited by our fast food and convenience food companies to dire consequences. (My speaking calendar is increasingly packed with presentations to primary school-aged children learning about agriculture, local food and permaculture systems.) The discussions around urban agriculture has finally tasked our elected leaders to consider lasting solutions to food deserts, food insecurity, hunger and malnutrition that lurks in every corner of our communities, sapping our children's potential to live full, productive and happy lives. While Cohen does touch on some cultural shifts in attitudes promoting of citizen engagement and valuing agricultural work, I feel strongly that these ideological shifts are just as important as the structural shifts. In fact, it's the combination of the practical and the ideological that will weight the future in favour of making urban agriculture part of our cities' fabric of tomorrow.

As structures become more permanent and mainstream – such as continuing to create more growing spaces in cities, continuing to educate people on local food growing practices, and building permanent food hubs which can provide true, convenient alternatives to supermarkets stocked with well-travelled foods – then pro-urban agriculture behavior and value systems will also become more mainstream. And just as we've changed social attitudes towards littering, against smoking in public spaces, and ingrained recycling practices in the matter of just one or two generations, perhaps we can create cities where it would be unthinkable not to have urban farms, local food hubs, abundant community garden and orchard space, and vertical farms.

As the benefits multiply and the barriers to urban food production and distribution diminish, we may find ourselves questioning why we got away from growing and raising food in cities in the first place. I'd like to imagine a day in the not-too-distant future in which there are textbook chapters on the anomalous period from the 1950s to early 2000s addressing why cities were devoid of food production and local food economies. Yes, perhaps the next question for academics, historians and writers will be: Why didn't we, for a period, grow food in cities?

Notes

1. Fernando Funes et al., *Sustainable Agriculture and Resistance: Transforming Food Production in Cuba* (Oakland, CA: Food First Books, 2002), p. 5.
2. Ibid., p. 235.
3. http://www.capitalgrowth.org/big_idea/. Accessed November 28, 2013.
4. See http://solefoodfarms.com/ (Vancouver, BC) and http://www.greencity-acres.com/. Accessed November 28, 2013.
5. Elizabeth Royte, 'Street Farmer,' *New York Times* Magazine, July 1, 2009. Available online at http://www.nytimes.com/2009/07/05/magazine/05allen-t.html?pagewanted=all&_r=0. Accessed November 28, 2013.
6. Will Allen, talking at 'Growing Out of Hunger' event, Vancouver, BC, January 27, 2011.
7. See http://www.hantzfarmsdetroit.com/. Accessed November 28, 2013.
8. See http://www.plantchicago.com/. Accessed November 28, 2013.

www.ingramcontent.com/pod-product-compliance
Lightning Source LLC
Chambersburg PA
CBHW050526300426
44113CB00012B/1977